DRIVEN

DARKNESS

"And they shall look unto the earth,
and behold trouble and darkness,
dimness of anguish,
and they shall be driven to darkness."

Isaiah 8:22

DRIVEN TO DARKNESS

Jewish Émigré Directors
and the Rise of Film Noir

VINCENT BROOK

RUTGERS UNIVERSITY PRESS
New Brunswick, New Jersey, and London

Library of Congress Cataloging-in-Publication Data

Brook, Vincent, 1946–
  Driven to darkness : Jewish émigré directors and the rise of film noir /
Vincent Brook.
       p.   cm.
  Includes bibliographical references and index.
  Includes filmography.
  ISBN 978–0–8135–4629–2 (hardcover : alk. paper)—ISBN 978–0–8135–4630–8
(pbk. : alk. paper)
  1. Film noir—United States—History and criticism. 2. Jewish motion picture
producers and directors—United States. I. Title.
  PN1995.9.F54B76 2009
  791.43'6556—dc22

                                                                2009000772

A British Cataloging-in-Publication record for this book is available from the British Library.

Visit our Web site: http://rutgerspress.rutgers.edu

Manufactured in the United States of America

Typesetting: BookType

For Karen

Contents

Acknowledgments

That all the Jewish émigré directors in this study were no longer alive when I began researching obviously deprived me of an invaluable resource. For many of the filmmakers, however, I was blessed with excellent alternatives: extensive interviews and oral histories; biographies, autobiographies, and film studies, many of them quite recent; files at the Margaret Herrick Library of the Academy of Motion Pictures Arts and Sciences; the resources of the Goethe Institute of Los Angeles and the Deutsche Kinemathek in Berlin; and special collections of the University of Southern California and the University of California, Los Angeles (UCLA). I also contacted via e-mail, telephone, or in person as many relatives or close friends of the deceased directors as possible. Of these I must give special thanks to Fritz Lang's close friends Cornelius Schnauber and Kevin Thomas; Robert Siodmak's nephew Geoff Siodmak; Billy Wilder's wife, Audrey Wilder, and daughter Victoria Roberts; Willy Wilder's son Miles Wilder, Miles's wife, Bobbe Wilder, and their daughter Kim Wilder-Lee; Edgar G. Ulmer's daughter Arianné Ulmer Cipes; Curtis Bernhardt's son Tony Bernhardt; John Brahm's daughter Sumishta Brahm; and Henry Koster's son Bob Koster. Fellow scholars who contributed information, counsel, or constructive feedback include Marc Dolezal, Thomas Elsaesser, Lester Friedman, Jan-Christopher Horak, Klaus Kreimeier, and Michael Meyer. The excellent editors at Rutgers University Press, Leslie Mitchner and Marilyn Campbell presiding, did their yeoman's duty, as usual. And access to some of the rarer films, which were legion, came courtesy of the treasure troves at Eddie Brandt's Saturday Matinee video store, Video Journeys, Danger and Despair, and the UCLA Film and Television Archives. The greatest godsend was my dear wife, love of my life, and research assistant extraordinaire, Karen Brook, without whose guidance, inspiration, and abiding love this book would never have seen the dark of night, much less the light of day.

DRIVEN TO
DARKNESS

1 Introduction

I am a German writer. My heart beats Jewish. It's my thoughts that belong to the world.

—Lion Feuchtwanger

"History," said George Santayana, "is always written wrong, and so always needs to be rewritten."[1] This study of Jewish émigré filmmakers of the 1930s and 1940s aims to rewrite a wrong in the historiography of American cinema generally and film noir specifically. The error is one of omission, and relates to the crucial contributions of Jewish, German-speaking, refugee directors to the emergence and evolution of film noir. Not that these directors' importance to the noir cycle per se has been neglected; quite the contrary. The disproportionate number and seminal influence of Austrian and German film noir directors—Fritz Lang, Billy Wilder, Otto Preminger, Edgar G. Ulmer, and Fred Zinnemann among the Austrians; Robert Siodmak, Curtis Bernhardt, Max Ophuls, and John Brahm among the Germans—has been duly acknowledged in regard to their refugee status, the infusion of expressionist aesthetics into the cycle, and the canonical status of many of their films. But the significance of these individual's *Jewishness*, and the impact of their ethno-religious identification on their work, has remained almost wholly unexplored.

Occasionally, a noir scholar will allude to the repercussions of exile in a manner that hints at its Jewish inflection, such as Tom Gunning on Fritz Lang ("The insecurity of the refugee status shapes his new mode of filmmaking"), James Paris on Billy Wilder ("Perhaps it took a European who had lost an entire world to see life with such a bittersweet sense of irony"), or Foster Hirsch on the expatriates in general ("They . . . shared a world view that was shaped by their bitter personal experience of living and then escaping from a nation that had lost its mind").[2] But even Susan M. White and Neil Sinyard, who actually name their subjects' Jewishness and consider it as a component (among others) in their films, still apply it (and rather cursorily) only to a *single* filmmaker—Max Ophuls for White, Fred Zinnemann for Sinyard—and only to their body of work *as a whole*. No writer that I'm aware of has *collectively* analyzed the import of the émigré directors' Jewishness, or done so *specifically* in regard to their film noir output.[3]

The consequences of this oversight are not merely related to identity politics. Certainly the accomplishments of émigré Jewish film noir directors deserve to be recognized from an ethno-religious standpoint as much as from a national one, all the more so given the fraught historical circumstances, both nationally and internationally, under which film noir emerged. My concern, however, goes beyond settling the multicultural score. In eliding the Jewishness of a substantial portion of noir filmmakers, an important piece of the film noir puzzle has been left out, leaving a gap in our understanding of this complex and still controversial cinematic form.[4]

The Jewish identity of a significant portion of noir's prime practitioners affected the noir cycle in several ways. First, all the Jewish émigré directors came to the United States when they did, namely in the 1930s or early 1940s, not because they were German or Austrian (or Ukrainian, in the case of Anatole Litvak) but because they were Jewish. They had left Germany and, most of them, later France (or Austria, in the case of Otto Preminger) under duress. Undoubtedly, some might have been lured to work in the United States at some point anyway, as had a coterie of their Jewish compatriots in the 1920s, such as Ernst Lubitsch, E. A. Dupont, William Wyler, Charles Vidor, and Bertolt Viertel.[5] All the "second-wave" European Jewish directors, however, rather than mainly *drawn to* Hollywood, were *driven from* Europe by Hitler. They were not merely *immigrants*, but *exiles*. As Billy Wilder explained in an interview: "Basically you would have to divide the influx of picture makers from Germany to the United States into two categories: First there were the ones that were hired in the 1920s by the American studios because they were outstanding geniuses like F. W. Murnau . . . and Ernst Lubitsch. . . . Then, in the mid-1930s came an avalanche of Jewish refugees who were looking for jobs on the basis of their experience in the German industry, such as Fred Zinnemann, Otto Preminger, and myself. Most of us didn't come because we were invited like the first group. We came to save our lives."[6]

Second, the expressionist style that historians (not without controversy) identify as foundational to the noir aesthetic, and which German-based filmmakers are credited with importing to the United States, already bore a strong Jewish trace.[7] The overwhelming Jewish influence on German cultural life generally, from the fin de siècle through the Weimar era, has been extensively charted. Peter Gay's *Weimar Culture: The Outsider as Insider* already in its title connotes the extent of the Jewish impact.[8] Walter Laqueur baldly asserts, "Without Jews there would have been no 'Weimar culture,'" which is especially impressive given that Jews had been full participants in German society only since the mid-1800s and by the 1920s made up less than 1 percent of the total German population.[9] From artists to impresarios, publishers to patrons, critics to curators (not to mention the media, the sciences, politics, and finance), Jews "were in the forefront of every new, daring, revolutionary movement."[10] Similarly in Austria, where they were also a "minute minority," Jews, Stefan Zweig wrote, "with their more agile perception less burdened by tradition, became everywhere the champions and sponsors of everything that was new."[11] Jewish novelist Jakob Wassermann went further, noting how, in Vienna, "the entire public life was dominated by Jews": from doctors, lawyers, and professors to actors, journalists, politicians, and poets, "Jews gave their imprint to the city."[12]

As for German Expressionism specifically, Jews did not "invent" this art movement to the degree that they helped build the Hollywood film industry, but here also—and to a greater extent than generally has been acknowledged—they played an overarching role.[13] Just as Expressionism's imprint on the German stage is inconceivable without the towering figure of Jewish impresario Max Reinhardt and the seminal plays of Frank Wedekind, Ernst Toller, and Walter Hasenclever, so is its cinematic incarnation—first in the horror film, then in offshoots such as the Kammerspiel, street, and crime film—unimaginable without the pioneering efforts of Jewish producers Erich Pommer and Seymour Nebenzahl; directors Lang, Dupont, Bernhardt, Robert Wiene, Joe May, Paul Czinner, Karl Grune, and Lupu Pick; writers Carl Mayer, Hans Janowitz, Henrik Galeen, Norbert Falk, and Robert Liebmann; actors Elizabeth Bergner, Fritz Kortner, Alexander Granach, Peter Lorre, Curt Bois, and Greta Mosheim; cinematographers Karl Freund, Eugen Schüfftan, and Curt Courant; and set designers Ulmer, Hans Dreier, Ernö Metzner, Kurt Richter, Ludwig Meidner, and Hans Poelzig, among many others.[14] A 1932 Nazi Party survey of the German film industry, unlikely to be an undercount, found that 41 percent of the scenarists, 45 percent of the composers, 47 percent of the directors, and 81 percent of the distribution company heads were Jewish.[15]

Third, even the influence of French poetic realism on film noir can be linked substantially to the Jewish émigré directors. It may well be true, as Raymond Borde and Etienne Chaumeton claim, that non-émigré American noirists such as John Huston and Howard Hawks were unfamiliar with the poetic realist work of Julien Duvivier, Jean Renoir, and Marcel Carné.[16] On the other hand, as Ginette Vincendeau points out, several of the Jewish refugees who would help jump-start film noir were not only aware of French films of the 1930s, but in fact had made many of them. Before moving on to Hollywood, figures such as Lang, Siodmak, Wilder, Bernhardt, and Ophuls spent time—some only a year (Lang and Wilder), others the entire decade (Siodmak, Bernhardt, and Ophuls)—working in the French studios.[17] Given that among filmmakers who came to the United States after working in France, only two non-Jews, Jacques Tourneur and Rudolph Maté, made any significant formative contributions to classical noir (*Out of the Past* [1948] for Tourneur; *The Dark Past* [1948], *D.O.A.*, and *Union Station* [both 1950] for Maté), it would seem, as with German Expressionism, that Jewish émigré directors were prime carriers of poetic realism into the noir aesthetic.[18]

Fourth, as Nazism advanced in Germany and then throughout Europe, and, concomitantly, as anti-Semitic acts increased (the Nuremberg laws, *Kristallnacht*, the Final Solution), the disturbing effects of these developments on the consciousness of Jewish émigré filmmakers would have been particularly acute. The bleak worldview and stark exposure of society's underbelly, which had already characterized Weimar cinema and would permeate film noir, also arguably found greater, or at least more overdetermined, resonance among Jewish émigré directors than among their American-born (Jewish or non-Jewish) counterparts. As for the deep psychological and moral ambivalence of the noir universe, who could possibly have *experienced* this aspect more profoundly than "wholly assimilated" German and Austrian Jews?[19] Beyond the Freudian divided self that all humans are purported to develop upon entry into the social order, and which is said to find its most overt expression in film noir, German-speaking Jewish refugees brought with them to the United States another deeply conflicted yet historically grounded and culturally specific syndrome.

Jews' post-emancipation assimilation into mainstream Germanic society in the 1800s precipitated a bifurcated lifestyle and a schizoid consciousness, captured in the folk adage, "A Jew at home, a gentleman on the street." Further duality resulted from assimilated Jews' alienation from their eastern Jewish cousins, who remained an embarrassing and potentially threatening reminder of their own ghetto roots. Once in the United States, those Jewish émigrés who had become "more German than the Germans" were confronted with a singular irony and an agonizing dilemma. The irony came from the fact that many of the studio and production heads the émigré Jews ended up working for, and often creatively struggling against, were themselves *Ostjuden* (eastern European Jews). What resulted, as Lawrence Weschler points out, "was a ritual of class revenge. Back in Europe the highbrow cultural figures of Vienna and Berlin had looked upon these peasants and shopkeepers with disdain, and now they were getting a touch of their own treatment."[20]

The dilemma derived from the fact that it was, after all, the émigrés' *Mutterland/Vaterland* (for Austrians, their cultural patrimony) that had begun devouring its own and was running roughshod over Europe, if not the world. The effect of this "shadowlike awareness" of personal and collective trauma, with its "antinostalgic resonance of 'home'"—to extrapolate from Janet Burstein's analysis of émigré Jewish women writers—"cannot be overestimated."[21] Moreover, such ambivalence was compounded, especially from a psychoanalytic perspective, once the United States entered the war, as the Jewish refugees now found themselves allied, patriotically speaking, with the potential perpetrators of matricide/patricide. Separating good parent (German Kultur) from bad (Nazism) helped mitigate the crime, but the stigma remained.

Animus toward the United States, meanwhile, although significantly alleviated by the sanctuary (and employment) their host country provided, was exacerbated by a superiority complex and critical stance similar to that which grounded their disdain for the Ostjuden. Émigré anti-Americanism had both cultural and political components, perhaps most cogently expressed in the critical theory of Jewish émigrés Theodor Adorno and Max Horkheimer. In

Dialectic of Enlightenment (1944), the two Frankfurt School theorists argued that the "germ of regression" that had led to the fascist outbreak in central Europe was also apparent in the institutional structures of the United States.[22] Thus, despite their cognizance of and gratitude for U.S. involvement in the war against fascism, Adorno and Horkheimer "were eager to point out similarities in the forms of mass control and mass entertainment used in Nazi Germany and the United States."[23]

Los Angeles, on the one hand, was a "model of the modern city" that "shared with Berlin the exile's uprootedness, modernity, artificiality, and a constant flow of newcomers in a never-ending process of renewal and transformation."[24] But it was also, for many, a cultural backwater, "a wasteland, anything but a civilized place to the cultivated Europeans," with *Ostjüdische* Hollywood representing the epitome of vulgarity and philistinism.[25] Yet these "two competing mythologies"—"between innocence and corruption, unspoiled nature and ruthless development, naivete and hucksterism, enthusiasm and shameless exploitation"—are precisely what allowed the exiles, in Ehrhard Bahr's words, "to adopt a dialectical stance toward the image of Los Angeles as a natural paradise in order to perceive it as a cityscape of modernism."[26]

The result, for Joseph Horowitz, was a form of "cultural exchange . . . a twofold posture of openness and retention, a percolating mixture of new ways and old."[27] And film noir, especially—as a challenge to both classical Hollywood cinema and U.S. society, and through its associations with Weimar cinema's artistic aspirations—offered exile filmmakers the nearest thing to dialectical exchange with the culture industry as was possible from within the belly of the beast. Furthermore, that exchange cut both ways, because not only the émigré filmmakers but also their studio bosses saw the benefit of, if not burying the hatchet, then at least blunting its blade. For the moguls, whose antipathy toward their émigré "brethren" extended to the aesthetic and budgetary excesses of the UFA (Universum Film AG) "style," more artistic films also served their business interests by weakening the émigrés' industries of origin while also appealing to both European and U.S. highbrow audiences.[28]

Attitudes and policies of the Americans themselves compounded the émigrés' ambivalence toward their host (and in most cases, adopted) country. The strict immigration quotas imposed by the National Origins Act of 1924 had been aimed to a large extent at Jews; much to the country's lasting shame, the legislation persisted, into World War II, even after the U.S. government knew of the Final Solution. Of course, the émigré directors (and many other refugee artists and intellectuals) were able to circumvent these restrictions, but the sense of collective unwelcomeness was palpable. Also unavoidable was its personal flipside, survivor guilt, as the comparative safety and comfort the émigrés enjoyed clashed irreconcilably with anxiety over the fate of their loved ones abroad and newsreel images of their homeland "being bombed to smithereens."[29]

Overt anti-Semitism in the United States, meanwhile, which had risen with the Depression of the 1930s, continued even after *Kristallnacht*, with polls in 1939 indicating that upward of 80 percent of the American public "were opposed to increasing quotas for Germany to help refugees."[30] Moreover, those who had already entered the country, particularly the cultural elite, came in for special opprobrium. A letter in *Life* magazine of 1940, titled "Refugees De Luxe," decried the "well-to-do refugees taking over expensive hotels, filling fashionable resorts, and dining in expensive restaurants, displaying assertive and flamboyant behavior."[31] Articles in *American Magazine*, with headings such as "Refugees—Burden or Asset?" "Spies Among Refugees," and "Refugee Gold Rush," "all contributed to the impression that refugees were a problematic issue in America."[32] Adding injury to insult, after Pearl Harbor the German émigrés found themselves "classified as 'enemy aliens,'" "had all their foreign royalties and accounts impounded," and "were also required to observe a strict curfew" during the war—not as stiff a penalty as Japanese citizens had to pay, certainly, but more bitterly ironic.[33]

The early cold war period proved especially threatening for the émigrés, although in this case there was some method to the madness. None of the Jewish émigré noir directors was a card-carrying communist, but all, like most Jews, were left-leaning, and the strong linkage between anti-Semitism and anticommunism made them ripe targets for the witch-hunters.[34] Only one Jewish émigré involved with the film industry, composer Hanns Eisler, was actually called before the House Committee on Un-American Activities (HUAC), which began investigating alleged subversive activity in Hollywood in 1947, but he was also the first to be interrogated by the committee, preceding the Hollywood Ten by a month. Called "the Karl Marx of music," a title that might have earned him praise in Weimar Germany, Eisler, despite claiming never to have joined the Communist Party, left the United States of his own accord to avoid deportation.[35]

The direct repercussions to the émigré directors were, in the end, comparatively slight: Lang claims to have been blacklisted for a year in the early 1950s; Bernhardt barely escaped blacklisting despite being denounced, by a fellow refugee, for his German communist affiliations in the 1920s. Billy Wilder and Fred Zinnemann were briefly tainted in the Director's Guild fight over loyalty oaths mounted by Cecil B. DeMille, during which DeMille notoriously questioned his foreign-born colleagues' patriotism by emphasizing their German names: "Vilder" and "Zinne*mann*."[36] Although DeMille's ploy backfired—the guild membership booed him, and even fellow right-winger John Ford openly chastised him—the émigrés' anxiety over their leftist sympathies was palpable. Billy Wilder was afraid his first wife Judith's communist ties might come back to haunt him, and Ulmer urged his daughter Arianné not to make political waves in high school for fear of the consequences, both to her and to him.[37]

Besides their concern over their susceptibility to persecution, the eerie echoes of Nazism in the anticommunist crusade appalled the émigrés. As Thomas Mann stated in a radio address in 1948: "I am painfully familiar with certain political trends. Spiritual intolerance, political inquisitions—and all in the name of an alleged 'state of emergency'—that is how it started in Germany. What followed was fascism and what followed fascism was war."[38] Partly from these concerns, partly due to more favorable political conditions in Europe, Mann and many other émigré artists and intellectuals returned to the Continent, some even to Germany, in the late 1940s and early 1950s. And as the decline of the Hollywood film industry continued into the 1950s, some of the refugee noir directors (Lang, Siodmak, Ophuls) followed suit. An added bitter irony here, corollary to the *Ostjude/Westjude* conflict limned above, is that the anticommunist crusade in the film industry was spearheaded by the still largely eastern European Jewish studio heads with whom the Jewish émigrés had already crossed swords socioculturally. As Billy Wilder sardonically summarized, "We went from Adolph Hitler to Adolph Zukor [head of Paramount Pictures]."[39]

To claim an overdetermined ambivalence for Jewish refugees is not to grant them a monopoly on historically based suffering. The situation in Europe leading up to and including World War II may have affected refugee Jews most adversely, but Americans of all stripes experienced their share of economic hardship, social turmoil, and psychological anxiety in the Depression and wartime years, and even more apocalyptic fears in the cold war years that followed. What I am proposing is that a Jewish *factor* be added to the "Zeitgeist theory" of film noir, which holds that "the pessimism, cynicism, violence and paranoia that typifies film noirs" can be explained as "an articulation of the cultural and social mood of [wartime and] postwar America; a mood that was itself pessimistic, cynical, violent and paranoid."[40] The emotional and psychological trauma induced in all who lived through these trying times, and which found at least partial expression in the emerging cycle of films retroactively labeled film noir, was necessarily heightened in a group of Jewish filmmakers who had been driven from a homeland and a culture to which they still felt strongly attached—and yet which in the interim had become the mortal enemy not merely of their adopted country, the United States, but of all humankind.

Fifth, and related to all the above, is admittedly the most problematic, but also the most intriguing, issue to pursue in regard to the Jewish émigré directors: Jewish sensibility. Beyond the more immediate influences of German Expressionism, French poetic realism, and the heightened ambivalence of exile, are their other aesthetic and thematic features in film noir that can be ascribed to uniquely Jewish ways of experiencing and looking at the world? If "unique" is understood here in historically grounded and culturally constructed terms, and "Jewish" is taken to embrace an array of identifications and expressions, then I propose that there can be. And through close readings of individual films by the Jewish émigré directors, I will explore the possibilities, and the limitations, of such a proposition.

Jewish Émigré Noir: Defined

Film noir's retroactive identification as a distinctive filmic type by French critics in 1946; the lack of awareness of this attribution among most American film-makers, critics, and filmgoers during the classical noir period (circa 1940–1960); and the broad range of films subsequently designated as film noir have led scholars to eschew a generic categorization in favor of more fluid concepts such as cycle, series, movement, historical construct, or cultural phenomenon.[41] For our purposes, this "category crisis" poses less of a problem conceptually than practically, where the issue becomes, first, identifying which films by Jewish émigré directors should be considered film noir; and second, determining who should be considered a Jewish émigré noir director.

The identification issue is notoriously slippery. Even leaving aside absurdly broad noir taxonomies such as Raymond Bellour's, which manages to include *King Kong* (1933) and *2001: A Space Odyssey* (1968) in the category, the differences among scholarly listings are striking.[42] My solution was to interact with and adjudicate among four prominent film noir encyclopedias: Michael F. Keaney's *Film Noir Guide*, Spencer Selby's *Dark City: The Film Noir*, Paul Duncan's *Film Noir*, and Alain Silver and Elizabeth Ward's *Film Noir: An Encyclopedic Reference to the American Style*.[43] The result is certainly not the final word on noir classification but rather a compromise of convenience among these reputable, but still significantly divergent, surveys.

The who's who of Jewish émigré directors begins with the historical distinction between first-wave Jewish *immigrants* and second-wave Jewish *émigrés*. That only four of the immigrants—Michael Curtiz, Lewis Milestone, Charles Vidor, and William Wyler—made *any* film noirs (and only Curtiz, who was Hungarian, made any significant number) renders the distinction somewhat moot,[44] except for its reinforcement of the notion that the "separation anxiety" experienced by Jews who had "arrived in flight" from Europe (rather than by choice) was a significant factor in these filmmakers' noir orientation.[45] As for those Jewish directors, such as Hugo Haas and László Benedek, who *were* driven from their homelands and might otherwise be considered part of the Jewish émigré noir grouping, the lack of direct involvement with the Weimar film industry is grounds for exclusion. Haas, a noted Czech film actor and director, came to the United States directly from Czechoslovakia following the Nazi invasion and occupation in 1938. Benedek worked as a screenwriter and film editor in Hungary until World War II, whence he escaped to Hollywood and began directing in 1944. Another second-wave arrival, Boris Ingster, a Latvian-born filmmaker who directed a key early film noir, *Stranger on the Third Floor* (1940), is left out of the grouping because he lacked direct contact with Weimar cinema *and* because he came to the United States of his own accord. Having worked with Sergei Eisenstein on *The Battleship Potemkin* (1925), Ingster joined Eisenstein on his trip to the United States in the early 1930s, and—unlike his mentor, who returned to the Soviet Union in disillusionment—remained in Hollywood for the rest of his career.

One exception to the above criteria is Willy Wilder (aka W. Lee Wilder), who came to the United States in the mid-1920s yet did not become involved in filmmaking until the mid-1940s. I include Willy among the Jewish émigré noir directors for several reasons: first, because of his near total neglect in the field until now; second, because his noirs are surpassed in number only by Lang, Siodmak, and Alfred Hitchcock, and one of them, *The Pretender* (1947), figures prominently in the noir canon; third, because of his sibling relationship to Billy Wilder, with whose life and work Willy's significantly interfaces; and finally, because several of his noirs relate intriguingly to Jewish themes.[46] Another mildly exceptional case, for a different reason, is Anatole Litvak. Born in the Ukraine and raised in Russia, Litvak is the sole non-German or -Austrian in my Jewish émigré noir director grouping. He makes the cut because, unlike Haas, Benedek, or Ingster, Litvak had considerable contact with Weimar cinema, having worked in Germany off and on from the mid-1920s until his escape to France in the early 1930s.

Jewish Émigré Noir: Quantified

No serious observer can (or does) deny that Jewish émigré directors—Fritz Lang, Robert Siodmak, Billy and Willy Wilder, Otto Preminger, Edgar G. Ulmer, Curtis Bernhardt, Max Ophuls, John Brahm, Anatole Litvak, and Fred Zinnemann—directed a disproportionate number of the earliest and most definitive examples of the noir canon. The following list highlights only some of their more salient films released in or before 1950: *Fury* (1936), *You Only Live Once* (1937), *The Woman in the Window* (1945), *Scarlet Street* (1945) [Lang]; *Phantom Lady* (1944), *The Killers* (1946), *The Dark Mirror* (1946), *Criss Cross* (1949) [Siodmak]; *Double Indemnity* (1944), *Sunset Boulevard* (1950) [Billy Wilder]; *The Pretender* [Willy Wilder]; *Laura* (1944), *Fallen Angel* (1945), *Where the Sidewalk Ends* (1950) [Preminger]; *Detour* (1945), *Strange Illusion* (1945), *Ruthless* (1948) [Ulmer]; *Conflict* (1945), *Possessed* (1947) [Bernhardt]; *Caught, The Reckless Moment* (both 1947) [Ophuls]; *The Lodger* (1944), *Guest in the House* (1944), *Hangover Square* (1945), *The Locket* (1946) [Brahm]; *Out of the Fog* (1940), *The Long Night* (1947), *Sorry, Wrong Number* (1948) [Litvak]; *Act of Violence* (1949) [Zinnemann]. (See the appendix for more details.)

And the following computation underscores the numerical predominance of Jewish émigré directors (again based on cross-referencing): Lang stands alone as the most prolific noir director with fifteen films; Siodmak ties Anthony Mann for second with ten; Hitchcock comes in third with nine; John Brahm and Willy Wilder are close behind with eight; Joseph L. Lewis is next with seven; Preminger and Ulmer join Nicholas Ray, Jean Negulesco, Robert Wise, Richard Fleischer, Joseph Losey, Lewis Allen, and Andrew L. Stone with six; and Bernhardt and Litvak are among a crowd with five that includes Curtiz, Edward Dmytryk, Henry Hathaway, Phil Karlson, John Farrow, and Maxwell Shane. In sum, five of the top seven, and eight of the top twenty-four, film noir directors (in number of films made) are Jewish émigrés.

Further down the noir list one finds Billy Wilder with three films, Ophuls with two, and Zinnemann with one. But three of these films, Wilder's *Double Indemnity* and *Sunset Boulevard* and Ophuls's *Caught*, are quintessential to the noir canon, and Zinnemann's *Act of Violence* is not only a key Jewish émigré noir but a vastly underrated noir altogether. Alain Silver, the Andrew Sarris of noir criticism, provides additional, if inadvertent, support for the preeminence of Jewish émigré directors when, in naming his "ten best" film noirs (four of which are by Jewish refugees), he states, "I did have one rule: a single movie per director, otherwise Siodmak, Lang, Ophuls and Wilder might have overwhelmed the field and made it an all-émigré list."[47]

Jewish Émigré Noir: Qualified

"There is no history of mankind," wrote Karl Popper, "there is only an indefinite number of histories of all kinds of aspects of human life."[48] Similarly, although the Jewishness of the refugee directors undoubtedly played a crucial role in the formation of film noir, this is only one of several, sometimes overlapping determinants. The other important factors have been amply rehearsed in the vast and ever-burgeoning film noir scholarship.[49] These include first and foremost, besides the German Expressionist and poetic realist influences already mentioned, the so-called hard-boiled American crime novels of Dashiell Hammett, James M. Cain, Horace McCoy, Raymond Chandler, and (to a less hard-boiled extent) Cornell Woolrich. These (non-Jewish) writers' work, which formed the basis for several noteworthy noirs (*The Maltese Falcon*, 1941; *The Glass Key*, 1942; *Double Indemnity*; *Phantom Lady*; *Murder My Sweet*, 1944; *Mildred Pierce*, 1945; *The Big Sleep*, 1946; *The Postman Always Rings Twice*, 1946), features noir's telltale clipped, tough-guy, Hemingway-esque dialogue; frequent first-person narration by an alienated, anti-hero protagonist; a gritty urban environment that includes forays into the haunts of the rich and famous; and, frequently but not obligatorily, a femme fatale.

If we look at the Jewish émigré noir output, however, an alternative pattern emerges. Although Jewish émigrés directed a few noirs based on hard-boiled novels (*Double Indemnity*, *The Brasher Doubloon*, 1947), these are exceptions. Far more prevalent are works that take a quite different, often decidedly un-tough-guy tack. *The Woman in the Window* and *Scarlet Street*, for example, two of Lang's early American noirs, feature pointedly soft-boiled protagonists—ordinary men who, like the petty bourgeois antiheroes of the 1920s German street film, venture at their peril from their drab middle-class existences into the pulsating nightlife of the city.⁵⁰ In some ways, shop cashier Christopher Cross of *Scarlet Street* and professor Richard Wanley of *The Woman in the Window*, both roles played against type by Edward G. Robinson, seem more like the British-type detective hero to which the hard-boiled American version was concocted as an alternative. These were men, in Gilbert Seldes's words, of "effeminate manners, artistic leanings, and elaborate deductions," who compare to a "real man" like "a shop-window full of dummies."⁵¹ The British detective hero, however, at least got his man; the Lang antihero is barely a man at all. Tellingly, he lacks access even to the tough noir's first-person, voice-over narration, denying him even partial control of events through interpretation and commentary. And although he is, like the libidinous tough hero, strongly attracted to the femme fatale, he is also, unlike the tough hero, physically unsuited for the role.

The effeminately coded "artistic leanings" of the British detective appear in protagonists and other main characters of Jewish émigré noirs to a striking degree. Chris Cross is a Sunday painter, and Professor Wanley falls for the woman portrayed in a painting. Harry Quincy (George Sanders), the avuncular title character in *The Strange Affair of Uncle Harry* (1945), is a frustrated painter working as a pattern designer, and Douglas Proctor (Ralph Bellamy), who falls for the femme fatale in *Guest in the House*, is a painter and magazine illustrator. *Detour*'s ill-starred hero, Al Roberts (Tom Neal), is a classical pianist stuck playing nightclubs; and two other figures, *Hangover Square*'s George Harvey Bone (Laird Cregar) and *City for Conquest*'s (1940) Eddie Kenney (Arthur Kennedy), are frustrated composers. Joe Gillis (William Holden), the "victim hero" of *Sunset Boulevard*; Stephen Byrne (Louis Hayward), the murderer-protagonist of *House by the River* (1950); and Gaston Morel (John Carradine), the eponymous serial killer of *Bluebeard* (1944), are, respectively, a down-on-his-luck screenwriter, a struggling novelist, and a demented puppeteer. Jack Marlow (Franchot Tone) of *Phantom Lady*, the leading man's best friend but also the arch villain, is a schizophrenic sculptor; Mark Lamphere (Michael Redgrave), the Jekyll-Hyde husband of the protagonist in *Secret Beyond the Door* (1948), is an architect and a magazine editor; *The Locket*'s Norman Clyde, played by iconic tough guy Robert Mitchum, is here a sensitive artist; and art plays perhaps its most pivotal role in *Laura*, in which a painting of the eponymous career girl (played by Gene Tierney) embodies the romantic obsession of both the epicene villain, fashion maven Waldo Lydecker (Clifton Webb), and the ostensible tough-guy hero, Mark McPherson (Dana Andrews). In addition, three of the refugee-noir protagonists, *The Suspect*'s (1944) Philip Marshall (Charles Laughton), *Uncle Harry*'s Harry Quincy (Sanders), and *Bluebeard's Ten Honeymoons*'s (1960) Henri Landru (Sanders again), are played by British actors.

As for female protagonists, an inordinate number of these, constituting a veritable subset within the noir cycle, appear in Jewish émigré noirs: Celia Lamphere (Joan Bennett) in *Secret Beyond the Door*; Carol "Kansas" Richman

(Ella Raines) in *Phantom Lady*; Jackie Lamont/Abigail Martin (Deanna Durbin) in *Christmas Holiday* (1944); Helen Capel (Dorothy McGuire) in *The Spiral Staircase* (1945); Terry and Ruth Collins (identical twins played by Olivia de Havilland) in *The Dark Mirror*; Katie and Pat Bosworth (also identical twins, played by Bette Davis) in *A Stolen Life* (1946); Louise Howell Graham (Joan Crawford) in *Possessed*; Leonora Eames (Barbara Bel Geddes) in *Caught*; Lucia Harper (Bennett) in *The Reckless Moment*; Margie Foster (June Havoc) in *Once a Thief* (1953); and Jenny Hager (Hedy Lamarr) in *The Strange Woman* (1946).

That Jews, as a historically disenfranchised and maligned people, should identify with other marginalized and oppressed groups such as women and gays, as well as people of color and the lower classes, is psychologically self-evident and empirically documented in Jews' American voting record and highly dispro-portionate involvement in various progressive social movements. Additionally, if more subtly, the linkage of Jewish masculinity with effeminacy, and by extension with homosexuality, has a long and ambivalent history. Sander Gilman, in his psycho-semiotic study *The Jew's Body*, describes how the European image of the male Jew as feminized was overdetermined: first, by his stereotypically stunted physiognomy, flat feet, and awkward gait, which rendered him "innately unable to undertake physical labor"; and second, by his circumcised penis, which was deemed analogous to the clitoris of the woman.[52] The Jewish/gay connection was made discursively explicit in the late 1800s, when anti-Semitism was labeled a "scientific" term for Jew hating at the same historical moment that homosexu-ality was being clinically designated a new disease.[53]

Jewish male internalization of the feminizing discourse is evident in the early Zionist movement, whose emphasis on physical exercise and manual labor must be viewed partly as a reaction against the stereotype of the Jewish weakling. Physician and Zionist leader Max Nordau's notion of the *neue Muskeljude* (new muscle Jew) was devised as an antidote to Jews' alleged physical, and thus also political, puniness and ineffectuality.[54] Nordau's therapeutic prescription would be realized, of course, in the new state of Israel's kibbutznik, Mossad opera-tive, and army soldier. The muscle Jew ideal would infiltrate the United States in the twentieth century also, albeit with a more working-class, less patriotic tinge. Where would American organized crime have been without mob kingpins Meyer Lansky, Bugsy Siegel, and Mickey Cohen, or American boxing without champions Benny Leonard, Max Baer, and Maxie Rosenbloom?[55]

Despite what some might see as healthy responses to, and others as overcom-pensation for, the Jewish weakling syndrome, the image of the feminized—or at least less ruggedly masculine—Jewish male persisted, if not prevailed, even in the United States. Harvard president Charles W. Eliot announced in 1907, shortly before the university instituted anti-Jewish enrollment quotas that would last into the 1960s, "Jews are distinctly inferior in stature and physical development . . . to any other race."[56] Sociologist Edward Alsworth Ross historicized the assessment in 1914, contrasting the American pioneers who crossed the continent by wagon train with the immigrant Jews who came over by ocean liner. These Jews, Ross proclaimed, were "undersized and weak-muscled," and shunned "bodily activity."[57] Über-anti-Semite Henry Ford summarized the Jewish weakling sentiment in the 1920s, declaring flatly, "Jews are not sportsmen."[58] Little wonder that second-generation American Jew Irving Howe, in his memoir *World of Our Fathers*, concluded that the "suspicion of the physical, fear of hurt, anxiety over the sheer 'pointlessness' of play . . . all went deep into the recesses of the Jewish psyche."[59]

Although the existence of the Jewish runt stereotype is beyond dispute, not everyone agrees that it was constructed entirely from without and internalized by Jews, or even whether such a self-image was, or is, "bad for the Jews." Daniel Boyarin, in *Unheroic Conduct: The Rise of Heterosexuality and the Invention of the Jewish Man*, argues that the sensitive, scholarly male Jew devoted to religious study developed in the early rabbinic period, and was encouraged thereafter, partly as a defense mechanism, partly as an overt rejection of and alternative to the more physical, aggressive masculinity espoused and practiced by the larger, and largely hostile, gentile society.[60] Boyarin's queer reading of the gentle rabbi's legacy is aimed primarily, and polemically, at the muscle Jew of modern-day Israel. Philip Roth's alter ego, Nathan Zuckerman, applies a similar revisionism to the American scene when he states, in *American Pastoral*, "Physical aggression, even camouflaged by athletic uniforms and official rules and intended to do no harm to Jews, was not a traditional source of pleasure in our community."[61]

Nor would such aggression, even camouflaged by a private investigator's license or a Wild West honor code, likely have been a source of pleasure to the Jewish refugee community that helped pioneer film noir. Heirs to a Jewish legacy and historical circumstance that privileged intellect over action, brokering over building, the luftmensch ("air man," or occupational schlemiel) over the man of the world, Lang, Siodmak, Ulmer, and the others were preternaturally less disposed than their American cohorts toward the virile, gun-toting, tough-talking detective.[62] Their antiheroes thus tended toward the artist and intellectual, the bank clerk and insurance agent, and to a character they were said, and perhaps sensed themselves, most to resemble: the woman.

This is not to assert, of course, that the attitudes of Jewish émigré noir directors toward this and other aspects of the noir aesthetic were monolithic or monocausal. Just as Jewish émigrés were by no means solely responsible for the formation of film noir, neither is their European-based, Nazi-inflected Jewishness the sole factor to consider in analyzing their noir films. Despite their shared history and experience, differences *within* difference—of class and region, of background and personality, of psychological motivation and cultural orientation—existed among the refugee Jewish directors and expressed itself in their work, to which the case studies that make up the bulk of this book will attest.

Conversely, the refugee Jews were not impervious to the various historical, cultural, socioeconomic, and ideological factors that influenced all filmmakers working in the United States during the classical noir period. What I am arguing is that crucial similarities among the Jewish refugees, and differences between them and non-refugees from a *Jewish* standpoint, have previously been ignored and deserve to be addressed as part of a reassessment of the ontology and epistemology of film noir.

Wartime Effects

The relevance of World War II to the Jewish/noir question goes beyond the unique psychological conflicts this universally tragic event may have induced in Jewish émigré noir directors. Recent work by Sheri Chinen Biesen, regarding the war's importance to the noir formation in general, has special pertinence here. Countering influential views, such as those of filmmaker-historian Paul Schrader, that noir was predominantly a "postwar trend pre-empted by the war," Biesen argues that the war generated "a complex array of social, economic, cultural, political, technological, and creative circumstances" that spurred rather than blunted noir's emergence.[63] To the wartime influence most frequently cited—namely, that the studios' wartime rationing of lights, electricity, and film stock, and the need to recycle sets and props, encouraged noir's emblematic low-key lighting and sparse décor—Biesen adds several other factors: (1) increased anxiety over loved ones in combat, fear of possible invasion at home, and hardship caused by government rationing and war-related shortages made moviegoers more receptive to the dark visions of film noir; (2) labor-driven migration to the cities made noir's urban milieu more familiar; (3) nighttime settings and darkened backgrounds resonated with those forced into twenty-four-hour production shifts and with everyone confronting "the shadowy abysses of blacked-out wartime cities at night"; (4) viewers' experience with dark themes and styles was foreshadowed before the war and reinforced during it through other popular cultural forms such as dime novels, comic books, and radio dramas (e.g., *Black Mask* novels, *Marvel* comics, Orson Welles's *War of the Worlds* and *The Shadow* broadcasts), which likewise grew darker during the war; (5) the federal Office of Censorship's lifting of its ban on depicting war-related atrocities in documentary films established, in 1943/1944, a precedent for increased screen violence in narrative films that was tailor-made for film noir; (6) the vaunted sexuality of film noir also responded to the shifting gender roles of independent working women and appealed to the desires of combat-hardened military men, both overseas GIs and returning veterans; (7) the studios' wartime labor needs, with many filmmakers pressed into wartime service but with most foreign directors over the age for combat, "gave greater creative . . . authority to European émigré filmmakers (for example Michael Curtiz, Fritz Lang, Billy Wilder, and Rudolph Maté)."[64]

Other points add further weight to Biesen's wartime noir ontology and its connection to the Jewish refugees. First, although film noir was initially identified as an emerging film cycle and given its distinctive name by the French after the war, this designation was prompted mainly by a group of films made *during* the war: *The Maltese Falcon* (John Huston), *This Gun for Hire* (Frank Tuttle, 1942), *Double Indemnity* and *The Lost Weekend* (Billy Wilder), *Murder My Sweet* (Edward Dmytryk), *Laura* (Preminger), and *The Woman in the Window* (Lang).[65] Four of the seven were directed by Jewish émigré directors, and a fifth, *Murder, My Sweet*, was strongly influenced by *Double Indemnity*.[66] Second, the years 1944–1945 saw a dramatic increase both in the number of film noirs released in the United States and in the number of noirs directed by Jewish refugees, and *Double Indemnity*, again, played a crucial role in the spurt. Silver and Ward's survey of film noirs by year lists only two noirs for 1943, neither directed by a Jewish émigré. In 1944 the total jumps to eight, and in 1945 to fifteen, with five of the eight and seven of the fifteen, respectively, directed by Jewish émigrés.[67]

Although the government's relaxed censorship policies in wartime documentaries encouraged reduced content restrictions in Hollywood fiction films, the Production Code Administration's (PCA) approval of a treatment for *Double Indemnity* in 1943 (an earlier version based on the 1935 Cain novel had been summarily rejected) was regarded by producers as an "an emancipation for Hollywood writing," and led to a flood of film proposals dealing with murder and eros.[68] Third, according to Biesen, eight of sixteen films that "heralded the first definitive phase of film noir" (*Double Indemnity, The Lost Weekend, The Woman in the Window, Scarlet Street, Ministry of Fear, Phantom Lady, Laura,* and *Detour*) were by Jewish refugee directors; and those that "represent the most expressionistic, stylistically black phase of film noir" include *Double Indemnity, Phantom Lady,* and the *Double Indemnity*–influenced *Murder, My Sweet*.[69] Finally, *Double Indemnity* marks, for Biesen (and most noir scholars), the "definitive, full-blown exemplar of the early noir crime cycle's steady emergence."[70]

Creative Control

The alleged "greater authority" granted émigré directors during the war is significant from an auteurist standpoint as well. It certainly lends support to the proposition that film noirs made by these directors might have reflected—within commercial and ideological constraints, and given the collaborative nature of the medium—their personal creative concerns. This contention must be further reconciled with the conventional view of a classical Hollywood system—operating under Fordist conditions of production—that tended to quash, or at least severely restrict, individual expression. Of course, qualifications to such a monolithic judgment were already present in the text that most firmly established it: David Bordwell, Janet Staiger, and Kristin Thompson's *The Classical Hollywood Cinema: Film Style and Mode of Production to 1960* (1985). Thomas Schatz, Richard

Maltby, and Steve Neale and Murray Smith, among others, have offered further revisioning, and outright debunking, of the strict constructionist line.[71] To summarize: even in its most orthodox phase, the Hollywood studio system allowed for, indeed demanded, a measure of independence—"controlled variation," in Bordwell, Staiger, and Thompson's phrase—varying according to the particular studio, producer, director, genre, and other contingencies.

Many of these factors worked in favor of the émigré directors, who were predisposed to a more autonomous approach due to their work in the director-oriented German and French systems, and inclined to be granted (somewhat) greater creative freedom due to their established artistic credentials or European branding potential. As for the studio-producer dynamic, Lang, although he began his Hollywood career at quintessentially classical Metro-Goldwyn-Mayer (with the early noir *Fury*), went on to make two noirs for independent producer Walter Wanger (*You Only Live Once*, and *Scarlet Street*); a third for the smallest and most independent-minded of the majors, United Artists (*Hangmen Also Die!* 1943); a fourth for mini-major International Pictures (*The Woman in the Window*); a fifth for the studio regarded as the most European in Hollywood, Paramount (*Ministry of Fear*, 1944); and two others for his own production company, Diana Productions, *Secret Beyond the Door* and *House by the River*.

Siodmak made most of his noirs for semi-independent producers (Joan Harrison, Mark Hellinger, Nunally Johnson, Sol Siegel) who granted him comparative independence, and, when they did not, he found other ways to circumvent the system, such as by cutting "with the camera" (reducing editorial choices) and inserting key scenes of his own devising (requiring other new scenes to be built around them).[72] Billy Wilder spent his entire early American career at Paramount, where he also became one of the first U.S. writer-directors (or cowriters, in his case), thus gaining a correspondingly greater measure of creative control. Preminger became one of the first classical-era producer-directors on his first noirs, *Laura* and *Fallen Angel*, made for Twentieth Century Fox, which, despite being one of the vertically integrated Big Five studios, was headed by the (somewhat) more artistically inclined Darryl F. Zanuck.[73] In addition to directing, Litvak produced some of his films as well; and Bernhardt and Brahm, similar to Siodmak, claim to have "pre-shot" their films to minimize outside tampering.[74] Ophuls directed *Caught* for the newly formed and creative freedom–oriented Enterprise Studios, and *The Reckless Moment* for Wanger.[75] Ulmer made his first noirs, *Detour* and *Strange Illusion*, at the mini-studio Producers Releasing Corporation, and he continued to work outside the classical studio system—despite the lower budgets, tighter shooting schedules, and lesser talent—because of the greater autonomy that such relative independence afforded.[76] Willy Wilder, meanwhile, not only produced but also partially financed all his pictures.[77]

Industry-wide developments in the Hollywood system of the early-to-mid-1940s further fueled resistance to the classical studio model. The Consent Decree of 1940, which curtailed block booking and eliminated blind selling and thereby encouraged "that all films, A or B, be sold to exhibitors on an individual basis . . . , greatly opened up the marketplace for the proliferation of independent production companies."[78] The Revenue Act of 1941, which raised top-bracket taxes to as much as 90 percent, was another "strong incentive for top talent to engage in independent production or seek freelance profit participation deals that allowed taxation at lower capital gains rates."[79] Several prominent directors, including John Ford, William Dieterle, Allan Dwan, Edmund Goulding, and Sam Wood, began freelancing in 1941 or earlier.[80] Frank Capra formed Liberty Films in 1940–1941 (revived, after his government documentaries, in 1944); James Cagney founded Cagney Productions in 1942; and Orson Welles's landmark film *Citizen Kane* (1941), a major influence on film noir, was coproduced (together with RKO) by his Mercury Productions. Other director-producers who flourished during the studio era include Howard Hawks and Ernst Lubitsch. Howard Hughes and Preston Sturges briefly formed California Pictures, and Hughes later formed his own company, as did Alfred Hitchcock and John Ford. On a more contentious note, actor Olivia de Havilland successfully sued Warner Bros. in 1943–1944 over the talent-contract system, and the Society of Independent Motion Picture Producers (SIMPP)—formed in 1941 by Walt Disney, Charlie Chaplin, Samuel Goldwyn, Mary Pickford, Walter Wanger, David O. Selznick, and Orson Welles— although less immediately successful in combating the studio oligarchy, played a crucial role in effecting the Paramount decision of 1948 that dismantled vertical integration in the industry and paved the way for the New Hollywood.[81]

Talent agents, whose ascension would radically transform Hollywood's power relations in the postwar years, first emerged as major players in the early 1940s. Some forged independent production partnerships with their former clients, such as Charles K. Feldman did with Siodmak on *Uncle Harry* and with Howard Hawks on his first two noirs, *To Have and Have Not* (1944) and *The Big Sleep*. The most important agency to emerge in the war years was Jules Stein and Lew Wasserman's Music Corporation of America (MCA), future owners of Universal Studios. Starting as early as 1942 with the formation of Bette Davis's independent production company, B.D. Inc., MCA began brokering lucrative talent deals, eventually becoming *the* key decision maker in postwar Hollywood.[82] All this is not to maintain that the historical moment of postclassical Hollywood should be shifted back from the late to the early 1940s, but rather to indicate that an incipient climate more compatible with creative independence was concurrent with the onset of film noir.

The Genre Question Revisited

The ambiguity of film noir's relation to genre further inscribes Jewish émigré directors in the noir discourse. If anyone in the United States would have been privy to the term "film noir," émigré directors—with their strong personal, cultural, and industrial ties to Europe, and France specifically—were the most likely candidates. But direct knowledge of the French designation may have been irrelevant in any event, because the domestic press had recognized already by 1944 "a bold new trend" in American films, featuring unprecedented levels of crime, violence, and sexuality, which they called the "red meat crime cycle."[83] By 1947, *Life* magazine, in referring to the films of the year before, went further, describing in detail many of the traits now universally attributed to film noir: "deep shadows, clutching hands, exploding revolvers, sadistic villains and hero-ines tormented with deeply rooted diseases of the mind . . . in a panting display of psychoneuroses, unsublimated sex and murder most foul."[84]

The constitutive elements of crime, violence, and sexuality that the mid-1940s discourse and subsequent scholarship regard as essential to the noir-type film do not by themselves separate Jewish émigré directors from the pack. Once the telltale figure of the ambivalent protagonist, the femme fatale, and expressionist mise-en-scène are added to the mix, however, a critical mass congeals linking noir to the Jewish émigré element. Significantly, all these components were evident in, if not fundamental to, the Weimar era in which the Jewish émigré noirists cut their filmmaking teeth. As I will describe more extensively in subsequent chapters, the German Kammerspiel and street film in particular, with their dark look, claustrophobic feel, and everyman antihero caught in a web of urban angst and transgressive sexuality, must be regarded as clear precursors of film noir, a notion that is reinforced through these tropes' foregrounding in several classical American noir titles: *City Streets* (1931, 1938), *Street of Chance* (1942), *Scarlet Street, The House on 92nd Street* (1945), *The Street with No Name* (1948), *Panic in the Streets* (1950), *Side Street* (1950), *Road House* (1948), *Roadblock* (1951), *Drive a Crooked Road* (1954), *Plunder Road* (1957), *Nightmare Alley* (1947), *Thieves' Highway* (1949), *Sunset Boulevard, Where the Sidewalk Ends, 711 Ocean Drive* (1951), *The Strip* (1951), *The Hitch-Hiker* (1953), and *Detour.*

The femme fatale is a more complex issue. This archetype's genealogy in western culture extends at least as far back as the biblical Eve and extra-liturgical Lilith, with several variants in Greek mythology and a major literary revival in the nineteenth-century gothic novel. The femme fatale's filmic incarnation can be traced pre-Weimar, and extra-Germanically, to Fox Films star Theda Bara's exotic vamp of the mid-1910s. Nonetheless, "the licentious adulteress or vice-ridden flapper, the lascivious high-society lady and the man-destroying Lulu of [Frank] Wedekind's invention," which had appeared in literary and stage form in Germany before World War I, flourished there again, and for the first time on film, in the 1920s.[85] To add that Wedekind was Jewish (as were Hungarian immi-grant William Fox and Cincinnati-born Theda Bara, née Theodosia Goodman) is, again, not to deny other, in this case specifically American, influences on film noir's predilection for the femme fatale (such as her privileging in the hard-boiled novel or the threat posed to men by women's unprecedented wartime entry into the workplace). Framing the spider woman in relation to her ethno-religious aspect does, however, serve to ground the figure's cross-cultural appeal for Jewish émigré directors' squarely in the Jewish-inflected Weimar period.

Visual style, for many *the* distinguishing mark of film noir, is for others the main reason to regard noir as a cycle or movement. Paul Schrader's gloss of the noir aesthetic, for example—nighttime scenes, rain-drenched streets, compositional tension rather than action, a fondness for oblique lines—both fits the street film like a velvet glove and leads him to posit greater kinship between noir and German Expressionism than with the thriller or gangster film. A group of like-minded filmmakers working in a specific time and place, reacting to particular historical conditions and expressing themselves through unconventional or alternative cinematic means—a thumbnail definition of a film movement—are what sets noir apart, for Schrader, more than shared narrative conventions defined by plot and character.[86] Janey Place bases her "movement" claim for noir exclusively on "a remarkable homogeneous visual style with which it cuts across genres."[87] As with Schrader, Place's delineation of the noir style could serve as a brief for cinematic expressionism—chiaroscuro, low-key lighting; an opposition of light and darkness; claustrophobic framing devices; unbalanced compositions; oblique shadows; obtrusive and disturbing close-ups juxtaposed with extreme high-angle shots—in all, a disorienting antirealism.[88]

Schrader's division of classical noir into three, sometimes overlapping phases—wartime (1941–1946), postwar realism (1945–1949), and psychotic action/suicidal impulse (1949–1953)—while it appears to contradict Place's antirealist ascription (and to some extent the *Life* article quoted above), comports exceedingly well with the Jewish émigré thesis. Schrader's first phase, typified by the detective and lone-wolf protagonist, was dominated numerically and in its expressionist aspect, as we have seen, by Jewish émigré directors. The second phase, in which tension between a dominant expressionist and an emergent neorealist style created an intriguing dialectic, also provides an uncanny parallel to the Weimar period's mid-1920s shift from Expressionism as its dominant cultural influence, to its reactive opposite, *Neue Sachlichkeit* (New Objectivity). This stylistic and philosophical paradigm shift will be elaborated on in subsequent chapters, but one can readily perceive how the turn from subjectivity to objectivity, which also crucially informed the street film, mirrors—mutatis mutandis—the aesthetic transition of Schrader's second noir phase (whose definitive works Schrader himself dubs "'street' films").[89] The third phase, when "the noir hero, seemingly under the weight of ten years of despair, started to go bananas," also appears to have resonated strongly with the Jewish refugee directors, and for similar, culturally specific reasons. The deranged personae in third-phase Jewish émigré noirs such as *Sunset Boulevard, Ace in the Hole* (Wilder, 1951), *Where the Sidewalk Ends, The Big Heat* (Lang, 1953), and *Angel Face* (Preminger, 1953)—not to mention earlier-phase "pathological noirs" by Jewish émigrés such as *The Lodger, Bluebeard, Hangover Square, Possessed, Guest in the House,* and *Caught*—may well have functioned as alter egos for the cold warrior paranoiacs of those post-Holocaust times. But they also found unmistakable Weimar antecedents in the monsters and serial murderers of *The Cabinet of Dr. Caligari* (Robert Wiene, 1919), *Nosferatu* (F. W. Murnau, 1922), the *Mabuse* trilogy (Lang, 1922, 1932), *Pandora's Box* (G. W. Pabst, 1928), and *M* (Lang, 1931).

Again, I am not claiming that Jewish émigrés were the only directors to indulge in third-phase Grand Guignol, as attested by Lewis's *Gun Crazy* (1949), Raoul Walsh's *White Heat* (1949), Norman Foster's *Kiss Tomorrow Goodbye* (1950), Maté's *D.O.A.,* and Ray's *They Live By Night* (1949) and *In a Lonely Place* (1950), among others. But, as before, I *am* making a case for the substantial influence and unique motivation, in both the third noir phase and overall, of a group of Jewish filmmakers who during the Weimar era had experienced firsthand, and subsequently were most traumatically affected by, Germany's devolution from Caligari to Hitler.[90]

The Jewish Question

Because my case for a Jewish factor in film noir obviously hinges on the Jewish identity of the émigré directors, the question naturally follows, how Jewish were they? As with questions of class, region, and personality, differences in Jewish identification and consciousness obviously existed among the Jewish émigré noir-ists. Moreover, these differences shifted over time in response to circumstance, some gradually and subtly, some suddenly and starkly. The individual case studies will explore the differences in greater detail, but one can generalize about one factor: these filmmakers were raised, without exception, in nonobservant, largely secular households and remained detached from religious observance in their adult lives. Almost all married, at least somewhere along the way, non-Jewish wives (Siodmak is the lone exception). Ulmer, however, who himself converted to Christianity upon marrying his first (non-Jewish) wife, reverted to Judaism upon marrying his second (Jewish) wife, and became perhaps the most religiously Jewish of the group. Lang, born to a non-Jewish father and a Jewish mother who converted to Catholicism, is no doubt the most complex case. Protesting his Catholicism to his dying day yet considered a Jew by both the Nazis and his fellow émigrés, Lang lived with a Jewish woman, Lily Latté, from the time that he fled Germany, and he granted her a Jewish wedding before his death. More important for the study of Jewish émigré noir, however, neither interfaith marriage nor secularism, as I can attest from my own situation and experience, necessarily implies a dearth of Jewish consciousness or commitment.

Another aspect of Jewish awareness that applies to all the émigrés, and which again separates them from their immigrant coreligionists, is captured in Billy Wilder's famous (if not necessarily original) quip that Hitler made him a Jew.[91] Although the émigrés had been exposed to anti-Semitism since childhood, through personal confrontation and the pervasive anti-Jewish atmosphere, the full ramifications, individually and collectively, of Jew hatred only became evident with the rise of the Nazis. And although the existential threat, physically and financially, was lessened once sanctuary in Los Angeles and a film job in Hollywood had been secured, the fate of relatives or friends left behind (several of whom perished in the Holocaust) remained for many an especially fraught issue.

Social interaction among the émigrés (many of whom had already known and worked with one another in Germany) in the various European-style salons that emerged in "Weimar on the Pacific" reinforced a kinship now heightened by their mutual refugee status. Their common background and current predicament occasionally translated into career assistance, such as Siodmak's help in securing Max Ophuls a directing assignment at Universal-International, and even collaboration, such as Siodmak's story idea for Bernhardt's film *Conflict*. Not that the narcissism of minor differences, and the cutthroat nature of the film business, didn't also generate rivalry—"every refugee was jealous of the next one," as Curtis Bernhardt put it.[92] But when it came to their identities as refugee *Jews*, not filmmakers, the men put aside their selfish interests and collaborated, most tangibly on the European Film Fund—started by the émigré community to help Jews still caught in Nazi-occupied Europe, but which also aided those who were struggling financially in the United States, such as Ophuls in his early Hollywood years.[93]

The various commonalities, although certainly not canceling the differences, do encourage what R. Barton Palmer terms "a group auteurist" approach to the study of the Jewish émigré directors.[94] My partial adoption of such an approach comes with full awareness of the pitfalls of auteur theory in general: namely, its tendency to downplay collaboration and to privilege intentionality at the expense of sociocultural and political economic factors. Group auteurism, however, while not eliminating these concerns, does at least offer, especially in regard to Jewish émigré noirists, a more nuanced method of addressing them. The fact that several Jewish Weimer-era actors (Curt Bois, Alexander Granach, Fritz Kortner, Reinhold Schünzel), cinematographers (Eugen Schüfftan, John Alton), set designers (Hans Dreier, Hans Jacoby), composers (Franz Waxman, Frederick Hollander, Hanns Eisler), and editors (Rudi Fehr) worked on noirs directed by Jewish émigrés actually expands, rather than contracts, the collaborative aspect. The focus on an ethnically distinct body of directors making films of a specific type in the same movie industry at a particular historical moment also allows for an analysis that radiates outward into the larger sociocultural sphere. By combining elements of authorship, genre, film movement, and historical analysis, the group auteurist approach thus provides a useful framework not only for the study of émigré Jewish noir, but hopefully also for the broadening and enriching of our understanding of film noir as a whole.[95]

2 *Jews in Germany*

TORN BETWEEN TWO WORLDS

Jews may not have invented the term "ambivalence"—its coining is credited to the non-Jewish Swiss psychoanalyst Eugen Bleuler in 1911—but their relationship to the notion of a conflicted self is uniquely overdetermined, both discursively and experientially. The biblical banishment of the ur-couple from paradise planted the seeds of a primal spirit/matter split, not only for Jews but for all humanity. Early Christian theologians reified the schism in the concept of original sin, Cartesian philosophers rationalized it in cogito ergo sum, and the Romantic poet Goethe gave it voice through the figure of Faust:

> Two souls, alas, are dwelling in my breast,
> And one is striving to be separate from the other.
> One holds, with sensual, passionate desire,
> Fast to the world, with clinging organs;
> The other rises strong from earthly mist
> To the ethereal realms of high ancestral spirit.[1]

But it would take the Jewish Freud, in shifting ambivalence's center of gravity from the metaphorical breast to the unconscious mind, and the Jewish Kafka, in historically grounding the phenomenon in existential angst, to lay the foundation for what Jewish filmmaker Henry Bean calls "the ambivalent, self-doubting, self-hating modern condition."[2]

That Freud's and Kafka's mother tongue was the same as Goethe's is more than coincidental to a discussion of the phenomenological dimension of ambivalence. Jews' "lived" relation to ambivalence expanded exponentially among modern German-speaking peoples, both in regard to non-Jewish Germans and among Jews themselves. The eighteenth-century Jewish enlightenment, or *Haskalah*, although indebted to the larger European Enlightenment, emerged and found its greatest affinity in Germany. Christian dramatist Gottfried Lessing's philo-Semitic play *Die Juden* (The Jews, 1749) literally set the stage for the *Haskalah*, which Lessing's friend, Jewish philosopher Moses Mendelssohn, carried to fruition.[3] Together with Jewish disciples Hartwig Wessely and David Friedländer, and with the continued non-Jewish support of Lessing and Christian Wilhelm von Dohm, Mendelssohn succeeded in opening the doors of German society to Jews and in coaxing them out of their ghettos and into the world of western culture.

The *Haskalah* could not have achieved its full cultural and political purpose, however, without the radical social transformation that the general Enlightenment (and its progeny, the French Revolution) set in motion. Although Hapsburg Kaiser Joseph II's Edict of Toleration in 1781 granted Jews freedom of movement and residence within the Austro-Hungarian domain, the nascent French Republic in 1791 was the first national government to grant equal rights to Jews. A few German cities followed suit in 1798, and Prussia as a whole, under Napoleonic pressure, officially freed its Jews in 1812, though the laws were annulled as part of the anti-Jewish reaction to Napoleon's defeat at Waterloo and the Congress of Vienna in 1815. The revolutions of 1848 brought with them full legal equality for Jews in Austria, but in Germany Jews didn't become equal citizens until the unified German state was proclaimed, under Prussian auspices and with Berlin as the new capital, in 1871.[4] Even then, Jews remained excluded from the military, the courts, the state bureaucracy, and, except for the less established academic fields, from the universities as well. Complete Jewish emancipation in Germany, de jure and de facto, wouldn't be achieved until the Weimar Republic (1919–1933), and then also, of course, not without contention.[5]

Given the comparatively recent and extremely short period of Jewish entry into German-speaking culture and society, and the substantial obstacles that Jews continued to face during this period, their accomplishments, especially in the cultural arena, are all the more remarkable—though also partly explicable. Similar to the United States in the late nineteenth and early twentieth centuries, where restrictions in the established professions shunted many immigrant Jews into the fledgling mass media and popular entertainment forms of the larger cities, marginalized German Jews gravitated to "the free professions" and "the less organized alternative public spheres that characterize urban life, such as the newspaper, the journal, the art gallery, the café, the theater, and the political group."[6] The reference to the city here is key, for as with the massive immigrant wave that carried eastern European Jews to burgeoning U.S. metropolises, emancipated German Jews who flocked to the fast-growing national capital were, as far as modern culture was concerned, at the right place at the right time. From 1871 to 1905, a stretch that corresponds with the ascendancy of mass media and modern art, Berlin's population more than doubled to over two million.[7] The Jewish population, which had begun the nineteenth-century urbanization process before most other Germans, saw their portion of the Berlin population double over the same period as well, to about eighty thousand.[8]

Further statistical analysis, however, reasserts the remarkable nature of Jewish cultural achievement. The Jewish *percentage* of the Berlin population never rose above 4 percent, and nationally it held steady at a little less than 1 percent.[9] Yet the *impact* of turn-of-the-century Berlin Jews on the creation and dissemination of modern art, literature, theater, and film was enormous. Few could contradict non-Jewish journal editor Ferdinand Avenarius's philo-Semitic claim, in 1912, that Jews dominated modern German culture. Berlin's press and theater, Avenarius noted, were virtual Jewish monopolies, and its musical life "would be unthink-able without the Jews." German literature and poetry, meanwhile, seemed "to be passing into Jewish hands," and the art world also was increasingly becoming a Jewish domain.[10] Of course not all cultural observers, much less the general public, viewed Jews' cultural influence as favorably as did Avenarius.

Here a comparison with an analogous situation in the United States is instructive, more for the differences than the similarities. Although Jewish enroll-ment quotas at some major American universities began in the 1910s, public complaints about Jewish "overrepresentation" in the cultural sphere extended mainly to the Hollywood movie industry, a "low" cultural form whose world prominence and Jewish dominance was only realized after World War I. German disaffection with Jewish cultural involvement, at least initially, applied mainly to high culture, and was evident well before the war. As early as 1821, a scant two decades since emancipation, fears of Jewish domination "in the cultural worlds of literature and journalism were voiced."[11] By the 1830s, anti-Jewish sentiment was directed at the "new Jews"—the modern Jewish intellectuals who had converted to Christianity yet were regarded as interlopers, who "do not belong to any state," who "roam the world like adventurers," and who flocked to Berlin because they thrived in "mechanical" rather than "organic" situations.[12] In 1850 Richard Wagner penned his infamous indictment of Jewish intellectualism, *Judaism in Music*. Wagner's anti-Jewish animus was aimed specifi-cally at the modern Jewish artist, whose cultural enterprise (as practitioner and patron) "was linked to the commercialization of culture and its concomitant vulgarization." And Wagnerian-style anti-Semitism would only intensify in the Wilhelmine period (1871–1918) with the rise of industrial capitalism, political liberalism, and popular culture.[13]

Wilhelmine Jews: Parvenus and Pariahs

Historian Werner Sombart, a leading anti-Jewish critic in the years leading up to World War I, provided "anthropological" grounding for Wagner's critique. Drawing on Orientalist associations that would color later American attacks on the Jewish studio "moguls" (evident in the sobriquet itself), Sombart, in 1912, alleged that Jews' nomadic roots encouraged both material avariciousness and insatiable intellectual curiosity. The intellectuality, however, owing to its nurtur-ance in the shiftless desert sands, tended toward superficiality, and its derivation in nomadic adaptability inclined it toward excessive empathy. Superficiality and empathy, meanwhile, predisposed Jews "to excel in journalism, jurisprudence, and theater—the three most distinctive and, to [Sombart's] mind, most troubling expressions of urban culture."[14] Virulently anti-Semitic publicist Philip Stauff, focusing on the art world, dispensed with analytical niceties in attacking the "alien element" of the Jewish dealers, critics, and painters (such as Paul Cassirer, Alfred Kerr, and Max Lieberman), "who are strangers in our land and to our blood, [and yet] who stand today at the apex of the fine arts."[15]

Countering the campaign against Jewish cultural influence, Jewish literary scholar Moritz Goldstein published an article in Avenarius's prestigious cultural review *Der Kunstwart* in 1912. Titled "The German-Jewish Parnassus," the article goes to the heart of the ambivalence being thrust on German Jews in their move from ghetto pariah to torchbearer of the avant-garde:

> We Jews are administering the spiritual property of a nation that denies our right and our ability to do so. . . . Among ourselves we have the impression that we speak as Germans to Germans—such is our impression. But though we may after all feel totally German, the others feel us to be totally un-German. We may now be called Max Reinhardt and have inspired the [German] stage to unanticipated revival, or as a Hugo von Hoffmannstahl introduced a new poetic style to replace the exhausted style of Schiller; we may call this German, but the others call it Jewish; they detect in us something "Asiatic" and miss the German sensibility, and should they—reluctantly—feel obliged to acknowledge our achievement, they wish we would achieve less.[16]

Goldstein's lament over Jews' lack of full acceptance as Germans has obtained, with historical hindsight, more than a touch of irony. At the time, and since, however, not all Jews, or non-Jews, took such rejection by the "host" culture as necessarily "bad for the Jews." The moniker *Grenzjuden* (border Jews), for example, became a popular code word to describe Jews' perceived straddling of the boundaries between cultures. Living in such a limbo state, sociologist Georg Simmel argued in his 1908 essay "Der Fremde" (The stranger), laid the basis for the cosmopolitan, universalizing outlook of the urban intellectual, of which Jews were considered the prime exponents.[17] Himself regarded as the typical Berlin Jewish intellectual despite his parents' conversion to Christianity before his birth, Simmel held that the modern "stranger's" lack of commitment "to the unique ingredients and peculiar tendencies of the group" made him "freer, practically and theoretically; he surveys conditions with less prejudice; his criteria for them are more general and more objective ideals; he is not tied down in his action and habit, piety, precedent."[18] American social critic Thorstein Veblen offered support for Simmel's view. In a 1919 essay, Veblen suggested that the German Jews who had attained "intellectual pre-eminence in Modern Europe"[19] owed much of their innovative, iconoclastic spirit to living "at the margins between cultures."[20] The "ingrained skepticism" derived from Jews' status as simultaneous insiders and outsiders "induced a lingering cognitive dissonance, an abiding irreverence that allowed them to assume a position at the forefront of modern inquiry and imagination."[21]

Both philo- and anti-Semites, then, whether from their perception of an innate or a more recently evolved Jewish sensibility, located a propensity for modernist thinking in Jews' marginalized status vis-à-vis mainstream society. Another contributing factor, however, can be assigned to Jews' marginalization from their own Jewishness, a *self-imposed* estrangement that was not only a precipitator but also a by-product of modernism. As Emily Bilski suggests, Jews' attraction to modernism was "itself a new expression of new possibilities available to Jews in post-emancipation Germany, and . . . their embracing the new art constituted a rejection of tradition that was also a declaration of emancipation from the bonds of Judaism and the Jewish community."[22] Indeed, such a "double marginalization" (from both Jewish and German traditions), Isaac Deutscher proposed in his 1958 essay "The Non-Jewish Jew," gave Jews an "epistemological advantage" that spurred some of the boldest thought of the modern age. "Marx, Freud, Trotsky, and Rosa Luxemburg" had in common "that the very conditions in which they lived and worked did not allow them to reconcile themselves to ideas which were nationally or religiously limited and enabled them to strive for a universal *Weltanschauung*."[23]

But these conceptual advantages came at a psychological cost: a painfully dual identity, both as Germans and as Jews. Jews' rejection as not fully German was a particularly bitter pill to swallow. Emancipated German Jews had been among the greatest champions of Enlightenment German culture and its liberal cosmopolitan perspective, partly because liberal humanism served as a gateway to bourgeois respectability and acceptance, but also because of their genuine belief in and admiration for these ideals' aesthetic and ethical value.[24] Indeed, *Kultur* (culture) and *Bildung* (education), with their presumption of a shared humanity and a quality of spirit based in a "quest for the good, the true, and the beautiful," became the equivalent of a new Jewish religion.[25] Kant, Goethe, and Schiller became the new prophets, universities the new shuls, and Jewish artists and intellectuals the new "meta rabbis."[26] *Deutschtum* (Germanness) and *Judentum* (Jewishness) had merged into a whole gloriously greater than the sum of its parts—so thought assimilated German Jews. Not to be accepted as equals by their non-Jewish countrymen was therefore deeply frustrating, hurtful, and troubling.

Additional discontent, if also liberation, stemmed from assimilated Jews' disconnect from their fellow Jews—particularly those from the ghettos of their own not-so-distant past, whose ranks were being refilled by immigrants and refugees from the shtetls of Russia and eastern Europe. Not only had these generally impoverished Ostjuden *not* experienced emancipation, but they would be driven in huge numbers into Germany, and a large portion eventually onward to the United States, by the pogroms that followed Tsar Alexander II's assassination in 1881. Even before this massive influx, assimilating German Jews were encouraged to view ghetto life, on whose renunciation their own emancipation was predicated, with loathing, dread, and disgust. This Jewish revulsion toward "their own" was facilitated by strong anti-ghetto sentiment within mainstream Enlightenment humanism.[27] The German intelligentsia, not to mention the average German, viewed the ghetto as a repository of religious fanaticism, economic parasitism, cultural barbarism, and material squalor; and its inhabitants were seen as physically disgusting and morally contemptible.[28] Even the personal traits of ghetto rabbis, according to Goethe, consisted of "fanatic zeal . . . repulsive enthusiasm . . . wild gesticulations . . . confused murmurings . . . piercing outcries . . . effeminate movements . . . the queerness of ancient nonsense."[29] Jewish poet Heinrich Heine concurred, calling the ghetto "a dreadful monument of the Middle Ages."[30]

Ostjuden were thus both an embarrassment and a threat to German Jews, given the latter group's newly achieved yet only partially realized and still precarious assimilation. The insecurity and concomitant sense of superiority further fueled antagonism between the "Cravats" and the "Caftans," as the Westjuden and Ostjuden, based on their contrasting dress styles (and class statuses), were called. Yet in sharing "the general distaste for the ghetto" and participating in "Othering" the Ostjude, Westjuden also renounced both their own past and a part of themselves, thereby compounding the internalized ambivalence and self-hatred generated by their own stubbornly second-class status within mainstream German society.[31]

Nothing demonstrates this double consciousness more than German Jews' reaction to the pogrom-driven immigrant wave of the 1880s. In coming to the aid of their fleeing Russian brothers, German Jews' compassion "was not feigned," Steven Aschheim suggests: "Social distance, cultural disparity, and political disenfranchisement served to reinforce rather than diminish the German Jewish sense of responsibility for the *Ostjuden*." But at the same time, although German Jews, just as their assimilated American Jewish counterparts, "wanted to help the East European Jews and alleviate their plight . . . nobody wanted them in his own country."[32] In Germany, the situation was exacerbated, compared to the United States, by the lack of an "ideology of ethnic and political pluralism" and, more ominously, by the beginnings of scientific racism and organized Jew hatred (labeled, for the first time in the 1870s, "anti-Semitism").[33] Although the rise in anti-Semitism was directed at the liberalism and capitalism associated with the German Jew as much as at the barbarity and depravity connected to the Ostjude, many German Jews, whether from self-hatred or self-preservation, pointed to Ostjuden as the source of the alarming trend.[34]

Ostjuden/Westjuden: Brothers and Strangers

German anti-Semitism in its various guises, like emancipation before it, generated varied and conflicting responses among German Jews. Although the emancipation pact permitted Jews to retain their religious affiliation, it also dictated that overt expressions of Jewishness—in dress, speech, and ritual—be restricted to the private sphere. The slogan, "A Jew at home, a gentleman on the street" describes, with some irony, the separation of public and private selves. What it fails to capture is the intense emotional conflict provoked by the imposed social division, or its perceived and actual relationship to material well-being. Moses Mendelssohn himself had struggled mightily, and against intense outside pressure, to "sustain within himself a two-fold spiritual bond" by embracing both enlightened German humanism and religious Judaism.[35] His grandson, however, the musical prodigy Felix Mendelssohn, would be baptized. Heinrich Heine converted to Christianity later in life, as did Karl Marx's father (like Georg Simmel's parents) before his son's birth.[36] An estimated two-thirds of intellectual Jews converted during the nineteenth century; for them, as for other Jews seeking to overcome obstacles to career advancement, conversion was seen as a solution to the "Jewish problem" up to and including the Weimar period.[37]

A compromise approach, although no less anathema to traditional Jews, was the establishment of a Jewish religious denomination more compatible with modernity. Reform Judaism, which "eliminated all those beliefs, rites, ceremonies and practices it deemed anachronistic and in disharmony with modern thought," first took root in Berlin and Kassel in 1815 and quickly spread throughout Germany and to other countries with assimilated Jewish communities.[38] Still other Jews eschewed both conversion and, like Deutscher's non-Jewish Jews, religious affiliation altogether, yet retained a sense of Jewish identity from broadly humanistic or progressive political ideals.

As the tide of anti-Semitism swelled in the late 1800s, two vastly different, often clashing Jewish movements arose to confront the worsening situation (as well as the overall crisis of liberalism). The majority of German Jews, "mainly well-established members of the prosperous middle-class," continued along a staunchly assimilationist course. Organizing themselves into the Central Society of German Citizens of the Jewish Faith, known as the *Centralverein* or CV, this mainstream group remained dedicated to "the ideals of liberalism and the Enlightenment."[39] Another, much smaller, but impassioned group of students, artists, and intellectuals advocated something far more radical: "a 'new beginning,' a return to nature, and a rejection of bourgeois values."[40] The latter movement, proclaimed the "Jewish Renaissance" in 1901 by one of its key figures, Martin Buber, was an offshoot of the fledgling Zionist movement that "sought to create a synthesis between Zionism, Jewish tradition, and modernity."[41]

The Jewish Renaissance, however, had a quite different view of early twentieth-century modernity. Drawing inspiration from avant-garde bohemianism and the "youth revolt" that proposed a merging of art and life, the Jewish Renaissance found itself at odds with political Zionism's bourgeois-liberal belief in a separation of culture and politics. Meeting in cafés, engaging in artistic pursuits, and circulating ideas via journals such as *Die Kommenden* (The up-and-comers) and *Ost und West* (East and West), the "cultural Zionists," as they came to be called, were concerned as much with establishing a new Jewish sensibility as a new Jewish homeland. Perhaps their boldest stroke was their rapprochement with eastern European Jewish culture and an attempted bridging of the Ostjude/ Westjude divide. The East was seen as contributing "a Jewish tradition that had remained authentic and vital," whereas the West would add "its vibrant and modern mores and values."[42] The political Zionists also made eastern European Jewry the cornerstone of their project; indeed, the proposed securing of a Jewish homeland in Palestine was, until the First World War, seen largely as a sanctuary for the unemancipated and impoverished Ostjude. This philanthropic project still essentially privileged modern western consciousness, however, and left the philo-Ostjude Zionist "with an old ambivalence in a new disguise."[43]

For assimilationist German Jews, the Zionist rehabilitation of the Ostjude compounded their own intra-ethnic conflict. Demeaning attitudes and discriminatory actions against the Ostjude, which assimilationist Jews in large part supported and even spearheaded, already violated their liberal principles; and reminders of the "authenticity and vitality" of an eastern European culture they had repudiated—be it voluntarily, opportunistically, or under duress—only exacerbated their sense of guilt and shame.[44] Eventually, as anti-Semitism increased and cultural and political Zionism radicalized in the post-1910 period, assimilationist Jews' unreconstructed self-hatred spilled over onto the Zionists, whose Jewish-nationalist sympathies had always been resented as antiliberal and misguided and who now also were "identified with *Ostjudentum* both in clientele and ideological spirit."[45]

Such intra-ethnic division both clashed and resonated with a larger, more positive Jewish-based ambivalence that cultural Zionist leader Buber identified and propounded in his *Drei Reden über das Judentum* (Three talks on Judaism) of 1909–1910. In these influential lectures, Buber spoke of a particular Jewish "sensibility" grounded in "the situation of being torn between two worlds," with a capacity for deep spiritual experience, suffering, and compassion—"all of this prefigured in the 'pathos of the prophets.'"[46] "Whoever confronts the pathos of his inner struggles," Buber stated, "will discover that something continues to live within him having its great, primeval national image in the struggle of the prophets against the diverging multitude of the people's drives."[47] Going Deutscher one better, Buber thereby located a basis for radical thought, action, and creativity that stemmed from both a marginalization from mainstream society and a centeredness within Jewish tradition. Moreover, and of particular genealogical interest to the Jewish émigré directors, Buber's emphasis on pathos found cultural expression in a group of mainly Jewish avant-garde artists calling themselves Die Pathetiker (The solemn ones). Emerging from the Expressionist movement, which emphasized intense

internal experience and affected all the arts in the prewar period, Die Pathetiker gave the "ecstatic-pathetic" character of their work the highest value,
"valorizing both deep spiritual experience and heroic posture—the 'pathetic'
artist portrayed as tragic seer or prophet without honor."[48]

World War I: Coming Together/Splitting Apart

World War I caused the various strands within German Jewry to lay their differences aside, at least initially. United against an enemy in the Russian tsar whose
tyrannical regime posed a triple threat—to the German nation, liberal values,
and Jewish existence—German Jews of all persuasions found, however briefly,
common cause. The internal and external rifts between Jews and their fellow
non-Jewish Germans also tended to subside temporarily as the country banded
together in support of what seemed, to Jew and non-Jew alike, a just war. As long
as the war went well, which it did for the first year, the detente generally held.
With a downturn in Germany's fortunes in 1915, however, came a commensurate
collapse of the tenuous domestic pact.

Renewed conflict between Jew and Jew, and Jew and German, was waged, like
the war itself, on an eastern and a western front. Yet while the issues remained
the same—anti-Semitism, Zionism, and how to deal with the Ostjuden—the
discourse around them became more volatile and politicized. Firsthand contact
with eastern ghetto and shtetl Jews, as well as a large influx of Ostjuden refugees
into Germany, "brought home" the *Ostjudenfrage* (eastern Jew question) in the
starkest terms. The sense of difference, between Ost- and Westjude and between
German Jew and non-Jew, heightened; views on how to address this difference,
among German Jews and anti-Semites, radicalized. Assimilationist Jews advocated more strongly than ever the westernizing of their eastern cousins; Zionists
constructed a hyper-romanticized "cult of the Ostjuden"; anti-Semites revived
the specter, first raised in the 1880s, of an eastern Jewish "invasion."[49] The Anti-
Semites' Petition of 1881—calling for the cessation of alien Jewish immigration
and signed by 250,000 Germans but never enacted into law—was resurrected in
the *Grenzschluss* (border closing) appeals of 1915. Demonstrating the perceived
threat that a flood of Ostjuden into Germany posed to German Jews themselves,
many actually supported the *Grenzschluss*. Even before it became official policy in
1918, however, German Jews had come to realize the futility of separating their
interests from those of the Ostjuden.

The *Judenzählung* (Jewish census) of 1916 was a hugely disillusioning event
for German Jews. Ostensibly aimed at quieting allegations that Jews were
shirking military duty, the census was insulting enough for a group that been
among the most patriotic supporters of the war effort. But when the army
refused to release data showing that Jews were serving in equal levels to other
Germans, German Jews "experienced a profound sense of betrayal. It was as
if the bubble of German-Jewish symbiosis had been burst."[50] The slight was

more than personal; the *Judenzählung* and the *Grenzschluss* were the first signs in twentieth-century Germany of political support for anti-Semitism. Jew hatred had, once again, become respectable.[51] Yet rather than bringing the various German Jewish factions together, as had the onset of the war, the latest rising tide of anti-Semitism widened the fissures between them. Assimilationist Jews increasingly, though not exclusively, scapegoated the Ostjuden, berated the Zionists, or converted as a means of entering the German fold; Zionists, for whom the *Judenzählung* and *Grenzschluss* demonstrated conclusively that Jews were doomed to second-class citizenship in Germany, now saw a homeland in Palestine as a necessary refuge not only for Ostjuden but for all Jews.

Philosopher Franz Rosenzweig, the father of postwar Jewish renewal, proposed a "third way": one that renounced neither *Judentum* nor *Deutschtum* but reinstated the essentialist integrity of both while maintaining a dialectical relation between the two. Unlike Moses Mendelssohn's attempted reconciliation of *Judentum* with *Deutschtum* while keeping the two spheres separate, Rosenzweig's goal was to recenter Judaism and reintegrate Jewish thinking into western culture. For Mendelssohn, the "and" between German and Jew did not suggest "any coordination, or covalescence." Mendelssohn may have been the first enlightened German Jew, Rosenzweig conceded, but he was, by his own admission, not "a unified human being . . . not one person but two."[52]

Rosenzweig's dialectical approach promised a synthesis of a higher order, one that would overcome Mendelssohn's dilemma and rectify the shortcomings of Jewish liberalism. Learning to be a German *and* a Jew, Rosenzweig reasoned, "was the challenge inherently posed by the Enlightenment and Emancipation." German Jews did indeed have "a dual destiny," but it need not tear them apart. Jews were a "metahistorical community," which placed them "simultaneously within and beyond culture, within and beyond time."[53] *Zweistromland* (Land of two rivers) was the title of the book that Rosenzweig devoted to this transcendent principle. The title's metaphorical association, fittingly, was to ancient Babylon—"where, at the convergence of two mighty rivers and several civilizations, Judaism attained new creative impulses and crystallized as a religious culture." In nascent Weimar Germany, "nurtured by two distinct spiritual sources—Judaism and European culture—German Jews could become paradigmatic for all modern Jews, indeed, by implication, for all individuals who lay claim to various, often radically contrasting, spiritual and cultural estates."[54]

Weimar Germany: Ambivalent Republic

Whereas Buber's prewar Jewish Renaissance would find fertile soil in the creative turbulence of the fin de siècle, Rosenzweig's utopian variant would run aground of the sociopolitical upheavals of the early Weimar Republic. The period from 1919 to 1923 was a Time of Troubles not only for Jews; the "shock of defeat, fear of revolution, unparalleled economic collapse, and brutalization of political life were inescapable realities" for all Germans.[55] The general crisis affected Jews disproportionately once again, however, because of the accompanying, ever-escalating anti-Semitism. Fanning the flames of postwar Judeophobia was the *Dolchstosslegende* (stab-in-the-back legend). This latest insult to German Jewish patriotism, like the *Judenzählung* before it, alleged Jewish sabotaging of the war effort. But the charges now went far beyond avoiding military service. As prominent capitalists and radical leftists, German Jews were held primarily responsible for war profiteering, fomenting labor strikes, espousing pacifist sympathies, and even harboring extra-national loyalties—in a word, selling Germany out to the enemy.

Such views were bolstered by the Russian Revolution, in which Jews had played a determining role, and by the short-lived Bavarian Soviet Republic, proclaimed for two weeks in Munich in 1919, many of whose leaders were Jewish. The Weimar Republic itself—its constitution drafted by the Jew Hugo Preuss and governed initially by the left-leaning, heavily Jewish-represented Social Democratic Party—was regarded suspiciously, if not conspiratorially, by the stab-in-the-back conspiracy theorists. The overall discourse of domestic betrayal resonated with a German populace yearning for somebody to blame for wartime humiliation and postwar suffering, and the scapegoating was easily funneled into the racialist nationalism of the emerging Nazi Party. By giving new credence to the old saw, "The Jews are our misfortune," the *Dolchstosslegende* contributed substantially to a collective Jew hatred during the early postwar years that historian Golo Mann regards as even more virulent than during the Nazi period.[56]

The increasingly dire situation further polarized tensions between German Jews and Ostjuden, fueling tendencies toward what Jewish psychoanalyst Anna Freud later would term "identification with the aggressor." Applied clinically to Jewish child survivors of Nazism who identified positively with their Nazi persecutors and negatively with themselves as victims, a similar behavior characterizes German Jews who "cringed at Jewish conduct" and, like Max Naumann's Deutschnazionale Juden (German national Jews), openly proclaimed political positions that placed "Jewish fate squarely in the conservative, nationalist camp."[57] In his 1921 novel *Mein Weg als Deutscher und Jude* (My life as German and Jew), Jakob Wassermann squarely confronted this uniquely Jewish self-hatred in his differentiation between the "Jewish" Jew and the German Jew: "Are those not two distinct species, almost two distinct races, or at least two distinct modes of thought?"[58] Wassermann's awareness that the source of the intra-ethnic division was as much a German as a Jewish problem is revealed in another passage: "The German and the Jew: I once dreamed an allegorical dream. . . . I placed the surfaces of two mirrors together; and I felt as if the human images contained and preserved in the two mirrors would have to fight one another tooth and nail."[59]

Although Wassermann's vision of a fight to the death between German and Jew was terrifyingly prescient of the catastrophe to come, violent conflict between the two camps was already well under way. In late 1919, the fledgling, and generally philo-Semitic, Social Democratic government, succumbing to relentless anti-Semitic pressure, announced the establishment of special detainment camps for "criminal" Ostjuden. Although the camps were not activated until 1921, raids and physical abuse of eastern Jews, beginning with a raid in Berlin in early 1920, occurred throughout Germany that year, apparently with official sanction. Matters became worse when the Social Democrats left office in 1921, and would not improve until their return in 1923. During this period, raids, expulsions, and violence escalated, with arbitrary, extralegal internment of many who had not been officially tried and convicted. The situation was worst in Bavaria, the hotbed of anti-Semitism, where political parties demanded the expulsion of Jews from public office and the immediate expulsion of Ostjuden. In 1923 a measure was passed expelling all Jews who had settled in Bavaria after 1914. Under the edict, not only many established and respected Ostjuden, but multigenerational Bavarian German Jews as well, were forced to leave Munich and other Bavarian cities.[60]

The lumping together of Ostjuden and German Jews in Bavaria underscored the hopeless fallacy of German Jews' attempts to distinguish themselves from the Ostjuden, whether through assimilation, ultranationalism, or anti-Ostjuden sentiment. Even conversion proved inadequate protection against the irrationality of anti-Semitism. Indeed, ever since emancipation, German Jews found themselves snared in an assimilationist double bind—literally damned if they did and damned if they didn't. On the one hand, Jews were regarded as preternaturally incapable of fully assimilating: no matter how hard they tried, some aspect of the ghetto Jew—bodily features, physical gestures, linguistic idiosyncrasies, behavioral traits—irrevocably clung to them and invariably "gave them away." A 1904 cartoon in the satirical magazine *Simplicissimus* acerbically made this point. Titled "Metamorphosis," the cartoon consists of three caricatures: the first depicts a rag peddler named Moishe Pisch; the second shows the same man as a middle-class clothing salesman, now calling himself Moritz Wasserstrahl (Water stream); the third finds the man "transformed" into a wealthy and fashionable art dealer named Maurice Lafontaine (fig. 1). Despite the name, dress, and status changes, Moishe/Moritz/Maurice is still marked as a salesman, of course, but also bearing the same stooped posture, bow legs, flat feet, and hook nose.[61]

On the other hand, those Jews who *could* successfully "pass" as Germans were in some ways even more maligned. Such "disguised" Jews were regarded either as "unsavory interlopers" not belonging "to any state, to any community," or as "estranged from their Jewish roots" and "betrayers of their 'true selves.'"[62] Most dangerous of all, these Jews' very "invisibility" put them "in an ideal position to

Figure 1.   His transformation from pariah to parvenu can't hide Moishe Pisch's lowly origins or Jewish appearance, in *Simplicissimus* (1904).

achieve, from within and unrecognized, the aims of Jewish power and domination."[63] A 1938 instructional illustration in the Nazi children's book *Der Giftpilz* (The poison mushroom) noxiously portrays this conspiratorial fear: a young boy offers a wild mushroom plucked from a fairy-tale forest to a beautiful maiden (fig. 2). The caption, in translation, reads, "To tell the difference between edible and poisonous mushrooms is often as difficult as to recognize Jews as cheats and criminals."[64]

Although the *Giftpilz* illustration is from the Nazi period, the degree to which a pathological strain of anti-Semitism had penetrated German consciousness already in the Weimar era is frightfully evident in an anecdote recounted by German Jewish historian Fritz Stern. Stern's father, a prosperous physician who had converted to Christianity and fought loyally in World War I, experienced the following incident shortly after the war: "In the medical auditorium in Breslau, while the case of a psychotic patient was being demonstrated, the patient suddenly began a nationalistic harangue full of violent outbursts against Jews and other criminals—and the assembled students and some of the doctors began applauding."[65]

Besides its resonance with the Holocaust, this chilling incident can't help but bring to mind the classic Expressionist and pioneering horror film that would launch Weimar cinema's golden age, *The Cabinet of Dr. Caligari* (Robert Wiene, 1920). Released to international critical acclaim, and a major stylistic influence on film noir, the film's narrative, told in flashback by a young man, centers on the sinister Dr. Caligari, the maniacal head of a mental asylum who travels from town to town murdering people with the aid of a somnambulistic giant that he keeps in a casket and displays at amusement parks. By film's end, however, we learn that the storyteller is the real maniac, whereas the doctor is

Figure 2.   Poisonous mushrooms as metaphor for Jewish duplicity, in *Der Giftpilz* (1938). (Courtesy Department of Special Collections, Charles E. Young Research Library, UCLA)

actually the (seemingly) benign head of the asylum in which the young man is confined. Film historian Siegfried Kracauer, in his seminal retrospective analysis of Weimar cinema *From Caligari to Hitler* (1947), sees the film as symptomatic of a fascist current in the collective German psyche and therefore prescient of the Nazi nightmare to come.

Although not unproblematic in its self-fulfilling prophetic thesis, Kracauer's psycho-historical reading of *Caligari* retains much of its currency, both textually and extratextually. Especially cogent is Kracauer's analysis of the film's controversial *Rahmenhandlung* (flashback framing device), which was not inherent to the film but apparently resulted from a suggestion by Fritz Lang, who was originally assigned to the project.[66] Lang's suggestion, intended "to intensify the terror of the Expressionist sequences," was adopted by the film's eventual director, Robert Wiene, and its producer, Erich Pommer, over the vehement protests of the film's coscenarists, Carl Mayer and Hans Janowitz, whose original story idea left Caligari the unreconstructed maniac.[67] Kracauer sides with the writers, arguing that the placing of this indictment of a German authority gone berserk "in brackets" turns the film into a mere pictorial "translation of a madman's fantasy."[68] Despite this aesthetic "compromise," however, the film's disruptive form belies its recuperative content. By having the angular, disorienting Expressionist sets permeate the film from start to finish, encompassing both the "fantasy" portion and the "real world" sections that bookend it, madness becomes the narrative's master trope. Thus even if, as Kracauer contends, "the *Caligari* style was as far from depicting madness as it was from transmitting revolutionary messages,"[69] the film's stylistic excess yet "organizational completeness" nonetheless reveals the scenery of a German soul and a Weimar society teetering between the poles of tyranny and anarchy.[70] And even in its content, Mayer and Janowitz, with Wiene's and Caligari portrayer Werner Krauss's assistance, may have gotten "the last laugh."[71] In the film's final iris-in on Caligari as he looms over the seemingly paranoid storyteller strapped in a straitjacket, the doctor's sinister expression bears eerie resemblance to his allegedly fictional persona, implying that the lunatics may be running the asylum after all.

For Jews, one partial refuge from the sociopolitical and economic insanity of the Weimar period was in the cultural realm. Of course, Jews had been a dominant force, as promoters and practitioners, in the rise of modern art and ideas since the Wilhelmine era. Given the hegemony of conservative forces led by Wilhelm himself, however, these modernist tendencies had been marginalized, if not demonized, before the war: "gutter art," the kaiser had declared it.[72] What Weimar's democratic foundation allowed for and its anarchic impulses encouraged was the movement of these tendencies from the margins to the mainstream. The Weimar "style" may not have been born with the Weimar Republic, Peter Gay reminds us, but it was liberated by it.[73] Germany's postwar experiment with democracy "gave new opportunities to talent ineligible for preferment in the Empire, opening centers of prestige and power to progressive professors, modern playwrights and producers, democratic political thinkers."[74] Hugo Preuss is a key figure here. As the architect of the Weimar Constitution, Preuss "was a symbol of the revolution; as a Jew and a left-wing democrat, he had been kept out of the university establishment . . . and now he, the outsider, gave shape to the new Republic, *his* Republic."[75] Poet Gottfried Benn put the matter more generally: "The overflowing plenty of stimuli, artistic, scientific, commercial improvisations which place the Berlin of 1918 to 1933 in the class of Paris, stemmed for the most part from the talents of this [Jewish] sector of the population, its international connections, its sensitive restlessness, and above all its dead-certain . . . instinct for quality."[76] As late as 1938, Nazi writer Tüdel Weller would baldly state, "Berlin is the domain of the Jews."[77]

Gay divides the Weimar period into three historical phases: 1918–1924, revolution, civil war, foreign occupation, political murder, hyperinflation, and artistic experimentation; 1924–1929, fiscal stabilization, abated political violence, renewed prestige abroad, widespread prosperity, and a more sober and optimistic turn in the arts; 1929–1933, rising unemployment, government by decree, decline of middle-class parties, resurgent violence, and a rising cultural tide of conventionality, propaganda, and kitsch.[78] Through all three phases, Berlin not only further solidified its position as Germany's political center but also became—wresting this distinction from Munich—its unrivaled cultural center as well.[79] The effect of this geo-cultural shift is nowhere more evident than in the evolution of the Expressionist art movement that would become, in its cinematic formation, indelibly associated with the Weimar period and, not uncontroversially, with film noir.

3   *Jews and Expressionism*

"PERFORMING HIGH AND LOW"

Just as the role of Jews qua Jews in the rise and evolution of film noir has tended to be underestimated or ignored, so has their contribution to the emergence and development of German Expressionism been downplayed or overlooked. Given that Expressionist cinema is seen as a major forerunner of film noir, the oversight in regard to the former widens the lacuna in regard to the latter. The twin attributional flaws can partially be explained by an epistemological similarity between the art form and the film type: both are notoriously difficult to define or categorize. As with noir's resistance to generic definition, Expressionism, due to the range of styles, philosophies, and cultural forms associated with it, has led art historians to describe it not as a coherent school or artistic approach but variously as a direction, tendency, movement, or Weltanschauung.[1]

The term Expressionism itself underwent considerable transformation during its formative period. It was first applied in 1911 to bold new trends in literature and painting that arose from "the great break with the cultural tradition in Germany, as elsewhere, between 1905 and 1914."[2] In painting, Expressionism referred broadly to the modernist avant-garde and alluded initially not to German artists at all but rather to other Europeans: Cezanne, van Gogh, Munch, Matisse, Picasso, and other Fauves and Cubists. The Jewish editor of the influential *Der Sturm* (The storm) journal and art gallery, Herwarth Walden, was the first to make the term nationally specific when he referred in 1913 to the Munich group Der Blaue Reiter (The Blue Rider), as "German Expressionists." Jewish critic Paul Fechter affirmed the national designation in a 1914 monograph, in which he defined Expressionism, as exemplified by the Blaue Reiter and Dresden (later Berlin) group Die Brücke (The bridge, founded in 1905), as "the German counter-movement to Impressionism, parallel to Cubism in France and Futurism in Italy."[3] As late as 1918, however, Walden's book *Expressionismus, Die Kunstwende* (Expressionism, the turning point in art), subsumed Futurists, French Cubists, and the Blaue Reiter under Expressionism.[4] Only after the postwar rupture of pan-Europeanism and the revival of ethnocentrism would the term Expressionism in painting shift conclusively to "German Expressionism," most commonly as an "umbrella appellation" for the works of the Brücke and Blaue Reiter.[5]

Today, the term refers to a period from about 1905 through the 1920s, emanating from and affecting Germanic art, literature, dance, theater, and film.

Jews, who played major if not definitive roles in all these areas, were attracted to Expressionism for the same reasons that drew them toward modernist movements in general. Besides emancipated Jews' historically determined disposition toward unconventional thinking, as Deutscher and others have proposed—as well as the links they perceived between certain Expressionist elements and the prophetic or mystical strands in Judaism—this new (but also *German*) direction in art offered Jews a way to both rebel and assimilate, to be both outsider and insider. By rejecting bourgeois values and aligning themselves with a radical movement they helped gestate and propel, German and Austrian Jews were able to embrace German culture without abandoning the Jewish tradition; indeed, for a time, Expressionism seemed the place where "the German-Jewish symbiosis" came "the closest to being realized."[6]

Expressionism in literature, for example, is unthinkable without the "father of the modern movement in the German theater," Frank Wedekind, as well as his fellow Jewish playwrights, novelists, and poets Ernst Toller, Walter Hasenclever, Jakob Wassermann, and Franz Werfel.[7] Expressionism in music arguably begins with the atonal works of Jewish composers Arnold Schoenberg and Alban Berg. The Jewish Adolf Loos (who converted to Catholicism along with Schoenberg) was among the first to apply Expressionist principles to architecture.[8] And although less prominent in the production of Expressionist painting (partly due to the residual influence of aniconic religious injunctions), even here—as art dealers, critics, and collectors—Jews were vital to this branch of the movement's emergence and ascendancy.[9] Major champions and disseminators of the new form included leading gallery owners and publishers Walden, Paul Cassirer, Heinrich Cohen, and Ludwig Jacobowski; critics Fechter, Alfred Kerr, Karl Kraus, Kurt Pinthus, Samuel Lubinski, and Max Hardin; art historians Oskar Wittgenstein, Otto Fischer, and Heinrich Schnabel; and collectors Ludwig and Rosy Fischer, Alfred and Tekla Hess, Alfred Fleuchtheim, Jakob and Rosa Oppenheimer, Ludwig Schames, Carl Sternheim, and Paul Westheim.

The café and salon cultures of Berlin and Vienna, also disproportionately hosted and populated by Jews, provided additional impetus, both inspirationally and promotionally, for the Expressionist and other modernist movements. Jacobowski founded the artists' journal and colloquium Die Kommenden (The up-and-comers), and Jewish writer Kurt Hiller started the influential Der Neue Club (The new club, later the Neopathetisches Cabaret).[10] Prominent Jewish salonieres included Felice Bernstein, Emma Dohme, Aniela Fürstenberg, Auguste Hauschner, Corneilie Richter, Bertha von Arnswalt, and Marie von Leyden. Rosa Siodmak, mother of Robert Siodmak, held salons in Dresden that included writers Toller and Hasenclever, as well as noted Expressionist painters Emil Nolde and Otto Dix.[11]

The inclusion of Dix, a Jew, indicates that Jewish Expressionist painters also participated in the movement; indeed, they would become increasingly prominent in its darker, urban offshoots most pertinent to Expressionist cinema. Among the darkest of these was the Martin Buber–inspired Pathetiker group, first exhibited at Walden's Sturm gallery in 1912 and composed of three Jewish artists, Ludwig Meidner, Jakob Steinhardt, and Richard Janthur.[12] The Pathetikers crucially affected the turn in Expressionist painting from its largely utopian, nature-driven early phase—exemplified by the Dresden and Munich-spawned Brücke and Blaue Reiter—toward its more angst-filled, urban-driven later period, centered in Berlin.[13]

The Brücke itself moved geographically from Dresden to Berlin in the early 1910s, and aesthetically from vibrant-colored, nude-cavorting idylls to ever harsher, more menacing cityscapes. As World War I and its turbulent aftermath accelerated Expressionism's drift toward the dystopian, Jewish artists such as Meidner, Dix, George Grosz, and John Heartfield would be key figures in pushing the movement toward its most apocalyptic and socially critical extremes. Meidner, in particular, mainly due to his 1916 series titled *Apocalyptic Landscapes*, has been called the "prophet of doom" and "the most expressionist of the Expressionists."[14] He was also one of the few major Expressionist painters to work in film, designing the sets for *Die Strasse* (*The Street*, 1924), a key Weimar-era precursor of film noir (fig. 3).

Urban Expressionism: Agony and Ecstasy

On the theoretical front, Jews were instrumental in laying the movement's conceptual underpinnings, defining its parameters, and articulating its agenda. Although exerting his greatest influence initially on the Viennese branch of Expressionism, Sigmund Freud's explorations of sexuality, subjectivity, and the unconscious found fertile ground in the overall Expressionist concern, if not obsession, with eroticism and inner experience. Kracauer described the Expressionist mind-set in starkly Freudian, or at least Oedipal, terms, when he wrote in 1920, "In its schematic personage of the 'father' the whole essence of the out-lived epoch often takes on its form, and against him, as the symbol of tradition, the preserver of what exists, there arises the 'son,' prepared to murder."[15] Analyzing the movement retrospectively, Peter Gay went further: "In their search for a new humanity, the Expressionists offered the public many heroes: the stranger, the sufferer, the suicide, the prostitute. But there was one theme that pervades their work: the son's revolt against the father."[16] Appropriately, the first true Expressionist play, by Hasenclever and staged in Berlin in 1912, was titled *Der Sohn* (*The Son*).[17]

Freud's paternal relationship to Germany became more overt in the late 1910s and early 1920s, when the war spurred interest in psychiatry's potential for treating soldiers' psychic traumas. The German-Freudian connection was nowhere stronger than in Berlin, where follower Karl Abraham (who was Jewish, as were most of the early Freudians) founded the Berlin Psychoanalytic

Figure 3.   Urban Expressionism: Ludwig Meidner's *Berlin* (1913).

Association in 1910 and where Freud himself introduced his theory of the id, the ego, and the superego in 1922.[18] Indeed, although Freud would return to Vienna and stubbornly remain there up until the *Anschluss* of 1938, Berlin by the 1920s "had replaced Vienna and Budapest as the capital of the [psychoanalytic] movement."[19] That Freudian theories were gaining a foothold in Germany at the very time that Expressionist film was emerging provides another uncanny comparison with film noir, whose emergence in the United States in the 1940s corresponded to a similar surge of interest in the "Jewish science"—driven, not coincidentally, by the influx of (largely) Jewish psychoanalysts from Germany and Austria.[20]

Martin Buber's considerable effect on Expressionist consciousness, most specifically that of the Pathetikers, through his talks in 1909 and 1910 on the Jewish prophetic tradition, has already been described. Yet Buber's earlier *Ekstatische Konfessionen* (*Ecstatic Confessions*, published in 1909) had an even more profound, and certainly more cross-cultural, impact. A collection of mystical writings from across the globe and throughout the ages, with a deeply empathetic introduction by Buber, the work is now regarded as "one of the most enduring documents of German expressionism."[21] The book's transcendental vision of "inner essential experience," however, was not the sole cause for Expressionism's early mystical bent; a neo-Romantic flair for the supernatural already pervaded the movement.[22] But Expressionist artists' quasi-religious striving (in their art and their lives) for "extreme subjectivity" on the one hand, and "individual immersion in and submission to the cosmos" on the other, received a compelling, ecumenically grounded boost from Buber and the mystical ideas his anthology revived and legitimated.[23]

Another Jew, Georg Simmel, shares with a non-Jew, Friedrich Nietzsche, the distinction as the most significant philosophical precursor of Expressionism. At least that was the opinion offered by cultural theorist Friedrich Huebner in his 1920 essay "Der Expressionismus in Deutschland." Nietzsche's notions of extreme subjectivism and individual transcendence were unquestionably fundamental to the Expressionist ethos, and his example of "self-liberation from authoritarian constrictions, bourgeois narrow-mindedness, materialist thinking" no less seminal.[24] Expressionist artists idolized the revolutionary philosopher and enthusiastically consumed his books, especially *Thus Spake Zarathustra* (1883–1885), whose exclamatory parole, "What does my shadow matter? Let it run after me! I—shall outrun it!" became the movement's credo.[25] Another passage in *Zarathustra* supposedly inspired the name of the first Expressionist group, Die Brücke: "What is great in man is that he is a bridge and not a goal: what can be loved in man is that he is a going-over [*Übergang*] and a going-under [*Untergang*]."[26]

If, however, Nietzsche was the "earthquake of the epoch," as Gottfried Benn declared, then Simmel was the era's hurricane.[27] Simmel's philosophy "prepared the ground for the new mode of thought," Huebner averred, "with his elaboration of the concepts of 'form,' 'self,' and 'life.'"[28] Simmel's influence on Expressionism derived largely from his 1903 essay "Die Grossstädte und das Geistesleben" ("The Metropolis and Modern Life"), which presciently and penetratingly analyzes the modern city's spatial configurations and their relation to consciousness and human interaction. Indeed, the essay reads like nothing less than a theoretical and aesthetic primer for Expressionism's urban phase. Simmel delineates the "exclusiveness and uniqueness" of urban space in city districts; the "individualizing of space" in the numbering of houses; the delimitations of spatial views in the "picture frame" and the "boundaries of darkness"; the "fixing of social forms in space" in the rendezvous (whose significance lies in "the tension between punctuality and the fleeting nature" of the meeting on the one hand, and "its spatio-temporal fixing" on the other); "spatial proximity and distance" in "the abstraction and indifference of the spatial proximity in the metropolis"; and "movement in space" in "the traveler, the stranger, and the dynamic of metropolitan encounters."[29]

Just as pertinent to urban Expressionism (as to film noir) is Simmel's analysis of the *psychological consequences* of the city's spatial dynamics, in which the endless interaction of networks, objects, individuals, and images within the "showplace of this culture," in Simmel's words, produces "an atrophy of individual culture and the hypertrophy of objective culture." Eventually, though always in flux, an uneasy equilibrium is established in which each of the cultures develops a "relative autonomy," with objective culture forming "a unity and autonomous self-sufficiency" and subjective culture taking on "the subjectivism of modern times." The unnerving result, for the individual and what remains of the collectivity, is a "particularly abstract existence."[30]

Simmel presages another of Expressionism's key principles in his description of the dialectic of objective and subjective culture in which "we can fully realize our subjectivity only in its *externalization in objective cultural forms.*" Such cultural transmutation was for Simmel, as for many (though not all) urban Expressionists, hardly a utopian prospect. The inability of objective culture to fulfill our desires, Simmel suggests, induces a permanent "feeling of tension, expectation and unreleased intense desires," a "secret restlessness" that leads to an endless quest for "momentary satisfaction in ever-new stimulations, sensations, external activities." Simmel elaborates, in a manner redolent not only of the urban Expressionists but also of postmodern critics Jean Baudrillard and Fredric Jameson: "We become entangled in the instability and helplessness that manifests itself as the tumult of the metropolis, as the mania for traveling, as the wild pursuit of competition, and as the typical modern disloyalty with regard to taste, style, opinions and personal relations."[31] The "inner barriers that are indispensable for the modern forms of life" are, in the end, insufficient, as David Frisby summarizes, to overcome "the experience of modernity as discontinuity and disintegration of time, space, and causality. Hence alienated forms of existence . . . become the forms in which we live."[32]

Although urban Expressionists would incorporate many of Simmel's spatial and psychological precepts into their work, their attitude toward his ideas, at least initially, was more ambivalent. Some artists translated their earlier ecstatic immersion in nature into a sensual engagement with, rather than a revulsion from, the metropolis, believing, like Meidner, that they should "paint what is close to us, our city world, the wild streets!" with their "tumult of light and dark"; or, like architect August Endell, that they should discover "the beauty of the city as nature" and "the street as living being."[33] The task for the pro-city Expressionists was "to regain 'those irrational, instinctive, sovereign traits and impulses' that Simmel believed metropolitan life excluded."[34] Jewish Expressionist writer Carl Einstein and Jewish philosopher Salmo Friedländer were other prominent celebrants, pre–World War I, of the city's liberating potential through its "dissolution of the individual into the apparent disorder of the world."[35] Einstein wrote of modern man's mind "as fragmented and capable of attaining unity only as part of a communal vision"; whereas Friedländer extolled the "new man," the "universal world-person," the *Erdkaiser* (earth emperor) of "presentism," who, as "the synthesis of the world," is an "eternal present."[36]

Armed with these utopian ideals, many Expressionists initially embraced World War I, not from blind patriotism but as a "powerful catharsis"—an Expressionism by other means that would destroy the old order and prepare the way for the "new man."[37] Max Beckman's letter from the front in 1914 captures this idealistic fervor: "Outside there was that wonderful, magnificent noise of battle. I went outside, through large groups of injured and worn-out soldiers coming back from the battlefield, and I could hear this strange, weirdly magnificent music. . . . I wish I could paint this noise."[38] As the horrors of trench warfare and Germany's sagging fortunes, on both the military and domestic fronts, punctured the early enthusiasm, Expressionism's malleability to circumstance, and its status as Weltanschauung, was further underscored. Future Jewish émigré noir director Curtis (then Kurt) Bernhardt relates how, as a young soldier in 1918, he stood up at a gathering of writers and journalists and proclaimed "that Expressionism was nothing but a protest against this insane war."[39]

Several practicing Expressionists, including Jews such as Meidner and Grosz, had resisted the patriotic euphoria from the outset. Their work, during and after the war, along with that of Dix—an early pro-war enthusiast who quickly became disillusioned—was at the forefront of an Expressionist turn toward a view of the city, and the world in general, more in line with Simmel's disturbing premonitions. Just as Expressionism's prewar ambivalence—"an art that shocked the bourgeoisie versus an art that mystically celebrated the German soul"[40]—congealed after the war around the movement's more irreverent strand, so did earlier notions of the metropolis as a "New Jerusalem" (whose "fragmentary mode of urban consciousness" promised psychological, social, and spiritual liberation) transmogrify into dystopian visions of "a darkened city," an "urban jungle," a "new Babylon."[41]

Max Reinhardt: Darkness and Light

Austrian-born Max Reinhardt was far and away the German-speaking world's, if not all of Europe's, most successful and influential theater director/impresario from the first decade of the 1900s through the early Weimar period: "the 'Kaiser' of the Berlin theater," Lotte Eisner calls him.[42] And although his connection to Expressionist aesthetics, and thus to film noir, is undeniable, the extent of his contribution, in degree and in kind, remains a matter of dispute. The two classic and still foundational texts on Weimar cinema, Kracauer's *From Caligari to Hitler* (1947) and Eisner's *The Haunted Screen* (1952), laid the groundwork for the debate. Kracauer maintains that Reinhardt's lighting effects in Reinhard Sorge's Expressionist play *Der Bettler* (*The Beggar*), first performed in 1917, set the stage for similar effects in early Weimar cinema. The play's creation of imaginary settings through the manipulation of light and shadow alone, Kracauer argues, moved Expressionist filmmakers "to breed shadows as rampant as weeds and associate ethereal phantoms with strangely lit arabesques or faces . . . to bathe all scenery in an unearthly illumination marking it as scenery of the soul."[43]

Eisner similarly acknowledges that *The Beggar*'s boldly chiaroscuro lighting "was the visual translation of the Expressionist axiom stipulating that a sole object chosen from the chaos of the universe must be singled out and plucked from its links with other objects. And everything, even the phosphorescent halo following the outline of a head and shading towards the regions of darkness, even the slash of piercing light screaming at the blur of a white face, was anticipated in this play."[44] She also grants Reinhardt's immense, if indirect, impact on Weimar cinema by virtue of the many actors, directors, and set designers who moved, sometimes back and forth, between his stage plays and the most notable of the proto-Expressionist, pure-Expressionist, or Expressionist-influenced films.

The actors included Albert Basserman, Elizabeth Bergner, Ernst Deutsch, Maria Fein, Alexander Granach, Emil Jannings, Fritz Kortner, Werner Krauss, Theodor Loos, Ernst Lubitsch, Alexander Moissi, Conrad Veidt, Paul Wegener, and Eduard von Winterstein.[45] Lubitsch and Wegener, of course, became major directors as well, and F. W. Murnau, perhaps the greatest of them all, had starring roles in two of Reinhardt's "very film-like" theater productions.[46] Expressionist-style writer/director Carl Grüne (*The Street*) was another Reinhardt alumnus, as were set designer/director Paul Leni (*Waxworks*, 1924) and set designers Kurt Richter (*The Student of Prague* [1913], *Sumurun* [1920], *Pharaoh's Wife* [1922]), Cesar Klein (*Genuine*, 1920), Marlene Poelzig (*The Golem*, 1920), and Edgar G. Ulmer (*The Last Laugh* and other uncredited films).[47]

Where Eisner balks, first, is in calling Reinhardt an Expressionist, an objection for which Reinhardt himself provided corroboration. Although he directed Expressionist plays, Reinhardt did not champion the style—or its Soviet relative, Constructivism—as did other leading (also Jewish) directors such as Erwin Piscator, Leopold Jessner, and Jürgen Fehling.[48] Reinhardt preferred the designation "Impressionist," and was, above all, anti-naturalist and eclectically experimental.

Second, although Eisner certainly finds *The Beggar* influential, she notes that much of Reinhardt's stage work during the war and before the production of *The Beggar* already had resorted to chiaroscuro, and not only for artistic reasons. In a materialist analysis strikingly consonant with Biesen's on the causes for film noir's aesthetic choices during World War II, Eisner points out how Reinhardt's creative decisions emerged in response to the exigencies of World War I. Criticized for the extravagance of his stagings while the country was asked to sacrifice for the war effort, and faced with wartime shortages in materials and financial resources, Reinhardt was forced to match invention to necessity. Innovative lighting effects, from this perspective, Eisner suggests, were "the only means of disguising the mediocrity of the ersatz materials used for sets and of varying the intensity of the atmosphere to suit the action."[49] Thus German filmmakers had far more than simply *The Beggar* to choose from in adapting that play's lighting style. As for proof that *The Beggar* did not single-handedly sire Expressionist cinema, Eisner points to a film released the year before Reinhardt's production of *The Beggar*, Otto Ripper's *Homunculus*, in which "the contrasts between black and white, the collisions between light and shade—all the classical elements of German film, from *Der Müde Tod* (*Destiny*) to *Metropolis*—are already present."[50]

Finally, Eisner's most provocative assertion about Reinhardt's, and Expressionism's, relation to Weimar cinema: that German Romanticism, not Expressionism per se, was the determining factor in the evolution of the distinctive Weimar style, "and that modern technique merely lends visible form to Romantic fancies."[51] Eisner invokes Spengler, Goethe, Novalis, and Hölderlin, among others, in their exultation of a primal German spirit that "instinctively prefers twilight to daylight, the mist, the enigmatic chiaroscuro, the 'Kolassal,' and infinite solitude"—a tortured soul "simultaneously both harsh and tender," attracted "by the dark maternal bosom of this dream- and death-dispensing night."[52] Yet curiously, and contradictorily, Eisner brings Reinhardt, and Judaism, back to center stage in her conclusion about Romanticism's cinematic legacy: "Nordic man's Faustian soul is committed to gloom, whereas Reinhardt—we should remember he was Jewish—created his magical world with light, darkness serving only as a foil to the light. This was the twofold heritage of the German film."[53]

As beguiling as Eisner's German/Jewish binary may be, its internal contradictions are multifold and telling. First, the Expressionist movement never denied its Romantic underpinnings; indeed, it drew sustenance from them, both philosophically and discursively, to differentiate the movement from the dizzying array of other early twentieth-century isms: Fauvism, Cubism, Orphism, Futurism, Suprematism, Constructivism, Dadaism, Surrealism, and so forth. Reinhardt himself was called, among many other things, a neo-Romantic.[54] Second, and more significant, the German-darkness/Jewish-light dichotomy, beyond its essentialism, is deeply flawed. Reinhardt was certainly Jewish, indeed piously so. But he was also, as were most Austrian artists and intellectuals from a cultural standpoint, intensely German.[55] And Germanic Jews in general, as I have shown, were themselves, in their post-emancipation formation, doubly torn—between *Deutschtum* and *Judentum*, and by interethnic divisions between Ost- and Westjuden. Moreover, modern Jews were drawn both to the darkness and the light of German Kultur generally, and of Expressionism specifically. The attraction derived not only from the entry into the Romantic tradition or avant-garde circles such engagement promised, but also from the deep affinities an ambivalent outlook held for the Jewish "soul."

Eisner's ascription of "lightness" to Reinhardt's art contains a measure of truth. Although clearly a serious artist, he was also highly popular. A master of all trades yet a slave to none, he veered from the intimate (pantomime, cabaret, and his pioneering *Kammerspiele* [chamber plays]) to the high cultural (ballet, opera, morality plays) to the grandly spectacular ("the theater of the masses for the masses") and back again.[56] This creative pluralism caused him to be many things to many people: "the illusionist, the impressionist, the neo-Romantic, the international impresario, the lighting wizard and manipulator of the revolving stage, the show-off showman, the circus man, the charlatan, the all-around genius."[57] He did, on occasion, speak of hoping to "bring joy back to the people" and to satisfy their desire, "given the gray misery of daily existence," for "brighter colors and a heightened sense of life."[58] But to attribute a privileging of light over darkness to Reinhardt's Jewishness is counterintuitive to say the least.

"All that is *not* Torah is levity," the Talmud teaches; and, indeed, the biblical Yahveh can hardly be considered a jocular, or even particularly compassionate, deity—even to his professed chosen people.[59] Nor can the Jewish historical experience be regarded as the most logical formula for a sunny disposition. Consequently, the association of Jews and comedy is a quite recent phenomenon. The public Jewish humor that did emerge—and then only in the post-emancipation period, first in Heine's poetry and in Yiddish folk tales, and subsequently in American popular entertainment—can be viewed as an ironic response to the cruel joke of God's singling Jews out to be a light among nations, then bequeathing them "a benighted existence." Confronted with this theological paradox and the anxieties of survival in a hostile world, Jews created a humor that served as a coping mechanism, "in which laughter and trembling were inextricably mixed."[60]

In high cultural forms, the laugh became a cackle. Jews' contribution to the dystopian turn in Expressionist painting has already been cited. In the literary arena, one need look no further than Freud and Kafka, Werfel and Hofmannsthal, Wedekind and Mayer, to recognize that no essential Jewish aversion existed to exploring the darker recesses of the human soul. When one takes into account the panoply of Jewish contributors to Expressionist cinema itself—from writers, directors, and producers to actors, cameramen, and designers—Eisner's Jewish "lightness of being" theory crumbles under its own weight. Whether "performing high or low," Jews have been the standard-bearers of a dialectic of darkness and light.[61]

Eisner's otherwise insightful formal analysis suffers also from its focus on Expressionist lighting at the expense of Expressionist space. Chiaroscuro lighting (which owes as much to Rembrandt and Caravaggio as to the German Romantics) or the emphasis on and choice of props and setting are only half the story. At least as important to the overall mise-en-scène is the manner in which lighting and setting are *composed* in the frame to establish—or *undermine*—a sense of place. From this perspective, the Expressionist privileging of angularity and distortion, fragmentation and exaggeration, geometric abstraction and cubist two-dimensionality, represents a uniquely modernist, rather than derivatively Romantic, stylistic intervention. And although aniconic injunctions may have impeded Jewish artists' involvement with the earliest elaborations of Expressionist space in painting, other specifically Semitic spatial orientations may have facilitated Jews' quick study and elaboration of Expressionist principles—in painting and in the other arts.

Jews as a people, according to Eli Barnavi, have evolved an anomalous spatial consciousness. Owing to their unique diasporic experience, Barnavi argues, Jewish perception of space has been marked by two characteristics: "a notion of multiple spaces, rather than of a single space; and between these spaces, a void." To a more heightened extent than humankind in general, in other words, the Jewish spatial sense has tended toward the *"differential* and *discontinuous."*[62] Due to its historical and geographical inflections, Jewish spatial awareness can be seen as alternately temporal and spatial, psychological and corporeal, constantly shifting "between awareness of physical spaces (the birth-place, for example) to spaces of reference (the ancestral homeland, Hebrew, etc.), a shift which actually *constitutes* the Jewish spatial experience."[63] The stereotype of the Jewish wanderer, in its relation to rootlessness, grounded the modern anti-Semitic discourse for the likes of Werner Sombart; in its relation to *mobility*, however, the wanderer trope might also help account for Jews' apparent special gift for adapting to and interpreting—per Georg Simmel, Ludwig Meidner, and Max Reinhardt—the radical instability and confusion of modern life.

Screening the Stage/Staging the Screen

Although Kracauer's analysis of Weimar cinema focuses on its thematic and narrative concerns, and Eisner's on its stylistic tendencies, Reinhardt's Weimar legacy requires attention to both content and form, separately and in conjunction. His initial contribution to content was indirect but major. In 1902, while working under then-reigning maestro of the German stage Otto Brahm (John Brahm's uncle), Reinhardt put on the first of Wedekind's "Lulu" plays, *Erdgeist* (*Earth Spirit*). Although not Expressionist in style, the play introduced, in the darkly seductive Lulu character, the prototypical modern femme fatale that would become a fixture of Weimar cinema and, later, film noir. Lulu herself would reappear in celluloid form in G. W. Pabst's 1929 film *Die Büchse der Pandora* (*Pandora's Box*), a composite adaptation of Wedekind's play of the same name and *Erdgeist*.

Jews' seminal role in adapting the primal figure of the evil temptress to the modern age is, once again, not coincidental. Proprietary claims to the femme fatale's origins are not the issue here. Whether one bases male ambivalence to female sexuality on its foundational archetypes—the Sumerian Lilith; the biblical Eve, Delilah, and Salome; the Hellenic Pandora, Medusa, and Circe—or on the Freudian notions of castration anxiety and the Oedipal complex, such ambivalence is indisputably a universal, ahistorical phenomenon. The modern variation on the black widow, however, bears distinctly Jewish markings. Renewed dread of the feminine coincided with the rise of modernity and its adjuncts, mass culture and the metropolis, and Jews were inextricably linked to all three.

The Jewish connections are echoed implicitly in an indictment of the cinema by critic Herman Kienzl in 1910: "The psychology of the cinematic triumph is a metropolitan psychology. Not only because the metropolis constitutes the natural focal point for all the radiations of social life, but especially because the metropolitan soul—that always hurried soul, curious and unanchored, tumbling from fleeting impression to fleeting impression—is also the soul of cinematography."[64] Mass culture as a whole, drawing on women's preeminence as cultural consumers and on mass culture's imbrication with desire, "was commonly personified as 'feminine,' as having the capacity to induce passivity, vulnerability, corruption."[65]

Most disturbing for the maintenance of social legitimacy, popular culture posed a threat "to the distinctions preserving traditionally defined male and female roles."[66] Here, once again, Jews and women conjoined in the gentile patriarchal imaginary. Long stereotyped as physically stunted and feeble—with a circumcised penis analogized with the female clitoris, and, in the late nineteenth century, disproportionately diagnosed with "female" mental disorders such as hysteria—the modern European Jewish male increasingly became identified, in scientific as well as popular circles, as the feminized Other.[67] As Patrice Petro has shown via popular magazine illustrations of the time, the city, and especially the "Jewish" city of Berlin, "served as the decisive metaphor for modernity. Modernity, in turn, was almost always represented as a woman figure." Moreover, these depictions were frequently androgynous and Amazonian, projecting male "anxieties and fears emanating from various phenomena of modernity that were recast and reconstructed in terms of an uncontrollable and destructive female sexuality."[68] The Jewish woman, meanwhile, as the inversion of the Jewish man, came to be constructed as the femme fatale in her most erotic and *exotic* form. Famed actor Sarah Bernhardt perhaps most epitomized this "Oriental exoticism," which "pointed eastward to Istanbul and beyond—to Judea, Herod's court, and the figure of Salome . . . she of the seven veils and John the Baptist's severed head."[69]

Expressionist thematic concerns were further spotlighted in another Reinhardt-Wedekind collaboration, *Frühlings Erwachen* (*Spring Awakening*), first staged in 1906. An explosive drama about the turmoil of adolescent sexuality so controversial that it had been banned in Germany for fifteen years, the play marked a major cultural "turning point," according to Peter Jalevich. The Expressionist movement was "prefigured by that play's theme of generational conflict, as well as by the fantastic final scene, in which Mortiz [the protagonist], having committed suicide in a previous act, arises from the grave with his blown-off head under his arm."[70]

As for formal innovation, Reinhardt had experimented audaciously with lighting, set design, and acting styles from the start of his stage career.[71] His first big coup came in 1905, when, two years after breaking away from Otto Brahm, he made headlines (and heads spin) with his revolving stage for a production of Shakespeare's *A Midsummer Night's Dream*. Not by itself Expressionist, the concept of making the set "as much an actor as the humans" would become a prime marker of the expressionist style in cinema.[72] Reinhardt's staging took another expressionist turn in 1906 in the lighting effects for his production of Henrik Ibsen's *Ghosts*. Predating by ten years the effects in his wartime work that would become the staple of Weimar cinema (as alleged by Eisner)—high contrast between dark and light, the symbolic use of shadows—the lighting scheme in *Ghosts* transformed mise-en-scène into a character in the drama.[73] Moreover, a photo detail of his 1909 production of *Hamlet*—reproduced, ironically, in Eisner's *The Haunted Screen*—indicates that Reinhardt's dynamic lighting schemes were no aberration. The tableaux, with its extreme chiaroscuro lighting, could pass for a de La Tour or a Rembrandt.

The allusion to Rembrandt is worthy of further consideration, given the Renaissance painter's relation to the debate around Reinhardt's impact on Weimar cinema. Barry Salt was the first to throw down the gauntlet in regard to Weimar cinema's genealogy of influence, with new research challenging both Kracauer's and Eisner's accounts. In a 1979 essay titled "From Caligari to Who?" Salt points out that the lighting style that both Kracauer and Eisner situate in Weimar cinema, and that Eisner attributes to Reinhardt's late-wartime theater work and the 1916 film *Homunculus,* can be found in 1914 and 1915 in the films of U.S. directors Ralph Ince and Cecil B. DeMille.[74] Indeed, the technical term "Rembrandt lighting," coined by DeMille as a marketing ploy, came into common use in the U.S. film industry at the time.

Of course, as I (with Eisner's help) have indicated, Reinhardt had done Ince and DeMille one better, using "Rembrandt lighting" on stage as early as 1909—nor is this precociousness surprising, chronologically or ethno-religiously. As Emily Bilski has shown, Rembrandt reemerged as an influence on modern German artists by the 1870s, when Jewish painter Max Lieberman, inspired by his yearly visits to Holland, began working in a Rembrandt vein. Decades later, in response to reactionary artists' "appropriation of Rembrandt as the model for a Nordic Germanic revival," Lieberman, from 1905 to 1909, turned to depicting scenes from Amsterdam's Jewish Quarter as a means of "reinstating a 'Jewish' construction of Rembrandt—as the artist who lived in Amsterdam's Jewish Quarter and portrayed the Jews there with sympathy."[75] Rembrandt's frequent depictions of Old Testament subjects further endeared him to Jewish artists, particularly Lesser Uhry, for whom Rembrandt provided "a source and inspiration" from the 1880s on.[76] Reinhardt's theatrical appropriation of Rembrandt thus can be seen, at least partly, as tapping into a collective Jewish consciousness surrounding the Dutch master. By extension, Weimar cinema's adaptation of chiaroscuro, given the profound influence of theater traditions in Germany as well as German filmmakers' propensity for cultural collaboration, would seem to owe at least as much to Reinhardt's, and other German artists,' innovations as to Hollywood's.[77]

Reinhardt's direct link with cinema begins in the early 1910s. Until this time, the movies in Germany generally had been held, at least by the middle and upper classes, in even lower esteem than in the United States, where they vied for cachet with the amusement park and the burlesque. The French Film D'Art company (1908–1911), through its presentation of classic plays featuring acclaimed actors such as Sarah Bernhardt, radically changed the perception of film's inferior cultural status among Germany's "upper world" of stage directors, actors, and writers.[78] Stirred by the new medium's creative potential, Reinhardt joined with Jewish movie theater owner and producer Paul Davidson—the latter moved more by the prospect of luring the bourgeoisie to his more elegant theaters—in founding a guild to promote and regulate exchanges between film and theater personnel. Reinhardt himself directed two films, and Jews in general—given their preponderance in the theater—became instrumental in raising the once despised medium to a level of respectability.[79] Jewish actors, set designers, and other members of Reinhardt's troupe alternated between stage and screen. Jewish playwright Arthur Schnitzler's romantic comedy *Liebelei* was adapted for film. And another Austrian Jew, poet/playwright Hugo von Hofmannsthal, wrote the script for *Das Fremde Mädchen* (*The Strange Girl*, 1913), one of the first "fantastic films" whose Weimar-era revival would herald the full-fledged arrival of Expressionist cinema.

German film's heightened artistic (though not necessarily critical) reputation, and its resultant broadened appeal for the middle classes (though not necessarily the masses), spurred the construction of new studios at Tempelhof and Neubabelsberg near Berlin.[80] Foreign films, especially from France and Denmark, continued to dominate the German marketplace, but the Berlin studios provided the resources for a group of *Autorenfilme* (author's films) that Henri Langlois calls the "sources of Germany's national film art."[81] As with Davidson's foray into more sophisticated film exhibition, the artistic pretensions of the *Autorenfilm* were both conscious and calculating. Predicting the Expressionist "branding" strategy that followed in the wake of *Caligari*'s international "art film" success, the *Autorenfilm* provided a means of gaining cultural capital while also differentiating the German film product from its more entertainment-oriented foreign competition.[82]

The two most noteworthy of the early *Autorenfilms* were *Der Student von Prague* (*The Student of Prague*, 1913) and *Der Golem* (*The Golem*, 1914). Regarded as key forerunners of Expressionist cinema, these short (one-reel) silent films have significant Jewish, as well as Reinhardtian, ties. *The Student of Prague*'s scenario by Hanns Heinz Ewers, a doppelgänger tale of a poor student who sells his mirror reflection to a diabolical sorcerer in exchange for wealth and love, is clearly indebted to Goethe's *Faust* and Edgar Allan Poe's short story "William Wilson."[83] Eisner, however, points additionally to two contemporaneous works as supplying inspiration: *Das Abenteur der Sylvester-Nacht* (*A New Year's Eve Adventure*) by E. T. A. Hoffmann, about a man who loses his reflection; and *Peter Schlemihl* by Adalbert von Chamisso, about a man who sells his shadow. The name Schlemihl, of course, references the classic fool of Jewish folklore, whereas the sale of one's shadow evokes the biblical story of Esau, who sells his birthright to his twin brother, Jacob, who, as the new Jewish patriarch, will bequeath his God-given name, Israel, to the Jewish people.

The Golem's Jewish bona fides are more unequivocal, given the film's basis in the Jewish legend of the clay monster created by a sixteenth-century rabbi to save the Jews of the Prague ghetto from a pogrom, but who ends up turning both on his master and his own people. Although Mary Shelley's *Frankenstein*, published in 1818, predates the first recorded publishing of the Golem story in 1847, and "homunculean" experiments were actually carried out by sixteenth-century alchemists, tales of golems associated with prominent rabbis proliferated in the Middle Ages and the principle of manmade super-beings is mentioned in the Talmud.[84] *The Golem's* significance, however, transcends its scriptural pedigree. In light of the ancient tale's modern-day resurrection and persistent appeal, as indicated by a 1920 German remake, and given a sociohistorical dimension at least as prescient as *Caligari's*, one wonders whether *From the Golem to Hitler* might usefully serve as a surrogate title for Kracauer's eschatological treatise.

Reinhardt's connection to the first *Student of Prague* and *Golem* films, besides supplying the talent—Wegener as star of both films and director of *The Golem*, and Kurt Richter as art director on *The Student of Prague*—relates, once more, both to content and form. Or, as Wegener described the two films' effect at the time, "the strange mixture of the natural and the artificial, in theme as in setting."[85] Because both films have been lost, we must rely on contemporary accounts to judge the expressionist resonance in Wegener's summation, but one critic's comparison of *The Student of Prague* to a Jusepe de Ribera painting offers support.[86] Ribera, a Spanish-born Baroque-era painter in the Caravaggio style, was not only noted, as was his mentor, for his extravagant compositions; he was, together with the Italian painter, one of the so-called *Tenebrosi*, or shadow painters, owing to their reliance on sharp contrasts of light and shade.

Another of Wegener's comments, on his own filmmaking approach, can be read as a direct extension of Reinhardt's dramaturgical principles to the new medium: "The real creator of the film must be the camera. Getting the spectator to change his point of view, using special effects to double the actor on the divided screen, superimposing other images—all this, technique, *form*, gives the content its real meaning."[87] Of course, while stroking Reinhardt with one hand, Wegener—in the Expressionist (and Freudian) tradition—was "killing the father" with the other. Beyond personally abandoning the stage for the screen, Wegener now proclaimed that cinema itself had to break free from the theater, the novel, and the other arts, and "create in its own medium, with the image alone."[88]

From Expressionism to expressionism

"Papa" Reinhardt would not go quietly into that good night. His specter would haunt German cinema well into the Weimar period, nowhere more so than in the Kammerspiel film, which—fundamental to the rise of film noir—is where the cinematic transformation of Expressionism into expressionism was most artfully achieved. Barry Salt counts only seven films that strictly qualify as pure Expressionist cinema through their artificially foregrounded visual design, exaggeratedly gestural acting style, and fantastic themes: *Caligari, Genuine, Von morgens bis Mitternacht (From Morning to Midnight,* 1920), *Torgus* (1921), *Raskolnikov* (1923), *Das Wachsfigurenkabinett (Waxworks,* 1924), and *Metropolis* (1927).[89] Five of the seven were directed by Jews: three by Robert Wiene (*Caligari, Genuine,* and *Raskolnikov*), one by Paul Leni (*Waxworks*), and one by Lang (*Metropolis*). All except *Metropolis* were made during, and help to characterize, what film historians regard as the first of the three Weimar cinema phases. These divisions roughly correspond to the larger German sociopolitical and economic changes as delineated by Gay: 1919–1924, failed revolution, rampant inflation; 1924–1929, economic stability; 1929–1933, economic depression, Nazi rise and takeover.[90]

The first and second phases overlap in the Kammerspiel/street films, which correspondingly serve as an aesthetic and thematic bridge between them. The Kammerspiel film begins with *Hintertreppe (Backstairs,* 1920) and *Scherben (Shattered,* 1921), and includes, to name some of the more prominent examples: *Sylvester (New Year's Eve,* 1923), *Der Letzte Mann (The Last Laugh,* 1924), *Varieté (Variety,* 1925), *Die Liebe der Jeanne Ney (The Love of Jeanne Ney,* 1927), and *Der blaue Engel (The Blue Angel,* 1930). *Die Strasse (The Street,* 1923) appropriately marks the onset of the street film, which continues through *Die Freundlose Gasse (The Joyless Street,* 1925), *Dirnentragödie (Tragedy of a Street,* 1927), and *Asphalt* (1928). Commensurate with the cultural shift in the mid-1920s from Expressionism to New Objectivity (*Neue Sachlichkeit*), the Kammerspiel and street films take place in the here and now, not, as with Expressionist films, in some supernatural nether region, futuristic dystopia, or lunatic's mind. Kammerspiel/street film acting styles and settings also comport to more naturalistic standards of representation (although sets are still largely studio-constructed). Incommensurate with the cultural shift, however, they retain a dark look and morbid sensibility more akin to Expressionism than the proudly utilitarian and optimistic New Objectivity.

Kammerspiel/street films are hybrids, in other words, combining elements of the receding and emergent art movements—but with a residual tilt toward the former. Rather than embracing the philosophical aims or aesthetic principles of New Objectivity, Kammerspiel/street films transfer Expressionist motifs into realistic surroundings.[91] Max Ernst's Expressionist dictate, "To give expression to something psychological by means of form alone"; Herwarth Walden's definition, to give not "an impression from the outside" but rather "an expression from the inside"; the Munich painters' manifesto, "To give material shape to the spiritual"; and Georg Simmel's admonition to use Stimmung to evoke the "inner quality" of nature, are all advanced, in modified form, in the Kammerspiel/street film.[92] The modification stems, primarily and crucially, from Kammerspiel's ability to merge, through mise-en-scène, the phantasmic and the everyday.

The Kammerspiel film, in other words, like purist Expressionist cinema before it, manages to transform "material objects into emotional ornaments," illuminate "interior landscapes," and emphasize "the irrational events of instinctive life."[93] These effects are achieved without resorting to patent artificiality, however, but rather are accomplished within a plausibly realistic representational format. Unusual camera angles and camera movement, atmospheric lighting, and stylized but believable sets do for the Kammerspiel/street film what painted backdrops and special effects did for *Caligari*. In the Kammerspiel/street film, Expressionism is stitched *into* the mise-en-scène rather than draped *across* it—ultimately, a more effective, or at least more seamless, cinematic means of externalizing internal reality (Expressionism's prime aesthetic trope). John Barlow's term for this more mimetic and pragmatic approach to Expressionism is "functional expressionism," defined as the manipulation of naturalistically motivated mise-en-scène for psychological or symbolic ends.[94] Its very name conveying the merging of Expressionism and New Objectivity, functional expressionism sought more economical and empirically credible means of "stretching the truth." As functional expressionism took hold, manipulation of light and shadow, composition and reflection, sets and props, and camera angle and movement (for aesthetic as well as economic reasons) became the preferred methods for connoting deeper meanings. Expressionist distortions were reserved (as they remain today) largely for depicting altered states of consciousness, the supernatural, alcohol- or drug-induced states, visions or dreams, mood swings, or insanity (figs. 4 and 5).

Reinhardt's significance to the development of Expressionist-style mise-en-scène has already been described. His bequests to the Kammerspiel/street film are even more direct, beginning with the very term and concept of Kammerspiel itself. In 1906, yearning for a more intimate experience than provided by his other two Berlin theaters, the Deutsches and Neues Theaters, Reinhardt converted a property adjacent to the Deutsches Theater into a more intimate "chamber theater" called the Kammerspiele. The first two productions at the smaller venue were none other than the two plays that launched German theater's foray into expressionist aesthetics, Ibsen's *Ghosts* and Wedekind's *Spring Awakening*.[95]

A second important Reinhardt contribution to the Kammerspiel film relates to acting style. Eisner notes how Reinhardt's emphasis in his stage work on unambiguous facial expression and gestural support was central to the discreet

Figure 4. Expressionism with a capital *E*: Conrad Veidt and Werner Krauss in *The Cabinet of Dr. Caligari* (1920). (Photofest)

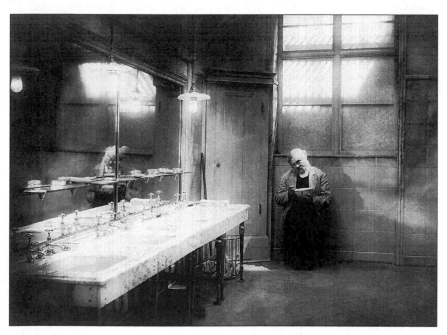

Figure 5. Functional expressionism: Emil Jannings in *The Last Laugh* (1924). (Photofest)

physical relationships demanded of the Kammerspiel film. She quotes from Heinz Herald, one of Reinhardt's collaborators, to this effect: "If an actor needs to lift his whole arm at the Grosses Schauspielhaus, he need only move his hand at the Deutsches Theater; and at the Kammerspiele it is enough if he moves his finger."[96] The subtlety of performance ushered in by the Kammerspiel stage drama, Eisner suggests, inspired a similar acting approach in the Kammerspiel film, in which the spectator "could feel all the significance of a smile, a hesitation, or an eloquent silence."[97]

Kammerspiel and street films' fusing of Expressionist motifs with contemporary concerns was made to order for film noir in several ways. Aesthetically, just as Expressionism may have served as a fitting representational analogue for the supernatural horror film, expressionism seemed ideally suited to presenting the horrors of the everyday. Thematically, Kammerspiel/street films incorporated two mainstays of the noir narrative: sexuality and violence. The street film, in particular, invariably turned on class- and gender-related conflict generated by the bourgeois male's simultaneous attraction/aversion to the nightlife of the city. From this approach/avoidance syndrome would emerge film noir's two most salient character types: the ambivalent protagonist and the femme fatale.

From an historical perspective, the transmutation of Expressionism into expressionism in the Kammerspiel/street film also counters a further challenge to the Expressionist-noir connection leveled by Marc Vernet. His deconstruction hinges on two main points: "first, that the 'expressionist' image is relatively rare in the period 1941–45 . . . and, second, it can also be found, and at least as frequently, in the films of the preceding decades."[98] Both points founder, however, on a fallacious premise; namely, "the contradiction that exists in putting expressionism together with the realism of the decors or situations that supposedly define film noir."[99] As I have shown, functional expressionism is precisely the means by which Weimar cinema *achieved* the symbiosis of Expressionism and realism, and to more concertedly psychological, symbolic, and phantasmic ends than the earlier American, Danish, French, and Russian filmmakers Vernet marshals as exhibits against the Weimar expressionist legacy.[100] Griffith and DeMille, Blum and Christensen, Perret and Feuillade, and Bauer and Protazanov (not to mention the Swedes Stiller and Sjöström) certainly made important strides toward functional expressionism, but it took the Weimar directors' proximity to and immersion in the Expressionist and New Objectivity movements to codify it into a formal *system*.[101] That American director King Vidor, regarding his consciously expressionist film *The Crowd* (1928), freely admitted his indebtedness to Weimar cinema in general and F. W. Murnau's *Sunrise* (1927) in particular, provides additional grounds for privileging the German connection.[102] And Vernet himself supplies the clincher when one of his prime examples of a later American proto-noir, Mervyn LeRoy's *Two Seconds* (1932), features a climactic scene clearly patterned, in style and content, on Lang's *M*, released one year before.[103]

Reinhardt's innovative stage work, his pioneering of the *Autorenfilm*, and the wealth of personnel and ideas he bequeathed to Weimar cinema clearly make him a prime progenitor of the expressionist turn in Weimar cinema and, by extension, film noir. Again, however, this by no means is to suggest a singular or straightforward through line from Reinhardt to noir—either via his own work, his influence, or from his (partial) progeny, the Kammerspiel/street film. The Kammerspiel/street film itself falls short of full-fledged film noir: First, because most of its examples were silent, whereas distinctive dialogue, often accompanied by voice-over narration, are important features of film noir. Two other notable noir ingredients, the figure of the private eye or police detective and his flip side, the master or pathological criminal, are also conspicuously absent from the Kammerspiel/street film—though not from Weimar cinema, as the work of Fritz Lang, in particular, will show.

4   *The Father of Film Noir*

FRITZ LANG

Auteurist caveats notwithstanding, Fritz Lang qualifies as the sire of film noir on several levels, both as progenitor and practitioner. After apprenticing as a writer and then director on a series of German films in 1919 and 1920, all commingling favored noir themes such as death, doubling, and the "destiny of woman," Lang's work in the Weimar period increasingly veered, with occasional mythic/romantic detours (partly prompted by his wife/collaborator, Thea von Harbou), toward cinema's dark side, both visually and thematically.[1] His *Der Müde Tod* (*The Weary Death*, aka *Destiny*, 1921) "defied all known standards" of the Reinhardtian "interplay of light and shadow," atmosphere, and mood, and the film's bittersweet fatalism would become a noir staple.[2] In the two-part *Dr. Mabuse: Der Spieler* (*Dr. Mabuse: The Gambler*, 1922), Lang became arguably the first director to merge expressionist mise-en-scène with the realistic crime film, as well as displaying a prototypically noirish horror/fascination with the criminal mastermind. The science fiction spectacular *Metropolis* (1927), although generically divergent from noir, features one of cinema's classic femme fatales, in the saintly/robotic Maria, and is considered, by Barry Salt and others, the visual culmination of Expressionist cinema.

Lang's first sound film *M* (1931), moreover—in its amalgam of expressionistic technique, subjective point of view, conflation of official and underworld "justice," and empathetic treatment of a serial child killer—ranks, for many noir scholars, as one of the first film noirs. Joseph von Sternberg's *The Blue Angel* (1930), Jean Renoir's *La Chienne* (1931), and Rouben Mamoulian's *City Streets* (1931) might compete for premier honors, but no other early proto-noir pushes the form's overall stylistic and thematic elements to the extreme of Lang's *M*. Before "Berlin's mid-war cynicism was married to the new hard-boiled style of the American novel in a low-budget environment demanded by Depression-era economics," David Wallace observes, "the early and among the most successful examples [of film noir] were created by Lang while he was at UFA."[3] Lang's work "is almost synonymous with film noir," Eddie Muller concurs, adding that *Metropolis* and *M* "etched the first blueprints of Dark City: omnipotent external forces dictating the fate of innocent people, and uncontrollable internal urges leading to self-destruction."[4]

Lang's life, almost as much as his art, is steeped in a noir ethos unmatched by his peers. Many of his personal actions and attitudes, and those of others toward him, betray an ambivalence uncannily commensurate with that found in his own films and in noir generally. The correlation of this ambivalence to Lang's biographical self, moreover, is both problematized and reinforced by what Patrick McGilligan generously calls Lang's penchant for "wishful hindsight" about his life.[5] Less forgiving descriptions of his suspect autobiographical accounts range from political opportunism to brazen dissimulation. And although one can dismiss as harmless embellishment Lang's claim that his father was an architect (he was a building contractor) or that Lang attended art school as a youth in Munich (no record of his enrollment exists), the linchpin of his biographical legend—his fleeing Berlin in a survivalist panic in 1933 after Joseph Goebbels offered him the "führership" of German film (Hitler reputedly loved *Metropolis* and had broken into tears over *Die Nibelungen*)—is less easily explained away.

Subsequent research, methodically culled by McGilligan, drills holes in Lang's account of the Goebbels affair. Passport records prove that not only did he not hop a late train to Paris the night of his alleged meeting with the Reich's propaganda minister, but that his final departure from Germany didn't take place till four months later. Documented currency transactions over this period also debunk Lang's claim that his hasty retreat precluded going to the bank, and Hollywood press releases listing Lang's prize Polynesian art collection contradict his assertions of having left it behind. Most damningly, Goebbels's published diaries—these from a man known for his "thoroughness and inclusiveness"—make no mention of any special meeting with Lang.[6] Lending credence to the notion that he may have concocted the story to shore up his shaky anti-Nazi credentials is the fact that Lang only began relating the incident in 1942, when a staunch anti-Nazi stance by a German-speaking émigré, especially one of Jewish heritage, had become de rigueur, and when "the chances of rebuttal" were "highly unlikely."[7]

Lang's interviews are littered with similar convenient untruths. Several of these again, such as those overstating his creative contributions to some of his films, can be rationalized as résumé padding. Other, more troubling fabrications concern his claims to political correctness. For example, although he later boasted of having fought in vain to cast an African American as the main character in *Fury* (1936), at the time of the filming he was planting racist jokes in magazines and newspapers, "often at the expense of 'colored people' he supposedly knew."[8] And his complaint of being blacklisted for over a year in 1952–1953 is discredited by evidence of his ingratiating himself with the HUAC inquisitors and landing a directing deal with Columbia's Harry Cohn.[9] The most damaging repercussion of Lang's pattern of prevarication is to cast doubt on his account of the most tragic event in his life: the death of his first wife.

In late 1920, the woman in question, a former cabaret dancer named Lisa Rosenthal, was found dead from a gunshot to the chest, fired from Lang's Browning revolver.[10] Lang claimed that he found his wife's body in the bathtub, the victim of an apparent suicide. His collaborator and mistress at the time (and soon-to-be second wife), Thea von Harbou, corroborated his testimony in a formal inquiry that found Lang free of any wrongdoing. Yet nagging doubts about Lang's innocence surfaced at the time and persist today. What appears indisputable is that Rosenthal had been distressed for some time over her husband's flaunting of his relationship with von Harbou, and that he was furious with Rosenthal for not dutifully accepting the affair. At one point, according to a witness, he had waved his revolver at Rosenthal during a heated argument about the matter. What remains in dispute is what happened when she later discovered him and von Harbou in a hotel room. Contrary to Lang's and von Harbou's version, newspaper editor Hans Feld and cinematographer Karl Freund, both of whom were around at the time and familiar with all parties, believed that Lang shot Rosenthal in a fit of rage, or even premeditatedly. One piece of circumstantial evidence, on top of the contentious backstory, lends the homicidal accusation credibility: shortly before her death, Rosenthal had called a girlfriend to go shopping with her after she took a bath.[11]

Whatever the actual cause of Rosenthal's death, McGilligan is not alone in speculating on the relation between the incident and Lang's work, which is haunted, "from the first film to the last, [with] guilt, complicity, false accusation, irredeemable crime, inadvertent crimes, and suicide."[12] And although Weimar cinema in general is distinguished by its characters'"suicidal state of mind," and self-destruction plays a role in two films Lang wrote before his wife's shooting—*Hilde Warren und der Tod* (*Hilde Warren and Death*, 1917) and *Lilith und Ly* (*Lilith and Ly*, 1918)—the theme of suicide is "elevated to ceremonial status afterward."[13] McGilligan lists the more striking examples:

> The suicide of Brunhild in *Die Nibelungen* [1924]
> The clown who shoots himself on stage in *Spione* [*Spies*, 1928][14]
> The astronomer who chooses to die by staying on the moon with her true
>   love in *Frau im Mond* [*Woman in the Moon*, 1929]
> Eddie and Joan, their flight from the law in *You Only Live Once* [1937], a form
>   of self-destruction
> Liliom, turning a knife on himself [in *Liliom*, 1934]
> The false justice of a mob lynching in *Fury*
> Jerry's "suicide," a murder faked by the Nazis in *Man Hunt* [1941]
> The killer who makes a mess of his suicide, and is pursued to the end of
>   his days by the ghost of his beloved, in *Scarlet Street* [1945]
> The suicide that triggers the plot of *The Big Heat* [1953]. The faked suicide
>   of a witness which is in fact a murder in the same film.
> The murder of a burlesque dancer, who turns out to have been the wife of
>   a clandestine marriage, in *Beyond a Reasonable Doubt* [1956][15]

(To which I can add: the three suicides in *Dr. Mabuse: The Gambler*, including one by Cara, a cabaret dancer, whose love for the nefarious title character is unrequited; the botched suicide of the female murderer in *The Blue Gardenia* [1953]; and, perhaps most resonant with the Rosenthal case, the frustrated writer's attempt, in *House by the River* [1950], to make his attempted murder of his brother look like a suicide!)

Two other Lang biographers, Cornelius Schnauber and George Sturm, suggest ways in which Rosenthal's death influenced not only Lang's work, but his life as well. Schnauber, a close friend of Lang's in the United States, observes that although the director's treatment of people was frequently harsh, "deep inside he was a very tender and soft person. . . . The death of his wife, whether or not it was a suicide, was a shock to him, became a part of his films, and influenced his whole life."[16] Sturm provides a potential concrete example of how the tragedy might have affected the director's psyche. In 1922, following the filming of *Der Müde Tod*, Lang spent some time in a mental institution—to research his next project, he later claimed. Sturm believes, not solely based on Lang's tendency to distort the facts, that he was actually there as a patient.[17]

The Man Who Got Away with Murder

One small but significant detail missing from the various accounts of the effect of Lisa Rosenthal's death on Fritz Lang, as filmmaker and as human being, is that Rosenthal was likely Jewish.[18] It doesn't take a psychiatrist (or perhaps it does) to fathom how heavily the responsibility—whether direct or indirect—for the death of a Jewish woman in Weimar Germany might weigh on the conscience of a man whose own Jewish identity—both internally and externally—was itself a matter of some contention.

Fritz Lang's mother, Pauline Lang (née Schlesinger), was born and raised Jewish. Although Austrian law forbade Christian-Jewish intermarriage, because Pauline's baptized husband Anton declared himself without religious denomination at the time of their wedding she was permitted to retain her Jewish affiliation. Given the rising anti-Semitic and assimilationist pressures in fin-de-siècle Vienna, however, which tended to exceed even those in Germany—not only Hitler, of course, but his Jew-hating guru, Adolf Josef Lanz, were Austrian—Pauline and Anton underwent a "double conversion" to Catholicism in 1900.[19] Lang himself, although baptized at birth in 1890 and raised Catholic by his mother, could still be considered formally Jewish based on the Judaic law of matrilineal descent. Informally, the tendency was even more persistent—among Jews and non-Jews—to regard Jews who converted, or whose parents had, as Jewish nonetheless. The flimsiness of the facade would become lethally evident during the Nazi era, when, the dark saying goes, Hitler had no trouble determining who was a Jew. For unconverted Jews, the perceived duplicity of self-denying "Jews under the skin" was cause from the start for a deep resentment that would only grow in bitterness with the Nazi threat.

Aside from the Jewish question, Lang's Viennese upbringing furnished a conflicted backdrop, which, again, in many ways surpassed that found in Berlin or other German cities. "Merry Vienna," Paul Hoffmann reminds us, the "city that inspired Mozart, Beethoven, and Schubert, the capital of *Gemütlichkeit*, of hand-kissing and the waltz, of coffeehouses and wine taverns in the green, of whipped cream and the annual opera ball, has long had one of the highest suicide rates in the world."[20] "The Austrian," Dutch composer Bernard van Beurden observed metaphorically, "lives in a two-room apartment. One room is bright, friendly, the 'cozy parlor,' well furnished, where he receives his guests. The other room is dark, somber, barred, totally unfathomable."[21] And let us not forget that although the carnage of World War I may have triggered its conception, it was "in the city of imperial and plebian suicide and 'beautiful' corpses" that Freud formulated the death wish.[22]

Adding to Lang's personal ambivalence toward his Jewishness—exacerbated by unavoidable contact with Jews in the German, and later American, film industries—was his emotional attachment to his mother, at the expense of his non-Jewish father, and his resemblance to her in his dark hair and features.[23] This overdetermined identity conflict no doubt partly explains the overcompensatory German, or rather Prussian, demeanor Lang affected as a director, from his tyrannical manner on the set to his trademark monocle.[24] The conflict is also manifest in his work from the very beginning. One of his first film scripts, *Lilith and Ly*, directed by Erich Kober in 1918 or 1919, "is clearly pinched from the Jewish legend of the golem."[25] The kabbalistic rabbi is here a scientist-inventor and the "monster" a statue of an ideal woman brought to life. The name of the reanimated statue itself, Lilith, references another figure from Jewish lore. Although of Sumerian origin, Lilith in her biblical, Talmudic, and folkloric variants is regarded alternatively as Adam's first wife or, again preempting Eve, as the ur–femme fatale: a succubus-like spirit that seduces men in their sleep and attacks children.[26]

Both the experimental scientist-inventor "embroiled in fantastic, macabre adventures" and the Janus-faced (occasionally superhuman) femme fatale crop up in various guises in Lang's subsequent films.[27] *Metropolis* offers the most blatant character resemblances in the neo-kabbalistic scientist Rotwang and the mechanical Maria; Alice Reed in *The Woman in the Window* (1944), as the "woman in the painting," patently extends the golem / Pygmalion allusion; the eponymous Dr. Mabuse is a master of telekinesis as well as criminality; and *Woman in the Moon* features both male and female scientists. As for Lilith's infanticidal aspect, the effeminate child murderer Hans Beckert in *M*, played by the Jewish (and "Jewish-looking") Peter Lorre, springs to mind. All-out spider women from Lang's Weimar period, besides Alice and Maria, include Resel Orla in the two-part *Die*

Spinnen (*The Spiders*, 1919/1920), the eponymous antiheroine of *Halbblut* (*Half-Breed*, 1920), Carla (most unwillingly) in *Dr. Mabuse: The Gambler*, and Kitty in *Spione*. In his American period, although changing social mores, studio politics, and his own increasingly leftist bent caused his male protagonists to morph from supermen to everymen, emerging noir conventions only encouraged Lang's propensity for portraying the black widow, as with Kitty in *Scarlet Street*, Rose in *The Blue Gardenia*, Debbie Marsh in *The Big Heat*, Vicki Buckley in *Human Desire* (1954), and, more ambiguously, Gina in *Cloak and Dagger* (1946) and Altar Keane in *Rancho Notorious* (1952).

Interestingly, and appropriately, given Lang's penchant for the *Caligari*-esque *Rahmenhandlung* (framing device), the Jewish references in his early work are revived toward the middle of his career and resurrected once more at the very end of his life. In 1942, Lang planned a remake of *The Golem*, adapted by the codirector of the 1914 silent version, Henrik Galeen. In the bitterest of ironies, this "homage to the Jewish tradition," to be set in Nazi-occupied France, was aborted in Hollywood just as the Final Solution was being fast-tracked at Wannsee.[28] In his last years, unable to direct anymore due to failing eyesight, Lang cowrote in German a short story called "Die Begegnung" (The encounter), whose protagonist, named Ahasverus, is the Wandering Jew. At the end of the story, Ahasverus encounters the figure of God ("the God of Sodom and Gomorrah," i.e., the Hebrew God), who says that He is a wanderer also, and the two wander off together.[29]

For a man haunted, and hounded, throughout his career by his connection to, yet rejection of, his Jewishness, the subject matter is deeply resonant. The figure of the Wandering Jew, which stems from the Christian apocrypha, became a popular anti-Semitic archetype in the Middle Ages, clearly relating to (and attempting to justify) the history and seemingly perpetual recurrence of Jewish banishment and dispersal. Ahasverus is one of several names for the Wandering Jew in European folklore, and a curious, but telling, choice for Lang's updating of the tale. Ahasverus is adapted from Ahasuerus, the Persian king in the book of Esther, who is not a Jew, and whose very name among medieval Jews was an exemplum of a fool.[30] Lang's "ur-story," written almost on his deathbed, thus becomes a striking confession-cum-disavowal, whether conscious or unconscious, of his own non-Jewish Jewishness. That he sensed something special about the story is indicated by his telling Cornelius Schnauber shortly before his death that his good friend must be sure to read it and that he, Lang, was "thinking about it all the time" ("Es beschäftigt mich immer zu").[31]

"Die Begegnung" can be added to other shards of Lang's life and work that, though they leave many pieces missing from the puzzle of his ethno-religious identity, also leave little doubt as to its profoundly conflicted nature. Upon his marriage to Thea von Harbou, Lang declared himself an agnostic, yet in public he steadfastly referred to himself as a Catholic.[32] Most of his German colleagues considered him Jewish, as did a French magazine article in 1929; a *New Yorker* article in 1933, however, called him a Nazi, because a swastika banner was reportedly seen hanging from his Berlin apartment window, and he was listed as a founding member of the "directors unit" of the Nazi workers union. At his alleged meeting with Goebbels, he purportedly "divulged" that his mother was born Catholic, but to Jewish parents; no evasion, however, could prevent the Nazis from using a clip from *M* in the pseudo-documentary *Der Ewige Jude* (*The Eternal Jew*, 1940) as an example of "degenerate Jewish art."[33]

In the United States, Lang outdid all the German and Austrian refugees in his anti-Nazi stance and most of them in his left-leaning politics. He lived from 1933 onward with the Jewish Lily Latté, with whom he had fled from Germany. He opposed Leni Riefenstahl's visit to the United States in 1938, became a U.S. citizen, and recommended that the atomic bomb be dropped on Germany. In 1942, as indicated, he tried to remake *The Golem* and, upon the U.S. release the same year of his Weimar-era, Nazi-banned *Testament of Dr. Mabuse*, claimed that *Mabuse* had been intended as an anti-Nazi allegory. Then again, he eliminated all Jewish references in his Nazi-resistance picture *Hangmen Also Die!* (1943).[34] And a *Current Biography* entry for 1943, with which Lang cooperated, labeled him an Austrian Christian who had fled Nazi Germany "only because he is a believer in democratic government."[35] He spoke solely English to German actor Lilli Palmer on the set of *Cloak and Dagger* (1946) but retained his monocle into the 1950s and a German cook for his Beverly Hills mansion. He joked, while working on *Cloak and Dagger*, that he was the only Catholic in the office, whereas Marlene Dietrich, with whom he had had an affair in the 1930s and a falling out in the 1950s, called him a Jew. Similarly, Thea von Harbou, to whom Lang's alleged Nazi associations in the late-Weimar period can at least partly be ascribed, referred to her divorced husband, in her post–World War II interrogation papers (no doubt self-servingly), as "the Jewish director Fritz Lang."[36]

When he grudgingly returned to Germany in 1956, he said that he both loved and hated it very much.[37] He protested the anti-German animus in Lotte Eisner's sympathetic book about him, writing her in 1968: "You at one time (just as I did) appreciated the German-cultural milieu, stood up against German anti-Semitism. . . . Can you abolish from your life Schiller, Kleist, Heine? I loved *Faust* from the bottom of my heart! . . . No, dear Lotte, these are things which belong to us, which we cannot tear from our hearts."[38] Shortly before he died, he asked Lily Latté for a copy of the "Our Father," and requested a priest to visit him at his bedside.[39] His lifelong friend, actor Howard Vernon, tried to diagnose Lang's Jewish identity complex: "Somehow he was a religious man. He needed it. I don't know if it was a faith built on fear, or respect of God. But he did consider himself a Catholic, which I found amusing, and *not* Jewish. But he also felt himself Jewish. He felt both, maybe according to the circumstances—a rabbi for marriage [to Lily Latté, shortly before his death], a priest for dying."[40]

In short, the dialectics of exile and the dualities of film noir, which inform all the Jewish émigré directors who helped launch the noir cycle, appear to have informed Lang's life and work to a pronounced degree. And Lang's work in Germany, specifically, was the first to bring both the noir aesthetic and many of its principle narrative tropes into stark relief. "More than any other director," Anthony Heilbut elaborates:

> Fritz Lang remained a guide to the moral ambiguities that came to dominate the century. His most famous German movie, *Dr. Mabuse* (1922), anticipated Heydrich, Himmler, and Hitler. . . . While the child murderer in *M* is a monster, by the film's end Lang forces us to identify with his terror: his final rescue by the law, represented by a monolithic and slightly totalitarian Shadow, almost makes us cheer. Twenty-five years later, in his last American film, *Beyond a Reasonable Doubt*, Lang presented rather curiously a man who almost gets away with murder, until his fiancée, while attempting to save him, discovers his guilt. The film makes her disloyalty appear worse than his crime. Lang's departing message to America remained one of moral ambivalence, the distillation of both his political history and his professional career.[41]

The Master-Criminal Films

Dr. Mabuse: The Gambler was by no means the first crime film. The French invented the genre in the early 1910s, and Lang himself, in his pre-directing days, apparently contributed a scenario to its German variant.[42] The silent *Mabuse*'s two-part structure, as well as its "cinema of attractions" form—"a series of spectacular visual moments strung loosely together"—bear the stamp of the conventional crime series as well as of a broader German cinematic type termed the "sensation film."[43] More significant for film noir, the crime film also offered a platform for confronting the anxieties, and excitements, of modern life. The crime genre, in Tom Gunning's words, served "as a form in which modernity is both displayed and defamiliarized, modern urban spaces and technology providing a modern form of mystery that Lang (and his predecessors) freely combined with older motifs of the exotic and magical."[44] Where Lang superseded his predecessors, in *Mabuse*, was in allegorizing the crime film to the historical moment.

The subtitles of the film's two parts leave no doubt as to their topical intentions: "Part I: The Great Gambler—A Picture of the Times" and "Part II: Inferno—A Play of the People of Our Times." Presentism permeated the movie's marketing campaign, which trumpeted the film's transcendence of the sensation and detective film to become the first "German film in modern dress."[45] Lang called the film a documentary,[46] and newspaper critics parroted the theme: "a mirror of the age," "an archive of its time," "a document of our time."[47] That such a document would be a dark one is not surprising. By 1922, the year of the film's release, Germany had reached, or was fast approaching, the nadir of its postwar Time of Troubles. The Versailles treaty, the Spartacist revolt, the Kapp Putsch, rising inflation, and withering poverty (alongside staggering wealth) were recent memories or ongoing realities, and, when combined with Foreign Minister Walter Rathenau's assassination, Hitler's Beer Hall Putsch, hyperinflation, and an ever-widening gulf between chronic poor and nouveau riche, would push German society to the brink of total collapse. The program notes for *Dr. Mabuse: The Gambler* capture the mood and set the scene of a world "fallen prey to lawlessness and depravity":[48] "Mankind, swept about and trampled down in the wake of war and revolution, takes revenge for years of anguish by indulging in lusts . . . and by passively or actively surrendering to crime."[49] The film plunges into the middle of this sociocultural maelstrom, with the eponymous master criminal both symbolizing and driving the manmade disaster.

But Mabuse represents more than just an archetype of Weimar decadence, devilry, and despair; he is, as Gunning suggests, "the evil genius of modernity."[50] Gunning sees Lang's films in general, and his German ones especially, as allegories of modernity, propelled by a destiny machine that enmeshes communication networks, the money economy, sexual desire, urbanism, mass culture, and cinema itself in its techno-mythic web. In the character of Mabuse, Lang and von Harbou—as well as Norbert Jacques, author of the novel to which the character and film hew quite closely—created a "Nietzschean superman, in the worst possible sense," as Lang described him, yet who also embodies "the whole of society."[51] In his fracturing yet manipulation of space and time, Mabuse is "everywhere present but nowhere recognizable"; in his effacement yet control of his identity, he is a ubiquitous threat that "cannot be localized"; and in his turning of technology into a weapon against itself, he is, like Lang the filmmaker, the "Grand Enunciator" of postmodern life (fig. 6).[52] The direct translation of "Spieler," after all, is "player," a synonym for actor, on the one hand, but also a reference, in this instance, to someone "who plays with cards, roulette, people, and death."[53]

As cogent as this assessment of *Dr. Mabuse: The Gambler*'s broader significance certainly is, nowhere in Gunning's masterful analysis of the film—or its later master-criminal variants, *Spies* and *The Testament of Dr. Mabuse* (1932)—does he, or any other commentator I'm aware of, mention a possible Jewish connection. Yet such a connection could hardly be more blatant—connotatively and denotatively—and in a largely pejorative sense. Intimations of anti-Semitism have been attached to some of Lang's other German films, notably *Die Nibelungen* and *Metropolis*. At the time of the former's release, Frank Aschau, in the Berlin weekly *Die Weltbühne*, complained that the evil dwarf Alberich "is, it can't be mistaken, depicted as a Jew. Not as a handsome Jew, naturally, but as a vile Jew."[54] Kracauer went further, reading the characterization as "a deliberate gesture of

Figure 6.   Dr. Mabuse (Rudolf Klein-Rogge) as master criminal and alien presence. (Photofest)

anti-semitism."[55] Nor has it gone unnoticed that the evil scientist/black magician Rotwang in *Metropolis*—besides "looking Jewish" with his beard and hook nose, and having a name redolent of leftist politics—employs explicitly kabbalistic practices to transmogrify the Madonna-like Maria into her inhuman twin. The master-criminal types in Lang's German films, when taken together, offer a veritable compendium of negative Jewish stereotypes.

Dr. Mabuse and the Haghi/Nemo character in *Spies*, with their exotic-sounding names and, in Mabuse's case, superhuman powers, announce themselves from the outset as distinctly alien figures.[56] That they also purport to represent "the times," or to allegorize "modernity," in no way contradicts their foreignness. Jews, as we know, since emancipation and increasingly during the Weimar period, had come to epitomize the modern age. Paradoxically, however, Jew's reputed domination of economic, political, and cultural life only reinforced their reputation as interlopers bent on destroying western (read: Christian) norms and traditions. By the time of *The Testament of Dr. Mabuse*, Mabuse's psychoanalyst-disciple, Dr. Baum—indicating his mundane stature but also the extent to which Jews had infiltrated the mainstream—is given a more commonly Jewish name.[57]

Mabuse's and Haghi's multiple disguises further expose the men behind the masks as Jews. First, because prior to E.T.A. Hoffmann's doppelgängers and Louis Feuillade's Fantômas, which provided clear literary and cinematic antecedents of shape-shifting, emancipated Jews were already notorious for their allegedly self-serving (but ultimately self-defeating) mastery of camouflage. Second, and more to the point, the chameleonic overkill in Lang and von Harbou's creations (inspired, at least in the first Mabuse film, by Jacques) bear a manifestly Semitic imprint. As for Dr. Mabuse's primary identification as a psychoanalyst, and Haghi's as a banker, no more need be said—except that the alienist's use of his hypnotic powers for conspiratorial ends and the banker's financial operation fronting for a spy ring aimed at world domination turns the two criminal masterminds into literal executors of the *Protocols of the Elders of Zion.*

The association to the *Protocols* is not meant glibly and should not be taken lightly. This invidiously forged tract about a Jewish plot to control the world through manipulation of media and finance, though concocted and first publicized in czarist Russia in the early 1900s, received its first major western translation in Germany in 1920. Despite its exposure as a forgery in the *London Times* in 1921, the *Protocols*, by melding centuries of church-fueled Jew hatred with more recent anxieties about the encroachments of modernism, retained a strong hold on western consciousness—nowhere more so than in crisis-riven Weimar Germany, where the *Protocols* seemed to prove "beyond any shadow of doubt that it was not the Germans who were to blame for the apocalyptic events which had occurred in their country, but foreign plotters and agents who for a long time had been at work to bring about its downfall."[58]

For Hitler and the Nazis, the *Protocols* took on the authority of holy writ and became a pillar of their anti-Semitic propaganda. But the *Protocols'* stipulation of the specific means that Jews would employ to achieve their conspiratorial ends clearly resonates with the Weimar period in general and with Mabuse and Haghi in particular: addiction to alcohol (and, by extension, drugs), the evils of materialism, the uses of brainwashing, the undermining of the financial system, and the precipitation of economic depression—all supposedly leading to anarchy, chaos, and the replacement of the social disorder with a new, more horrific "order" based on mass manipulation.

It wasn't by accident that the *Protocols* caught on in the West immediately following the Bolshevik Revolution. Their extrapolation of Jewish domination onto the ostensibly antithetical systems of capitalism and communism, however counterintuitive, seemed both empirically justified (Jews were prominently represented in both systems) and in keeping with Jews' alleged Janus-faced nature. This systemic duplicity is perfectly embodied in the character of Haghi, whose appearance was consciously patterned by Lang after Trotsky, and whose Haghi Bank is both an architectural and operational facade for his Soviet-based spy ring.

Haghi's alter ego, the double-agent stage clown Nemo, meanwhile, ties this figure further to the theater and, by extension, to the film medium, both of which Jews were reputedly remaking in their image.[59] Mabuse's myriad impostures, meanwhile, read like Hitler's Jewish hit list: Sternberg, the financial magnate/stock-market manipulator; the ugly, hook-nosed Dutch professor-cum–card shark who uses Oriental magic (and Expressionist cinema) to do in his opponents; the political rabble-rouser who incites a working-class mob to attack the police paddy wagon; the slum-dwelling street peddler (the only character that McGilligan identifies as a Jew); and, most climactically, Dr. Weltmann, the stage magician/hypnotist extraordinaire. Besides being another psychoanalyst, purveyor of Oriental spells (the Chinese syllables, "Tsi-Nan-Fu"), and conjurer of images (here pointedly Semitic ones, given the Arab caravan!), Weltmann's name, which means "world man," clearly encodes him as *the* modern Jewish prototype: the cosmopolite.

As if all this wasn't overkill enough, the portly, cigar-chomping Schramm, although seemingly a secondary character, is given a set-piece montage that showcases his stereotypically Jewish rise (remember Moishe Pisch/Moritz Wasser-strahl/Maurice Lafontaine?) from ragpicker to wartime profiteer to millionaire casino owner. Lang, in a later interview, expressed particular distaste for this paradigmatic Weimar-era parvenu, whom he derisively referred to by the slang term *Raffke* (roughly: money-grubber).[60]

Responsibility for the anti-Semitic imagery in the master-criminal films, of course, cannot be laid at Lang's feet alone. The characters, if not the characterizations, were created by Norbert Jacques, and one is inclined to regard von Harbou, given her later associations with Nazism, as having played no small part in emphasizing their odiousness and specificity. On the other hand, Jews themselves were not averse to pointing out their own group's less flattering traits. Philosopher Hannah Arendt's pariah/parvenu binary, although formulated during World War II, encapsulated the self-criticism that middle-class Jews had engaged in since emancipation. Pariah Jews, in this admittedly overgeneralized schema, were held to possess all the laudable Jewish qualities—such as humanity, humor, and disinterested intelligence—whereas parvenu Jews, much like Lang's *Raffkes*, represented all that was degrading—tactlessness, political stupidity, and money-grubbing.[61]

Jewish artists had indulged in a less erudite, but no less potent, form of character self-assassination for some time, and not only in Germany. Jewish vaudevillians in the early 1900s in the United States mixed Jewish stereotypes into an unkosher brand of minstrelsy termed "Jewface," albeit intended primarily for Jewish audiences. In Berlin, Max Reinhardt's cabaret Schall und Rauch (Sound and smoke), founded in 1901, similarly included skits about Jews that were performed, initially, only for invited, largely Jewish guests.[62] The Jewish cabaret owner and songwriter Rudolph Nelson (born Rudolph Lewysohn) wrote broadly popular material in the 1910s that riffed on Jewish types, and Ernst Lubitsch first became famous as a portrayer of characters with pointedly Jewish names (Pinkus), occupations (clothing or shoe store salesmen), and appearance (short stature, dark features, large hook nose, and an otherwise "wholly un-Teutonic physiognomy").[63] During the war, however, as anti-Semitic tensions rose, such self-deprecating portrayals seemed increasingly in bad taste, if not dangerous. Even Reinhardt had run into trouble when his Schall und Rauch parodies of Jews went public, and Nelson received angry letters from Jews incensed over the use of "vulgar" Yiddishisms, particularly by a fellow Jew.[64] Working in the silent medium of film, Lubitsch was able to get away with his Jewish send-ups longer than most, but by the late 1910s the issue became moot when he began directing the historical epics that would buy him his ticket to Hollywood. For Jewish artists who remained in Germany, things came to a head in 1926, "when Jewish organizations held massive meetings to protest the telling of jokes about Jews by Jewish cabaret performers."[65]

Satirizing one's own is one thing; indeed, critics and practitioners often defend such an approach—most recently with the mockumentary Borat (2006)—as a salutary or even subversive form of humor.[66] For "nonmembers" to sling barbs at the tribe, particularly in a serious vein and with intent to harm, is another story. Any anti-Semitic representations produced during the Weimar era bear the added burden of speculation as to their effect on subsequent events. Subjecting Lang, or his master-criminal films, to a posthumous Nuremberg Trial, however, is neither fruitful nor the main purpose here. My interest is rather in determining how Lang's problematic relationship to his Jewish identity may have colored his cinematic vision of the "times." Instead of shifting the onus of anti-Semitism onto Jacques or von Harbou, or onto other creative personnel (such as Eisner does with makeup artist Otto Genath in regard to Die Nibelungen's Alberich),[67] I would submit that anti-Semitism was an integral part of "the times," and that Lang, precisely because of his Jewish self-denial, was especially prone to traffic in it.[68]

Further compounding the psychological and moral complexity of Lang's position in relation to Dr. Mabuse: The Gambler—and his master-criminal films in general—is that during this film's production, and indeed throughout much of the Weimar period, the director was known to indulge in the very hedonistic excesses the film purports to condemn. As McGilligan relates, Lang knew only too well the milieu he depicted in Dr. Mabuse: "the floor shows of the posh hangouts, the deviant sex clubs, the Spielklubs (card-playing dens) for jaded women and rich gambling addicts, the hangouts for prostitutes, séances, or cocaine. These addresses were part of his nightly routine. Lang himself was addicted to sex and not a little to drugs."[69]

Jewish self-hatred and nocturnal debauchery are not the only problems Lang faces in judging his Weimar films' possible role, however inadvertent, in the rise of the Third Reich. Historians have implicated form as well as content in this regard, with his oeuvre's glorification of technology, geometry, and spectacle—in particular the arrangement of the masses into grandiose ornamental designs—seen by some as anticipating Leni Riefenstahl's infamous *Triumph of the Will*.[70] Of course, here again von Harbou's influence cannot be discounted, nor for that matter can Max Reinhardt's, whose decoratively stylized, elaborately orchestrated crowd scenes were among his trademarks.[71]

Kracauer, although acknowledging these qualifications, remains the harshest of Lang's critics, and the most inclined (as part of a broader critique of Weimar cinema) to find latent fascism in Lang's German work. *Die Nibelungen* and *Metropolis* bear the brunt of such criticism, not surprisingly, given the films' notoriety as Hitler's favorites. But the master-criminal films are not granted immunity. Although good ultimately overcomes evil in the Mabuse films and *Spies*, the films also exhibit, for Kracauer, a moral "neutrality" that manifests itself "in the absence of any distinction between legal and illegal pursuits."[72] Even the Nazi-banned *Testament of Dr. Mabuse*, despite Lang's alleged placing of Nazi slogans in the mouth of Mabuse's phantom image, "betrays the power of the Nazi spirit over minds insufficiently equipped to counter its peculiar fascination."[73] In the end, Kracauer observes—in what is intended as an indictment of all of Lang's master-criminal films, but which could just as easily serve as an advertisement for film noir—"the law triumphs and the lawless glitters."[74]

The First Film Noir

Nearly all the prime aesthetic and thematic elements that later would become associated with film noir were an accepted part of Weimar cinema by the time Lang and von Harbou set to work on *M*. The transmutation of Expressionism into expressionism as a visual style was complete; horror and crime films had established murder as a main action; Kammerspiel and street films had unleashed the psychodynamics of desire and exposed a forbidding inner-city milieu; a combination of all these films had produced a catalog of ambivalent protagonists, doppelgängers, and femme fatales; and a gloomy fatalism had permeated the atmosphere of a society caught in a perpetual downward spiral. To be sure, the romantic melancholy of French poetic realism had not yet been added to the mix, nor had hard-boiled private eye and tough-guy lingo contributed their distinctive American stamp (not to mention that Nino Frank and Jean-Pierre Chartrier's naming of film noir was still fifteen years, a Great Depression, and a world war away).

What *M* managed to accomplish, similar to what Griffith's *The Birth of a Nation* (1915) had done for the classical Hollywood style and what Welles's *Citizen Kane* (1941) would do to counter that style, was to refine, expand on, and consolidate previous cinematic developments into a coherent, if loosely defined, *system* that would come to be known (largely after the fact) as film noir.[75] While the Kammerspiel film had pioneered psychological intensity, repressed desire, and explosive instincts of the petty bourgeois male, *M*, without weakening the social dimension, magnified the inner conflict to pathological proportions. *M*'s pathetic antihero Hans Beckert is not merely a murderer but also a maniacal one, and he doesn't kill from revenge or romantic rivalry but rather from a clinically diagnosable, if societally induced, compulsion.

Here a comparison with *Caligari*, which also features a homicidal madman, is instructive. As Kracauer points out, Beckert "is a direct offspring of the somnambulist Cesare. Like Cesare, he lives under the compulsion to kill. But while the somnambulist unconsciously surrenders to Dr. Caligari's superior will power, the child-murderer submits to his own pathological impulses."[76] In other words, the destabilizing of identity in *M* is neither a matter of disguise, as in Lang's master-criminal films, nor of allegory, as in *Caligari*, but rather internally realized. Beckert's divided self has not developed supernaturally, as in Robert Louis Stevenson's *The Strange Case of Dr. Jekyll and Mr. Hyde* (1886), but "organically," through a psychosocial process. Ultimately, as Kracauer further suggests, *M* combines elements of both the Kammerspiel/street films and the horror film; Beckert "is the link between two screen families; in him, the tendencies embodied by the philistine and the somnambulist finally fuse with each other."[77]

The doubling and splitting of identity, or in Kracauer's words, "a deep and fearful concern with the foundations of the self,"[78] had been an obsession of German cinema since Wegener's *The Student of Prague* in 1913. During the Weimar period (particularly in the Kammerspiel, street, and crime films), the doubling motif extended into the social realm, representing, as class divisions widened and crime mounted, "two social spheres separated by an abysmal gulf."[79] While street and home, crime and the law, demimondaine and *Burgertum* perpetually clashed, they also, as with all binaries, revealed a symbiotic interdependence. *M* blurs the lines of symbiosis to the extreme, positing not merely interdependence but also interchangeability. Visual and sound montages start the suturing process: parallel editing between cop and robber strategy meetings; cross-fading of dialogue between the two groups. Structural rhyming ratifies the merger: a mutual effort by the police and the mob to capture the killer who's ruining both licit and illicit "businesses"; an underground tribunal replete with "prosecutor," "defense attorney," and "jury." The "absence of any distinction between legal and illegal pursuits" that Kracauer discerned in Lang's master-criminal films is foregrounded in *M*.

A similar structural amplification is achieved in the street film's inner-city locale. Whereas the city became a character, and a determining one, in the street film, in *M* it has become, as Gunning observes, "the protagonist."[80] This is partly by default, since the film has no clear human main character. Through much of the film Beckert is more spoken about than seen, and he has no meaningful dialogue (though he compulsively whistles) till the very end. Even his murders either took place in the past, occur off camera, or are portrayed through indirection (the rolling ball, the floating balloon).[81] Most all the action involves and revolves around the city. An occasional subtitle for the film, "The City Searches for a Murderer," literalizes the urban environment's proactive role in the narrative, which is achieved, as Gunning perceptively points out, through "process and setting."[82] Communication, media, and transportation networks had dominated Lang's master-criminal films, but there they were put into play and manipulated by Mabuse or Haghi. Here the workings of the city seem to have "a will of their own."[83]

This weblike will is imposed on the mise-en-scène as well. Whether shown as starkly empty or as magnets for mobs, the anonymous city's streets, tenement houses, cheap dives, and office buildings are equally ominous and imprisoning. Yet the imprisoning theme so paradigmatic of the (largely silent) Kammerspiel/ street film, as with Beckert's pathological impulses, is rendered materially *and* psychologically, crucially reinforced through spoken dialogue. Beckert is trapped by his urban surroundings and by his own uncontrollable urges, an intertwined predicament poignantly expressed in his plea to the underworld kangaroo court: "I have to roam the streets endlessly, always sensing that someone's following me. It's me! I'm shadowing myself! . . . I must, must take the path that's hunting me down, and run and run down endless streets! I want to get away! . . . I want to run—run away from myself! But I can't! I can't escape from myself!"

But what of the femme fatale, that common catalyst of the Kammerspiel/ street film and fixture of film noir? In the classical sense, of a woman who lures the leading man to his doom, she seems to have gone missing. Yet even here, *M* turns apparent lack into excess. From Beckert's psychological perspective, at least, the femme fatale's physical absence is a structuring one. Beckert, as Gunning puts it, is partly "attracted to children because he is a reject from the adult world."[84] Each young girl thus represents for him the future mature woman, embodied both in the girl's and his own absent (or withholding) mother, of whose sexuality he is both desirous and deathly afraid. In an Oedipal sense, the femme fatale is not merely present, but *omni*present—in the endlessly reappearing figure(s) of the little girls who, from the standpoint of the infantilized Beckert, are his maturational equals. Finally, one can hardly avoid reading a subtle seductiveness, if not self-destructiveness, in the behavior of the "sweet young things" who, despite myriad warnings from parents, teachers, peers, and the media, cheerfully choose to buy goodies and traipse off with the lethal little man.

Stylistically, *M* displays Lang's complete command of functional expressionism, which by this time had replaced Expressionist exaggeration except in instances of heightened subjectivity. Lang had incorporated Expressionist sets "realistically" into his first pair of Mabuse films, in the casino and aristocratic mansion scenes. There, however, the sets were taken to be faithful renderings of actual Expressionist interior designs and artwork, thereby commenting, pejoratively, on Expressionism's reflection of and influence on Weimar society. In another exceptional case, *Metropolis* had lent itself to Expressionist treatment due to its sci-fi/futuristic setting.

Famous examples of functional expressionism in *M*, besides the overall oppressiveness of the cityscape, include: Beckert's shadow on the kiosk, swooping in from off camera like a bird of prey, as he makes initial contact with young Elsie; the various "prison shots," visualized in the barred gates of the office building courtyard and the wooden slats of the storage compartment in which Beckert, quite literally, is caged; and, most originally, the double framing of Beckert as he peers into the shop window (framed once by the window itself, and more pronouncedly by a reflection of a smaller frame created by a row of knives in the window display). Connected to this shot is a reverse shot from Beckert's point of view, in which a little girl is shown reflected within the same smaller frame that had previously isolated Beckert. Besides the self-reflexivity of the device (implicating cinema, as in the master-criminal films, in both the film's surveillance narrative and the larger social context), the two shots, in a similar "double move," imbricate Beckert's "zeroing in" on his next victim with his being "framed" for his multiple crimes by the underworld (and, by extension, the larger society). As the working title of the film ambiguously suggested, Hans Beckert is "the murderer among us" (figs. 7, 8, and 9).

As for the Jewish aspect in *M*, in this rare instance neither Gunning, nor other noted *M* commentators, have neglected to address it; the Nazis wouldn't let them. Hitler and his henchmen lavished attention on the film, both at the time of its original release and after they came to power. Yet unlike the case with their adoration of *Die Nibelungen* and *Metropolis*, or their banning of *The Testament of Dr. Mabuse*, overall Nazi reaction to *M*, befitting Lang's ambivalent Weimar legacy, was decidedly mixed, if not contradictory. Goebbels, along with Hitler a Lang fan since *Die Nibelungen*, raved in his diary upon attending *M*'s gala premiere in May 1931: "Fantastic! Against humanitarian soppiness. For the death penalty. Lang will be our director one day."[85] Once the Nazis assumed power in 1933, however, the film joined *The Testament of Dr. Mabuse* in being removed from domestic circulation. Then in 1940, *Der Ewige Jude* featured a clip of Beckert's defense before the underworld tribunal as a triple whammy against the Jews: as an example of "degenerate Jewish art"; as an indication of Jewish dominance of the Weimar film industry (besides Lang, producer Seymour Nebenzahl and, of

Figure 7. Beckert's (Peter Lorre's) predatory shadow in *M* (1931). (Photofest)

course, "the Jew actor" Peter Lorre); and, in Lorre's character, as a display of "psychotic Jewish behavior."[86]

Nazi rhetoric itself is perhaps less extensive in *M* than in *The Testament of Dr. Mabuse*. But the figure who espouses it, the underworld leader Schränker—with his cane, military manner, and black leather jacket and gloves—is even more blatantly patterned after one of Hitler's minions, who were increasingly making their presence felt at the time the film was made. Schränker's harangue about "an outsider" who "is ruining our business," about a "monster who has no right to survive" and "must be killed, eliminated, exterminated, without mercy or compassion," sounded like Nazi-speak in 1931, and sounds ever more disturbingly

Figure 8.   Tables turned: Beckert as caged animal. (USC Special Collections)

so afterward. *M*, like *The Testament of Dr. Mabuse*, "indeed like all Lang's German films," Gunning suggests, "exists under the shadow of the Third Reich and the holocaust. . . . The echoes and anticipations of Nazi policies appear everywhere for contemporary viewers of this film: . . . the image of an SS officer, the rhetoric of final solutions, . . . the euthanasia of mental patients, Beckert's inscribed M as the star of David—all recall the Shoah."[87] As harrowing as Gunning's litany of contemporaneous and retrospective Nazi allusions in *M* is, however, here again, as with the master-criminal films, his otherwise penetrating analysis fails to register the full range and extent of *M*'s anti-Semitic referents.

The Nazis were far from the first to require Jews to wear yellow badges to identify their religious affiliation. The invidious practice, borrowed from Muslim countries (where it applied to Christians as well), was introduced in Europe by

Figure 9.   Self-reflexivity in *M*. (Frame grab)

papal decree in 1215, with its first appearance in Germany in 1294. Friedrich Wilhelm I of Prussia "abolished" the requirement in 1710, albeit only in return for 8,000 thaler, or about $360,000. An additional Jewish, or at least Old Testament, association with a mark for someone guilty of murder is of course the mark of Cain, stamped on Adam and Eve's firstborn for his slaying of his younger brother Abel. Here the reference to Beckert as "der schwarze Mann" (the black man) is especially pertinent, given racist interpretations of Cain's "mark" as signifying black skin, thereby "explaining" and "justifying" the suffering of an entire black *people* destined to live under Cain's curse.

Although Jews have had their own New Testament–based murderous curse to contend with, their historical association with blackness has added yet another stigma. As Sander Gilman reminds us, "Medieval iconography always juxtaposed the black image of the synagogue, of the Old Law, with the white of the church." This imagery, moreover, "is incorporated, not merely as an intellectual abstraction, but as a model through which Jews are perceived, and thus treated, and thus respond as if confronted with their own reality."[88] In the nineteenth century, as "scientific racism" became not only respectable but an essential prop of western colonialism, the Jewish-black connection was made into biological "fact." For

Jews, who were already seen as a preternaturally "mongrel race," their most recent "hybridization," explained British "scientific" racist Houston Stewart Chamberlain, "was the admixture of Negro blood with Jewish in the Diaspora of Alexandria."[89] Empirical "proof" was provided by Jews' and blacks' purported physical resemblance. As Adam Grotowski, a Polish noble, observed about a trip to the United States in 1857: "Jews [in Poland] have the greatest resemblance to the American mulattoes: Sallow complexion, thick lips, crisped black hair. On my arrival in this country I took every light-colored mulatto for a Jew."[90]

And if the various dark marks against Jews weren't enough to justify Beckert's merciless elimination on anti-Semitic grounds, his relation to the "blood libel" sealed the deal. This especially odious canard alleged a Jewish propensity for ritually murdering Christian (or Muslim) children in order to drain their blood for the making of Passover matzoh. Originating with the Greco-Egyptian philosopher Apion in the first century, the myth proliferated in Europe from the twelfth century on, invariably leading to revenge pogroms. Some more recent related incidents include the Damascus affair in Syria in 1840, the Leo Frank trial and lynching in the United States in 1913, and the Mendel Beilis trial and execution in Kiev in 1915.[91] Given the blood libel's long history and the virulently anti-Jewish climate in 1931 Germany, it would seem that a Weimar audience confronted with a serial child murderer who readily passes for Jewish, is played by a Jewish actor, and who confesses that "I can't help it! . . . Don't I have this cursed thing inside me?!" could scarcely avoid connecting, if only unconsciously, the conspiratorial dots.

Whether the rising Nazi tide, his alleged meeting with Goebbels, or his relationship with Lilly Latté (which began around this time) increased Lang's own sense of Jewish stigmatization will likely remain unresolved. What seems clear is that from being a "sleepwalker through history," as Lang claims he had been through much of the Weimar period, the director did, with the making of *M* and *The Testament of Dr. Mabuse*, start to "come of age" politically.[92] Along with an already advanced noir style, this emerging political consciousness is something Lang would bring with him to Paris, and soon thereafter to the United States, where his work would play a crucial role in the rise of film noir in its classical American formation.

5   *Fritz Lang in Hollywood*

Had he not made another film after the Weimar period, Lang's place in the film noir pantheon, based on the seminal *M* and his overall influence, would be assured. That he went on to make some of the earliest, most influential, and most highly regarded noirs in the United States only adds to his preeminence. His pioneering role in American noir is not surprising given his predilection for dark-themed films from the onset of his career. Indeed, Lang is the émigré director whose noir orientation can be traced most directly and unequivocally to his work in Weimar Germany. Siodmak and Bernhardt had made some borderline German noirs, and Edgar Ulmer had contributed to some as a set designer, but no other émigré director was typecast as a "master of the macabre" to the extent that Lang had been and would continue to be. Lang's patriarchal position among the Jewish émigré directors is further enhanced by his being the first refugee director to make a film noir in Hollywood (Ulmer and Zinnemann arrived earlier, but neither directed any noirs until the mid-to-late 1940s).

Jewish émigré filmmakers can be broken down into two contingents. The first, spurred by the Nazis' rise to power in the late 1920s and early 1930s (and, for some, delayed by stopovers in France or England) included Lang and six others: Preminger, Ulmer, Brahm, Litvak, Zinnemann, and Billy Wilder. The second, which carried Siodmak, Bernhardt, and Ophuls onto Southern California shores, was propelled by the outbreak of World War II, the Nazi invasion of France, and the London bombings. Both contingents, unlike the first immigrant wave of the 1920s, were political refugees—but also, for the most part, somewhat privileged ones.[1] Although their and other (Jewish and non-Jewish) émigré artists' status as strangers in a strange land should not be discounted—and several, such as Ophuls, Bertolt Brecht, Arnold Schoenberg, and, eventually, Salka Viertel struggled financially—most came with formidable pedigrees, existing or soon-to-be-acquired sources of income, and, most important, a ready-made and ever burgeoning support group.[2]

The Salon, California-Style

The cohesiveness of the German émigré community lay not merely in its intellectual, professional, and ethno-religious affinities, but, perhaps most crucially, in its social structures. The touchstone of the latter was another European import, the cultural salon, which in Los Angeles, as on the Continent, existed both on the lofty artistic and more mundane professional planes. One of the latter (which included my parents) consisted of former lawyers, doctors, businesspersons, and their spouses that generically dubbed itself "Die Gruppe" (the group). Experts on various subjects would be invited to speak, and occasionally someone from the higher-profile gatherings, such as actor Alexander Granach, would make a guest appearance.[3] No wonder that Los Angeles in the 1930s and 1940s—a sudden Parnassus of European artists, intellectuals, and the cream of the German film industry, as well as a sanctuary for the German-Jewish middle class that had composed a sizeable portion of their audience—took on the monikers "Weimar by the Sea," "Weimar on the Pacific," or simply the "New Weimar."

Formed as an offshoot of the French court by the Marquise de Rambouillet in the early seventeenth century, salons consisted of weekly "open house" gatherings in private residences hosted primarily by women. Coextensive with the *Haskalah*, the salons that emerged in Germany in the late eighteenth century became the almost exclusive province of Jewish women.[4] The assimilationist advantages to emancipated Jews of promoting *Bildung* and *Kultur* have already been discussed. But salons were not merely social stepping stones for their hostesses or their guests; they also served, at their best, a progressive function. Taking their cue from the formative role that French salons had played in the Enlightenment, the first German-Jewish salons promoted cultural and political advancement and grew to become, in the Wilhelmine era, an integral part of the German modernist enterprise. The salon's disappearance in Germany after 1914 can be traced partly to the war and its traumatic aftermath. Other factors, posited by a contemporary chronicler of the demise of salon life, Marie von Bunsen, are especially pertinent to the German salon's revival in 1930s Los Angeles: "the acceleration, the *Americanization* of our existence, the restless need for travel and variety, the increase in hotel hospitality, the clubs, the passion for sports."[5]

How ironic, then, that the German-accented salons of Alma Mahler, Marta Feuchtwanger, Nelly Mann, and, most prominently, Salka Viertel, would resurface in that most Americanized of places, Southern California. Of course, that these were salons "in exile" crucially differentiates them from their Continental forebears, but the salons' exilic aspect also partly underwrites the basis for their reemergence. Salons had always operated on the margins as a kind of "underground high culture," and German-Jewish salonieres, in particular, had functioned as the "ultimate outsiders on the inside."[6] In the salon's diasporic formation, the circle around and within the salon grew tighter, the sense of difference more acute, and the survivalist angst more urgent. Max Reinhardt's son Gottfried, himself a noted Hollywood screenwriter and producer (and Salka Viertel's decadelong live-in lover), captured some of the ambivalence of the New Weimar (as well as its Jewishness) in his counter-sobriquet, "A Ghetto Under Pacific Palms."[7]

Thomas Mann, in a speech for his brother Heinrich's seventieth birthday at Salka Viertel's home, addressed the German exile's predicament: "What today is the meaning of foreign, the meaning of homeland? . . . When the homeland becomes foreign, the foreign becomes the homeland."[8] Yet in spite of intense alienation from the erstwhile *Heimatland*, a bittersweet longing for Kultur, of which the salon was a part, persisted. Lang certainly embodied such mixed emotions with his intense anti-German stance during the war on the one hand, and his glorification of Goethe, Schiller, Kleist, and Heine on the other. Brecht went Lang one better (or worse), calling Germans "a shitty people" while continuing to write in "their" language.[9] Otto Preminger couched the contradiction in comic terms when he famously admonished Hungarian-spouting fellow expatriates at a restaurant: "Goddammit, guys, you're in America! Speak German!"[10]

Viertel herself, who spearheaded efforts to rescue stranded writers and artists in Europe and cofounded the European Film Fund for those left behind, was wont to quote a line from Heine: "I had a fatherland, but it was a dream."[11] Yet the Free Germany Committee, which she also helped found, formulated a manifesto declaring the German people the victims, not the architects, of Nazism.[12] And in her memoirs, Viertel describes her salon guests as representing "the true Fatherland to which, in spite of Hitler they adhered, as they adhered to the German language."[13] "This nostalgia for German culture," Shira Bisman suggests, "blended with the horror at what was happening in Europe, characterized the ambivalence felt by Viertel and her circle."[14] As Gottfried Reinhardt indicated (and which cannot be overemphasized), a Star of David squared this circle. Or as Max Reinhardt poignantly put it in a letter to his son about his daughter-in-law's use of German, "It delights the ear of an old theatre man and awakens—despite everything, despite everything—in a racially alien Jew, not rooted, of course, in that soil, the longing for his ardently loved mother tongue."[15]

Salka Viertel's Sunday afternoon gatherings at 165 Mayberry Road in Santa Monica, from the late 1920s through the 1940s, constituted the longest-running and most popular of the New Weimar salons. Also, given Viertel's position as a screenwriter—and *the* screenwriter for another of her lovers, Greta Garbo—her salon tended to attract the most movie people. Thus, besides Thomas Mann, Max Reinhardt, Arnold Schoenberg, Rudolph Schindler, and Theodor Adorno, one might find in her living room on any given weekend Garbo, Alexander Granach, Franz Waxman, Billy Wilder, Edgar Ulmer, and Fritz Lang.[16] The sheer range, prestige, and intellectual firepower of Viertel's coterie was truly extraordinary. Of course, owing to their refugee origins, the various émigré salons had an unprecedented wealth of talent from which to draw. It is estimated that as much as one-half of the European and four-fifths of the German-speaking cultural elite sojourned in Southern California, at one time or another, from the 1930s to the 1950s.[17] Yet although the cultural, political, and therapeutic value of the New Weimar was surely enhanced by its tropical-paradise setting and eye-of-the-hurricane situation, these same qualities assured that all would not be pacific by the Pacific.

Artist colonies are not noted for their equanimity, but the pall of Nazism and World War II politicized the émigré community to an uncommon degree—and the politics cut both ways.[18] Although the fact that all the émigrés, pre- or post-Hitler, were now exiles tended to paper over broad ideological and artistic disputes, the very personal stakes involved caused more immediate issues to surface. A particularly bitter rift developed between Brecht and Thomas Mann over Mann's withdrawal of his signature from the Free Germany Committee's manifesto because it was "too patriotic" and might be considered a "stab in the back" by the Allies.[19] Although the political and cultural differences between the two writers made them uneasy bedfellows to begin with, their opposing views about the nature of Germany once again spoke to the deep ambivalences the expatriates felt toward the land of their birth. As Erhard Bahr describes the dispute, "Brecht espoused the so-called 'two Germanys theory,' which posited that a good Germany was being suppressed by evil Nazi Germany, while Mann believed that there was only one Germany, both good and evil."[20] As for the overall tensions in the émigré community, Brecht observed, "Even in the backwoods of Finland I never felt so out of the world as here. Enmities thrive like oranges and are just as seedless [groundless]. The Jews accuse one another of anti-Semitism, and the Aryan Germans accuse one another of Germanophilia."[21]

Fritz Lang's self-distancing from his Jewish heritage, combined with his suspect history in Germany, made him an easy target on both scores. His monocled presence alone—despite and because of his very public anti-German pronouncements—must have been off-putting to many. Gottfried Reinhardt, for example, couldn't forget the Nazi banners he claims were seen hanging from Lang's Berlin apartment in the early 1930s, and which, Reinhardt believed, could not be blamed solely on von Harbou.[22] Peter Viertel, Salka's son, related to McGilligan how, as a teenager, he observed Lang on several occasions at his mother's gatherings. When Lily Latte, whom everybody knew and liked, accompanied the director, Lang seemed to blend in. When he came alone, however, "he seemed remote, unapproachable, sitting off by himself and nursing his martini. Distinctly uncomfortable in the group setting, he always behaved with meticulous formality."[23]

Schnauber believes that fellow émigrés had more reservations about Lang's personality than about his Jewish self-denial.[24] But whether he was subject to charges of anti-Semitism or Germanophilia, face-to-face or behind his back, any real or perceived slight to his (by this time no doubt genuine) anti-Nazi bona fides could only have heightened his already considerable insecurities and ambivalences. As for the tensions produced by an exilic life in la-la land, these also, Hollywood compromises notwithstanding, might have worked to his creative advantage. The dystopian realities behind Southern California's utopian facade would drive some, such as Brecht, to distraction and, eventually, renewed flight. "I / Who live in Los Angeles and not in London," Brecht infamously wrote, "Find, on thinking about Hell, / that it must be / Still more like Los Angeles."[25] Yet Brecht could also claim, around the same time if in another frame of mind: "Emigration is the best school of dialectics. Refugees are the sharpest dialectic thinkers."[26]

Bahr argues that this "dialectical stance" toward the failed Edenic promise of Southern California provided an essential grounding for the New Weimar artists' and intellectuals' modernist artistic pursuits during a time of crisis.[27] Although Bahr focuses primarily on the high cultural forms of serious literature and classical music, it would seem that a popular form such as film noir, with its art-film ancestry in Weimar cinema, would have added yet another dialectical layer. Steeped in an expressionist aesthetic that challenged the classical Hollywood style—and conveyed through tales of frustrated desire, deception, and death that potentially subverted the culture industry's ideological underpinnings—film noir brought the dialectics of exile and the "competing mythologies" of Los Angeles together to a profoundly overdetermined degree. In the films (and life) of Fritz Lang specifically, the overdetermination was compounded by a Weimar past tarnished through links to Nazism and the possible murder of his Jewish wife, and by an American present predicated on anti-Nazism and a long-term relationship with another Jewish woman.

The Uncredited Collaborator

The differences between the Weimar art cinema and the classical Hollywood studio system, in terms of the collaborative process, are well documented. And although we also know that the purity of the former's artistry and the crassness of the latter's commercialism have been exaggerated, what remains uncontestable is that the German film industry, on the whole, favored a more interactive process than did the U.S. industry, and that Weimar directors generally enjoyed more creative freedom and control than their producer-dominated Hollywood counterparts.[28] In his move from Berlin to Hollywood—following one film, the romantic fantasy *Liliom* (1934), made with Erich Pommer in Paris—Lang faced an especially difficult adjustment. Not only had he relinquished his position as the greatest filmmaker in Germany (Lubitsch's, Murnau's, and Pabst's earlier exoduses had removed any serious competition), but he also had lost his chief screenwriter, collaborator, and wife (whom he divorced in 1932), Thea von Harbou.

The change of environment and working conditions were by no means a disaster; in some ways, quite the opposite. For one thing, the commercial censorship and Production Code Administration (PCA) restrictions imposed by classical Hollywood paled in comparison to what he would have faced (had he been able to survive) in Nazi Germany or its occupied countries. For another, the material resources and professional expertise afforded by the Dream Factory (enhanced, of course, by an ever expanding font of European talent) offered considerable creative benefits. Lang also, despite the constrictions of the line-unit system of production, managed to exercise at least some control over the scriptwriting and even the editing stages of many of his American films, and eventually even formed his own production company.[29] Finally, although von Harbou's contribution to Lang's work during the Weimar period was invaluable, his "emancipation" from her (both professionally and personally) also carried with it distinct advantages, at least from a film noir standpoint. Freed from her tendency toward the epic, the mystical, and the overblown, not to mention from her Nazi leanings, he could more readily give himself to subjects, if not always to treatments, that were more on a human scale and that engaged his more progressive impulses.

One can counter that a turn toward smaller-scale, more politically liberal films was already evident in Lang's last two Weimar productions, *M* and *The Testament of Dr. Mabuse*, both of which were written by von Harbou. And the downscaling must be attributed significantly to the commercial failure of the more expensive and technically ambitious *Metropolis* and *Woman in the Moon*. Another, largely neglected determinant remains to be considered, however, both in Lang's late Weimar shift and, even more crucially, in the increasingly socially conscious films that marked his early American period. The factor, as with von Harbou, is a professional and a personal one, though unlike with von Harbou, the creative collaboration of this "other woman" was, and remains, officially uncredited.[30] I am speaking, of course, of Lang's lover in the early 1930s who joined him in exile and remained his lifelong companion and personal assistant until his death: Lily Latté.

Like Lang's first wife, Lily Latté (née Schaul) was Jewish. Although she also had long legs and bore a resemblance to Marlene Dietrich, she was no chorus girl. She came from a wealthy Berlin family, was well educated, and had married first a prominent Berliner, Richard Bing, in the mid-1920s and, after Bing's death, married a cofounder of the Tobis-Klangfilm company, Hans Latté. She had drifted into the periphery of both the film business and left-wing politics by the early 1920s.[31] A strong woman and as big a flirt as Lang was a womanizer, she became the mistress of Conrad von Molo, an assistant editor for Lang; via von Molo she met, set her sights on, and began an affair with Lang. Whether Latté was primarily responsible for Lang's seeming political awakening in the later Weimar years, or rather reinforced an already ongoing leftward drift on his part, it is striking that the change occurred not only just as he was becoming intimate with Latté, but also just as von Harbou, together with her new lover (and future husband), the young Indian journalist Ayi Tendulkar, were becoming ever cozier with Nazism.[32]

Several people, including Schnauber, lend support to the notion that Latté's influence was crucial to Lang's political thinking—and not only in Germany. In the United States, she assisted him with production details, helped him with his English, and became "not only his right hand and secretary but also his most trusted confidante."[33] Throughout their lives together, according to Schnauber,

Latté remained the more politically aware and committed of the two (fig. 10). It was she, more than Lang, who maintained a strong relationship with Theodor Adorno and his wife after the two couples met in the early 1940s in Los Angeles.[34] And even when Lang did express more radical views, they were frequently gleaned from discussions with Latté (although he would never admit it). As Schnauber observed in regard to his own wife as well, Lang's dismissive attitude in public toward women's views was largely a chauvinist pose, belied by his echoing their remarks to others in the women's absence. Latté's Jewishness, of which she was highly conscious, though not religiously so, also quite likely affected Lang's anti-Nazi tilt in the later Weimar years and beyond. It crucially affected his decision to leave Germany when he did, Schnauber believes, for, as Latté told him, she had warned Lang that having a Jewish mistress was sure to come back to haunt him: "One day they will also be after you."[35]

Despite an ocean's separation from the immediate Nazi threat, Latté's politics and her Jewishness, and Lang's connection to them, would continue to haunt Lang and his work in the United States. "One day they will be after you" could easily serve as an alternate title for his first three American films, a triad that critics have grouped together for their pointed social criticism: of a lynch mob in *Fury* (1936), the "three-time loser" law in *You Only Live Once* (1937), and parole laws in *You and Me* (1938). Indeed, one of the first projects that Lang considered upon his arrival at MGM in 1934 was working-titled *The Man Behind You*. The

Figure 10.   Fritz Lang and Lily Latté in Los Angeles. (USC Special Collections)

scenario transposes to the United States a Mabuse-type master criminal who this time drives an attorney, rather than a psychiatrist, "into a life of crime and madness."[36]

Fury

The first two American films that Lang ended up making instead of *The Man Behind You* manage even more telling transpositions than those proposed by the shelved project. Crime and madness in *Fury* and *You Only Live Once*—rather than emanating, no matter how allegorically, from a single master criminal as in the *Mabuse* films and *Spies*, or from a lone psychopath as in *M*—emanate directly from society. And the emanation, and thus the critique, travels both ways, continentally speaking—denotatively onto the mid-1930s United States, where the films are set, but connotatively back onto the Third Reich.

The Depression-era climate and rising fascist threat in Europe and, to a lesser extent, in the United States no doubt contributed to this broadening of political perspective, not only for Lang but also for his American story originators and screenwriters: Norman Krasna (story) and Bartlett Cormack (script) on *Fury*, and Gene Towne (story/script) and Graham Baker (script) on *You Only Live Once*. The films also must be seen as part of this period's fascination with social-problem pictures.[37] Although "one can overstate the degree of true political analysis in his social problem films," as Gunning rightly suggests, one must also grant Lang's refugee status, his companionship with the Jewish (and Marxist-leaning) Lily Latté, and his membership (however peripheral) in the New Weimar community as significant inducements for the pointedly progressive films of his early American period.[38] Gunning lists Lang's "revulsion at the Nazi takeover" as a contributing factor to the antifascist aspect of *Fury* and *You Only Live Once*, but to this revulsion must be added intense ambivalence, as Lang's nostalgia for German culture dueled with the images of swastikas, jackboots, and Hitler salutes.[39]

The parallels between German and American fascism, in *Fury* especially, could hardly have escaped American audiences. The district attorney in the film—prosecuting twenty-two citizens accused of torching and dynamiting the jail in which a man, falsely arrested on kidnapping charges, was incarcerated—provides empirical evidence that mob violence in the United States goes beyond this single gruesome incident: "In the last forty-nine years, mobs have lynched 6,010 human beings in this proud land of ours—a lynching about every three days." As for the German connection, the scenes of a crowd of ordinary folk whipped into a vigilante frenzy couldn't help but evoke images of mass hysteria captured in contemporary newsreels of Nazi gatherings or in Leni Riefenstahl's *Triumph of the Will* (1935). Nor would the Reichstag fire have been far from informed viewers' (and certainly Lang's) understanding of the jailhouse burning's "spectacle of pious sadism."[40] The hapless victim turned avenging angel, Joe Wilson (Spencer Tracy), who miraculously survived his attempted immolation, underscores the Nazi connection in his harangue to his brother and a friend after his furtive escape: "You know where I've been all day? In a movie, watching a newsreel, of myself, burned alive. I watched it ten times or twenty maybe, over and over again, I don't know how much. The place was packed. They like it, they get a big kick out of seeing a man burned to death. A big kick!"

Expanding the human blood-lust associations, but with a Freudian twist, the town barber (a somewhat rehabilitated version of Hans Beckert) had earlier admitted to his own barely suppressed desire to cut his customers' throats while shaving them: "People get funny impulses. If you resist 'em, you're sane. If you don't, you're on your way to the nut house or the pen. An impulse is like an itch, you gotta scratch it." But when Joe appears in court at the end of the film to set the record straight about his assailants' guilt, his diatribe goes beyond cultural or psychological convergence to moral equivalence: "A belief in justice, and an idea that men were civilized, and a feeling of pride that this country of mine was different from all others—the law doesn't know that those things were burned to death with me last night." Horowitz sees the anti-American influence of Adorno (with whom, via Lilly Latté, Lang had significant social contact in Los Angeles) in the film's blistering societal critique: "Like the caustic immigrant social theorists of the Frankfurt School, Lang [in *Fury*] is an Old World Cassandra debunking New World illusions of democracy, justice, and freedom. Like Theodor Adorno . . . he embodies a corrective analysis arguably prescient, arguably acute, but cruelly tendentious and cold."[41]

Yet the indictment of "good" Germans and Americans alike need not have plunged the already disillusioned Lang into complete despair. The implication that evil knows no national bounds, that people are amoral creatures subject to debilitating social and psychological forces, is certainly vastly troubling. But for Lang the refugee, it also would have provided a measure of consolation for the personal betrayal he had suffered due to his native country's and cultural patrimony's descent from grace. "It *can* happen here!" becomes *Fury*'s mantra from an Austro-German exile point of view, to which Lang's Jewish self-denial supplied additional parallax. Lang's sense of betrayal, enhanced by his relationship with Latté, intersected with that of his Jewish émigré colleagues, yet it also significantly diverged from theirs. However painful the Jewish people's exclusion from the European mainstream had been, all the more frustratingly following emancipation, it also offered the compensatory moral righteousness of marginalization and disenfranchisement. Lang's personal dissociation from his Jewishness left him doubly exiled—from German culture and society, and from the Jewish majority within the New Weimar community.

This double marginalization goes a long way toward explaining the extreme narrative "excess" in Joe's shocking transformation, after his near-death experience, from mild-mannered everyman to Mabuse-like monster, as well as the film's radical shift from lighthearted romance to violence-tinged near-tragedy.

The opening and closing street scenes underscore this tonal and generic turn-about. The film begins with the same streets and shopwindows that haunt Joe at the end. At the outset, the furniture store's bedroom display that Joe and his fiancée, Katherine (Sylvia Sidney), longingly gaze at serves as the film's "staging of desire," in Gunning's apt phrase.[42] Unlike the German street films, however, the desire connoted here—despite some ominous foreshadowing (the ripped coat, the rain storm)—is hopeful rather than perilous. But by film's end the streets have returned, stylistically and thematically, to their expressionist roots—driving the protagonist to the brink of insanity and back to the comfort and security of home.

The thematics of doubling and splitting heavily informed Lang's filmmaking from his earliest Weimar days. And, similar to M, the multiplications and bifurcations occur in Fury on the structural as well as the characterological level. As Alain Silver points out, the "fury" of the title can be applied both to the lynch mob in the first half of the film and to Joe in his hyper-vengeful state in the second half. By dividing the movie into matching social and individual parts, "Lang suggests the potential for transference between the two, that alienation or angst are both personal and mass ills."[43] Where the film's, and its protagonist's, split personality enters virgin territory (which can be mapped to Lang's conflicted refugee condition) is in the lack of transference between Joe's mild-mannered and infuriated characters.

Mabuse's and Haghi's serial disguises, and Hans Beckert's evil internal twin, destabilized their identities, but the instabilities were established early on and remained consistently turbulent throughout; Joe Wilson's transmogrification occurs abruptly midway through the film and without the slightest previous hint of the demonic aspect that subsequently overtakes him. Joe's volcanic rage represents more than a change in heart; it is a sea change in character, a diegetic rupture (at least in classical Hollywood terms) that appears motivationally unsupportable until one factors in the extreme internal and external tensions of Lang's self-denying Jewish identity.[44]

Broader Jewish connotations are inherent in the lynch mob theme. Lang claims that early in preproduction he suggested making Joe's character a black man accused of raping a white woman. Whether this "patently absurd" proposal (for the time) was another of Lang's fabrications or merely reflected his naïveté about Hollywood studio (and American) politics, the notion itself does bear on the historical reality of lynching in this country, and therefore on domestic (and other informed) audiences' perceptions.[45] From this perspective, Joe's attempted lynching could be read allegorically, applying collectively to its most common victims, African Americans. For Jews, however, especially Jewish refugees, victims of an even longer history of violent oppression and unjust treatment, some of it quite recent (the Mendel Beilis trial, the Leo Frank lynching, the Nazi anti-Jewish laws), the racial displacement would have been unnecessary and the allegorical juxtaposition just as pertinent.[46] If *M*'s Hans Beckert could be seen as the average Jew-cum–ritual child murderer, then *Fury*'s Joe Wilson certainly qualified as the average Joe turned persecuted Jew (fig. 11).

Yet despite its harsh truths and cautionary allusions, *Fury* is not a wholly despairing film, and therefore is a somewhat compromised film noir. A new ingredient enters Lang's noir-oriented oeuvre at this point: romantic fulfillment. His lone French film, *Liliom*, had featured a love story because it was first and foremost a romance. In his Weimar period, however, romantic relationships were always peripheral and rarely consummated. The classical Hollywood mandate for resolving narrative conflict through heterosexual coupling is fully, if uncomfortably, in force in *Fury*, as is the PCA's baseline of moral restitution. Katherine is the Breen Office's mouthpiece. When Joe's thirst for revenge causes his moral compass to swerve, she's the one who brings the needle back on point: "If those people die, then Joe Wilson dies—you know that, don't you? . . . I couldn't marry you now, Joe. I couldn't marry a dead man."

It is not only Katherine's admonishment, however, that causes Joe's resurrection; film noir, compromised but not completely contained, ironically helps "saves the day." With his Mr. Hyde persona already seriously fraying (thanks to Katherine), functional expressionist mise-en-scène threatens to swallow him whole as he walks the city's lonely streets at night in the film's penultimate

Figure 11.   Average Joe turned persecuted Jew: Spencer Tracy in *Fury* (1936). (USC Special Collections)

scene—the funereal window display, the haunting subjective visions and sounds, the eerily (though not actually) empty restaurant, the even more eerily empty bar with its crowd noises and surrealistic pile (pyre?) of chairs. In addition, doubling motifs expand exponentially—Joe's mirrored image in the restaurant; the double bourbon he orders at the bar; the calendar pages tearing from 20 to 22 (the number of defendants in the lynching trial); and, finally, the tracking shot down the dark, deserted street that takes on a sinister life of its own, tailing Joe like a conveyor belt as he walks down the middle of it, splitting it (and him) in two.

Although *Fury*'s noir elements are partially muffled by Hollywood's constraints, these very limitations, coupled with Lang's inner demons, also appear to have nudged the film in an unconventional noir direction, one that Hitchcock would develop further in *Shadow of a Doubt* (1943) and Lang himself would return to, with more creative license, in *The Big Heat* (1953). D. K. Holm has dubbed this variant "film soleil," a useful description for a noir subset that eschews perpetual darkness and foreboding in favor of sunny-side up openings that turn broken-yoked and bloody as the films progress.[47] *Fury*, with its contrived, Hollywood-mandated embrace between Joe and Katherine at the end, doesn't totally follow the "film soleil" trajectory, but it points the way.

You Only Live Once

Lang's second American film offered another alternative direction for film noir, and in more fully realized form. Ironically, it uses the romantic couple—the very thing that hobbled *Fury*'s noir aspirations—to accomplish the feat. Even more than *Fury*, *You Only Live Once* places a love story at its narrative center. Eddie Taylor (Henry Fonda), in this instance a reconstructed criminal, and Joan Graham (Sylvia Sidney), his newlywed wife, attempt to flee to Canada to avoid Eddie's execution under the "three-time loser" statute for a crime he didn't commit (and for which he eventually, though unknowingly, is pardoned). Rather than having Sidney's character's moral rectitude undermine the film's darker, socially critical message (as in *Fury*), her decision here to stick by her husband and also become a victim of the law reinforces it. The result is the first clear example of another noir subset: the fugitive-couple film.

Although another Hollywood film featuring lovers on the lam, *Mary Burns, Fugitive* (1935), had been released two years before *You Only Live Once*, a comparison of the two film texts and the circumstances of their production supports both the latter's pride of place as a fugitive-couple film noir and Lang's as a key forerunner of the noir cycle. On the first point, *Mary Burns* lacks the moral ambivalence, dark look, and harsh worldview that are essential components of *You Only Live Once*. On the second, the fact that *Mary Burns* shared the same producer (Walter Wanger), screenwriters (Baker and Towne), and female lead (Sylvia Sidney) as *You Only Live Once*, but was directed by William K. Howard, not only affirms Lang's claim to authorship but serves as a prime exhibit for the auteur theory itself.

You Only Live Once is replete with noir's archetypal tropes. From the atmospheric nighttime pond scene where Eddie explains how frogs mate for life and Joan compares them to Romeo and Juliet, to the prison escape scene choked with fog and slashed by searchlight beams, to the prison-bar and cross motifs, to the doomed couple caught in the crosshairs of a police sniper's rifle at the end, the film's iconography, in the finest expressionist tradition, "becomes an extension of Eddie's frightened and disoriented state of mind," and an "evocative metaphor for the entire narrative."[48] Silver further comments on the film's ambivalent protagonists for whom, "as for numerous noir figures to follow, the only way to freedom is through death."[49] "Progressive nihilism" is how Gunning describes the film's tragically romantic theme, "founded in the demonstration that faith and desire have no place in the world as presently constituted."[50]

The film's "refugee connection," meanwhile, could hardly be more pronounced, and, as in *Fury*, the allegorical allusion has both an American and a European component. The dark saga of a couple driven from their home, as Gunning notes, obviously resonated, even pre–*The Grapes of Wrath* (1940), "with Depression era images of Oakies and other displaced and migratory people."[51] But as the pair try to make it across the border to Canada, the associations become transnational, invoking "not only America's migrant population of the 30s, but the plight of the refugee, with the irony that this couple is trying to escape from the land of liberty." Lang and his collaborators, Gunning avers, were clearly "counting on a recognition and sympathy for Joan and Eddie's exile from the American dream."[52] Eddie and Joan's exchange in the car, after she leaves her baby with her sister, affirms such a stance (fig. 12):

EDDIE: Back there I watched through the cabin window. You and the baby looked so warm and safe, inside a house. We were inside a house once. For a few minutes. Lots of people in love get to live inside a house.

JOAN: That doesn't matter now, Eddie. Maybe anywhere's our home—in the car, out there on that cold star. Anywhere's our home.

For Lang, in exile with Lilly Latté from the *German* dream, the refugee aspect also resonated on a personal level, with strong Jewish connotations—both immediate, in relation to the Nazis, and allegorical, in relation to the Wandering Jew archetype. The star-crossed couple's flight to a foreign land in *You Only Live Once* served an additional "morally equivalent" function (as in *Fury*). Yet although the equivalence in *Fury* extended mainly to the common man, in *You Only Live Once* the cross-cultural critique casts a wider net. In *Fury*, social institutions, primarily the justice system and, to a certain extent, the media (newsreel footage provides the incriminating evidence), come to Joe's rescue. In *You Only Live Once* the common man is by no means let off the hook; Eddie even steals a few lines from *Fury* in his harangue to the crowd following his false conviction: "Go ahead!

Figure 12.   Fugitive couple: Sylvia Sidney and Henry Fonda in *You Only Live Once* (1937). (USC Special Collections)

Take a good look, you monkeys! Have a good time! Get a big kick out it! It's fun to see an innocent man die, isn't it?!" But the suspicious innkeepers, lying gas station attendants, and heartless bosses act more as abettors than perpetrators of the crime against Eddie and Joan. It is the justice system itself, with the media's complicity, that is the protagonists' arch nemesis. Justice, thanks to love, ultimately prevails in *Fury*; in *You Only Live Once*, justice triumphs at love's expense.

Although he didn't initiate the film's story, it's hard to imagine that Lang didn't identify strongly with Eddie Taylor, as with Joe Wilson before him, both allegorically and personally. Both Eddie and Joe are falsely accused of a crime, as Lang either was or believed himself to be, in regard to his first wife's death, to his Nazi sympathies, and, though more complexly, to his Jewishness. And, just like Eddie and Joe, at least extratextually—for Sylvia Sidney was Jewish—he had a loving relationship with a Jewish woman with whom he had fled for his life. Moreover, it was Sidney who not only chose to work with Lang on *Fury* but also was instrumental in getting him to direct her in both *You Only Live Once* and their next film, *You and Me*. "I loved him as a friend," she would later recall. "He was bright, he was witty, he was giving. I still have a picture of him stuck up in my kitchen—with a monocle."[53]

Female affection notwithstanding, romantic coupling does not compromise the dark ending of *You Only Live Once*, as it did with *Fury*. On the contrary, à la *Romeo and Juliet*, the tragic love story is the film's most redeeming feature. Even the PCA, although it managed to leave its mark, couldn't entirely gum up the works. As conceived and shot by Lang, the final scene retains a vibrant ambiguity that rescues it from sentimental moralizing. First, the disembodied-crosshairs shot reflexively adds cinema, as a cultural practice, to the broader societal indictment in the killing of Eddie and Joan. Second, the voice of the deceased prison priest, Father Dolan, calling out to a dying Eddie as he peers at the forest tableau—"You're free, Eddie! The gates are open!"—is open to interpretation. The one that the PCA no doubt preferred sees Dolan's metaphor, and Eddie's point of view, as the "gates of heaven," to which the choir music on the soundtrack lends ample support. But within the context of an emerging noir cycle, a more "fatalistic and materialist" reading applies. As Gunning, echoing Silver, observes, *You Only Live Once* played a role in the "transformation toward more sympathetic gangsters, one continued in Raoul Walsh's *High Sierra* [1941] when Ida Lupino greets Bogart's death with the statement, 'Free, free!' In the trajectory of the gangster series, death itself became a deliverance, not necessarily a transcendence, but simply a way out of the trouble of the world."[54]

The forest image places a literal roadblock in front of a religiously redemptive reading, at least from a Christian perspective. The crosshatched trees with their thick, angular branches appear, expressionistically and existentially, to bar rather than facilitate any exit. Even the radiant beams of light, as Gunning reminds us, recall the prison searchlights.[55] One is ultimately thrown back, rather than forward, onto Joan's line, "I would have done it all over again—glad!" and onto the film's title, *You Only Live Once*, with its "plea to live life to the fullest, to be adventurous."[56] From a Jewish perspective, however, such a life-affirming stance—"and the devil take the hindmost"—is not at all sacrilegious.

Judaism, in perhaps its starkest contrast to Christianity, places prime emphasis on life as it is lived here and now—not as a means to a better life beyond, but as an end in itself. This is not a call to hedonism, but rather to *tikkun olam* (healing of the world) and to *shomrei adamah* (guarding creation); heaven is something to be *achieved*, on earth, through human striving, not something that *awaits* one in the afterlife as a reward for faith or good works. The refugee and Wandering Jew motifs sustain a Jewish interpretation of the ending of *You Only Live Once*, and name symbolism further encourages such a reading. Eddie Taylor, like Joe Wilson, was patently conceived as a prototypical, if not proletarian, American name. The surname Taylor—as Eddie is referred to most often in the film—in its relation to the occupation from which it derives, however, begs to be associated, in the European and American context, with Jews. Other Jewish occupational stereotypes (such as banker, lawyer, psychiatrist, journalist, gallery owner, and media mogul) prevailed in the 1930s as well (as most still do today), but all these are middle- to upper-class professions and had emerged post-emancipation. The Jewish tailor, befitting Eddie's everyman status, is timelessly archetypal and decidedly working class.

Joan—as she is most commonly addressed in the film—clearly evokes Joan of Arc. Yet although this places her squarely in the Christian camp, the French saint's legendary heresy and martyrdom in no way contradicts her filmic namesake's attraction to a persecuted, symbolic Jew. Jesus Christ, after all—as it never (or perhaps always!) hurts to recall—was Jewish.

The Woman in the Window and Scarlet Street

Although several of the six films that Lang made in the eight years between *You Only Live Once* and *The Woman in the Window* (1945) are of interest, both cinematically and in regard to their Jewish aspects, I gloss over them here because only three of the six even peripherally qualify as film noir: *Man Hunt* (1941), *Hangmen Also Die!* (1943), and *Ministry of Fear* (1944). *The Woman in the Window* and *Scarlet Street* (both 1945), on the other hand, are key to the noir cycle.

You and Me (1938), made directly after *You Only Live Once* and with greater creative freedom than Lang's previous Hollywood efforts, has noir elements and is even included in Universal's home video "Noir Series." The film is actually a mélange of genres: gangster film, romantic comedy, musical, and Brechtian *Lehrstück* (instructional piece).[57] The genre mixing itself is in keeping with Brechtian alienation principles, and Brecht's *Threepenny Opera*–collaborator Kurt Weil even contributed the musical numbers, some of which are delivered in the *Sprechstimme* (spoken voice) style. But the experiment in meshing populist politics and broad entertainment fails both aesthetically and ideologically. The fluctuation among comedy, melodrama, and didacticism frays the thematic through line, and romantic coupling as plot resolution corrupts the capitalist (and Hollywood) critique. The Jewish facet is in some ways the most overt but also the most sentimentalized of any Lang film. The film's trailer starkly reprises the Jewish refugee theme in its description of *You and Me* as a story about "people without a country" who cannot vote, who have no civil rights, and who must live "under the watchful eye of the parole officer."[58] And the film contains the first (and only) explicitly identified Jewish characters in a Lang film: the Levines, the female protagonist's (again played by Sylvia Sidney) landlords. Although presented sympathetically, the plump, lovable, Yiddish-prone Mrs. Levine (with her gaunt, sheepish husband) comes across as a clichéd translation of the popular radio (and later television) character Molly Goldberg.[59]

Man Hunt, *Hangmen Also Die!* and *Ministry of Fear* come closer to classical noir, and the last two are included on the standard film noir lists. The subway scene in *Man Hunt* introduces an iconic noir image of urban hell; the carnival scene in *Ministry of Fear* recalls *Caligari*; and the representation of "a city under the threat of terror" in *Hangmen* (the script was cowritten by Brecht from a story by Brecht

and Lang) evokes the "dual power system" of *M*.[60] The three films'"Jewish"
bona fides are also buttressed by their anti-Nazi themes. Yet it is precisely the
unequivocally evil nature of the Nazi villains and the films' unavoidable function
as wartime propaganda that ultimately cripple their noir aspect.

An element Gunning identifies in *Hangmen Must Die!* that bears most fruitfully
on the noir-Jewish connection is its theme of paranoia. Present in Lang's films
from the outset, the representation of paranoia shifts during the Weimar period,
specifically in the protagonists' relationship to it: from masters of a paranoid
world, in the Mabuse films and *Spies*, to its victim in *M*. The Hollywood trilogy
of social-problem films, although continuing the centering of paranoia in the
victim, compromises this "totalizing view" by specifying its source and offering
a possible recompense for it. Given paranoia's emanation in *Hangmen Must Die!*
from a totalitarian world without recourse to appeal, this film "anticipates the
full blown emergence of paranoia in Lang's cinema," beginning with *The Woman
in the Window* and *Scarlet Street*.[61]

Although Gunning's analysis of the function of paranoia in Lang's work
in general, and in *The Woman in the Window* and *Scarlet Street* in particular, is
insightful, a blind spot remains (once again) in regard to Jewishness. This lacuna
is all the more surprising given Gunning's description of paranoia as "a form
of delusion" whose "defining characteristic lies in its . . . relation to a *persecution complex*."[62] If Jews didn't sire the persecution complex, they surely must be
counted, as with ambivalence, among its patron saints. From Freud's "Jokes and
Their Relation to the Unconscious" to Kafka's *The Trial* to Hitler's *Mein Kampf*,
Jews have been the prime theorizers and victims of the paranoid modern condition. Gunning even cites, without drawing any Jewish conclusions, Andrew
Sarris's observation that "Lang's films might be said to recall the century of
Hiroshima and Hitler with the post-Freudian punch-line: 'I'm not paranoid. I am
being persecuted.'"[63]

When one adds that the self-persecuted antiheroes of *The Woman in the
Window* and *Scarlet Street* are, respectively, a doctor of psychology and an effeminate bank cashier, that the former rips his coat on barbed wire while disposing
of a corpse and the latter's identity is doubled with a woman's, and that both
characters are played by Edward G. Robinson (born Emanuel Goldenberg),
paranoia's relation to Jewishness in these texts is all but conspiratorial. An
immigrant born in Romania to Yiddish-speaking parents, Robinson not only
"looked" Jewish—diminutive, dark-complexioned, "Semitic"-featured—but as a
cousin of the Yiddish stage actor turned Hollywood star Paul Muni (born Muni
Weisenfreund), he was clearly identifiable as a Jew in the popular imaginary. This
made congressman John Rankin's infamous "outing" of Robinson, along with
other Jewish supporters of the Hollywood Ten, all the more redundant. As part
of the HUAC's investigation of the Ten in 1947, the notoriously racist Rankin
listed Robinson's and other Jewish actors' stage names, followed by their real (i.e.,

Jewish) names, thereby implying, via their "hidden" identities, an insidious link between Jews and Communists.[64]

Robinson's ties to Jewish-type characters didn't begin with the two Lang films. Making his name as the mobster "Rico" in *Little Caesar* (1931), and typecast as tough guys throughout the 1930s (*Smart Money*, 1931; *Tiger Shark*, 1932; *Kid Galahad*, 1937; *A Slight Case of Murder*, 1938), Robinson showed a more sensitive, and explicitly Jewish, side in *Dr. Ehrlich's Magic Bullet* (1940), a biopic about the German-Jewish discoverer of antibiotics. Then there was Robinson's physical resemblance to Peter Lorre, which, as already described, had been exploited once before in the *M*-inspired finale to *Two Seconds* (1932). Whatever it was about Robinson that caught Lang's eye, his staid professor and meek bank-cashier characters allowed Lang to return, more overtly than before or since, to his Weimar roots.

The German genre patently referenced in *The Woman in the Window* and *Scarlet Street*, explicitly in the latter's title, is the street film. *Scarlet Street*'s derivation from Jean Renoir's 1931 film *La Chienne* (*The Bitch*), an adaptation of a novel by Georges de la Fouchardière, does not contradict this assertion. On the contrary, Renoir's film indicates, on the one hand, the cross-cultural appeal of the Kammerspiel/street film's bourgeois rebellion/submission theme; on the other hand, it shows that the German expressionist style remained dormant, and French poetic realism embryonic, in France at this time. Both versions share the same basic plot and characters, but Renoir's visual treatment is more naturalistic and only sporadically noir, even introducing comedic moments, a puppet-show framework, and, unlike Lang's bitterly sardonic ending, a rather lighthearted conclusion. The starkest contrast comes in the depictions of the protagonist, where divergent casting (in relation to body type), between *La Chienne*'s hulking Michel Simon and Robinson's gnomish figure, carries over onto their characters' behavior (and names), with Simon's Maurice Legrand displaying far more marital *and* extramarital assertiveness than Robinson's henpecked and sexually timid Christopher Cross.[65] As Foster Hirsch describes the overall differences, "The light touches and humanist grace notes, always a part of Renoir's lexicon, are erased in Lang's more morose, Germanic remake, as in classic noir generally."[66]

In both *The Woman in the Window* and *Scarlet Street*, the main elements of the street film are on bold display: the "philistine who longs for the sensations and splendors of the nocturnal city"; the middle-class, middle-aged antihero whose rebellion starts too late and ends in submission; and the petty bourgeois whose repressed instincts explode in his face.[67] The paradigmatic street film, Jewish director Karl Grüne's *The Street* (1923), as Gunning points out, can be taken as a model for Lang's two American variants. In *The Woman in the Window*, Richard Wanley's late-night seduction by a woman's portrait in a gallery window, whose subject (played by Joan Bennett) miraculously materializes on the sidewalk beside him, leads to a nightmare of killing, attempted cover-up, and ultimate retreat to the safety of home (fig. 13). In *Scarlet Street*, Chris Cross's after-hours excursion into unfamiliar redoubts leads to enticement by Kitty (Joan Bennett again), a streetwalker posing as an actress, whom he eventually murders from jealousy and then goes insane for getting away with it. Compare this with Grüne's *The Street*, in which the "tempting shop windows" of the city at night "give rise to fantasies," and where the protagonist, "lured by a prostitute," "becomes involved with murder," and eventually "returns to the security of his wife and apartment" and "willingly submits to the domestic regime."[68]

Perhaps growing out of their generic ties to the Weimar period, Lang's two American street films also resonate, more consciously than most, with his own life. *The Woman in the Window*, as McGilligan relates, "was a film in which Lang invested a great deal of himself. The character of Professor Wanley represents another of his civilized alter egos. . . . The Old World gentleman, the professor who loves art and literature, after-dinner drinks and cigars." As for Wanley's "feeling lonely, undergoing a mid-life crisis . . . so was the director."[69] Whereas *The Woman in the Window* may have drawn more on Lang's condition at the time the film was made, *Scarlet Street* appears to have harkened back to his European youth. Lang's personal attachment to the film's protagonist is evident from a

Figure 13. "Looking" Jewish: Edward G. Robinson and Joan Bennett in *The Woman in the Window* (1945). (USC Special Collections)

Figure 14. Feminized Jew (Robinson) stuck between desire (Bennett) and the law (Tom Dillon) in *Scarlet Street* (1945). (USC Special Collections)

backstory he outlined for the character, in which, adding an Oedipal twist to Lang's wannabe artist days in the 1910s, Chris Cross's "youthful ambitions are thwarted by his father." As for Cross's painting style, his artistic credo, "I paint what I feel," aligns him conceptually with the Expressionists. Most specifically, recall also that Lang's first wife, Lisa Rosenthal, whom Lang was suspected of killing, was a chorus girl or, in other words, a glorified prostitute—another of the "professions" regarded, from medieval times through the early 1900s, as stereo-typically Jewish. The long list of suicides or attempted suicides in Lang's films, including Wanley's imagined overdose and Cross's failed hanging, have already been connected, if only unconsciously, with Rosenthal's death. Evidence that the incident continued to haunt Lang *consciously* more than two decades later, and indeed would till the end of his life, is demonstrated by his keeping a meticulous diary, which, he explained to a friend, partly served as protection against further "unfounded" allegations.[70]

Compare such sublimated paranoia with the reporter's sermon to Cross on their way to the execution of Johnny (Dan Duryea), the pimp falsely convicted of Cross's crime: "Nobody gets away with murder . . . no one escapes punishment. I figure we have a little courtroom right in here—judge, jury, and executioner. Murder never solves anything. . . . The problem just moves in here where it can never get out. Right here in solitary . . . so you go right on punishing yourself.

You can't get away with it. I'd rather have the judge give me the works than have to do it for myself." The sermon serves as a sop to the PCA, of course, but its narrative excess points to a paranoia that existed within Lang as much as within his psychologically tortured antihero, who eventually goes mad.

Christopher Cross's overtly, if ambiguously, symbolic name adds another Jewish link to Lang, specifically to his self-denying, half-Jewish identity. Both Christopher and Cross are clear allusions to Christ the Savior, and Chris Cross does share with his namesake a long-suffering, quasi-martyred quality. Yet given Chris's double murders—one of commission, the other of omission, and his lack of overt repentance for either crime—he can scarcely be called a Christlike figure. Film noir offers a clue to the contradiction: "cross," as word and symbol, denotes doubling and splitting; connotes ambivalence; and punningly conjures, in many noirs, the double-cross by the femme fatale or other characters. Seen from Lang's Jewish/non-Jewish perspective, Chris Cross's betrayal of his sacred name signifies a double-crossing of Christ himself, while the final shots of him sleeping in the park and meandering down Main Street in a lunatic haze make him another of Lang's Wandering Jews.

A comparison with the Wandering Jew theme in *You Only Live Once* is telling, reinforcing the sense of Lang's reversion to a Weimar worldview in *Scarlet Street*. Whereas Eddie and Joan Taylor's unjust persecution allies their heroic Jewish and Christian aspects and elevates the couple to the hallowed status of martyrs, Chris Cross's capital crimes, compounded by his lack of repentance, parallels Jews' alleged defiant complicity in the killing of Christ and "justifies" Cross's lunatic stranding on the far side of redemption. The two films' final images reinforce the Judeo-Christian contrast, with the "heavenly" forest seeming to offer, however problematically, far greater succor to Eddie and Joan than the "deserted" city street, subjectively evacuated (in a high-angle long shot) of fellow human beings, possibly can for poor Chris.

The Woman in the Window's and *Scarlet Street*'s privileged status in the noir canon stems partly from the former's inclusion in the short list of wartime American films on which postwar French critics first pinned the term film noir (*Scarlet Street* was released after the term had been coined). Further grounds for valorization come from the films' unlikely protagonists. The repressed pedagogue and bank clerk, one refined, the other naive, are a far cry from the virile, hard-bitten private eyes, police detectives, and loners of early noirs such as *High Sierra*, *The Maltese Falcon*, *This Gun for Hire*, and *Murder, My Sweet*, or even the wronged everyman and three-time loser of Lang's own *Fury* and *You Only Live Once*. The shift was more than one of degree, for the notion that the alienated antihero need not be extraordinary, but rather could be "one of us," and that horror threatened from within *and* from without, meant that hell lay not only in the "Others" but in ourselves as well. This heaping of Freudian dread onto existential angst was nothing new, of course, evoking Weimar cinema from *Caligari* to Kammerspiel

and culminating in *M*. Nor was the admixture of Freud and Kafka (with a sprin-
kling of Sartre and Camus) unique to American noir. Hitchcock's *Shadow of a
Doubt* had broached similar terrain in the doubling of a deranged, worldly uncle
and his wholesome, small-town niece, both named Charlie. Lang's interposing
of derangement, wholesomeness, and gender in *Scarlet Street*, however, and all of
these *within a single protagonist*, extended noir's boundaries—and, once more, in
a Jewish direction.

The linkage between Jewish males and females has a long legacy in European
culture, dating back at least to the Middle Ages. As glossed in the first chapter,
this linkage stems psychoanalytically from "the analogy of the circumcised penis
and the clitoris: each seen as a 'truncated penis.'"[71] Indeed, as Sander Gilman
has shown (with unintended pertinence to Lang), "The clitoris was known in
the Viennese slang of the time simply as the 'Jew' (*Jud*)."[72] "Consequently," Ruth
Johnston extrapolates, "the Jew in Europe was seen as a feminized male, that
is, as sexually deviant, and circumcision functioned as both a racial and sexual
sign."[73] The internalizing of gendered and racial stigmatizing is evident even
(or especially) in Freud, who, Gilman argues, "constructed in his image of the
woman . . . the absolute counter image of the Jew," translating Jews' racial
difference "strictly into a definition of femininity as a defense against the representation of Jewish males as feminized."[74] Thus, again according to Johnston,
"a difference internal to masculinity (i.e., between Aryan and Jewish males) is
projected onto the heterosexual model of difference." Or as Daniel Boyarin
puts it, "The binary opposition phallus/castration functions to conceal the third
term: the circumcised penis."[75]

Scarlet Street may be faithful to Freud in regard to repressed sexuality, but
Christopher Cross's "circumcised penis"—that is, his feminization—far from
concealed, is on perpetual display. Besides his emasculated cashier's job and dandi-
fied artist's avocation: Chris, the name he's mostly called, can pass for male or
female; he cowers at home before a larger woman; his primary domestic spaces
are the kitchen, where he does the dishes apron-clad, and the bathroom, where
he sneaks in his painting; he responds to Kitty's attaching her name to his artwork
not with resentment but with barely suppressed glee, declaring ecstatically that
his picture of her will be called *Self-Portrait*; and when he asks Kitty to marry him,
she laughs in his face, declaring that Johnny, her true love, "could break you into
pieces—he's a man!"

Secret Beyond the Door, House by the River, and Beyond

Lang's "coming into his own" or, alternatively, "returning to form" on *The
Woman and the Window* and *Scarlet Street* must be attributed at least partially
to the greater creative control that he had been granted on the two films. *The
Woman in the Window* was produced independently by Nunnally Johnson, who
gave Lang free rein on the film, and *Scarlet Street* was made through Lang's own

company, Diana Productions.[76] Lang's next major noirs—following *Cloak and Dagger* (1946), an undistinguished reprise of the anti-Nazi espionage thrillers that preceded the two neo–street films—also were made under comparatively auspicious production conditions. *Secret Beyond the Door* (1948) was produced through Lang's Diana Productions, and *House by the River* (1949) for the financially strapped but directorially unobtrusive Republic Pictures. Here again, the wider berth that Lang was granted bore creative fruit.

Visually, both *Secret Beyond the Door* and *House by the River* maintain, in some ways even magnify, the dark look and expressionist mise-en-scène of Lang's previous work. And although *Secret Beyond the Door's* narrative is somewhat derivative, generically both it and *House by the River* signal a shift in Lang's oeuvre (if only momentarily) from the urban to the gothic strand of film noir. The films' titles, in their foregrounding of the house over the street, are the first indication of the shift. That the houses are mansions, are haunted to some degree, and are situated in the country rather than the city further align the films, spatially and thematically, with the gothic mode. As does, at least for *Secret Beyond the Door*, a woman protagonist—the first for a Lang noir, though not by a long shot for Jewish émigré noir in general, as Ulmer's *The Strange Woman* (1946), Litvak's *Sorry, Wrong Number* (1948), Bernhardt's *A Stolen Life* (1946) and *Possessed* (1947), and Siodmak's *Phantom Lady* (1944), *Christmas Holiday* (1944), *The Spiral Staircase* (1945), and *The Dark Mirror* (1946) amply attest.[77]

Secret Beyond the Door's story is also faithful, perhaps to a fault, to the gothic thriller formula, Hitchcock's *Rebecca* (1940) in particular: upper-class newlyweds; sensitive but unstable husband; inter-spousal paranoia fueled by a jealous, sinister servant; all taking place in a mansion, "haunted" by the former wife, that ultimately goes up in flames. Even the film's overt Freudianism, among the more sympathetically deployed and openly articulated of any film during this famously philo-psychoanalytic period, has a direct antecedent in *The Dark Mirror* and Hitchcock's *Spellbound* (1946). Yet the psychoanalytic aspect is also where *Secret Beyond the Door* goes furthest, and comes closest to noir's archetypal dialectic of Thanatos and Eros.

During the troubled husband Mark Lamphere's (Michael Redgrave) guided tour of the mansion's rooms, which he has had replicated from the scenes of—and, to his mind, inspirations for—actual brutal murders of passion, Mark explains to his guests: "He [one of the murderers] never intended to murder. What he hoped for was an ultimate and lasting love. But that *something*, he spoke of an unholy emanation from this room, drove him inevitably to kill." A young psychology student will have nothing of this supernatural explanation, however, offering instead a more clinical, and for the husband himself, uncannily acute diagnosis: "In many cases the murder of a girlfriend or wife has its psychological roots in an unconscious hatred of the mother. Perhaps in his childhood he'd made a resolution in this room to kill. His conscious mind had forgotten all about it, but . . . if he'd been able to tell someone about it, like a psychoanalyst, no murder would have been necessary." And, of course, with Mark's wife, Celia (Bennett again), cloaked in the psychoanalyst's mantle, a talking cure is what barely prevents Mark from murdering her—with a final-scene caveat that extends the love / death coupling. "That night you killed the root of evil in me. But I still have a long way to go," Mark admits, on their second honeymoon. "*We* have a long way to go," she replies (fig. 15).

House by the River underscores the distance Lang still had to go to exorcise his own inner demons. A film about a frustrated novelist who is unfaithful to his wife, hates his brother, stages the brother's apparent suicide, kills (unintentionally) a housemaid of loose morals, and fulfills his artistic promise only by transposing his dastardly deeds into semiautobiographical fiction, recapitulates the themes of Lang's life and work to a remarkable degree. The trope of the river, a symbol of life but also of the unconscious—into which people pour filth, from which they dredge up actual corpses, and whose current ebbs and flows with the tide of history—also resonates, on multiple levels, with Lang's life script and cinematic corpus (fig. 16).

Following his two-film dip into gothic waters, Lang returned, in the 1950s, to the wet streets of urban noir with a vengeance, making some of his most potent and highly regarded noirs: *The Blue Gardenia* (1952), *The Big Heat* (1953),

Figure 15.   Subject and object of desire: Bennett in *Secret Beyond the Door* (1948). (USC Special Collections)

Figure 16.   Sublimating desire: Louis Hayward and Jody Gilbert in *House by the River* (1950). (USC Special Collections)

Clash by Night (1953), *Human Desire* (1954), and *Beyond a Reasonable Doubt* (1956). Although the visual style becomes more muted in these films, the recurrent themes of revenge, paranoia, sexual betrayal, moral and institutional corruption, alienation, and anomie loom just as large, actually clashing more than ever with the mainstream mood of a country embarking, however equivocally, on the good ship *Eisenhower*. Because the main concern of this book is with the lighting rather than the passing of the noir torch, however, I leave Lang at this point and turn to the director who, at least from a Jewish émigré noir standpoint, is his closest rival.

6   *The French Connection*

ROBERT SIODMAK

Whether one agrees with Michael Walker's claim that Robert Siodmak "contributed most extensively to *film noir*" (Lang is more commonly given the nod), Mark
Bould's assessment is indisputable: "Two émigrés—Robert Siodmak and Fritz
Lang—are absolutely central to the development of film noir."[1] Yet while these
two Jewish émigré directors are comparable in their noir output and impact,
they diverge considerably in their noir trajectories.

Lang, as we have seen, exhibited a noir bent from his earliest efforts in the
Weimar period, contributed substantially to the noir vocabulary, and continued
his pioneering role upon his arrival in the United States in the mid-1930s. Siodmak,
with sporadic exceptions, was a comparative latecomer to full-fledged noir. Ten
years younger than Lang, Siodmak also began his filmmaking career a decade later
than the Austrian director. Born and raised in Dresden, Siodmak came to Berlin
with his brother Curt in 1923.[2] His first film job was as assistant director to Kurt
(later Curtis) Bernhardt in 1925; his first directorial effort, the legendary *Menschen
am Sonntag (People on Sunday)* in 1930. The latter film, shot with no written script,
nonprofessional actors, and in a documentary style, is more proto-neorealist than
proto-noir. But it remains a pivotal event in film noir history (and film history
as a whole) due to its credits list of then-unknown collaborators that now reads
like a Who's Who of Jewish émigré noir: codirectors, Siodmak and Edgar Ulmer;
coscenarists, Siodmak, Billy Wilder, and Curt Siodmak; cinematographer, Eugen
Schüfftan; camera operator, Fred Zinnemann; and producer, Seymour Nebenzahl
(Siodmak's cousin and producer of Lang's *M* and *The Testament of Dr. Mabuse*, as
well as Joseph Losey's 1951 American remake of *M*).[3]

Siodmak's subsequent Weimar films did not veer consistently in the noir
direction either, although Thomas Elsaesser's assertion that France, not Germany,
prepared the director for his Hollywood crime and mystery films is overstated.[4]
Two of the six films that Siodmak made in Germany after *Menschen am Sonntag*
have dark crime themes: *Voruntersuchung (Inquest, 1931)* and *Stürme der Leiden-
schaft (Storms of Passion, 1932)*. Two others are relatives of noir's psychosexual
cousin, the Kammerspiel: *Abschied (Farewell, 1930)* and *Brennendes Geheimnis (The
Burning Secret, 1933)*. Even *Der Mann, der seinen Mörder sucht (Looking for His Own
Murderer, 1931)*, a musical comedy about a depressive paranoiac who botches his
own suicide, cowritten by Billy Wilder and Curt Siodmak, is described by Wilder

biographer Ed Sikov as a "proto-film noir."[5] In contrast, five of the nine films that Siodmak made in Paris between 1933 and 1939 were either light comedies or musicals, with only two, *Mollenard* (1938) and especially *Pièges* (*Snares*, 1939), exhibiting noir characteristics. Yet even if we grant that the French influence was greater than the German in these latter two films, as Elsaesser proposes in his critique of the Weimar-noir connection in general, this argument, in the end, falls back on itself—and into the lap of my Jewish émigré noir thesis.

In seeking to explain Siodmak's remarkable ten-film spurt of quintessential American noir from *Phantom Lady* (1944) through *The File on Thelma Jordan* (1950), Elsaesser asks facetiously whether suddenly, "in exile, Siodmak 'remembered' the lighting style of Murnau, Pabst and Dupont."[6] Yet this presumption, however valid in eroding a strict linear correspondence between Weimar cinema and classical noir (at least in Siodmak's case), actually supports the notion that the ambivalences of exile, both toward the corrupted German "homeland" and the American "sanctuary," made noir a uniquely attractive cinematic option for émigré Jewish directors. Moreover, the *longue durée* of expressionist consciousness need not have been funneled solely through the Weimar channel. The French noir tradition, notably in the poetic realist cycle of the 1930s, rather than an "interference" in the through line from Weimar to Hollywood (as Elsaesser proposes in his otherwise brilliant analysis), actually served in significant ways as a bridge between the two.

Poetic Realism

The term "poetic realism," drawn from French literature, was first applied in cinema to *La Rue sans Nom* (*The Street with No Name*, 1933) by Pierre Chernal. Just as the word "street" in the title gave instant notice of the film's Weimar inheritance, its narrative description, and those of other poetic realist films, supported the notion: an urban drama set among the lower middle classes, as well as a romantic/criminal story emphasizing doom and despair.[7] Visual motifs found in *La Rue sans Nom* and subsequent poetic realist works expand the German expressionist connection to the point of plagiarism: nighttime urban landscapes "bathed in strong shadows and pools of light from street lamps," "patterned lighting on characters faces and bodies," and "sleazy locations, of which the night club and bar . . . is the epitome."[8]

French filmmakers' adoption of a "German style" in the 1930s should have come as no surprise. Similar to French critics' later anointment of wartime American films as "film noir," their earlier reaction to *The Cabinet of Dr. Caligari* upon its release in Paris in 1919 propelled the film's canonical status. The French even coined the term "Caligarisme" to describe the horror film's unique visual style, and (despite Erich Pommer's preference of the homegrown term "Expressionism" as a brand name for German art films abroad) the reputation that *Caligari* garnered from its championing by the French, which "allowed it to become one of the few world-wide export successes the German cinema has ever had," also led to its being "almost regarded as a 'French film.'"[9]

Gallic affinity for a German film in the early Weimar period must be taken in the context of post–World War I political as well as cultural internationalism: the League of Nations on the political front and the avant-garde film movement in the cultural arena. Conversely, as with American film noir, adding French luster to a foreign product—particularly one seen as critical of the society of origin—massaged the national ego. By the late Weimar/early Nazi period, however, when a climate more hostile to all things German prevailed, the notion that poetic realism was essentially a "German aesthetic" became less propitious. As Ginette Vincendeau has shown, acknowledgment (and criticism) of the German connection to poetic realism crossed the political spectrum in the 1930s: fascist writers like Maurice Bardeche and Robert Brasillach saw "the gloom and despair" of poetic realist films as not merely German but "Judeo-German"; more liberal (and less anti-Semitic) critics pointed, not always depreciatively, to the "marks of German [Jewish] cameramen (Eugen Schüfftan, Kurt Courant, as well as Otto Heller and Franz Planer) or French assistants enamored with their style (Henri Alekan)."[10]

Germanofilia and -phobia aside, there was, and remains, something distinctively French about poetic realism. Just as French filmmakers such as Chernal, Jean Renoir, Julien Duvivier, and Marcel Carne absorbed "Caligarisme" and its offshoots, German filmmakers working in France had to adapt to French cinematic traditions and cultural sensibilities. These included "the representation of communities" and a more "well-defined social milieu" rather than the "abstract cities of German films"; and the emphasis on character motivation and the "showcasing of actors' performances" rather than the subsuming of people within the mise-en-scène. [11] Although such an approach suggests a privileging of realism over expressionism, the style's "poetic" aspect should not be dismissed: a "Gallic melancholy"; a fascination with "the poetry and mystery of everyday objects and settings"; and an affinity for romantic, world-weary characters "acutely conscious of their existentialist traps."[12]

Elsaesser argues that the realist element in French cinema created a mismatch with the German expressionist style, and Jean Renoir's telling Kurt Courant on the set of La Bête humaine (Human Desire, 1938) to stop "getting on the actors' nerves with your UFA photography" supports such a notion.[13] Moreover, according to Elsaesser, this "culture clash" caused the émigré directors to make "hybrid," "heterogeneous," or even "incoherent" films during their Paris sojourn.[14] Vincendeau counters that the mélange of styles the émigré films exhibit "was itself a feature of the French cinema of the 1930s. . . . Directors like Siodmak and Bernhardt not only adapted to harsh new working conditions"—economic crisis, political instability, anti-Semitism—"they also successfully integrated French generic practices, something which again, would come in useful in Hollywood."[15]

I would add that the alleged conflict between French realism and German Expressionism, besides aiding refugee directors' adjustment to classical Hollywood's filmic practices, also benefited the development of film noir. Moreover, as we have seen, a similar tension between realist and expressionist modes had already characterized the Weimar-era transition from Expressionism to expressionism in the Kammerspiel and street films, and would recur in the post–World War II United States as the expressionist orientation of the early American noir cycle collided with Italian neorealism. The realist/expressionist dialectic that characterized the poetic realist formation in the 1930s, in other words, far from an indication of "irreconcilable differences," points, if not quite to the through line between Weimar and Hollywood that Elsaesser rejects, to a rather sturdy historical link in the noir chain.

The French connection to American noir is further evinced in the host of noir-tinged French films from the 1930s and early 1940s that were remade, most often by Jewish émigré directors, in the classical period in Hollywood. Besides the aforementioned *La Chienne,* remade by Lang as *Scarlet Street,* and *La Bête humaine,* remade, again by Lang, as *Human Desire* (1954), these include *Pepe le Moko* (1937), remade as *Algiers* (1938) and *Casbah* (1948); *Le Jour se lève* (1939), remade by Litvak as *The Long Night* (1947); *Le Corbeau* (1943), remade by Preminger as *The Thirteenth Letter* (1950); and Siodmak's own *Pièges,* remade by another German (albeit non-Jewish) émigré, Douglas Sirk, as *Lured/Personal Column* (1947). Even *The Postman Always Rings Twice* (1946), based on James M. Cain's 1936 novel, that was initially rejected for U.S. production by the Breen Office, can be seen as a remake of the earlier French version, released in 1939 as *Le Dernier Tournant* (The last bend in the road).[16]

The Jewish émigré aspect of the French connection comes into even sharper focus when one considers that only two films made by non-Jewish émigré directors working in France in the 1930s are regarded as significant contributions to the classical noir canon: Jacques Tourneur's *Out of the Past* and Rudolph Maté's *The Dark Past* (1948). (Renoir is credited with one quasi noir, *Woman on the Beach* [1947], while Tourneur's two other noirs, *Experiment Perilous* [1944] and *Nightfall* [1957], are, respectively, of secondary interest and a straggler.[17]) Given, by comparison, the far greater number and significance of noirs made by Jewish directors who had worked in France (besides Siodmak, these include Lang, Billy Wilder, Bernhardt, Litvak, and Ophuls), it seems fair to conclude that the carryover of poetic realist elements onto classical film noir must be attributed largely to Jewish émigré noirists. Siodmak's "remembrance" of a lighting style past was, in effect, a *double* remembrance—of a German style combined with a French style that itself had German stylistic roots.

Of course, neither the German style nor its French variant was exclusively reliant on recent émigrés (Jewish or otherwise) for its dissemination into American cinema. The aesthetics of Expressionism/expressionism, beginning with silent-era forays and expanded through Weimar-era imports and earlier German immigrant waves, had long been absorbed into classical Hollywood, particularly the gangster and horror genres. And among the few French films to which American audiences and filmmakers were likely to have been exposed in the 1930s, poetic realist films headed the list.[18] Yet, as we will see in the work of Robert Siodmak, perhaps more than with that of any other noir director, what had gone around came around.

Universal Authorship

As with Lang and every other established European director starting out in Hollywood in the classical period, Siodmak faced greater obstacles to directorial autonomy than he had in Berlin or Paris. An additional challenge, confronting Siodmak more than Lang, was that the former's reputation, while impressive in Continental terms, lacked the latter's crossover critical acclaim and (as with *M*) box-office success. Although dubbed the "Wunderkind of UFA" in Germany following *Menschen am Sonntag,* and having risen to the top again in Paris by the late 1930s, Siodmak was lucky to land a B-film contract with Paramount in 1941—more than a year after arriving in Hollywood, and even then only through the intercession of star writer-director Preston Sturges.[19]

Of the three programmers he churned out at Paramount, one, *Fly-By-Night* (1942), was a film noir parody that mixed slapstick comedy and thriller elements patterned after Hitchcock's *The 39 Steps* (1935). After two other B films for Twentieth Century Fox and mini-major Republic, Siodmak got his first real chance to show his stuff at Universal, where, through the aid of brother Curt, who had established himself as a screenwriter, he signed a seven-year directing deal in 1943.[20] Although still a "major" studio (as opposed to mini-majors Republic, Monogram, and Producers Releasing), Universal's relatively smaller size and idiosyncratic production protocol combined to make it a comparatively hospitable place for collaborative filmmaking in the 1940s. As Thomas Schatz has shown, Universal's "curious combination of discipline and disorganization" under the regime of Nathan Blumberg and Cliff Work countered the common perception of the studio as "the most factory-like of all the major studios" and further challenges the conventional wisdom of classical Hollywood's "assembly-line filmmaking."[21]

Industrial changes wrought by the 1940 consent decree's curtailing of block booking (the forcing of independent theaters to purchase several of a studio's films in advance) expanded prospects for creative license at Universal. Although not as far-reaching as the Paramount decision of 1948, which eliminated studio ownership of exhibition outlets and block booking altogether, the 1940 government action boosted the ability of theater owners to choose films based on quality, not quantity.[22] As Joseph Greco points out, "The [1940] Consent Decree made the first-run market more accessible to the minor studios," and "Blumberg and Work were now able to tackle the first-run market with A-class projects, like René Clair's *The Flame of New Orleans*, Alfred Hitchcock's *Shadow of a Doubt*, and Siodmak's *Christmas Holiday* and *The Suspect*."[23] More significant than the push for A-class projects, from a directorial autonomy standpoint, was the package-unit system of production that Blumberg and Work, through their newly hired production team of Leo Spitz and William Goetz, instituted to accomplish it. Borrowing from the mode of production long in place at the "prestige" studio, United Artists, the package-unit system (which would come to dominate Hollywood in the postwar years) consisted of contracting with independent producers on a film-by-film basis, with the studio supplying financing, production facilities, marketing, and distribution. The first of Universal's "in-house independents" was Walter Wanger, through whom Lang would make *Scarlet Street*.[24]

Of course, the degree of director control, even in the early package-unit system, varied according to the producer. Some, such as Wanger, and producers with which Siodmak worked such as Joan Harrison, Nunnally Johnson, and Sol Siegel, maintained a comparatively loose grip on the director; others such as Mark Hellinger and Hal Wallis, with whom Siodmak also worked, held a comparatively tighter one.[25] Even when creatively hampered, however, Siodmak found ways to end up with something close to what he wanted. Like Lang, he aggressively sought, and increasingly gained, access to the screenwriting process; and, mining his early Weimar experience as an editor, he joined Lang and other émigré directors, as well as non-émigrés such as John Ford and Alfred Hitchcock, in cutting "with the camera." By filming with a shooting ratio (footage shot to footage used) of three-to-one, compared to the standard Hollywood ratio of ten-to-one, and by carefully selecting camera angles and gauging shot length, Siodmak compensated for the producer's obligatory control of "final cut" by shooting a scene in a way that all but required it to be edited as he had envisioned.[26]

Fortunately, thanks to the yeoman efforts of Joseph Greco, we needn't rely exclusively on historical generalizations, interviews with Siodmak, or his memoirs to affirm the degree of personal input in his films. From a scouring of studio production files, Production Code Administration memos, and comparisons of shooting scripts with the finished films, Greco is able to make a convincing case for Siodmak's substantial participation in all facets of the filmmaking process from *Phantom Lady* (1944), his first A film noir, through his last, *The File on Thelma Jordan* (1950): "Siodmak's oeuvre holds together not only in his collaboration with screenwriters (. . . he had a hand in developing the story lines of *Uncle Harry* [1945], *Cry of the City* [1948], *Criss Cross* [1949], and *Thelma Jordan*), but also in collaboration with cinematographers, and especially in his direct supervision of and active involvement in editing."[27] He was apparently unencumbered on the editing of *The Spiral Staircase* (1945), was paid for his editing work on *The Suspect* (1945), and, in the absence of producer Nunnally Johnson, was entirely responsible for the editing of *The Dark Mirror* (1946).[28] Siodmak's personal style, both in montage and mise-en-scène, is clearly stamped on *Phantom Lady*, most especially in the famous jam-session scene that serves "as a metaphor for sexual climax." And already by his second noir, *Christmas Holiday* (also 1944), "where love and death are fitted equally to the images as to the film's thematic purpose, Siodmak is able to extend his artistic vision throughout the whole of the script."[29]

Phantom Ladies, Fatuous Gents

Adding irony to the paradox of Siodmak's creative flowering in Hollywood, Andrew Sarris claims that his American films are "more Germanic than his German ones, and that is as it should be. Why should Germans want to look at Germanic films?"[30] Although the rhetorical question, posed in the 1960s, was directed at Siodmak's postwar German films, Sarris's overall assessment holds conversely for Siodmak's Weimar-era films, which are also less Germanic (read: less noir) than his American ones. But what, again, of the Jewish component? Are Siodmak's American films also more Jewish than his German ones, pre- and postwar? In terms of *affect*—that is, emotionality—the darker aspect in Siodmak's American noirs renders them, by definition, more Jewish; and this also, in accordance with the dialectics of exile, is "as it should be." In terms of *effect*—that is, signification—feminization is the Jewish trope that leaps most immediately to mind. More than those of any other director, including Hitchcock and the "woman's directors" Bernhardt and Ophuls, Siodmak's noirs feature female protagonists, or strong women in key secondary roles not exclusively relegated to the femme fatale.[31] Conversely, Siodmak's male leads and important secondary characters tend (to an uncommon degree compared to non-Jewish émigrés) to be weak, soft, or otherwise to counter conventional notions of heteronormative masculinity.

Siodmak's individual noir cycle begins with two films, *Phantom Lady* and *Christmas Holiday*, both of which have strong female leads: Carol "Kansas" Richman (Ella Raines) and Jackie Lamont/Abigail Martin (Deanna Durbin), respectively. Richman (the name itself bespeaks maleness, and the nickname "Kansas" evokes a Midwestern toughness) is especially noteworthy in her pointed, and extremely rare, inversion of standard noir character conventions: she plays the streetwise private investigator whereas her male love interest plays the passive victim. Richman takes on the tough-guy role when her boss/love interest Scott Henderson (Alan Curtis) ends up on death row for his wife's murder—actually committed by his "best friend," the demented sculptor Jack Marlow (Franchot Tone) (the name Marlow, of course, taking a potshot at Raymond Chandler's detective-hero, Philip Marlowe).[32]

With Henderson stuck in prison, Richman not only shows her street smarts, posing as a prostitute (thereby sending up the femme fatale) to get information from a lascivious drummer, but courage and physical prowess as well. She more than holds her own against the male bartender-witness whom she first stares down (appropriating the gaze) at the bar and then stands down (waving off male bystanders) in the nighttime streets. She stumbles along the way (both the drummer and bartender are killed), and requires the assistance of the police to forestall her own murder by Marlow (who leaps to his death to avoid arrest), but she ends up getting the evidence she needs (finding the phantom lady, Henderson's alibi) on her own (fig. 17).

Jackie Lamont/Abigail Martin (the *first* of the given names can pass for male) is not as physically active or imposing as Richman, but she's easily her match in inner strength. A quasi–fugitive couple film, *Christmas Holiday* (based on a W. Somerset Maugham novel) finds a nice girl (Abigail) turned nightclub singer/"hostess" (Jackie) pining for her husband, Robert Manette (Gene Kelly), a two-bit gambler convicted of murder shortly after their marriage. Unlike *You Only Live Once*, however, Manette *is* guilty—but that doesn't make any difference to Jackie/Abigail. Even after he rejects her following his prison break (he's put off by her new "profession"), she remains faithful, offers to flee with him, and clings longingly to his limp body after he's killed by the police in a film-ending shoot-out. Jackie/Abigail dominates the narrative (and screen time) in other ways as well. She voices the narration over flashbacks of her meeting and marrying Manette, and sings, among other tunes, the film's theme song (Irving Berlin's "Always") in a proud, straight-backed manner signifying not that she is "on the

Figure 17. Prison visit or boxing match? Ella Raines and Alan Curtis in *Phantom Lady* (1944). (USC Special Collections)

side of the law" but rather "registering resistance to the degradation she has forced upon herself."[33]

Other uncommonly forceful women, not counting the femme noirs of *The Killers*, *The Dark Mirror*, and *Criss Cross* (Ava Gardner's Kitty Collins; Olivia de Havilland's Terry Collins; Yvonne de Carlo's Anna, respectively), include Mrs. Manette (Gale Sondergaard), the Oedipal mother in *Christmas Holiday*; Cora Marshall (Rosalind Ivan), the shrewish wife in *The Suspect*; Lettie Quincy (Geraldine Fitzgerald), the incestuous sister, and Deborah Brown (Ella Raines), the sexually aggressive fashion designer, in *The Strange Affair of Uncle Harry*; Mrs. Warren (Ethel Barrymore), the clairvoyant, filicidal mother in *The Spiral Staircase*; and Thelma Jordan (Barbara Stanwyck), the black widow turned penitent lover in *The File on Thelma Jordan*. Another of the female leads, Helen Capel (Dorothy McGuire) in *The Spiral Staircase*, although meek to the point of parody (she is psychosomatically mute), still manages to fend off a suspected assailant, ultimately speaks, and is, when all is said and done, the film's protagonist.

As for Siodmak's male characters, starting with the protagonists, *The Suspect*'s Philip Marshall and *Uncle Harry*'s Harry Quincy vie with *Woman in the Window*'s Professor Wanley and *Scarlet Street*'s Chris Cross for effeminacy in behavior and appearance. Indeed, these two Siodmak films, although less expressionistic in style, can be taken as companion pieces in character and story to Lang's two noirs of bourgeois repression.[34] All four films were released the same year (*The Suspect* and *Woman in the Window* within a day of each other) and feature stodgy, middle-aged men who resort to murder to extricate themselves from stultifying, middle-class existences.[35] Both Philip Marshall and Chris Cross are married to monstrous shrews (both played by Rosalind Ivan), and both men, although they elude the arm of the law, succumb to pangs of conscience, though Philip's remorse leads not to insanity but to turning himself in. Both Harry Quincy and Professor Wanley commit "accidental" killings, though Harry's is accidental only in missing his target (he aimed to poison domineering sister Lettie instead of innocuous sister Hester); and more significant, and for the same Code-induced reason, both Harry's and the professor's killings turn out to be "bad" dreams.[36]

Philip is played by the famously gay (though straight-playing) Charles Laughton, and Harry by another notoriously effete, "soft-bodied" British actor, George Sanders. Minus the accent and a few pounds, Laughton's lumpish manager of a tobacco shop could easily be taken for a close relative of Robinson's prissy professor and cashier. Harry's "unmanliness" is characterized in several ways: besides his pattern designer's occupation and closet painter's avocation (à la Chris Cross), and the Quincy family's (like the Manette's) financial decline, Harry is controlled, not to say commandeered, by women. Not only is he surrounded in the family house by the maid and his two sisters, one of whom (Lettie) is incestuously attached to him, but even his apparent ticket to freedom, his eventual fiancée Deborah, plays the male role in their relationship.

On their first date she has them go to a girl's softball game, after which he responds, when she thanks him for taking her out, "At times I wondered who was taking whom?" Dressed in suit-like outfits, Deborah consistently plays the sexual aggressor, saying, still on their first date, "I'm not ready to turn in," then asking to see Harry's nine-inch telescope at home. Once in his studio/observatory, she grabs a brush to add color to one of his still lifes and suggests turning off the lights so that they can see the stars. Such bold stokes, surprising even for a femme fatale, are here all the more striking in that Deborah is painted as the good, not the evil, woman.

Siodmak's subsequent male main characters are not as overtly unmanly as Philip and Harry. Jim Reardon (Edmund O'Brien), the insurance company investigator in *The Killers*, and Scott (Lew Ayres), the psychiatrist in *The Dark Mirror*, are more conventionally appealing male types. Yet Reardon is a particularly ineffectual detective, clearly out of his element in the noir world. He doesn't even know how to handle a gun, allowing one of the villainous thugs to grab his and beat him up, and requiring the police to handle the climactic gunfights. Scott, meanwhile, rather slight of build to begin with, as a psychiatrist obviously relies more on brains than brawn. He also needs the police to prevent the destruction of the woman he loves. Moreover, neither Scott nor Reardon can be viewed as unequivocal protagonists. *The Dark Mirror* was, above all, a vehicle for star Olivia de Havilland, playing identical twin sisters: one sweet and innocent, the other lethally deranged (fig. 18). Although Scott, in unraveling the distinction between the twins, solves the murder case, it is de Havilland's dual performance, and Siodmak's visual effects (that innovatively allow her to appear as two characters in the same shot), that steal the show.[37] *The Killers*, meanwhile, as Michael Walker observes, has a "double narrative" and two "sorts of *noir* hero": the seeker hero (Reardon) and the victim hero (Peter Lunn, aka "the Swede," played by Burt Lancaster). The latter's mob-style killing at the film's outset triggers the former's subsequent investigation, with much of the remainder of the story related through *Citizen Kane*–like multiple flashbacks.[38]

Even if we move Lancaster's character to center stage, however, we are still left with a compromised hero in normative masculine terms. This was Lancaster's first film, and although he had yet to develop the macho persona that would make him a matinee idol, his towering height, muscular physique, and boyish good looks are already on display. Yet these are all undercut by his character's strange passivity, subpar intelligence, and physical handicap (symbolic of impotence)—he breaks his hand in the boxing ring, ending his career—that ultimately render him a patsy in crime and in love. Far from a tough-guy hero, or tragic antihero, the Swede is, as Greco describes him, "just a big, dumb lug . . . a luckless, lovesick manchild," who, narratively, in the ultimate slight to his manhood, "is denied a living point of view."[39] Lancaster's other role in a Siodmak film, Steve Thompson in *Criss Cross*, gains a "living point of view" (his voice-overed flashback governs

Figure 18.   Olivia de Havilland(s) in *The Dark Mirror* (1945). (USC Special Collections)

the story) and adds a few points to his IQ (the big heist is his idea), but he is still a hapless man-child, as easy a prey as ever for both the underworld boss and the femme fatale (fig. 19).

Another ostensibly potent male main character whose masculinity takes a hit is Cleve Marshall (Wendell Corey) in *The File on Thelma Jordan*, Siodmak's last American noir. A tall, imposing (if somewhat pudgy-faced) district attorney, Marshall, falls in love with the woman he's trying for murder. Marshall/Corey, like Scott/Ayres in *The Dark Mirror*, however, not only must share marquee billing and protagonist duties with a bigger female star, Barbara Stanwyck (the title character and the woman he falls for), but he also plays second fiddle in the narrative, occupationally and conjugally, to his father-in-law, judge Calvin Blackwell (Minor Watson), whose intrusion into his marriage Marshall deeply resents but cannot overcome.

Other notably "soft" male characters include the already mentioned love interests Scott Henderson in *Phantom Lady* and Robert Manette in *Christmas Holiday*. Henderson is actually described as soft by Richman, and he is even "allowed" to cry. In addition, his occupation was changed from broker to engineer in the adaptation of the Cornell Woolrich novel, as was Marlow's from engineer to artist. Although Henderson's job change appears to distribute gendered

Figure 19.   Crossed up inside and out: Yvonne de Carlo in *Criss Cross* (1949).
(Photofest)

attributes along more conventionally acceptable lines, "a weak, helpless engineer,"
as Walker points out, "is *more* of a threat to gender stereotypes than a weak, helpless broker."[40] As for Manette, the name is literally a feminization of the word
"man." His humbled social status—as last in the line of a once influential, since
fallen, Southern aristocratic family—further deflates his manhood. What most
undermines his masculinity, however, is his relationship to his mother. His being
more than your usual "mama's boy" is made explicit in Jackie/Abigail's flashback
voice-over, which quotes a psychoanalyst as claiming that "Robert's relations to
his mother were pathological." The same voice-over reveals the homosexual
subtext of such a claim—"He was so gay, so charming, so . . . different." An
anachronistic imposition, perhaps, but as Walker reminds us, by the mid-1940s
"'gay' was already in currency within gay (and showbiz?) subculture with its since
commonly accepted meaning."[41]

Walker also discerns gay resonance in the relations between Manette and the
slimy, Jewish-looking journalist/procurer Simon (Richard Whorf), and additional
queerness in the Martin Rome (Richard Conte)/Lieutenant Candela (Victor
Mature) relationship that forms the crux of *Cry of the City*. Candella's obsession
with hunting down the hoodlum Rome, whom he has known since childhood,
is heightened through obsessive doubling in the film's narrative: besides having

grown up in the same Italian neighborhood as Rome, Candella receives a gunshot wound, goes to the hospital, and escapes near the end of the film, just as Rome was shot, went to the hospital, and escaped at the film's outset. The repressed gay elements "return," for Walker, "in one of the most fascinating subtexts of the 'forties. The gun that Candella takes from Rome belongs to Niles [the sinister lawyer]; the knife that Rome flicks open in his dying reflex is the one that killed Niles. The weapons, charged with potential Freudian meaning, circulate between the moralistic cop, the sadistic villain and the gangster hero in a highly suggestive way" (fig. 20).[42]

Clearly, an unusual number of strong, good women and weak, good (and not-so-good) men inhabit Siodmak's film noirs. But what are the Jewish ramifications of these unusual, by 1940s Hollywood standards, gender reversals? Film noir's sexual politics have long been looked at in terms of modernity's crisis in masculinity, exacerbated by wartime and postwar renegotiations of gender roles and changing attitudes toward sexuality. Even the "tough" hero's putative potency, as Richard Dyer and Jonathan Buchsbaum have shown, is itself a cover for an internal conflict "over the existence and definition of masculinity and normality" and a "core generative anxiety about passive homosexuality."[43] The classical noir male hero's "aggressive masculinity" and his reliance on the femme fatale are means of denying those conflicts and anxieties, just as gay or gay-coded characters have functioned to contrast and highlight the hard-boiled

Figure 20.   A weapon charged with Freudian meaning: Victor Mature and Richard Conte in *Cry of the City* (1948). (USC Special Collections)

hero's masculinity. Such characters have therefore appeared more frequently in film noir than in other classical Hollywood genres and have developed a distinctive iconography: upper-crust (or foreign) accent, prissy mannerisms, impeccable taste, and a soft or corpulent body.[44]

Prominent secondary characters exhibiting these characteristics, in non-Siodmak noirs, include Peter Lorre's Joe Cairo in *The Maltese Falcon* (1941), Laird Cregar's Ed Cornell in *I Wake Up Screaming* (1942), Douglas Walton's Lindsay Marriot in *Murder, My Sweet* (1944), Charles Laughton's Earl Janoth in *The Big Clock* (1948), and Clifton Webb's Waldo Lydecker in *Laura* (1944). The crucial difference in Siodmak's noirs (as in some of Lang's work, and that of other Jewish émigré noir directors to be discussed later) is that they have altered the terms of the discourse. Siodmak's "soft" characters, and their strong female counterparts, do not act as counterpoint to the tough hero; rather, they have replaced him altogether. Even the police in Siodmak's noirs generally lack typical tough attributes. Huxley (Stanley C. Ridges) in *The Suspect* and the policeman (James Bell) in *The Spiral Staircase* are more akin to British "constables" or "inspectors" than American cops or detectives (because *The Suspect* is set in London, Huxley actually hails from Scotland Yard). Most of the other police officers either have "soft or corpulent" bodies—Lieutenant Burgess (Thomas Gomez) in *Phantom Lady* and Lieutenant Stevenson (Thomas Mitchell) in *The Dark Mirror*—or fail to meet "all-American" standards of masculinity through ethnic typing: either by character name, actor's name, appearance, or some combination, Burgess (Gomez) can be taken as Latino; Stevenson (Mitchell), as Irish; Lieutenant Ramirez (Stephen McNally, in *Criss Cross*), as Latino; and Lieutenant Lubinsky (Sam Levene, in *The Killers*), as Jewish.

The history and ideology of Jewish associations, both negative and positive, with the "soft" male have already been explored. But what of Jewish connections with the strong, dynamic woman? Not surprisingly, the two ethnically gendered constructions are linked, discursively and experientially. The notion of the powerful Jewish woman far precedes more recent, and largely offensive, manifestations in the American Jewish mother or Jewish American Princess stereotypes. Alongside the *yeshiva-bokhur* (religious scholar) models of Jewish masculinity—gentle, introverted, bookish, isolated from the larger society—that arose in early Roman and Christian times and congealed in the European diaspora, a contrasting female image, and reality, emerged.[45] Propelled by practical necessity (the husband's engrossment with Torah and Talmud), but also supported by biblical precedent (Miriam, Judith, Deborah, Esther), Jewish wives and mothers often found themselves not only as heads of what came to be perceived as a matriarchal family, but as the major breadwinners of the household as well.[46]

By the High Middle Ages, as David Biale has shown, Jewish women in western European communities "enjoyed rather astonishing freedom" due to "their active role in business and other public professions."[47] This freedom apparently extended to romantic as well as financial matters. According to Daniel Boyarin, cases are recorded, pre–Freud and Marx, where, "first of all, the dominant, desiring subject is clearly the female one. . . . Second, in order to find the sort of husband she desires, she must be economically well established."[48] Moreover, the strong woman/soft man nexus was apparently satisfactory, and satisfying, both socially and sexually: "There is . . . sufficient evidence to make it plain that the notion of the pale, thin, side-curled, studious *Yeshiva-Bokhur* as erotic object for young women is not a mere nostalgic construction à la *Fiddler on the Roof*."[49] The most famous nonbiblical exemplar of the strong, desiring Jewish woman is Glikl of Hameln, a member of the trading class of seventeenth-century Hamburg and Altona. Extremely capable, economically autonomous, and "the first great female literary voice in Jewish history (since Miriam and Deborah in the Bible)," Glikl describes her husband "as the ideal male Jew of her time," emphasizing "his inwardness, piety, and especially 'meekness.'"[50] Despite the sublimation of Jewish female strength and independence within the regime of bourgeois gentility in the post-Enlightenment period, carryovers of dynamic Jewish womanhood are evident in the European and Southern Californian cultural salons, and in progressive political movements from socialism and labor unions to civil rights and feminism.[51]

Of course, just as the positive valence of Jewish male softness had its homophobic counterimage, manifested most blatantly in the Zionist ideal of the muscle Jew, so did sympathetic regard for Jewish female power confront its misogynistic shadow. Jewish women were (and continue to be, in strict Orthodox Judaism) disenfranchised in the religious sphere—segregated in the synagogue and barred from religious training—and subject to male hegemony in the domestic and social spheres as well. In the broader society, again with ample precedent from biblical and other sources, the assertive (read: phallic) Jewish woman easily transmogrified, in post-Enlightenment Europe, into the anti-Semitic variation of the femme fatale: the carnally voracious *belle juive*. Nor did Jewish émigré noir directors shy away from perpetuating, albeit in non-denomi-national form, the evil temptress archetype: Siodmak's Kitty Collins and Anna (*The Killers, Criss Cross*), Lang's Kitty Marsh (*Scarlet Street*), Billy Wilder's Phyllis Dietrichson (*Double Indemnity*), Preminger's Stella and Diane Tremayne (*Fallen Angel, Angel Face*), Ulmer's Vera and Jenny Hager (*Detour, The Strange Woman*), and Brahm's Nancy Blair and Evelyn Heath (*The Locket, Guest in the House*) are among the cycle's most ruthless examples.

Then again, a strong, independent woman, even if she's "bad," has much to recommend her—as Mae West famously reminded us and feminist critics have further elaborated.[52] In a classical Hollywood narrative system and a patriarchal society given to relegating women to passive, objectified, or self-sacrificing roles, a woman who resists or, all the better, transgresses such restrictive and demeaning norms can hardly be deemed the villain (in a progressive political sense).[53] This is even less the case when Jewish linkages with the feminine are added to the mix, along with the moral righteousness of marginalization that both Jews and women can claim as their rightful (or wrongful) inheritance. This is not to claim higher moral ground for the chosen people, much less for Siodmak and the other Jewish émigré noir directors in regard to gender representation. It is to say, however, that Siodmak and company, given a Jewish discourse of polymorphous sexuality reinforced by the circumstances of exile, did gain privileged access to a counter-narrative of queered gender construction that is clearly legible in a substantial number of their films.

Unfashionable Fascism

Although Siodmak made no overtly anti-Nazi propaganda films during his American period, as did several other of the Jewish émigré directors, two of his noirs made his stance on matters Hitlerian abundantly clear.[54] Artist Jack Marlow and zoology professor Albert Warren, the murderous villains of *Phantom Lady* and *The Spiral Staircase*, respectively, appear eager recruits (or recruiters) for the Nazi cause. "A fascist modernist in thin disguise," the pathological Marlow is a sculptor whose works recall the monumentality of Nazi art.[55] Steeped in a twisted Nietzschean philosophy by way of Ayn Rand, he expounds his world-view to Richman while rubbing his hands in preparation to strangle her: "I never liked cities. The noise, confusion, and the people in them—they hate me because I'm different from them. . . . You'd be happier if you'd never come to New York, never met Scott. The world's full of men like him. You could buy stupid people like him a dime a dozen. . . . What's his life worth compared to mine? A mediocre engineer working in sewers, drain pipes, faucets. What's any life compared to mine!"

Lutz Koepnick, in a brilliant analysis of this aspect of the film, explains the fascist underpinnings of Marlow's melding of the aesthetic and the political: "Marlow's massive works hope to ground art in the vitalistic roots of collective life and, in order to do so, not only challenge abstract modernism and bourgeois utilitarianism but also promote the artist as charismatic 'prophet, educator, and *Führer* of his *Volk*.' . . . [He launches] a double attack on modern life, one against the postaesthetic rule of mass art and diversion and one against liberal democracy and the equalizing rationality of social engineering. Henderson represents what aggravates Marlow most . . . [he] upsets Marlow's call for the aura of genius art."[56]

The fascist politics of Warren's "aesthetics of horror" carry over into the film medium. His serial murders, exclusively of women with some sort of physical disability or imperfection, are preceded by extreme close-ups of Warren's eyeball (fifteen years before *Psycho* and *Peeping Tom*) as he "voyeurs" his female victims. This visual trope need not be interpreted in purely Mulveyian (or Hitchcockian) terms, however, as Koepnick explains: "Far from implying that cinematic specta-torship per se exhibits a natural tendency toward a delight in the art of murder, the shots instead expose the way Warren's politics of social hygiene rely on a manipulation of the cinematic apparatus and its peculiar pleasures. . . . These shots draw attention to the way Warren . . . appropriates the special effect that is cinema in order to pursue his antimodernist vitalism."[57] Nazi associations become explicit in the black gloves Warren puts on before strangling his victims, and in the rant he delivers to his last intended one, the mute Helen: "There's no room in the whole world for imperfection. . . . Steven [his dandyish brother] is weak, as I once was. What a pity my father [a big-game hunter] didn't live to see me become strong, to see me dispose of the weak and imperfect of the world, whom he detested. He would've admired me for what I'm going to do."

But his (until-then-bedridden) stepmother doesn't! Marshalling the strength to descend the eponymous staircase, she shoots Warren—eliciting a scream from Helen that cures her of her trauma-induced muteness (as a child she had witnessed her parents perish in a fire) (fig. 21). The film's final image, however, undermines the therapeutic storyline. As Helen phones the doctor whom she loves and with whom she will presumably, in the Hollywood afterlife, live happily ever after, the camera pulls back from her ever dwindling figure encased in shadow and dwarfed by the sinister mansion, whose darkest mysteries, unlike those in Lang's *Secret Beyond the Door*, have yet to be revealed.

Coming "Home"

In his memoirs, Siodmak describes his wrenching career shifts and geographical dislocations as part of a pattern that intersects with pivotal world and film-historical events: "One day after Hitler came to power I left Germany; one day before the war broke out I left for America; one year before Cinemascope was invented I gave up Hollywood and moved back to Europe."[58] Perhaps more accurate, if less compelling, than Lang's tale of his flight from Goebbels and the Nazis, Siodmak's biographical gloss nonetheless reveals a similarly glorified sense of self-importance—as if his global wanderings were driven as much by Destiny as by historical circumstance. The parallel between Siodmak and Lang extends, as we have seen, to several of their American noirs, as well as to their career trajectories. Lang, too, would return to Europe in the 1950s; although reversing the chronology of his and Siodmak's prewar French intermezzos, he would remain in the United States well beyond the shift to widescreen, making a number of noirs in that format before leaving in the late 1950s.[59]

The most uncanny correlation between the two directors' career arcs is Siodmak's 1957 West German film *Nachts, wenn der Teufel kam* (*The Devil Strikes at Night*). An anti-Nazi crime film about a mentally deficient serial killer tracked down by the police and the SS, the film's premise bares obvious resemblance to Lang's *M*. Adding to the similarity, both films were based on true-life cases:

Figure 21.   Gothic noir, Weimar style: Dorothy McGuire in *The Spiral Staircase* (1945). (USC Special Collections)

Lang's on that of mass killer Peter Kürten, the so-called Monster of Düsseldorf, whose multiple murders "resounded throughout Germany in 1930"; and Siodmak's on that of Bruno Lüdke, murderer of more than eighty women across Germany over an eleven-year period that spanned the Nazi era.[60] As for their filmic representations, Lang's bifurcation of the search for the killer into police and underworld strands is mirrored in Siodmak's division of the dragnet into police and SS strands, with the SS easily readable as the legalization of organized crime under Hitler. Two major differences, however, separate the two films: first, Siodmak's version, rather than evoking the looming threat of Nazism, is set toward the end of World War II as the Nazi regime was collapsing. Second, and of greater retroactive significance to Jewish émigré noir, the serial murderer and his terrorization of society that form the crux of Lang's film serve in Siodmak's mainly "as a pretext for a coming-to-terms with the Nazi era."[61]

Except for the initial murder scene (shot in deep shadow by a staircase) and a subjective point of view of the killer as he reenacts an earlier killing for the benefit of the police, *The Devil Strikes at Night* is pedestrian stylistically and completely lacking in expressionist aesthetics. It also retreats from noir's moral ambivalence in a way that exceeds Lang's wartime anti-Nazi films. Not only are Siodmak's Nazis, and the gestapo in particular, portrayed as utterly vile and despicable, but the German people are presented as "captive of an evil force"—both in relation to the serial killer and to the Nazi regime.[62] The SS initially views the killer's capture as "justification for the extermination of mental 'degenerates,'" which is reprehensible enough.[63] But when Hitler regards the case as casting doubt on the efficacy of Nazi law and order and has official records of it erased, the denial of reality and interment of the truth become the more historically resonant crimes—of which, however, the German people are absolved.

Similar to the need of many in the Weimar Pacific community to distinguish the evils of Nazism from traditional German culture and society, *The Devil Strikes at Night* paints a portrait of a German homeland and its citizens "awakening from the Nazi nightmare."[64] Although the death camps are briefly acknowledged in a scene where a Jewish woman is hidden away, Anne Frank–style, by a German couple, the purpose seems less to expose the horrors of the Holocaust than to spare ordinary Germans from retroactive complicity with the Final Solution. The handsome, sympathetic investigator is a true hero, unwavering in his pursuit of justice and with a soldier's limp, signifying both his patriotic service and the moral scars inflicted by the Nazis. Average citizens are also shown as distanced from, if not openly hostile to, Nazi ideology and policy, or simply, as Bernhard Hemingway describes, "enduring of their lot in an atmosphere of intimidation and suspicion, and so effectively disassociated from the Party, its rhetoric and acts."[65]

Such an ameliorative treatment of the Nazi period is understandable, perhaps even necessary, in the context of early postwar Germany, where healing wartime trauma, both material and emotional, may have been a prerequisite for confronting wartime guilt. The film certainly struck a sympathetic chord in German and international critical circles, garnering ten German Film Awards, including Best Feature Film and Best Director, and an Oscar nomination for Best Foreign Language Film. That *The Devil Strikes at Night* is the closest Siodmak came to a film noir in his post-Hollywood period, however, lends further support to the notion that Jewish émigré noir was nurtured by conditions, specific to an American refugee colony shadowed by Nazism, that were scarcely to be found in a newly carved West Germany.[66]

Of course, film noir as a cycle was on the wane by the mid-1950s, the double-barreled victim of Eisenhower-era optimism and Hollywood-studio malaise. Indeed, some argue that noir's decline was a factor in Siodmak's exodus from the film capital.[67] But it is also "as it should be" that Siodmak's American films are more noir than his German ones, not only because postwar Germans were disinclined to watch Germanic films, but also because Jewish refugee directors found in an American film form with Germanic roots the most effective means for confronting their multiply entwined and conflicted Germanic, Jewish, American, and human identities. Émigré Jewish filmmakers and film noir were a natural fit, both for the Hollywood studios that benefited from the foreigners' bent for the "black film" and for the exiles who found in the noir cycle an outlet and partial anodyne for their experiencing, on multiple levels, a sense of traumatic dislocation, frustration, and loss.[68]

7   *Viennese Twins*

BILLY AND WILLY WILDER

The chapter title is a bit of a fudge (or a Sachertorte), but that's part of the point. The Wilder brothers were not joined at the hip at birth, but rather were born two years apart: Willy in 1904, Billy in 1906. And they both entered the world not in Vienna but in Sucha, Galicia, a town in the Polish region of the Austro-Hungarian Empire. But the two boys did spend their formative years in the imperial capital, where they moved with their German-speaking Jewish parents in 1916, and where they were exposed to the bounties of cosmopolitan culture and to its Hapsburg flipside, anti-Semitism. They did not need the (later assassinated) Weimar statesman Walther Rathenau to tell them that there comes a time when every German-speaking Jew "realizes he's a second-class citizen."[1] The Wilders' estrangement from mainstream society, exacerbated by their low economic and social status, was legally affirmed when their father's application for Austrian citizenship shortly after World War I was denied because "Mr. Max Wilder was not able to bring proof that he belongs to the German majority of the population of Austria according to race and language."[2]

Then there are the names. Billy was officially named Samuel at birth, after his paternal grandfather. His mother, Eugenia (called Genia), who had visited an uncle in New York City as a young girl and fallen in love with the United States, had formed a crush on Buffalo Bill, whom she had seen perform in his Wild West Show in Madison Square Garden. Subsequently, along with regaling the children with stories about the New World, she nicknamed Samuel "Billie," a German-ized diminutive of Bill (Billy changed the "ie" to the more gender-appropriate "y" upon his own arrival in the United States).[3] Linguistically, then, Billy and Willy *were* conjoined from childhood, with obvious psychological repercussions. If identity formation wasn't troubled enough by the two nicknames' phonetic and spelling similarities, as well as a common etymological source in the formal name Wilhelm/William, Genia's proclaiming Billie "her American boy," as biographer Ed Sikov avers, all but assured heightened sibling rivalry.[4]

Nor would the Torah have encouraged a rapprochement. Cain's murdering of his younger brother Abel, and Jacob's wresting the patriarchal mantle from his older brother Esau, to name just the most high-profile examples from the Pentateuch, provide archetypal precedent for the sibling rivalry complex.[5] As for Billy and Willy's exposure to the Jewish scriptures, neither boy was raised religiously; their grandmother on their mother's side, who lived with the family, however, was an observant Jew, and their mother's brother was an ardent Zionist who eventually migrated to Israel.[6] Galicia also had a sizable Jewish population (9 percent), and in Vienna the Wilders lived near the *Judenplatz* (Jewish district). Thus, whether or not they imbibed the book of Genesis with their mother's milk, the boys would surely have absorbed the gist of this ur-text from school or the overall milieu.

With or without biblical reinforcement, birth order by itself would have ensured familial conflict. Older children, and firstborns especially, naturally feel resentful at a younger child's usurpation of their privileged position in the home, particularly in relation to motherly affection, physical contact, and, in some cases (as one can assume was the case with Willy), suckling. The resulting power struggle invariably generates "a set of strategies to compete with siblings for parental investment."[7] The phenomenon is exacerbated if the parents, despite their better judgment, play favorites, as empirical studies have shown to be the rule, and which certainly appears to have been the case with the Wilders.[8] Moreover, as with all unresolved childhood complexes, sibling rivalry persists throughout life. As Steven Pinker summarizes, "Siblings never completely escape the orbit of their parents, but compete all their lives."[9]

Another developmental model with particular resonance for the Wilder brothers is Melanie Klein's notion of object relations, which proposes that all young children are prone to view people and things in all-good/all-bad extremes based on their role in satisfying or frustrating the child's needs.[10] Older siblings, in this framework, would tend to regard younger siblings as decidedly more bad object than good—and Billy Wilder, already as a young boy, played into the bad-object syndrome in spades. A precocious schmoozer and scam artist, he was allegedly hustling pool at five years old, moving on to "outright thievery"—swiping waiters' tips from tables when nobody was looking—soon thereafter.[11] Although not the sole cause of his bad-boy behavior, Billy's (mother-induced) identification with his Wild West hero namesake would surely have contributed to it.[12] And although the family name Wilder (pronounced *"vill-der"* in German and referring, as its English equivalent, to wildness) conceivably influenced both boys' characters, it was Willy whom his parents sent to fetch Billy during the rapscallion's frequent truancies from school.[13] Billy's unruly behavior got an additional, Jewish-inflected boost from his Zionist uncle, who immersed the boy in the muscle Jew tradition of Judah Maccabee and Bar Kochba, a tradition reaffirmed by Billy's toughness and muscular frame.[14]

Given the convergence of internal and external forces, it seems not only plausible but inevitable that Billy and Willy's emotional connection would have been more than normally conflicted. Constrained by family protocol during the boys' youth, and held at bay in early adulthood by geographical separation, their problematic relationship finally found expression, although even then largely subliminally, when the Viennese twins' paths crossed again in middle age in Hollywood.

The West Gets Wilder and Wilder

Billy's nominative connection to the United States eventually carried over to American popular culture, with which, spurred by his mother's stories as a youth, he became obsessively enamored, from westerns and adventure movies to jazz music. His love for and deep knowledge of the latter led to an early career coup: After (barely) graduating high school and on the rise as a fledgling reporter, Billy schmoozed his way into a touring Paul Whiteman's good graces, escorting the jazz superstar and his band to Berlin in 1926. There Billy resumed his reporter's job, resorted for a brief time to *Eintänzerei* (dancing for hire), and moved into filmmaking. His cinematic involvement in the Weimar period consisted mainly of scriptwriting, including on Siodmak's breakthrough feature *Menschen am Sonntag*; after that film, as with Siodmak, Billy's film career briefly took off with the aid of Erich Pommer, yet was abruptly cut short by Hitler. Unlike Siodmak, Billy's emigration in 1933 to Paris, where he directed his first film, *Mauvais Graine* (*Bad Seed*, 1934), was envisioned from the start as a stopover on the way to Hollywood—a goal that was accomplished, even before the release of the French film, thanks to a deal secured by another Jewish émigré director, Joe May.[15]

The seemingly less impetuous Willy, although he would trail his younger brother by sixteen years in embarking on a film career, made it to his mother's beloved United States a decade before Billy. Although accounts vary, Billy Wilder biographers Maurice Zolotow and Ed Sikov have Willy leaving Vienna short of finishing high school in 1922, staying first with relatives in London, then moving on to live with the uncle in New York who had introduced Genia to Buffalo Bill.[16] "He wanted to be here [in the United States]," Willy's son Myles explained in an interview, adding as rationale for his father's abrupt departure from home at such an early age, "He was a very adventurous man, a big risk-taker."[17] Although Willy's adventurousness can be seen partly, as with Billy's, as living up to the family name, an Oedipal perspective aligns the risk taking once again with the sibling-rivalry syndrome. In exchanging his parents' home in Vienna for a strange new one in New York, Willy was both "pleasing" his mother by realizing her "American dream," and "winning back" the love he sensed she had bestowed on her "American boy." Whatever the motivation, by the time he met the Hollywood-bound Billy at New York Harbor in 1934, Willy had a wife, an infant son (Myles), and a Long Island mansion with live-in servants made possible by a thriving ladies' handbag business. For the next ten years, Willy would remain ensconced on the East Coast, content, but not entirely satisfied, with his financial success and upper-class respectability. Then in 1944, just as brother Billy had reached the upper strata of the film business with his smash critical and box-office hit *Double Indemnity*, Willy pulled up his stakes and decided to try his own hand at the Hollywood game.[18]

As for Billy, his rise to the top of the movie business had not come easy. With fewer credits than Siodmak at the start of his U.S. career, and lacking the Weimar-era stature of a Lang or even a May, Billy also had to start from scratch. Contacts made through Salka Viertel's salon helped, as did Paul Kohner, the émigré agent extraordinaire—both in terms of his own background and that of his client list, which included, besides Billy, at one time or another, Siodmak, May, Salka and Bertolt Viertel, Ulmer, Ophuls, Litvak, William Wyler, and Gottfried Reinhardt, among others. Brother Willy, before coming to Hollywood, had also lent Billy a helping hand, according to son Myles: "For the record, my father was here [in the United States] and established and successful, and Billy . . . came out to Hollywood, didn't get work, and was supported by my father. . . . My father kept him alive, before he became *Billy Wilder*."[19]

Billy began as a screenwriter, which wasn't necessarily a problem: he was a gifted writer and his experience on *Mauvais Graine* had left him with a distinct distaste for directing. What did irk him, as it has many film writers before and since, was the sometimes glaring discrepancy between what he committed to paper and what ended up on the screen. He began observing the work of directors he wrote for and respected, such as Lubitsch (*Bluebeard's Eighth Wife*, 1938; *Ninotchka*, 1939) and Howard Hawks *(Ball of Fire*, 1941).[20] And when some key dialogue lines in the refugee drama *Hold Back the Dawn* (1940), one of the earliest American films to deal openly with the fascist threat, were deleted by director Mitchell Leisen in deference to star Charles Boyer, Billy decided he'd had enough of playing second fiddle. The jettisoned lines are worth recalling, because they so clearly emerge from and speak to Billy's own refugee experience. In the scene in question, a Romanian gigolo named Iscovescu (played by Boyer), desperately seeking to immigrate to the United States, paces in his room in a shabby hotel (in which a Jewish refugee has just hanged himself to avoid being taken by the Nazis). Spotting a cockroach crawling along the wall, Iscovescu says to the bug: "Where do you think you are going?! You're not a citizen, are you? Where's your quota number?!" According to the script by Wilder and writing partner Charles Brackett, Iscovescu then "smashes the cockroach with a stick."[21]

Billy began training and campaigning to join Preston Sturges and John Huston among the fledgling ranks of writer-directors, and he got his chance with the screwball comedy *The Major and the Minor* (1942). The film was a hit, as was his next, *Five Graves to Cairo* (1943), a war film about the North African campaign, with Erich von Stroheim playing the "Desert Fox," Erwin Rommel. His third directorial effort would not only be his first film noir, but also one that would help establish the noir cycle's stylistic and thematic tropes and establish Billy as a major director. *Double Indemnity* (1944) was nominated for seven Academy Awards, including Best Picture and Best Director, losing out in both categories to the more upbeat *Going My Way* and the Bing Crosby vehicle's director, Leo McCarey.[22] Billy's next film, *The Lost Weekend* (1945), turned the tables. Although up against another McCarey-directed and Crosby-starring crowd-pleaser, *The Bells of St. Mary's*, and in some ways even darker-tinged than *Double Indemnity*, *The Lost Weekend* garnered both Best Picture and Director honors for Billy. The difference this time, of course, was that *The Lost Weekend*, a social-problem drama on the evils of alcoholism, unlike *Double Indemnity*'s romanticized tale of adultery and murder, had moral suasion on its side.

For Willy Wilder, the message of his brother's dark films was bright and clear: if Billy could do it, why not him? At least that's how Billy interpreted Willy's sudden move to Hollywood in 1944. "He sold his business, he bought a house here, and started making pictures, one worse than the other, and then he died," Billy curtly told writer-director Cameron Crowe in a 1998 interview.[23] Myles offers a more nuanced explanation for his father's Hollywood gambit. Although he acknowledges that Willy, as a savvy businessman, was keen on availing himself of Billy's industry connections, he also recalls Willy telling him many times "that he had the first inklings of becoming a movie producer, director, a creator of film, long before Billy. . . . He was always fascinated with it. . . . He would have done that [moved to Hollywood] if Billy were a dentist!"[24]

Whatever his motivation, Myles's wife, Bobbe, who came to know both Willy and Billy, relates that Willy "would have loved to have a relationship with the man. I don't think I ever heard Willy say anything bad about Billy."[25] "My father wanted to be Billy's brother," Myles confirms. "Billy wanted my father to be a third cousin. Billy wanted very little to do with him."[26] Although these comments seem to contradict my sibling rivalry thesis, at least from the older brother's side of it, Willy's masochistic persistence in trying to "win over" Billy—who as a budding Hollywood auteur had regained, if not magnified, his position as mama's "American boy"—points rather to classic overcompensation for the syndrome, whether from identification with the mother or from sublimated guilt. As for Billy's rebuffing of Willy, some of his other personality traits—egocentrism, cynicism, disdain for bourgeois protocol—undoubtedly contributed to his conde-scension. But a sense of having assumed his "rightful" position of preeminence, both on a familial and a professional plane, certainly resonates with a younger sibling's sense of entitlement, as mythologized in the saga of Jacob and Esau and empirically confirmed.[27]

However painful Billy's rejection of his brother may have been in Willy's lifetime, it turned downright nasty after Willy's death: a "fool" who "fell flat on his ass" and a "dull son of a bitch" were Billy's standard put-downs of his brother in statements to interviewers (when he deigned to mention Willy at all). And of Willy's films, besides the "one worse than the other" dismissal, Billy offered this somewhat contradictory but similarly abject appraisal: "I saw one. I didn't expect much, and it didn't let me down. It wasn't even bad, which is worse. He should have stuck with leather purses."[28]

Billy's cavalier panning of Willy's films out of hand and en masse, apparently on the basis of having seen only one, is both unwarranted and—except for what it says about sibling rivalry—irrelevant. My analysis of Jewish émigré noir directors hinges less on a qualitative evaluation of specific films than on the function of the noir mode as a channel for the unique conflicts generated by the exilic condition. On this score, the work of Willy Wilder—or W. Lee Wilder, the filmmaking sobriquet that Willy took on to avoid confusion with the likes of Billy Wilder, William Wyler, and "Wild Bill" Wellman—is of inordinate interest.[29]

Whether as W. Lee or Willy Wilder, Billy's brother has been almost completely neglected in previous studies of film noir, this despite his having made more noirs than any other director except Lang, Siodmak, and Hitchcock—a total of eight, by my reckoning, and nine if one considers the first film he produced but did not direct, *The Great Flamarion* (1945). Only this film and his third directed one, *The Pretender* (1947), receive any serious mention in the voluminous noir literature, and this largely because the former film stars Erich von Stroheim and was directed by Anthony Mann, and because the latter was filmed by legendary Austrian Jewish cinematographer John Alton. Sikov certainly betrays the pro-Alton bias when he avers that one critic's deeming Willy "one of the more extreme of the noir directors" likely had more to do with Alton than with Willy.[30] And Todd McCarthy elides Willy's contribution entirely in his introduction to the 1995 reprint of Alton's pioneering 1949 book on the art of cinematography, *Painting with Light*: "John Alton pushed film noir to its most exciting visual extremes. . . . no one's blacks were blacker, shadows longer, contrasts stronger, or focus deeper. . . . Alton's [expressionist style] certainly represents the purest visual correlative for fatalistic existentialism yet seen in motion pictures."[31]

Yet, after all, it was under Willy's direction that Alton shot *The Pretender*, which McCarthy considers the "turning point" in Alton's career and noir historian Spencer Selby deems Alton's "first noir."[32] Moreover, not only was *The Great Flamarion* also Anthony Mann's first noir, but Mann, off of Alton's work on *The Pretender*, chose him to shoot both men's second noir, *T-Men* (1948), after which Mann and Alton worked together on three more classical noirs: *Raw Deal* (1948), *Border Incident* (1949), and *He Walked by Night* (1949).[33] Thus even without the eight noirs he himself directed, Willy Wilder's contribution to film noir would be immense. When his own oeuvre is added to the mix, his near total neglect in the critical literature seems inexplicable except as deference to his inarguably more significant younger brother, with whom, as one critic opines, "W. Lee's films aren't fit to share the double bill."[34]

The fact that all Willy's films (including his several science fiction ventures) are B films (or less), made on the fly with shoestring budgets, is certainly no ground for the critical aspersions. Canonical noir director Edgar Ulmer worked almost exclusively, indeed often intentionally, on the B-film plane, and several noir commentators regard film noir as quintessentially, and to its considerable advantage, a B-film mode. One would think that the "B" factor, plus the revisionist inclination to retrieve previously ignored or slighted directors from obscurity, if not to admit them into the auteurist pantheon, would work in Willy's favor. Or is it simply that, as brother Billy gibed, Willy's films are not "even bad, which is worse"? To my mind, quite the contrary: several of Willy's films are of considerable interest both aesthetically and thematically, not only from a Jewish émigré perspective but also in their own right.

As for Willy's auteurist credentials, in terms of property selection and creative control these likely surpassed those of the high-flying Billy—at least through the early 1950s, when Billy remained contractually bound to Paramount Studios—and even those of most B-film directors, including Edgar Ulmer. For starters, Willy not only produced all the films he directed, but also, according to Myles, who wrote many of them (and went on to a substantial television writing career), financed most of them with his own money: "He would put up the collateral . . . he would go to the Bank of America to get swing loans. He would finance these pictures and release them, the early ones, through Republic." Having total creative control, however, didn't always work to the films' advantage: "My father had this heavy-handed way of doing everybody's job. And he wasn't good at everybody's job. And people resented that, particularly the writers." Nor was he that interested in pioneering new cinematic styles. But he did have an artistic bent (he had designed his company's handbags) and, Myles believes, deserves much of the credit (when credit is due) for the look of his films, including the pathbreaking imagery of *The Pretender*: "I remember Alton very well, and Floyd Crosby [*The Snow Creature*, 1954], and he had some Academy Award–winning people—Bill Clothier [*Once a Thief*, 1950; *Phantom from Space*, 1953] was his favorite cinematographer. . . . [But] no one ever told him where to put the camera, never! He would have the cutter in it, maybe, he would have Johnny Link there: 'Left to right, right to left, which way do I want to do this, quick—okay, fine.' He was completely in charge."[35]

The Two Wilders: A Comparative Analysis

Unlike Bill Wilder's long-since canonized oeuvre, Willy Wilder's body of work, noir and otherwise, can scarcely be considered without reference to that of his younger brother. Yet surprisingly, at least from a Jewish émigré noir perspective, Willy's work actually benefits from such a comparison. Beginning with his first film, *The Great Flamarion*, which Willy produced on his own and released through Republic Pictures, the connection to Jewish émigré noir generally and to Billy specifically is unmistakable. *The Great Flamarion*'s adaptation from a short story by the Austrian Jew Vicki Baum front-loads the Jewish émigré aspect, which is further amplified in the narrative when Flamarion's spurning by his true love turns out to be a reprise of his Austrian wife's rejection of him fifteen years before. The direct connection to Billy begins with a distinctive narrative feature *The Great Flamarion* shares with *Double Indemnity*: a Clytemnestra plot, in which a wife conspires with a paramour to murder her husband.[36] In these modern American variations, however, the cannibalistic desires of the black widow trump the moral imperatives of Greek tragedy, with neither *Double Indemnity*'s Phyllis Dietrichson (Barbara Stanwyck) nor *The Great Flamarion*'s Connie Wallace (Mary Beth Hughes) content simply to replace one male consort with another but rather preternaturally disposed to serial husband killing (fig. 22).

The casting of Erich von Stroheim in *The Great Flamarion*, and the type of character he portrays, also strongly intersects with both Billy's work and personal life. It could hardly have been coincidental that Willy would choose as the eponymous star of his first film the same Austrian Jewish actor who had played Rommel in Billy's *Five Graves to Cairo*. An automaton of parodically Teutonic temperament

Figure 22.   Anthony Mann, Eric von Stroheim, Mary Beth Hughes, Dan Duryea, and Willy Wilder on the set of *The Great Flamarion* (1945). (Courtesy of Myles Wilder)

in both films, von Stroheim's Flamarion is a vaudevillian sharpshooter whose stage assistant, Connie, brings out his softer (but also his homicidal) side, getting him to shoot her husband, Al (Dan Duryea), on stage, accidentally on purpose. That the Flamarion is ultimately a failed artiste whose career and love life both literally misfire (Connie shoots him in the end, as he's strangling her) adds a pathetic quality to his character that begs to be read in relation to Jewish émigré noir generally and Willy and Billy's Viennese-twin relationship specifically. The émigré aspect is embedded reflexively in the Hollywood lowbrow associations with the vaudevillian stage on which Flamarion, the foreign artist manqué, plies his penny-ante, sex-and-violence-inspired trade (his act begins with his character's cuckolding and climaxes with his sharpshooting revenge). The interpersonal relation with Billy lies in Flamarion's romantic misalliances (onstage and off-), which, to fully understand, must be supported by additional biographical information.

Billy, as we know, had worked briefly as a taxi dancer, or nightclub gigolo, in his pre-screenwriting days in Berlin. During the last years of his stormy first marriage to Judith Coppicus (the left-leaning American non-Jew whom he had wed in 1936), he either continued, or resumed, his womanizing ways. He boasted in a later interview of having "used" women to help him with his English ("That's the best way to do it"); Raymond Chandler complained of the endless calls from assorted women that Billy received during their tumultuous cowriting of *Double Indemnity*; and Billy managed to juggle two rather high-profile affairs during the shooting of *The Lost Weekend*: one with the film's costar, Doris Dowling, and the other with his future second wife, jazz singer Audrey Young.[37] As for how he conceived of women's roles for his films, Billy brazenly, as was his wont, took the standard misogynist line: they're either virgins or whores.[38]

According to Shirley MacLaine, a close friend of Billy's who played a glorified and then an actual prostitute in two of his non-noirs, *The Apartment* (1960) and *Irma La Duce* (1963), Billy's cinematic treatment of men and women was equally problematic. "He has never worked it out, this conflict between love and money," she averred, pointing to the gigolo-like main characters in *Ninotchka*, *Hold Back the Dawn*, *Sunset Boulevard* (1950), and *The Apartment*. "Imagine having to resort either to a pimp or a whore as representative of men and women."[39] Biographer Maurice Zolotow provides another explanation for Billy's sexual cynicism. Based on information supplied from interviews with Billy, Zolotow concludes that Billy's romantic disillusionment stemmed from a traumatic event he experienced as an eighteen-year-old in Vienna. Fresh out of high school and about to enter the university, Billy fell madly in love with a blond-haired, blue-eyed damsel named Ilse, whom he dreamed of marrying and moving with to the United States—until he discovered that she was a prostitute. The "unhealed wound of Ilse's seeming betrayal," Zolotow maintains, "drove him into making a career as a reporter and confirmed him in his cynical philosophy. He could not trust a woman."[40] Whether one accepts Zolotow's interpretation, which Billy himself protested (perhaps a little too much), one can hardly deny that Billy's post-Ilse existence, and especially his cinematic characterizations, display to an inordinate degree "the dilemma of money/love/lust/money/sex/men/women."[41]

If *The Great Flamarion* is taken partially as Willy's scornful commentary on Billy's ill-fated or sordid romances, it remains a rather generous exercise (especially compared to Willy's subsequent films). Although the Flamarion character is hardly sympathetic in the conventional sense, he is neither morally corrupt nor money hungry. He is merely the prisoner of his erotic desires. As Duryea's Al Wallace, Connie's husband in the film, describes the syndrome: "You're [Connie] a bad habit I can't cure, even if I wanted to. Any guy who wouldn't fall for you is either a sucker, or he's dead." In almost all Willy's other noirs, however—and these are the ones he produced *and* directed—the femme fatale scenario is reversed. Perpetrators rather than victims of the romantic double-cross, the male leads function as *homme fatals*—men who for their own vile and selfish motives lure hapless women to their doom, rather than the other way around.

This definition, it should be noted, differs sharply from the one deployed by Jans B. Wager in *Dames in the Driver's Seat: Reading Film Noir*. Wager's homme fatal, whom she claims "appears in almost every film noir," is a man of "visibly antisocial desires" who "wants more than he should, more money and often a dangerous dame as well," and who functions "much as the typical female archetypes do."[42] Contradicting this presumption, however, is the fact that the key elements of sexual allure, ruthlessness, and treachery—directed toward the male—for which the femme fatale is infamous, are precisely those that are lacking, toward the female, in Wager's homme fatal. To the contrary, Wager's archetypal male figure, as her own prime exhibits demonstrate—Burt Lancaster's Swede in *The Killers*, Robert Mitchum's Jeff Bailey in *Out of the Past*, John Garfield's Frank Chambers in *The Postman Always Rings Twice*, John Dall's Bart Tare in *Gun Crazy*, Sterling Hayden's Johnny Clay in *The Killing*—rather than inherently antagonistic toward the femme fatale, generally remain obsessively drawn to her to the bitter end (often even after recognizing her selfish designs).

The true homme fatal, as I see him, serves as the mirror image (spitting image, if you will) of the femme fatale; and he need not, indeed most often does not, appear in the same film with his gender reflection. Moreover, such a figure, far from appearing in "almost every film noir," is comparatively rare. Yet six of Willy's eight directed noirs—*The Glass Alibi* (1946), *The Pretender* (1947), *Once a Thief* (1950), *Three Steps North* (1951), *The Big Bluff* (1955), and *Bluebeard's Ten Honeymoons* (1960)—contain homme fatals, a clear plurality, by one director, of the total number of classical noirs featuring such figures (eighteen films total, by my estimation, with no other director making more than three). It's as if, similar to Hitchcock, who once his mother died was able to vent his ambivalence toward mother figures in his films, once Willy went from using Billy as a Hollywood stepping-stone to carving his own career niche, his critique of the Billy-type character was given freer, and increasingly obsessive, rein. Even his son Myles, although contending that his father's content decisions were largely commercially motivated, admits that Willy "did like a gigolo . . . kind of character."[43]

"Like" is a telling understatement, and a highly ambiguous one. In fact, it is hard to imagine a more Machiavellian gang of male chauvinist murderers than are found in Willy's noirs. Neither should the unlikelihood of such an unlikable character choice, nor its Jewish émigré noir implications, be underestimated. Of the twelve non–W. Lee Wilder homme fatal noirs, by my reckoning—*Bluebeard* (1944), *Cornered* (1944), *Conflict* (1945), *Strange Illusion* (1945), *Fallen Angel* (1945), *Monsieur Verdoux* (1947), *Ruthless* (1948), *Caught* (1949), *Whirlpool* (1949), *The Thirteenth Letter* (1950), *Sudden Fear* (1952), and *The Blue Gardenia* (1953)—nine are by Jewish émigré directors: three by Ulmer (*Bluebeard, Strange Illusion, Ruthless*); three by Preminger (*Fallen Angel, Whirlpool, The Thirteenth Letter*); and one each by Ophuls (*Caught*), Bernhardt (*Conflict*, from a story by Siodmak), and Lang (*The Blue Gardenia*). Thus it appears that although Willy's sibling rivalry complex may have contributed to his obsession with the homme fatal, the disproportionate leaning toward such a figure among Jewish émigré directors in general points to a group auteurist link as well.

A partial explanation for this collective predilection toward the homme fatal lies in a dialectical relation—psychosexually and politically—with its obverse: the tendency among Jewish émigré directors toward sympathetic *female* protagonists or *weak or effeminate* male leads. Psychosexually, the virile male who preys on women has obvious Oedipal implications, complicated in Jewish men by their historical identification with women; politically, the powerful patriarchal figure who exploits or destroys those deemed weak or inferior would also have had, for left-leaning Jewish refugees especially, clear associations with the depredations of Nazism and the inequities of American capitalism.[44] With problematic ties both to sexual and national identity, the homme fatal was thus fraught with an ambivalence uniquely attuned to, and compounded by, the Jewish émigré experience.

W. Lee Wilder: A Case Study

The Glass Alibi was the first film Willy directed, and it shows. Although it boasts solid performances from noted character actors Paul Kelly, as the police captain, and Douglas Fowley, as the black widower protagonist, it suffers otherwise from overacting, underexposed lighting, slapdash plotting, and frenetic pacing unsuited to the putatively suspenseful subject matter. Some of these flaws can be written off to the exigencies of a B-movie budget and crew, but given the aesthetic leap of Willy's subsequent work under similarly strapped conditions, lack of experience must be held at least partly accountable. That Willy himself regarded his initial directorial effort as unworthy of the material is partly indicated by his remaking the film less than a decade later as *The Big Bluff* (aka

Worthy Deceivers).[45] Although the later film slightly alters the original film's characters and situations, the basic story line remains the same: A slimy gold digger
seduces and marries a wealthy heiress with a terminal heart ailment and only
a short time to live. When the romantically revitalized heiress's condition not
only doesn't worsen but actually improves—despite the gold digger's replacing
her heart pills with a placebo—he gets desperate and concocts a convoluted
murder scheme. After planting fingerprint evidence of an ostensible meeting
with his girlfriend/partner-in-crime in a hotel room some distance away, he
sneaks into the heiress's mansion and shoots her while she's apparently asleep
in bed, then reappears at the scene some time later. Of course, the scheme
backfires. First, it turns out that the heiress had died from heart failure before
she was shot, seemingly absolving the gold digger of murder even if his alibi
doesn't hold. But when his girlfriend is murdered the same night by another
of her shady boyfriends, the evidence the gold digger had planted to clear him
leads to his arrest for a murder he didn't commit (fig. 23).

The other four of Willy's homme fatal noirs also fit, if somewhat more
broadly, into pairs. *Once a Thief* and *Bluebeard's Ten Honeymoons* both feature serial
"Spider Men"; *Three Steps North*'s and *The Pretender*'s "Evil Tempters," conversely,
are the least lethal of the bunch.

Figure 23. Homme fatal and prey: John Broomfield and Martha Vickers in *The Big
Bluff* (1955). (USC Special Collections)

Once a Thief and Bluebeard's Ten Honeymoons

In *Once a Thief*, suave con man Mitch Moore (Cesar Romero) uses a laundry business as a front for a bookmaking ring and his Latin lover charm as the key to women's purses. Once he has sucked one woman dry, romantically and financially—one victim, that we see, is driven to suicide—he moves on to the next. In Margie Foster (June Havoc), however, Mitch meets his match. Basically a sweet young gal who, from poverty and another woman's bad influence, turned to a life of high-end shoplifting, Margie tries to go straight, and appears to be succeeding, until a chance meeting with Mitch derails her again. Madly in love to the point of reverting to thievery to help Mitch out of a jam, she ends up in jail for her crimes (past and present). But when she learns that her arrest was Mitch's doing, to clear the way to her roommate, Marjorie breaks out of jail, fools Mitch into thinking she still loves him, then pulls a gun—which she can't bring herself to use because, as she tells him, "You're not worth shooting." When he grabs for the gun to shoot her, an ensuing struggle causes the gun to go off, killing Mitch.

At least this is the story Margie tells the police after turning herself in—a story whose rendering in flashback supplies the film's main narrative and which, with no alternative version to challenge it, we are forced to accept as true. Margie thus emerges as one of the most complex and sympathetic of the female noir protagonists, toward which Jewish émigré directors seemed inordinately inclined. Neither goody-two-shoes nor pathetic victim, she is able to straddle the worlds of crime and respectability and emerge morally, if not legally, unscathed (fig. 24).

The second of Willy's serial homme fatal films, *Bluebeard's Ten Honeymoons,* is one of several cinematic renderings of the actual life and deaths of the Parisian Henri-Desire Landru, including Edgar Ulmer's *Bluebeard*, to be discussed later.[46] A down-on-his-luck secondhand furniture dealer and father of four, Landru, between 1914 and 1918, murdered ten women (and a teenage son of one of the women), most of whom were lured into marriage via newspaper ads and then cut up and burned in an oven in Landru's country villa. The epicene George Sanders plays Landru here, minus the four children (and teenage son), but with the same spousal body count, modus operandi, and ultimate capture and guillotining through the efforts of one of the victims' sister.

One of the fictional noir twists to this true-life Grand Guignol is the character of Odette (Corinne Calved). A chorine of ill repute, Odette, together with her *La Chienne*–like pimp/lover Pepi (Sheldon Lawrence), prompts Landru into committing his grisly crimes. Not that Odette and Pepi mastermind the murders, or are even aware that Landru is committing them, but Landru's erotic obsession with Odette ignites their plan to seduce him into lavishing her with expensive clothing and jewelry. His upper-crust appearance is only a pose, of course, and after one heiress killing succeeds, only momentarily, in satisfying

Figure 24. Not ready for her close-up: June Havoc in *Once a Thief* (1950). (USC Special Collections)

Odette's material needs, the homicidal practice becomes a necessary means of meeting Odette's insatiable demands. When Landru proposes marriage after the first four murders, for example, Odette replies, "You can't afford me yet." But six honeymoons and murders later, when he spies Odette in Pepi's arms, she becomes, sans honeymoon, his final victim. Thus, besides adding one of the more loathsome homme fatals to Willy's already exceptional collection, *Bluebeard's Ten Honeymoons* provides perhaps an even greater rarity: an homme fatal and a femme fatale, operating separately but to similarly insidious ends, in the same film. Also, unlike the usual distribution of evil in film noir, where, as in *Double Indemnity*, both sexes "are rotten" but the female of the species is "a little more rotten," in *Bluebeard's Ten Honeymoons* the rottenness ratio is reversed.

Landru's first victim's sister, meanwhile, whose relentless investigation leads to Landru's demise, joins *Once a Thief*'s Margie Foster on another of Willy's uncommon—for film noir generally, though not for Jewish émigré noir—character lists: that of the active and independent, but also decent and sympathetic, woman who defies and ultimately triumphs over the male villain. Other characters in Willy's noirs who fit this description are Marcia Jordan (Eve Miller), the heiress's best friend in *The Big Bluff*, and Elena (Lea Padovani) in *Three Steps North*. Marcia is not only the first person in the film to suspect the venal motives of the seductive con man, Ricardo de Villa (John Broomfield); she also sticks to her guns despite the contrary opinions of all those around her, including the heiress's physician, Dr. Kirk (Robert Hutton). Elena, an Italian woman initially abandoned by the American homme fatal, Frank Kieler (Lloyd Bridges), combines traits of the femme fatale and the good woman in one of Willy's most stylish and intriguing noirs.

Three Steps North and *The Pretender*

Three Steps North opens with an extraordinarily striking image: From the bottom of the pitch-black frame, after a few seconds of silence, first the sound of a motor is heard, and next the (as yet unidentifiable) hood of a transport truck appears. Looming from the dark depths like a resurrected sea monster, the truck grows to fill the screen, then gradually disappears as it exits out the top, returning the frame to darkness. This stunning below-road-level shot, with its figurative rising action (perhaps partly attributable to Italian cinematographer Aldo Giordani), both establishes the film's forbidding mood and encapsulates its theme of degradation and redemption. The truck, as subsequent shots and its driver Frank Kieler's voice-over reveal, is a U.S. Army vehicle transporting military supplies between Salerno and Naples during World War II. Kieler's main aim, however, is to sell some of the stuff on the black market for his own personal profit. And although he eventually gets caught and is sent to a U.S. brig for four years, he first had managed to bury his ill-gotten gains—three steps north of a tree in the Italian countryside. The bulk of the film concerns Kieler's postwar return to Italy to retrieve his buried loot.

Kieler's venal, illegal, and highly unpatriotic behavior, disturbing at any time for an American soldier protagonist, would have been all the more so in the early 1950s with the nation having launched the Marshall Plan in Europe, embroiled in the Red Scare and McCarthyist witch hunt at home, and with its troops newly engaged with communist forces on the Korean peninsula. And here again, as with *The Great Flamarion* and *Double Indemnity*, Willy's work intersects with Billy's at the same juncture. The amoral Frank Kieler is a close relative of the ethically challenged main characters in several of Billy's films—Joe Gillis in *Sunset Boulevard*, Chuck Tatum in *Ace in the Hole* (1951), and Sefton in *Stalag 17* (1953)—all of whom, last-minute comeuppances notwithstanding, dismantle exceptionalist notions of the United States and its citizens as morally superior.[47]

Going Billy's "anti-U.S." films one better, in *Three Steps North* even the comeuppances are at the expense of the United States (or its allegorical representative). Kieler's quest, as any (anti)hero's must be, is fraught with obstacles: some coincidental, some triggered by criminal elements who vie with Kieler (and among themselves) for the booty, and some by the police who suspect Kieler of a murder related to the underworld rivalry. The (bitterly ironic) coincidence is that a military cemetery now adjoins the spot where Kieler buried the money, and that a memorial chapel is being constructed adjacent to the cemetery. An added intertextual irony extends both to the casting of Pedro, the cemetery caretaker supervising the chapel's construction, and to the film's overall style. Pedro is played by Aldo Fabrizi, an Italian actor most noted, internationally, for his role as an anti-Nazi resistance priest who is tortured to death in Roberto Rossellini's seminal neorealist film *Open City* (*Roma, città aperta*, 1945). Pedro the caretaker serves as the conscience of *Three Steps North* as well, only this time he lives to deliver the moral. When Kieler finally unearths the box that once contained his four million lire, it's empty. Pedro had come on the stash during the construction of the cemetery and used the money to build the chapel. Kieler is thus redeemed in spite of himself, and an additional grace note is supplied by Elena. The "tough gal" that Kieler left behind when he was sent to prison, who appeared to be "sleeping with the enemy" at the outset, helps him retrieve his "loot" and appears destined to fill an empty spot in his heart as well.

As with the casting of Fabrizi, the stylistics of *Three Steps North* trade on neorealist principles—real locations, some nonprofessional actors, a gritty documentary look—that alternate with expressionist flourishes. Although this combination may again reflect the influence of the Italian setting and film crew, informed additionally by the experimental work of Rossellini at the time, the combining of neorealist and expressionist elements also coincides with an overall tendency in late-1940s/early-1950s noir toward a syncretism of these ostensibly diametrically opposed styles—a tendency uncannily consonant, as we've seen, with Weimar cinema's transition, more than two decades earlier, from Expressionism to New Objectivity.[48] Once again, though unsurprisingly, much of Billy's work at the time, notably in *Ace in the Hole* and especially in *Sunset Boulevard*, likewise exemplifies the expressionist/neorealist salmagundi.

In *Ace in the Hole* (aka *The Big Carnival*), a documentary-like treatment, in keeping with the reporter protagonist, clashes with a media circus and an actual carnival that was built to exploit the rescue of an Indian-artifact robber trapped in a cave. In *Sunset Boulevard*, the pointedly realistic locations (Schwab's Drug Store, the Paramount Studios lot, Sunset Boulevard itself) and casting (Paramount newsreel crews; celebrities Cecil B. DeMille, Hedda Hopper, and Buster Keaton; not to mention the *film à clef* representations of Gloria Swanson and Erich von Stroheim as a former silent movie queen and director) oscillate and intermingle with the surreal movie-star mansion and the star's demented state of mind, in which "the dream she had clung to so desperately" finally enfolds her (fig. 25). In *Three Steps North* the stylistic hybridization is exhibited in the juggling of the uncanny truck opening, overall low-key lighting, and sporadically symbolic mise-en-scène (barred shadows, cross patterns, a fragmented mirror on the wall of Elena's apartment) with everyday Amalfi street life that serves not only as backdrop for the action but occasionally takes center stage.

The Pretender is the only W. Lee Wilder film listed in Alain Silver and Elizabeth Ward's far from exhaustive yet widely referenced encyclopedia of film noir.[49] The inclusion is undoubtedly partly due to its being Willy's most

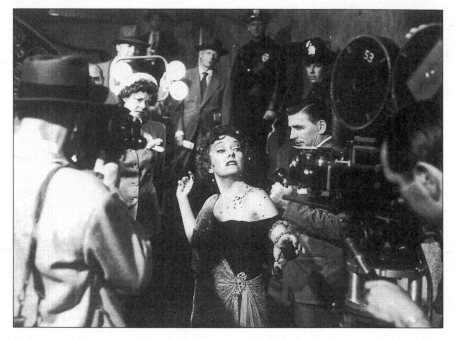

Figure 25.   Expressionist/neorealist salmagundi: Gloria Swanson in *Sunset Boulevard* (1950). (USC Special Collections)

distinguished noir visually, thanks to the contribution of John Alton. More than any other of Willy's films, or any of Billy's for that matter, *The Pretender* is awash in expressionist motifs, several of which self-consciously evoke the Weimar masters. Noir's standard-edition doubles/splits motifs, cross and striped patterns, and prison-bar shadows are joined here by deep focus and forced perspective indebted, most immediately, to *Citizen Kane* but, like Welles and Toland's work, even more redolent of *The Last Laugh, Variety,* and *Sunrise* (fig. 26).

Several subjective move-ins to the ambivalent protagonist Kenneth Holden's (Albert Dekker's) face isolated by spotlight in a sea of darkness are direct quotes from Lang's *Dr. Mabuse* series (perhaps also channeled through Ulmer's *Detour*). Given that neither Alton nor Willy had experienced the Weimar period firsthand, Jewish émigré filmmakers seem once again, per Elsaesser, to have "remembered" the German lighting style rather than to have brought it with them from Germany. Even Billy, whose Weimar and early American work consisted mainly of musicals and comedies, and whose first directed film, *Mauvais Graine,* was more proto–New Wave than noir, appears to have come, even more than Siodmak, to expressionism belatedly and through the backdoor.[50] Again, however, as with Siodmak's poetic realist trajectory, this delayed attraction to, or at least application of, expressionist aesthetics further supports the Jewish émigré thesis.

Figure 26. Jailed by the mise-en-scène: Albert Dekker and Linda Stirling in *The Pretender* (1947). (USC Special Collections)

The conditions of exile, and specifically Willy and Billy's relation to the Holocaust, although certainly not the sole cause for their delayed embrace of film noir, cannot be discounted as a factor propelling them to work in a darker cinematic mode at this particular historical moment. Their mother had remarried after their father's death in 1928, and had remained with their grandmother in Austria during the 1930s, even after the *Anschluss* (Germany's annexation of Austria) in 1938. Billy had detoured from France to Vienna to visit Genia before coming to the United States, and his failure to convince her to leave Europe would prove "one of the most painful experiences of his life."[51] Willy must have shared in the pain, and guilt, when knowledge of the death camps filtered through to the émigré community after 1942, and even more devastatingly when neither Genia nor her mother's whereabouts or status could be determined after the war; it was later confirmed that both had perished at Auschwitz.[52]

From this post-Holocaust perspective, the punishment of the "tough guy" protagonists in Billy's noirs (Walter Neff in *Double Indemnity*, Joe Gillis in *Sunset Boulevard*, Chuck Tatum in *Ace in the Hole*) can be seen as partial penance for Billy's not having done more to save his mother from extermination. By the same token, Willy's phalanx of homme fatals, who exploit and ultimately cast aside their often wealthy wives, can be taken not only as displacements for his conflicted feelings toward a gigolo-like younger brother whose first wife came with a father who headed Columbia Artists agency. These despicable characters, and the just desserts they receive, might additionally have served to exorcise Willy's own guilt over his sin of omission in regard to his mother's tragic demise.[53]

Added to the anguish over the deaths of their nearest and dearest were the profoundly mixed emotions the Wilder brothers, along with their Jewish refugee brethren, felt toward the former homeland in the war's aftermath. Lang, for example, upon his return to Germany in the 1950s, found that the "true tragedy" of the exiled individual lay in the realization that "when he then returns, he is a stranger in his own home."[54] Billy, upon a postwar tour of Germany sponsored by the Office of War Information (for which he was slated to supervise the German film industry), experienced a similar confusion: "We wondered where we should go now that the war was over. None of us—I mean the émigrés—really knew where we stood. Should we go home? Where was home?"[55]

Frank Kieler, conversely, and contrary to his initial mercenary motive, seems on the verge of finding a new home away from home at the end of *Three Steps North*. None of Willy's other homme fatals, least of all *The Pretender*'s Kenneth Holden, is so fortunate. Like the gold diggers in *The Glass Alibi* and *The Big Bluff*, Holden, a corrupt financial adviser, marries a wealthy heiress for purely pecuniary reasons—in this case, to cover up his previous embezzlement from her estate. The murder plot is aimed not at the heiress, however, but at the fiancé who stands in the way of his marital scheme. The plan backfires only partly from unforeseen happenstance: Holden's fear that he has become the target of the hit man he hired to kill the fiancé (who bowed out on his own, allowing Holden to replace him) grows into pathological paranoia shortly after the marriage. Imprisoning himself in a dark room in his newly acquired mansion, subsisting on meager rations and barely speaking with his wife, he eventually bolts from the house and speeds away when he thinks he's being watched and followed, crashing to his death beneath a broken bridge. The kicker is that the hit man was indeed after Holden, but only to return the money he had been given for the (now superfluous) murder of the fiancé.

A Foreign Affair, Vicious Circle, and *Fright*

If Willy's homme fatals can be taken, at some level, as exaggerated versions of Billy, this manifestation of sibling revenge was itself superfluous; the male characters in Billy's noirs—ambivalent at best, despicable at worst—already invite autobiographical associations. The cantankerous claims manager Barton Keyes (Edward G. Robinson) in *Double Indemnity* seems a dead ringer, looks and personality-wise, for the unprepossessing, "aggressive and prickly" Billy.[56] And Keyes's working relationship with his conspicuously goy subordinate, Walter Neff (Fred MacMurray), in its amalgam of the affectionate and the adversarial, bears more than passing resemblance to the film's volatile yet creatively fruitful screenwriting collaboration between Billy and Raymond Chandler. The protagonists of Billy's other two noirs are even more akin to him occupationally, and less flattering as characters. *Sunset Boulevard's* Joe Gillis (William Holden) is a frustrated Hollywood screenwriter who, similar to Billy in his salad days, sacrifices professional and ethical standards to become a ghostwriter and gigolo to a wealthy, much older woman. *Ace in the Hole's* Chuck Tatum (Kirk Douglas), an exiled (from New York to Albuquerque) newspaper reporter who craves chopped liver and garlic pickles, may be more ruthless than Billy was as a scribe in Berlin and Vienna, but neither did Billy always have the most spotless journalistic reputations. Dubbed a *Schlieferl* (bootlicker) by his colleagues, Billy also apparently was engaged in illegal activities for one of his papers, *Die Stunde*, which extorted advertising from businesses in exchange for favorable, or lack of unfavorable, publicity.[57]

Even Captain John Pringle (John Lund), the lead of his 1948 quasi-screwball comedy *A Foreign Affair* (as dark a film visually as any in Billy's oeuvre), can be read in autobiographical terms. Although neither Pringle's all-American good looks nor his army officer's position lend credence to such a reading, his ambivalent relations to war-ravaged Germany certainly do. Pringle is the fulcrum in a bizarre love triangle whose other two sides belong to a prominent Nazi's wife–turned–nightclub singer, Erika von Schluetow (Marlene Dietrich), and an Iowa congresswoman, Phoebe Frost (Jean Arthur), sent to Berlin to investigate the status of the postwar occupation. But like Billy's own transnational conflict, the triangular tensions are never fully resolved in this ultimately incoherent, yet personally revealing, film. Although Lund eventually chooses the "good woman," of course, this motivationally tenuous turnaround occurs only after the parodically Teutonic midwesterner (all blond-bun stiffness and by-the-book decorum) is taught to let her hair down by the Americanized blue angel, whom Pringle had alternately made love to and (emotionally and physically) abused. "Should we go home? Where was home?" resounds long after the end credits roll.

Willy's most direct filmic reference to the circumstances surrounding the war was made around the same time as *A Foreign Affair*. His *Vicious Circle* (aka *The Woman in Brown*, 1948), although set in nineteenth-century Hungary, is about a timeless but then uncommonly topical issue: anti-Semitism. Based on a play, and more period courtroom drama than noir, the film features former American silent star Conrad Nagel and noted Weimar Jewish actors Fritz Kortner and Reinhold Schünzel. The entire action takes place on a single courtroom set and consists of the trial of five Jewish farmers (Kortner plays one of these) falsely accused of murder by a local baron (Schünzel) whose motive is to gain control of the Jews' land, on which oil has just been discovered. Adding to the moral corruption, and the Jews' predicament, the district attorney is in league with the baron. Nagel plays the stouthearted defense attorney. By most accounts a flawed production despite the big names, the film's theme must have been not only personally poignant for Willy but also highly pertinent to contemporary audiences (however meager they may have been).[58] Given developing and subsequent events in the Middle East, this historical allegory of Jews threatened with expulsion from their oil-rich land has turned into gallows humor of the most diabolical sort.

Fright (aka *Spell of the Hypnotist*, 1956) is in some ways Willy's most personal film. Inspired by the Bridey Murphy reincarnation craze of the time (Murphy being the eighteenth-century Belfast barrister's wife "revealed" to a Colorado woman through hypnotic regression), the film beings with a psychiatrist, Dr. James Hamilton (Eric Fleming), using long-distance hypnosis, transmitted by megaphone, to prevent (yet another) serial killer from jumping to his death from the Brooklyn Bridge. A young woman, Ann Summers (Nancy Malone), who observed the bizarre incident, is drawn to seek Hamilton's help in dealing with her own highly suggestible state. In her subsequent treatment, Hamilton learns that the twenty-five-year-old Ann has a split personality, her "other self" belonging to an eighteen-year-old Viennese baroness named Maria Vetsera—she of the famed double suicide committed with her lover, the Austrian Crown Prince Rudolph, at Mayerling in 1889. Ann's alternative identity resulted from her having been raised, after her mother's death when she was four, by a beloved Austrian nurse who, upon the exposure of her affair with the father, was mercilessly cast from the house. Ann is cured when Hamilton hypnotizes the serial killer, in his jail cell, into thinking he's Crown Prince Rudolph, and gets him to shoot Ann, with blanks, in her Maria state. When Ann awakes from her phantom death, "Maria" has been vanquished as well. Hamilton ties things up by explaining that only a pathological killer could have played the Rudolph role because a normal person would not have pulled the trigger, even under hypnosis.

Whether *Fright* managed to scare off Willy's sibling rivalry and Oedipal guilt complexes is open to question, given that *Bluebeard's Ten Honeymoons* was still to come. A more viable diagnosis is that, as in Freud's *fort-da* game (in which a child allays anxiety over the mother's absence by casting out and pulling back a ball on a string), Willy's obsession with homme fatals and imperiled yet frequently triumphant women served momentarily to contain, though never to vanquish, his inner demons. These demons were, after all, an integral part of his being, and of the film noir mode to which he devoted the better part of his filmmaking career.

8   *The ABZs of Film Noir*

OTTO PREMINGER AND EDGAR G. ULMER

Though not blood-related, Otto Preminger and Edgar Ulmer constitute a Viennese-twin grouping of their own. Here the kinship, and contrast, relates not to psychological conflict between the two Vienna-bred directors but rather to the divergent production modes within which most of their work can be subsumed. All of Preminger's film noirs, like most of Lang's and Siodmak's and all of Billy Wilder's, were made within the comparatively privileged A-film category; the majority of Ulmer's, like Willy Wilder's, fit into the more marginal B-film type. The alphabetic differences are more than nominal, having strictly governed budget levels during the classical studio era and therefore substantially affecting talent choices, technical resources, and production schedules, not to mention distribution and exhibition strategies in promotion and theater billing. B-feature budgets, among the eight major Hollywood studios, were generally one-fourth to one-half of even A-programmers, and sometimes as little as one-twentieth of so-called superspecials.[1]

At Poverty Row companies limited exclusively to B pictures, such as Producers Releasing Corporation (PRC) where Ulmer spent much of his time, budgets were even more minuscule and production conditions often strayed "beyond the pale of the B's into the seventh circle of the Z's."[2] These monetary and material deprivations, however, should not be regarded, as they tended to be with the Wilder brothers, as a straightforward determinant of quality. Although Preminger's films made the most of their big-budget advantages, they also bore the burden of classical Hollywood's autocratic controls and aesthetic constraints. Conversely, what Ulmer's cheapies may have lacked (for the most part) in star power and production values were frequently compensated for in the greater creative freedom that working in the cinematic backwaters provided.

The upper- and lower-class niches associated with Preminger and Ulmer's films, while not preordained, seem to have suited the two men's similarly divergent backgrounds, personalities, and artistic aspirations. Preminger was more to the manor born (although not to the extent that he describes in his memoirs); and his creative instincts, like his aristocratic bearing and lifestyle, leaned toward the "tradition of quality" and the "well-made" cultural artifact.[3] Ulmer, who grew up under less privileged, at times even penurious circumstances, veered toward the bohemian in lifestyle and the experimental in his stage and film work. Yet once in Hollywood, both men, like most of the émigré filmmakers, had to not only prove themselves anew but also adapt their talents and proclivities to the exigencies of the American system. Adding uniquely, and ironically, to Preminger's and Ulmer's challenges, both directors, after some early American successes, faced occupational exile from mainstream Hollywood altogether. Preminger would claw his way back into the industry's good graces and rise to A-film stature and considerable prominence. Ulmer would stage a comeback as well, but—partly from choice, partly from circumstance—would work, with a few significant exceptions, in the B-to-Z rung for the rest of his career.[4]

Jewishness also figures uniquely in both directors' lives and careers. Preminger's lawyer father, who had risen rapidly in the Austro-Hungarian Empire's juridical ranks during World War I, was appointed state prosecutor (the equivalent of U.S. attorney general) at war's end—an unprecedented honor. No Jew, especially one who refused the pro forma demand to convert, had ever been granted such a high government post. His son's ascent in the theater world was similarly propitious. In 1923, the seventeen-year-old Preminger landed an apprenticeship at the prestigious Theater in der Josefstadt that Max Reinhardt was reviving (and Ulmer had helped redesign) in Vienna. By 1926 he was already appearing in starring roles in German-speaking regional theater; by 1927 he was directing; in 1928 and 1929 he opened his own theater companies in Vienna; in 1930 he was back with Reinhardt as a director; and in 1931 the twenty-five-year-old wunderkind replaced the maestro as manager of the Josefstadt. Uncannily mirroring his father's meteoric rise, Preminger was next offered the highest position to which any Austrian impresario could aspire: the director-managership of the Burgtheater, the Austrian state theater. And like his father, the offer was contingent on conversion to Catholicism, and like his father, Preminger refused—unlike his father, Preminger was denied the post.[5]

Preminger's unparalleled success and shocking setback compare (and contrast) tellingly, in regard to class and ethnicity, with the other three Viennese émigré directors discussed so far. Like Billy and Willy Wilder, Preminger was born not in Vienna but in Galicia, and his family, like theirs, only moved to Vienna at the start of World War I. By this point, however, the Preminger family had attained solid middle-class (soon to be upper-middle-class) status; they could, with only slight qualification until the rise of Nazism, regard themselves as fully Austrian. The Wilders, in Vienna as in Galicia, never rose above the lower middle class and were denied the basic privileges of Austrian citizenship in no uncertain terms. As for Lang, Preminger's and his father's firsthand experience of anti-Semitism, and their proud and stubborn assertion of their Jewishness in the face of it, contrasts sharply with Lang's complex yet persistent Jewish self-denial. Thus while Preminger, like the other three Austro-Jewish directors, was raised neither in a religious nor an observant Jewish household, the dialectics of Jewishness and Austrianness clearly played a prominent role in his identity formation.

Edgar Ulmer's convoluted relationship to his Jewishness is rivaled, among the émigré noir directors, only by Lang. Although Ulmer was born, like Preminger and the Wilders, in eastern Europe—Olomouc, Moravia, to be exact (then part of the Habsburg empire, now in the Czech Republic)—he was raised from infancy in Vienna.[6] Given his staunchly secular upbringing, he claims not even to have been cognizant of his Jewish heritage until, upon admittance to a Jesuit secondary school as an exceptional student, he learned of the "Numerus Clauses"—the 4 percent quota on Jewish enrollment.[7] His Jewish identity was literally imprinted on him shortly after the war when, after his father's death on the battlefield, he was sent to a home for war orphans in Uppsala, Sweden, where he was made to wear a Jewish star on his clothing. Although the marker was intended to identify the wearer as a needy child, not as a sign of Jew hatred, its negative associations could hardly have failed to rub off on a sensitive fourteen-year-old who had almost been barred from school due to his Jewishness and, consciously Jewish or not, had been raised in a city notorious for its openly anti-Jewish climate.[8]

Ulmer would largely be spared the effects of Austrian anti-Semitism upon his return to Vienna in 1920. This was partly because, with the fall of the empire and the rise of the Austrian Social Democratic Party, overt anti-Semitism briefly, if precariously subsided; the main reason, however, was that Ulmer did not remain in Vienna for any extended period of time.[9] Upon joining Max Reinhardt's theater academy in Vienna as an actor and art director in training, he traveled back and forth between Vienna and Berlin. More significant, for our purposes, he also began, as was the wont in Austro-German cultural circles, to move freely between the theater and film media.[10] In film this entailed, according to Ulmer, set construction (uncredited) on the cream of early Weimar cinema, including *The Cabinet of Dr. Caligari*, *The Golem*, and *Die Nibelungen*.[11] In theater it meant, still as a teenager, traveling with Reinhardt to New York and Los Angeles for the 1923 touring production of *The Miracle*.

Adding intercontinental travel to his intermedial meanderings, Ulmer, for the remainder of the decade, would divide time between Hollywood and Berlin, and between low-budget and more prestigious film productions. In Hollywood, he was hired as an art director by Universal, then a second-tier studio, and even directed a few B westerns for the company. In Berlin he did production design at UFA on F. W. Murnau's classic art films *The Last Laugh* (1924) and *Faust* (1926), then rejoined Murnau in the United States for work on his American expressionist masterpiece, *Sunrise* (1927).[12] It was during this last American interlude that Ulmer also married his first wife, Josephine, an American Episcopalian. Most remarkable, for the future director of landmark Yiddish-language films, Ulmer himself converted to Episcopalianism soon thereafter—not in Germany, where he had returned with Josephine in 1928 to work on *Menschen am Sonntag*, but rather in the United States, where, sensing the coming Nazi storm, he finally decided to settle in 1929.[13] Refugee status trumped conversion, however, and Ulmer was not only drawn into Salka Viertel's Los Angeles émigré circle but would become one of the closest of the exiled directors to Viertel herself, who would cowrite one of his later films and give acting lessons to the daughter from his second marriage, Arianné.[14]

Ironically, Ulmer's subsequent banishment from Hollywood would facilitate his return to his Jewish roots. Seemingly an up-and-comer following the success of his first significant directorial effort, the Universal horror feature *The Black Cat* (1934), Ulmer would be "blackballed not for politics but for love" when he became romantically involved with a Jewish script supervisor, Shirley Kassler Alexander.[15] Ulmer was by then divorced from Josephine, but Shirley was still married to Max Alexander, a nephew of Universal chieftain Carl Laemmle. By the time Shirley was granted a divorce and married a reconverted Ulmer in a Jewish ceremony in New York in 1935, a pall had been cast over his mainstream film career.

Hollywood's loss, however, was Yiddish cinema's gain. Together with director Joseph Green, Ulmer would instigate a "golden age" of Yiddish-language talkies with four films: *Grine Felder* (*Green Fields*, 1937), *Yankl der Shmid* (*The Singing Blacksmith*, 1938), *Di Klyatshe* (*Fishke the Cripple*, 1939), and *Americaner Shadkn* (*American Matchmaker*, 1940). As J. Hoberman, and I myself, have shown, these films deftly reflected both the darkening Jewish political and cultural attitudes of the time and Ulmer's own growing affinity for a darkly expressive cinematic style.[16] By the time he reemerged in Hollywood in 1941, albeit now along its Poverty Row fringes, Ulmer had established the schizoid modus operandi—A-film expressionist technique stuffed into Z-film production straitjackets—that would both become his trademark and serve him well at nightmare factories (both in their favored genres and working conditions) like PRC.

Although his adoption of an expressionist style this late in the game might again seem to provide support for Elsaesser's claim that émigré directors' "suddenly remembered the lighting style of Murnau, Pabst, and Dupont," Ulmer's career trajectory explodes such a notion.[17] He, like Lang, had actively participated in the style's development; it was part of his cinematic DNA. Preminger, on the other hand, provides a stiffer test for Elsaesser's "interference" theory. Alone among the Jewish émigré noir directors, Preminger had had no direct contact with German cinema, from a production standpoint, prior to his exodus to the United States in 1935. Other than for a brief stretch as a touring actor in German regional theater, he had worked exclusively in Vienna, and, except for one film, *Die Grosse Liebe* (*The Great Love*, 1931), had directed exclusively for the stage.

As biographer Foster Hirsch describes, Preminger, during this period, "knew nothing of the technique of filmmaking and, moreover, didn't have the same passion for the medium as he had for the theater. The plays of Shakespeare and Shaw meant far more to him than the silent film of F. W. Murnau, Ernst Lubitsch, or Fritz Lang."[18] As the impresario of a major Viennese theater in the postwar era, however, and as an acolyte of Reinhardt's, Preminger certainly would have been well versed in, even if personally averse toward, Expressionist aesthetics. And although it is interesting in this regard that his film noirs are often cited for their somewhat muted mise-en-scène compared to other noir directors, the very fact that he came to work in a darker palette at all, and that this shift occurred at the onset of the noir cycle, indicates that something beyond a "remembrance of styles past" is at issue here. A likely additional factor, for the principled Preminger as well as for the newly self-conscious Ulmer, was a remembrance of *Jewishness* past, a recollection whose reverberations from the 1930s on were waxed in black.

Rogue Cops and Fallen Angels

Preminger's blackballing from Hollywood was a matter neither of politics nor love, but rather of temperament—both his and that of Twentieth Century Fox chief Darryl Zanuck. Hired by Zanuck off his European theater reputation, Preminger left an increasingly Nazi-leaning Vienna in 1935 and began working for Fox in 1936. Given his inexperience in film directing, he was initially assigned B projects, from which he was expected to, and quickly did, work his way up to the As—and, for a time, into Zanuck's good graces. On his first A picture, however, Preminger's notorious temper, until then kept under wraps, clashed with Zanuck's legendary iron will, leading to Preminger's banishment not only from Fox but from the Hollywood film industry altogether. The cinematic diaspora lasted until 1942 when, after Preminger's considerable successes, as director and actor, on the New York stage, and with Zanuck off helping the war effort, Preminger was hired by interim Fox chief William Goetz first to reprise his signature Nazi stage role on-screen, and then to direct.[19] Finally, in an apparent studio power play, Goetz offered Preminger a seven-year contract in 1943 that included not only directing but—astoundingly, given his recent ostracism—producing rights as well.[20] And it was during this stretch of comparative creative freedom, which included significant involvement with screenwriting, casting, and crew selection, that the bulk of Preminger's film noirs were made.[21]

Several of these films contain elements that encourage analysis from a Jewish or an autobiographical perspective. Starting with *Laura* (1944) and the effeminate critic (and murderer) Waldo Lydecker (Clifton Webb), who writes "with a quill dipped in venom," Jewish connotations emerge that, for Jewish émigré directors, seem almost de rigueur. A twist on the weakling figure in this film, however, is Lydecker's contrast from, yet also doubling with, the tough-guy cop, Mark McPherson (Dana Andrews). Both the she-man antagonist and the he-man protagonist have perverse attractions to the eponymous Laura (Gene Tierney): Lydecker's love interest is largely proprietary (if I can't have her, nobody will), which is why he tried to kill her (but mistakenly killed another woman); McPherson's desire is necrophilic, because he thinks Laura *was* murdered yet (as Lydecker points out) he is in love with her corpse. The two men's transgendered relationship is underscored by a narrational strategy: Lydecker (Lie-decker) supplies the opening voice-over, and thus the governing point of view; McPherson (Mc-fear-son) plays the "good guy" who gets the resurrected Laura in the end, but only after being "softened up" by her painted portrait and confronting his own shadow (and feminine) side (fig. 27). Although the autobiographical aspect will loom larger in subsequent films, Preminger himself possessed opposing character traits: priding himself, on the one hand, as an artist and aesthete; notorious, on the other hand, for a violent temper and physical attacks on men by whom he felt insulted.[22]

Whirlpool (1949) revolves around two other Jewish émigré standbys: the female protagonist, Ann Sutton (Gene Tierney again); and the psychiatrist, of which there are two in the film, one benevolent—Dr. William Sutton (Richard Conte)—and the other malevolent—David Korvo (Jose Ferrer)—each portrayed by an ethnically ambiguous actor. The sexually repressed Ann, married to the upstanding if somewhat insipid Dr. Sutton, is irrepressibly drawn to the seductive quack Korvo after he intercedes on her behalf to prevent her arrest for shoplifting at a high-end department store. Aware that Ann is a closet kleptomaniac desperately trying to keep this dark secret from her loving husband, Korvo lures her—partly through his homme fatal charms, partly through the promise of a cure—into submitting to hypnotherapy sessions that accurately diagnose the

Figure 27.   Painted into a corner: Gene Tierney and Dana Andrews in *Laura* (1944). (USC Special Collections)

source of her illness but also drive her to implicate herself in the murder of another of Korvo's female victims. Ultimately, Ann is cured of her compulsion to steal and absolved of the murder committed by Korvo, but—dialectically, as in *Laura*—only after undergoing both Korvo's darkly revelatory and Sutton's cathartic hypnotherapy (fig. 28).

Where the Sidewalk Ends (1950) begs to be read semiautobiographically in relation to Preminger's notorious temper and tendency toward physical violence. The protagonist, police detective Mark Dixon (Dana Andrews again), is a rogue cop with a short fuse, prone to beating criminals into submission—but also into confessing to crimes they did in fact commit. Although initially reprimanded and later nearly suspended for his rash behavior, Dixon learns to curb his temper both through his accidental killing of a murder suspect and through the love of a woman (Gene Tierney yet again). Yet Dixon's excesses are also redeemed when the police chief urges Dixon's nemesis and immediate superior to use Dixon's harsh methods on a potential informant; these tactics, combined with Dixon's own persistence, lead to the apprehension of the actual murderer and his mob gang.

The Thirteenth Letter (1950) is another of the Hollywood remakes from the French poetic realist period to which Jewish émigré noir directors were disproportionately drawn—in this case, Henri-Georges Clouzot's *Le Corbeau* (*The Raven*, 1943). In an attempt to preserve some of the regional flavor of the original, the film is set in a French-Canadian provincial town (although actually shot in

Figure 28.   Déjà vu: Gene Tierney in *Whirlpool* (1949). (USC Special Collections)

New England). As an exemplar of film noir, *The Thirteenth Letter* fits into the subset of the American cycle foreshadowed by Lang's *Fury* (1936) and pioneered by Hitchcock's *Shadow of a Doubt* (1943), in which a cheery small-town facade is peeled away to reveal ever darker layers of depravity underneath. Preminger's film establishes this bipolar motif early on when, as Dr. Laurent (Charles Boyer), one of the town's most respected citizens and another quasi psychiatrist, enters his imposing house from the tree-lined sidewalk, lighting and music abruptly shift from sunlit and lilting to low-key and sinister. This audiovisual counterpoint also literally foreshadows the ultimate revelation of Dr. Laurent's true character (he is the source of the anonymous poison-pen letters that end up terrorizing the town), while also figuratively painting the town itself with a noir brush. As Laurent says of the possible source of the letters, "If my diagnosis is correct [about the pathology of the letter writer], it could be almost anybody in this town."

The Thirteenth Letter also contains one of the classic noir syntheses of rhetoric and mise-en-scène, which, although partially lifted from *Le Corbeau*, speaks eloquently to Jewish émigrés' keen awareness (further heightened by recent disclosures of the Holocaust) of humankind's fractured nature. As suspicion for the sadistic letters' author veers, through Dr. Laurent's machinations, toward his rival Dr. Pearson's (Michael Rennie) beloved, Denise (Linda Darnell), the following exchange occurs between the two doctors:

DR. LAURENT [standing above the seated Dr. Pearson]: Denise is not a vicious person. If she did it, there must be some explanation. Some twist in her mind.

DR. PEARSON: In that case everything can be excused. And no one can be held accountable for anything!

DR. LAURENT: Forgive me, doctor, but you are a little rigid, too ready to judge. You believe that people are either good or bad. Good and evil change places, like light and shadow. [Here he taps the lamp above his head so that it sways back and forth, casting alternate patterns of light and shadow across both their figures as he continues.] How can we be sure where one ends and the other begins, or which side we are on?

DR. PEARSON: Very simple. [He stands.] We can stop the swaying! [He reaches out to steady the lamp, and burns his hand.]

DR. LAURENT: You see?!

Eventually, Dr. Pearson *will* see—at least who the actual culprit is. And although the film concludes on a superficially happy and heterosexually romantic note, the audience is forced to acknowledge, if only subliminally, the cogency of Dr. Laurent's dialectic of good and evil.

No Jewish émigré noir, of Preminger's or any other émigré director's, is more expressionistic in style or more steeped in Jewish relations than *Fallen*

Angel (1945). Belying Preminger's reputation as a conservative aesthetician, the film, shot in extreme high-contrast black-and-white by the director's "discovery," Joseph LaShelle, qualifies stylistically—surpassing Willy Wilder/John Alton's *The Pretender*—as the German expressionist film noir par excellence, and thematically as a Judeo-Christian morality play of the highest (and lowest) order.[23]

Eric Stanton (Dana Andrews yet again), a one-time East Coast promoter turned drifter/scam artist, is booted off a bus in beachside Walton, California, with a dollar in his pocket. His character recalls the eastern European immigrant moguls who moved out west and "invented" Hollywood, of course, but also the archetypal Jewish luftmensch (air man)—a reference that is literalized when someone in Walton asks Stanton what he does and he answers, "Nothing." Stanton could almost pass for Sammy Glick as well, the slimy Brooklyn Ostjude in Budd Schulberg's novel *What Makes Sammy Run?* (1942), who bluffs and tramples his way to the top, financially and romantically, in Hollywood. Stanton's first "job" in Walton, soon after his arrival, is as the successful promoter of a bogus psychic. When Stanton's sultry love interest Stella (Linda Darnell) asks him, "What do you do when you're not telling fortunes?" he schmoozes, "I help make 'em for others. I passed actresses, directors, producers through a publicity mill I ran and they came out famous. . . . I know all people, in all places, like Twenty-one, the Stork Club—that's where you belong, smothered in mink. I can see you there."

Where we first see Stella is in that (eventually) most favored of noir hangouts, a cheap diner at night, and as the star of that (eventually) obligatory noir set piece, the introduction of the femme fatale. All male heads at Pop's Diner, including Stanton's and Pop's, turn with the camera as the door's jingling bell announces Stella's entrance, whence, before resuming her waitress duties, she struts over to a chair, exposes her long legs, and takes off a high-heeled shoe to massage a tired foot. Eroticism's stage, and the film's moral dialectic, has been set (fig. 29).

The antithesis hails from the sunlit, broad-leafed part of town, in the person of June Mills (Alice Faye), prim church organist and well-heeled daughter of Walton's deceased mayor. June's personality and her father's estate make her the perfect candidate for another of Stanton's scams, this one aimed at fleecing June, through a bogus marriage, of the money he needs to convince Stella to marry him. June has led a sheltered life but is no dummy, yet she lets Stanton woo her, half-knowing that his intentions are impure; she senses that he is essentially Stella's mirror image, an homme fatal. Her yielding to his ambivalent charms has two semiconscious motivations. The first is missionary: the hope of steering Stanton toward the better side of his nature (June: "You live by impulse, and you never bother to think if you're following the right impulse"). The second is exploratory: the desire to sample some of the impulses that Stanton overindulges (Stanton: "You're scared to live, that's why you bury yourself in books and music"). June represents Christian chastity and lofty ideals pointing to a sacred world beyond; Stanton, minus the scamming, represents a Jewish tradition that

Figure 29.   Outsider looking in: Dana Andrews, Percy Kilbride, and Linda Darnell in *Fallen Angel* (1945). (USC Special Collections)

honors simple pleasures, common humanity, and the here and now. "I love, you don't," he argues, not entirely disingenuously. "The things you look down on are the things that make up life. . . . Little things like a game of bowling or a swim at night. Or a dance, a kiss, the stuff that bubbles." She counters that this doesn't really amount to anything; he concedes that by itself it doesn't, "but you add up all the little things, that's what makes life."

As June begins to partake of the little things—a dance, a kiss, the stuff that bubbles—things begin to add up for both her and Stanton. She experiences a liberating change, even admitting, before fainting in his arms from too much bubbly, that she's been saving magazine ads for years: "Sometimes I feel I'm the girl in that ad, softly alluring, full of grace, gown by Scaparelli." His scam comes closer to fruition when they marry on the quick in San Francisco. But when Stella is killed by one of her many lovers and Stanton becomes a prime suspect, he is forced to flee; and June, despite her knowledge of his feelings for Stella, flees with him. Here, in their fugitive state, appropriately, is where Stanton's Jewish aspect, more historically specific than his airman existence or pseudo-Chasidic philosophy, is revealed.

June, naively trusting in the justice system, urges Stanton, whom she believes to be innocent, to turn himself in. The worldly wise but increasingly world-weary Stanton demurs. As if pleading the case for Preminger and his Jewish émigré cohorts, not to mention for Jewish victims of persecution through the ages, Stanton explains, "Maybe that's the way it works in your books, but when I was a kid, I was always being beaten up for something I didn't do. That's when I learned to run away before it was too late." And he's been on the run ever since. Most recently, after being snookered himself in a business deal in New York, he headed west—Chicago, Omaha, Las Vegas, Walton, and now San Francisco. "There you have it, folks," one can imagine a more self-aware Stanton announcing, "Luftmensch, pseudo-Chasid, and, through and beneath it all, Wandering Jew."

But all is not lost for our star-crossed lovers; quite the contrary. Holding Stanton in her arms, June recites from one of her books: "We were born to tread the Earth as angels, to seek out heaven this side of the sky. But they who race alone shall stumble in the dark, and fall from grace. Then love alone can make the fallen angels rise, for only two together can enter paradise."[24] And so the moral of the morality play is made explicit: a Judeo-Christian synthesis of the fugitive couple's once antipodal ideologies has been achieved. The saintly June has come down from her ivory tower, confronted the world's dark side, and learned to love life's little things. The grifter Stanton has climbed up from the gutter, glimpsed the redemptive power of love, and learned to strive for something beyond himself. One can almost envision a Yiddish version of the film (by Ulmer?) having Stanton, the reformed homme fatal, respond to June's recitation with Rabbi Hillel's Talmudic maxim: "If I am not for myself, who will be? If I am for myself only, what am I? If not now, when?"

When is now for Stanton. After June is nabbed by the police and sent back to Walton, he returns as well, but not to turn himself in. Instead, he fingers the real culprit, Mark Judd (Charles Bickford), the most rogue of rogue cops, who was seen earlier using Mark Dixon–like methods on an innocent suspect, and who murdered Stella from jealousy. As Judd is hauled away from the diner, June picks Stanton up in her car and asks him where he wants to go. "Home," he replies, but the normative-sounding ending is muffled by the noir mise-en-scène. As the car drives off and out of frame, the camera holds on an image all but lifted from Weimar-era outtakes: wet street and lone streetlamp set against a dark, distant ocean and a cloudy, partially moonlit sky.

Strange Women and Unmanly Men

Edgar Ulmer began working for PRC at an auspicious time in the Poverty Row studio's history. Via a multi-film contract with Weimar producer Seymour Nebenzahl's (and partner Peter van Duinen's) Atlantis Pictures, Ulmer signed on with PRC in 1942 just as the company, under production head Leon Fromkess, was embarking on an expansion program aimed at lifting it out of the cinematic gutter to the level of the "mini-majors" Monogram and Republic, if not beyond. The focus was to be more on quality than mere quantity, and to this end

Fromkess cut back on the number of films made at the studio from forty-four in 1941 to twenty-six in 1942.[25] PRC also broadened its generic spectrum, as Ulmer's daughter Arianné reports, moving beyond "a small schlock house that only produced Westerns," to adding "exploitation pictures, and as Ulmer came on, even higher-level quality productions."[26] The studio also did its part for the anti-Nazi cause, as did Ulmer, who contributed substantially to the preproduction and direction of *Hitler's Madman* (1943)—for which Douglas Sirk received sole directorial credit, however, after the film was picked up for completion and release by MGM.[27]

Although the somewhat boosted budgets and shooting schedules may have been lavish by PRC standards, they remained skimpy compared to even the majors' B-level output. For the eleven films that Ulmer made for PRC from 1942 to 1945, the average budget was twenty thousand dollars and the majority were shot in six days, according to Ulmer.[28] Up to eighty setups a day were filmed, with an average shooting ratio of two-to-one, and "his actors often were simply placed before an empty gray wall and his films were largely cut in the camera."[29] The restrictive working conditions and confined aesthetics led Bret Wood to characterize all of Ulmer's PRC films, somewhat ironically and certainly not pejoratively, as "Kammerspielfilms."[30]

As for subject matter, much of this, befitting the exploitation orientation, tended toward the derivative, often trading on the majors' recent successes. Ulmer even proposed a *Double Indemnity* knockoff titled *Single Indemnity*, but potential legal entanglements turned it into *Blonde Ice* (1948), with Jack Bernhard directing instead of Ulmer.[31] What ultimately became Ulmer's first film noir, and his most expensive PRC production to date, also derived from a mainstream hit—and from another film directed by a Jewish émigré. John Brahm's *The Lodger* (1944), a Jack the Ripper thriller, provided the impetus for Ulmer's *Bluebeard* (1944), whose titular rights PRC was able to wrest from Charlie Chaplin, causing his similarly Henri Landru–inspired film to be re-titled *Monsieur Verdoux* (1947).[32]

Ulmer, like Chaplin, had something more in mind than a straightforward retelling of Landru's real-life horror story. *Bluebeard* is set in Paris, but the serial killer, played by John Carradine, is named Gaston Morel and, more important, is not a furniture dealer but rather a painter and puppeteer. Once again we have the Jewish émigré noir director's predilection for the artist type, and again with clear personal autobiographical and cinematically self-reflexive implications. Ulmer had trained as a painter and set designer, was steeped in the classical theater, worked on some of Weimar cinema's greatest art films, and, as most of the émigrés, was broadly conversant with European high culture. He had a particular appreciation for classical music, as was affirmed by his choice as director of the semidocumentary musical drama *Carnegie Hall* (1947), featuring performances by Arthur Rubinstein and Yasha Heifetz.[33] In *Bluebeard*, Ulmer manages to bridge high culture and kitsch, while also foregrounding their dialectical relation to the

Hollywood film industry and his own place in it. Gustav Morel is not a purveyor of Punch and Judy shows but rather of puppet operas based on Charles Gounod's reworking of *Faust*, but he is also a B-movie monster whose desire to produce great art is traumatically bound up with his urge to kill beautiful women.

The metaphorical allusions to filmmaking can scarcely be avoided: Morel's most desired female object, Lucille (Jean Parker), is a costume designer whom he spies through a curtain peephole as she sits in the audience during one of his performances; he paints his last victim, Lucille's sister Francine (Teala Loring), by viewing her in a mirror with his back toward her, thus both mediating her image and withholding his gaze; and the necrophilic aspect of puppets themselves, with their embalming of life in wood and cloth replicating cinema's fossilizing of nature in celluloid. Steven Jenkins is not far off in comparing *Bluebeard* to Michael Powell's macabre disquisition on cinematic voyeurism, *Peeping Tom* (1960), in the linkage of the artist-subject connection to sexuality and power.[34]

The linkage to Ulmer's personal filmmaking predicament is also patently evident. Morel's confession to Lucille at the end—that he gave up serious painting after learning that his true love and prime inspiration was a whore, upon which he strangled her and now paints only for the money he owes his dealer, Lamarte—conforms strikingly with Ulmer's refugee experience of renouncing his once-beloved-turned-murderous motherland and succumbing to commercial straitjacketing at PRC. Even his ambiguous relationship to his own Jewishness comes out in the money-grubbing Lamarte (played by the German Jewish actor Ludwig Stössel), whose gnomish appearance, art dealer's profession, and French name at odds with a German accent dredge up archetypal anti-Semitic associations. Both the confessional and ambiguous aspects surface in Ulmer's interview with Peter Bogdanovich: "I yearn for absolution for all the things I had to do for money's sake."[35]

Stylistically, the film is like a Jewish trip down Weimar lane. *Bluebeard* demonstrates, more even than Ulmer's later noirs, as Stefan Grissemann describes:

the [German expressionist] school the director (as well as cameraman Eugen Schüfftan) passed though in his early years: the chiaroscuro in the streets and in Morel's studio, more dark than light; the wide-open, almost extruding eyes of the murderer in the deadly act; the underground tunnels in which the hunted man flees, and which he as easily navigates as the Phantom of the Opera in the underground hallways of his house; the canted street lamps and painted house fronts of Paris at night; finally, the music [by émigré Leo Erdody] which, unceasingly and above and beyond all the silence, accompanies the images.[36]

Eugen Schüfftan deserves more than parenthetical mention here. Noted earlier for his work (along with Ulmer, Siodmak, Billy Wilder, et al.) on *Menschen am Sonntag*, Schüfftan is another Jewish émigré whose contribution to Ulmer's films, Jewish émigré noir, and film noir in general should not—but unfortunately has—been underestimated. The oversight stems mainly from the fact that Schüfftan failed to gain admittance (until the 1950s) to the American Society of Cinematographers (ASC), the camera branch of the Hollywood crafts union, and thus was denied, despite his significant input, director of cinematography credit on several of Ulmer's (and Siodmak's) films. When Schüfftan *is* credited, it is generally as set designer (in which capacity he also served), executive producer, or technical consultant.[37] A special effects pioneer, Schüfftan devised some of the more spectacular imagery in Lang's *Metropolis*, partly through a see-through mirror technique thereafter dubbed the Schüfftan effect; he would also perform wonders with mirrors for the doubling effects in Siodmak's *The Dark Mirror*.[38] But his larger contribution to noir lies in the mnemonic link he provided to German expressionist cinema, as can be seen not only in *Bluebeard* (and in noirs by the directors mentioned above), but also in the other noir he filmed without screen credit for Ulmer, *Strange Illusion* (1945).

Ulmer's attempt in *Bluebeard* of mixing high and low culture on a comparatively lavish plane succeeded neither critically nor at the box office, moving the director to revert to a more modest project for his next film. Grissemann terms Ulmer's tendency at PRC to fluctuate between more and less ambitious work a form of "backlash"; Ulmer himself characterized his dilemma during this period as "schizophrenic": on the one hand, he was certainly interested in box office returns; on the other, he was continually striving to produce "art with substance and style."[39] *Strange Illusion*, which Grissemann aptly describes as *Hamlet* cloaked in a noir whodunit, admirably exemplifies the effort, or better the strain, of mixing high culture and kitsch.

Strange Illusion, like its Shakespearean antecedent, deals with a young man, Paul Cartwright (the Henry Aldrich series's Jimmy Lydon), bent on proving that the man about to marry Paul's mother is actually his father's murderer. Also like his Danish counterpart, Paul's suspicions, although eventually shown to be justified, are dismissed by everyone around him as paranoid delusions. A final *Hamlet*-like touch is the extrasensory means by which Paul is led to his suspicion: a harrowing dream that foreshadows the perilous events to come. Where Ulmer goes the Bard one better, or worse, is in the homme fatal's pathological character flaw: he is a pedophile obsessed with young girls, a fatal weakness that his psychiatrist and coconspirator, Professor Muhlbach (Charles Arnt), rightfully feared would lead to their downfall.[40]

The film was shot by Schüfftan in a starkly expressionist vein. Indeed, the lengthy dream scene that opens the film—in which Paul's ghostlike figure somnambulates across a dark sea of clouds and fog as other ghostly figures (his father, mother, sister, the homme fatal) drift in and out of the picture—is as Expressionistic as anything in classical noir.[41] The most Jewish émigré aspect of

the film, besides the homme fatal, lies in the familiar figure of the overly sensitive, mildly effeminate, or at least "less than fully masculine" male protagonist.
Alexander Horwath attributes such qualities not only to this particular character
type but to a characteristic of Ulmer himself, whom he describes as "an 'unmanly'
director of unmanly men."[42] Other prominent boy-men in Ulmer's noirs include
Ephraim Poster (note the Jewish first name), played by Louis Hayward, in *The
Strange Woman* (1946); Vic Lambdin (note the "gentle" last name), Hayward again,
in *Ruthless* (1948); and, most famously, Al Roberts (the surname was de-Judaized
from the novel's Alexander Roth), played by Tom Neal, in *Detour* (1945).[43]

Paul Cartwright fits the boyish bill literally through his high-school student's
age, but also figuratively through the "unmanly" methods that he uses to unmask
the homme fatal. An upper-class, British-style, cerebral "detective" rather than
a hard-boiled gumshoe, Paul possesses the smarts and the (feminine?) intuition
needed to nail the villain. But his physical deficiencies, like his paranormal visions,
nearly come back to haunt him when, in his climactic confrontation with his
archrival, the older man knocks him cold with a single blow, thereby requiring the
cops to come to the rescue. Additionally, though not surprisingly given the dialectical relation between the effeminate male and the homme fatal, the "Jewish"
aspects of the villainous figure are also foregrounded here. Cultured and refined
to a fault (at one point he woos Paul's sister with a poem from Omar Khayyám),
Brett Curtis (Warren William), Paul's mother's suitor, is pejoratively dubbed "a
cosmopolitan" by a jealous friend of Paul's. And of course Curtis's client/partner-
in-crime relationship with the sinister psychiatrist additionally qualifies as Jewish
guilt by association.

In *The Strange Woman* (1946), a period noir set in the rough-and-tumble
lumber town of Bangor, Maine, in the early-to-mid 1800s, Ephraim Poster's pris-
siness is evidenced in the opening sequence. Pushed into a creek as a youngster by
Jenny, the "strange woman" as uppity tomboy, Ephraim, who is unable to swim,
flails about yelling for help as young Jenny stands on a bridge taunting him.[44]
Sadomasochism colors their adult relationship as well, as the now stunningly
beautiful Jenny (Hedy Lamarr) carries on an affair with the pretty-boy Ephraim
under the nose of Ephraim's elderly father and Jenny's husband, Isaiah (Gene
Lockhart), a ruthless, unprepossessing lumber tycoon who wangled his way into
marrying the much younger woman. Eventually, Jenny manipulates Ephraim into
murdering Isaiah, then drives him to suicide in order to make way for the man she
truly loves, lumber company foreman John Evered (George Sanders). Conversely
to *Strange Illusion*, which combined the unmanly man and the homme fatal, *The
Strange Woman* combines (as in Willy Wilder's *Bluebeard's Ten Honeymoons*) the
homme fatal and the femme fatale. But what a strange variation on the devilish
vixen Jenny Hager Poster turns out to be (fig. 30).

The product of poverty, an abandoning mother, and an abusive, alcoholic father,
Jenny's ruthless behavior is rendered, if not justifiable, at least comprehensible.

Figure 30.   Hedy Lamarr is *The Strange Woman* (1946). (Courtesy of Arianné Ulmer Cipes)

Further sympathy accrues to her by virtue of the (only partially self-serving) good works she provides the community—much to the dismay of the miserly (and Jewish-named) Isaiah—through her generous charitable donations and ministrations to the sick. Most of all, unlike the classic femme fatale, she is ultimately able to love unconditionally; and John, a decent man, responds in kind despite deep suspicions of her dastardly deeds. And indeed, Jenny's newfound capacity for true love almost—but for the Production Code—redeems her in the end. Yet anyone of whom it is said, as Ephraim does to John, "She's so rotten. She's not even a human being!" must, by classical Hollywood's terms, die for her sins.

How the film ultimately dispenses divine justice, however, is not quite the way that Ulmer had envisaged. Instead of having Jenny perish penitently in John's arms at the end, confessing her wrongdoing and professing her undying love, Ulmer planned a denouement that thrust a critical lens back onto the barbarous town that had given rise to Jenny, Isaiah, and a host of other scoundrels, and that clearly serves, in its period setting, as a microcosm of the nascent United States. Resonant of, if not directly inspired by, Hitchcock's *Shadow of a Doubt*, Jenny's reverential funeral procession through the town—which we had just seen descend into a Dantean inferno of drunken revelry, fiery destruction, and rapaciousness—was to be *The Strange Woman*'s final image. As her flower-bedecked hearse is carried past the grieving citizens of Bangor, Jenny was to be eulogized with the words: "Oh, was she good. Oh, was she charitable."[45]

The Strange Woman was not made for PRC but rather as one of Ulmer's rare A films (produced by Hunt Stromberg and released through United Artists), thus the top-flight cast, more refined script, and higher production values, but also, crucially, more commercial pressures, less creative control, and a compromised ending. Ulmer's next major film, following the semidocumentary *Carnegie Hall*, was another A film, *Ruthless (1948)*. Produced by Arthur Lyons and released through Eagle Lion, the film's screen adaptation of a novel by Dayton Stoddart was cowritten (uncredited) by Hollywood Ten figure Alvah Bessie and another left-wing Jew, Gordon Kahn, both of whom would later be blacklisted.[46] The radical political patrimony no doubt contributed to the anticapitalist animus; rendered allegorically in *The Strange Woman*, that animus is more topically represented in *Ruthless*.

Dubbed "a *Citizen Kane* in miniature" by Myron Meisel, the film, set in the contemporary period, centers on high-powered financier Horace Vendig (Zachary Scott), whose Horatio Alger–like saga is presented, à la Welles's *film à clef* of William Randolph Hearst, as a series of flashbacks from various characters' points of view.[47] Not quite a Bluebeard in the serial-*killing* sense, Vendig does serially seduce, and subsequently discard, a bevy of women whose well-placed connections enable his rise to riches. Vendig's social Darwinist philosophy, and its relation to the capitalist system, is limned in a few lines: "I'm an adding machine. I can't afford a conscience," he tells his childhood best friend, Vic Lambdin (Hayward), just before his latest outfoxed business rival commits suicide. "When I saw something I wanted, I said, 'This I must have!'" he tells Vic's fiancée, Mallory (Diana Lynn), the second of Vic's girlfriends that Vendig has attempted to steal (he succeeded with the first, Martha Burnside, also played by Lynn). As Vendig and another of his vanquished rivals, Buck Mansfield (Sydney Greenstreet), battle to both their deaths in the dark waters beside Vendig's Xanadu-like mansion (fig. 31), Mallory, the first woman to resist Vendig's advances, sums up his surplus value to the film: "He wasn't a man, he was a way of life!"

As with *Citizen Kane* (and *The Strange Woman*), the protagonist's dysfunctional upbringing—absentee, ne'er-do-well father; emotionally withholding mother—engender sympathy for Vendig and offer a partial explanation for his ruthless drive to power. The ultimate effect, however, as with the eponymous Kane, is to imply synergy rather than incommensurability between Freudian and Marxist theory; the psychosocial and the socioeconomic, in other words, are shown to be mutually reinforcing. Certainly in no other of the homme fatal films discussed thus far is this figure shown to be more the product of internal as well as external forces, more psycho-economically overdetermined, than in Ulmer's *Ruthless*.

Figure 31.   Cutthroat competition: Zachary Scott and Sydney Greenstreet in *Ruthless* (1948). (USC Special Collection)

As if the conflation of Freud and Marx weren't Jewish influence enough, Ulmer provides a Judeo-religious connection as well. Yet here, once again, the moral(ity) is dialectical rather binary. "Good and evil in Ulmer's films," Grissemann suggests, are not polar opposites; they "are bound up with one another, live off one another, dissolve into one another."[48] Expressing the push-pull of Judaism and Christianity that affected his life and permeated his thought, Ulmer stated, "My films have religious force, but are not really Christian; the most solid of all religions is namely that which is based on the Old Testament. Its morality is stronger than that of the New Testament."[49] Extracting an existentialist strand from Ulmer's Judeo-Christian quilt, Grissemann elaborates, "He doesn't believe in angels who come down to Earth to seek a person out. How one thinks and acts is everyone's own business."[50]

Detour

Detour is the most critically acclaimed of Ulmer's film noirs and—thanks to François Truffaut and other *Cahiers du cinéma* critics—the one that, along with the dark western *The Naked Dawn* (1954), led to the retrieval of Ulmer's body of work from the dustbin of history. Although *Detour*'s fabled low budget and tight shooting schedule have recently been revised upward, the film still qualifies as a prototypical example of the B film's capacity, at least in Ulmer's hands, for mining noir's stylistic and thematic tropes.[51] Additionally, from a Jewish émigré noir perspective, *Detour* provides the richest vein for analysis of all of Ulmer's films.

Protagonist Al Roberts, "one of the weakest heroes the American cinema has produced," prototypically combines the "weakling's" lack of assertiveness with an uncommon artistic sensibility.[52] A pianist of classical training and considerable talent, Roberts is stuck playing second fiddle to his girlfriend, Sue (Claudia Drake), a pop singer whom he accompanies as the main attraction at the Break O'Dawn club in New York, where he is allowed to riff on his own in the wee hours. His supporting-actor billing in his personal relationship with Sue is underscored when she leaves him behind to go after the brass ring in Hollywood.

The theme of an artist of high cultural abilities and ambitions prostituting himself carries over from *Bluebeard*, of course, except that the biographical link to Ulmer's own situation is more direct in *Detour*, where the conflict is not between epic poetry and puppetry but between European classical and American mass culture. As for a similar "cross-cultural" conflict in *Strange Illusion*, the Hamlet/whodunit dialectic there was inter- rather than an intra-textual. In *Detour*, the "continental divide" is displayed in the film itself when Roberts, in his wee-hour riff, merges a pop tune, Brahms's "Wiegenlied," snippets of jazz, a Chopin waltz, and a hard-driving boogie in the same brilliant improvisation.[53]

Geography and biography also converge in the film's narrative. Ulmer worked on both coasts, outside the Hollywood system in New York and within it in Los Angeles. Roberts's trek west to meet up with Sue after she moves to Hollywood is redolent of Ulmer's own cross-country and career travels (and travails). Yet the dire conditions and tragic consequences of Roberts's antihero's journey bespeak something larger and more fraught than a mere trip from the East to the West Coast, or from independent to contract-director status. As his physical trials, psychological trauma, and moral tribulation mount, Roberts's existential ordeal once again resembles (à la *Fallen Angel*'s Frank Stanton) that of the Jewish émigré himself—a semblance brought into relief when, after the accidental (or natural) death of Haskell (Edmund MacDonald), the man who picked him up hitchhiking, Roberts becomes (à la *Fury*'s Joe Wilson, *You Only Live Once*'s Eddie Taylor, and Stanton again) another of Jewish émigré noir's "innocent fugitives."

Narrative structure and mise-en-scène reinforce the analogy. The film takes place in three main locations: New York, Hollywood, and the road. The first, representing "home," is shot as if on a UFA stage: pitch-black night, foggy streets, and canted street lamps as expressionistically rendered as any in the noir cycle. Hollywood, Robert's involuntary destination, by contrast, is depicted, at least in the exterior scenes, in broad, shadowless daylight; even night scenes in the hotel room, where Roberts plays married couple with the vicious Vera (Ann Savage), although claustrophobic and prison-like (Vera locks the door and keeps the key), are not exceptionally darkly lit. The road, geographically and cinematically an "in-between" space, is also aesthetically bifurcated: daytime scenes bright and sunny; nighttime scenes dark and rainy, most notably the fateful night when Roberts is literally "driven to darkness" when he exchanges identity with the deceased Haskell to avoid being fingered for his "killing."

The road section's chronotopal centerpiece is the diner, where the ill-fated story begins and ends with Roberts's voice-over narration, and meets midway, before and after Haskell's death. Brightly lit for the most part, the greasy spoon becomes simultaneously Expressionistic and surrealistic during Roberts's voice-over confessional. Recalling *Mabuse* (and perhaps influencing *The Pretender*), the diner interior gradually goes dark as the camera moves in to a close-up of Roberts's face, with a narrow band of light illuminating his eyes like the obverse of a bandit's mask—so much for Expressionism (fig. 32).[54] As Roberts's doleful narration drones on, the camera moves backward behind his eerily white coffee cup that now appears overlarge and surreally animate . . . then forward, past, and behind him to another circular object, the spinning record on the jukebox, whose love song triggers his tortured memory of happier times . . . which, in turn, are visualized through a form-match dissolve to the circular white surface of a base drum in the nightclub where Roberts, in flashback, accompanies sweet Sue. Roberts's voice-over underscores his limbo state, as well as the innocent fugitive's lament: "Did you ever want to forget anything? Did you ever want to cut away a piece of your memory, or blot it out? You can't, you know, no matter how hard you try. You can change the scenery, but sooner or later you'll get a whiff of perfume or somebody will say a certain phrase or maybe hum something—then you're licked again."

Roberts is not the only character whose condition connotes a historically specific relation to Jewishness. The film's other key figure, the femme fatale Vera (whom Roberts gave a ride in Haskell's car and who subsequently blackmails him over Haskell's "killing"), also suffers from an affliction with decidedly Jewish markings. The seriousness of Vera's condition is spelled out in a hotel room scene when, after coughing, Vera intimates she doesn't have long to live but she then offhandedly adds, "I'll be all right," to which Roberts responds, "That's what Camille said. . . . Nobody you'd know." The literary allusion, and Vera's ignorance of it, of course remind us, and Roberts, of his cultural alienation. Even more significant from a Jewish émigré noir perspective, however, are the implications that the reference to tuberculosis holds not only for Jews in general, but for Jewish prostitutes in particular. Indeed, heightened fear in the late-nineteenth and early-twentieth centuries of contracting tuberculosis (along with sexually transmitted diseases) from women of ill repute—to which group impoverished ghetto Jewish women belonged, of necessity, in disproportionate numbers—likely contributed to the Jewish female link to the femme fatale trope.[55]

Figure 32. Driven to darkness: Tom Neal in *Detour* (1945). (Frame grab)

As with so many anti-Semitic insinuations, however, that of the tubercular Jew(ess) is also a canard—although, for a change, somewhat counterintuitively. That Jews, or at least ghetto Jews, were thought to be predisposed to tuberculosis is understandable. People who dwell in large cities, particularly those living in crowded and insufficiently ventilated tenement houses, were generally the first victims of the deadly lung disease. Tailoring and other sedentary occupations traditionally favored by Jews tended to raise the probability of infection. And consanguineous marriages, common among Jews during the disease's rise, further heightened susceptibility. "All these conditions," according to Joseph Jacobs and Maurice Fishberg, "added to their poverty, constant grief, anxiety, and mental exertion, besides the ceaseless persecutions to which they [were] subjected, tend[ed] to make [Jews] ready victims to tuberculosis." Finally, the statistically greater physical stuntedness and gauntness of Jews seemed to confirm the suspicion, and the perception, that "many a modern Jew" suffered from the affliction.[56]

And yet, despite the odds seemingly stacked against them, Jews actually contracted tuberculosis with *less* frequency than non-Jews living under similar conditions. Although genetic factors have been offered to explain Jews' comparative immunity to TB, the most cogent causes were likely threefold: Jews were more apt to be "engaged in occupations which required no exposure to the vicissitudes of the weather"; kosher meat was more carefully inspected for bovine diseases of the lungs and pleura; and alcoholism, well recognized as a predisposing cause of tuberculosis, was less prevalent among Jews.[57] Epidemiological explanations notwithstanding, the fact that Jews, "particularly those residing in the congested tenement districts of large modern cities, like New York, London, Vienna, Odessa, etc.," did suffer from tuberculosis more than others would have encouraged a belief among anti-Semites and anti-Ostjuden—that is, the majority of "good citizens" in Austro-Germany during Ulmer's formative period—that tuberculosis was a Jewish disease.[58]

As such, it seems only fitting that Vera *is* a lush, and that she dies from lack of breath, partly by her own hand. As she goes to call the cops on Roberts and locks the bedroom door behind her, stumbling onto the bed and drunkenly wrapping the telephone cord around her neck, he yanks the cord to break it and accidentally strangles her. An innocent fugitive twice over, Roberts taunts the audience with a timeless Jewish plaint rendered more poignant by contemporaneous events: "How many of you would believe the killing wasn't premeditated? Everyone of you on the jury would say I murdered her! This was the kind of evidence [unlike with Haskell] I couldn't rub out. . . . I was cooked, done for."

Then, a minor miracle: "Haskell," not Roberts, turns into the suspected murderer of Vera and "Roberts," thereby exonerating Roberts himself of both deaths. Yet stripped of his official identity, Roberts by this point is a shell of his former self in every other way as well. As he told Vera, who wanted him to continue playing Haskell to glean his wealthy father's inheritance, "I don't even know what my religion is!" Poetic justice (even more than the Production Code) thus demands that he be brought to heel at the end, leaving an utterly resigned Roberts to speak the Kafkaesque words that have become noir's archetypal epitaph: "Some day a cop car will stop to pick me up that I never thumbed. Yes, fate, or some mysterious force, can put the finger on you, or me, for no good reason at all."[59]

9   *Woman's Directors*

A predilection for prominent, sympathetic women characters is, as we've seen, a distinctive feature of Jewish émigré noir. This gynophilic tendency in the work of Curtis Bernhardt and Max Ophuls, in particular, led them to be typed, somewhat pejoratively, as "woman's directors." That the American filmmaker most noted as a "woman's director," George Cukor, was also widely known (at least within the industry) to be gay, reinforced the derogatory connotations. Indeed, Bernhardt may have been attempting to even the score, orientationally speaking, when he pointed out, in an interview with Mary Kiersch in 1977: "It's funny, because in Germany all my films might be called 'male pictures' . . . [but being taken for a] woman's director [in Hollywood] saved me from doing Westerns. I was glad about that."[1] Leaving aside that Bernhardt's account of his Weimar filmography is myopic—he directed *Das Mädchen mit den fünf Nullen* (*The Girl with Five Zeroes*, 1927) and Marlene Dietrich's first film, *Die Frau, nach der Man sich sehnt* (*The Woman Every Man Desires*, 1929)—the conflation of sexism and homophobia in the "woman's director" designation, especially as applied to Jewish émigré directors, couldn't be more pertinent to our analysis.

From Kurt to Curtis

Among Jewish émigré noir directors, only Fritz Lang surpasses Curtis Bernhardt in the breadth and depth of his involvement with the Weimar film industry. Edgar Ulmer began working in Germany at about the same time as Lang, but he never directed a German film. Billy Wilder also worked during the Weimar period but only as a screenwriter. Robert Siodmak, who would direct a significant number of Weimar-era sound films, actually got his first break as an assistant director on Bernhardt's sixth German film, *Der letzte Fort* (*The Last Fort*, 1928). Where Bernhardt diverges from Lang and joins the majority of the Jewish émigré directors is in having segued into cinema from theater.

Born to a lower-middle-class Jewish family in Worms, Germany, in 1899, Kurt, as he was legally named, was bar mitzvahed but otherwise not religiously raised. His Jewish awareness, as with most Germans and Austrians, was thrust on him by the anti-Semitic environment. Neither he nor his more robust brother took the bigotry lying down. The much smaller Kurt held his own in school fights with Jew-baiting bullies, and his "muscle Jew" brother "beat the hell" out of a group of taunters in a movie theater.[2] Drawn along by the patriotic fervor, both brothers served in World War I, where Kurt formed both his radical political consciousness and his acquaintance with Expressionism. Indeed, ideology and culture were initially synonymous in Kurt's mind; at one coffeehouse meeting, he cut through an abstract discussion of formal aesthetics with the declamation "that Expressionism was nothing but a protest against the war."[3] By the end of the war he had joined the Spartakus (German communist) movement and began working in a regional Heidelberg theater as an actor.

Politics more than aesthetics eventually nudged young Kurt into film-making as well. Initially regarding cinema, even in its "art film" guise, as inferior to avant-garde theater, he was coaxed into directing *Namenlose Helden* (*Nameless Heroes*, originally titled *War*), a 1924 antiwar film made in Berlin for Prometheus Films, a Viennese company run by the Communist Party. Although Bernhardt was no longer a party member by this time, his involvement with *Nameless Heroes* would come back to haunt him in the McCarthy era (ironi-cally, given the film's title) when a fellow refugee would "name" him before the HUAC.[4] Fortunately—and lady luck would shine on him throughout his life—this combination of mendacity and betrayal did not lead to Bernhardt's blacklisting. Indeed, despite his early radical and continuing leftist leanings, Bernhardt's work as a whole has been slighted both for its ideological fluc-tuation in Germany—where it veered from *Nameless Heroes* to the Catholic Church–financed antiabortion film *Kinderseelen klagen euch an* (*Children's Souls Rebuke You!*, 1927) to the ultra-patriotic *Die letzte Kompanie* (*The Last Company*, 1930)—and for its quietism and political retreat in France and the United States—where it allegedly descended into the familiar and everyday. Although Bernhardt himself joked about his chameleonic propensity for being "on every side," critics such as Lothar Schwab have less sympathetically described him as "a bourgeois director uninterested in larger political issues . . . who leaned toward the everyday world of family relations."[5]

That Bernhardt was not an intensely individualistic director, but rather one adept at adapting to national styles, is incontrovertible.[6] This adaptability, however, was not a one-way street. Especially in the United States, Bernhardt, like the other émigré directors, displayed a knack for meshing European high-cultural proclivities with Hollywood's popular cultural demands. "I was a perfect symbol of the two cultures," he would tell Kiersch of his Hollywood period, "of two different sensibilities."[7] He would also serve, much like Siodmak (and contra Elsaesser), as a tripartite link among German Expressionism, French poetic realism, and the Hollywood classical style.[8] And, somewhat like Siodmak but even more like Lang, his films—despite their generic leap from compilation documentary (*Nameless Heroes*) to problem film (*Children's Souls Rebuke You!*) to historical drama (*The Last Company*) to melodrama (*The Woman*

Every Man Desires) to mountain film (*Der Rebell* [*The Rebel*], 1932)—already exhibited, in their Weimar phase, a noir bent.[9]

Bernhardt's escape from Nazi Germany, if one can believe his Keystone Kops account to Kiersch, qualifies as one of the more miraculous of any Jewish survivor, filmmaker or not. Following Goebbels's notorious speech to leaders of the German film industry—in which the propaganda minister singled out Bernhardt's *The Rebel* and *The Last Company*, along with Lang's *Die Nibelungen* and Eisenstein's *Potemkin* (for its aesthetics, not its politics), as exemplary films "that could not have been conceived in the degenerate brain of a Jewish director"—Bernhardt left immediately for France.[10] Soon thereafter, however, the French company he was working for sent him back to Munich to film *Der Tunnel* (*The Tunnel*). Being "the only Jewish director allowed to work in Germany in 1933" had its drawbacks, of course, and as soon as filming on *The Tunnel* was over, the gestapo paid him a visit.[11] But just as Jewishness had placed him in harm's way, chutzpah enabled his survival. "I told the Gestapo that I was the director of two big films—one German and the other French—and that I had special permission from the Ministry of Propaganda. They told me to stay put and they'd check in Berlin. I told them to do that. They went out the front door and I went out the back door and never returned."[12]

Rather than using Paris as a brief stopover, as had Lang and Billy Wilder, or as the base for a new career, as had Siodmak, Bernhardt ended up dividing time between Paris and London, where he also had business contacts. His first expatriate film was the French comedy *L'Or dans la rue* (Streets paved with gold, 1934), his second the British musical *The Beloved Vagabond* (1936). In its narrative of a rootless man in transition the latter, although neither proto-noir nor poetic realist, certainly adhered closely to Bernhardt's own refugee situation. The third film, and his last before coming to the States, *Carrefour* (*Crossroads*, 1937), a British-French coproduction shot in France, was a poetic realist variation, both in style and subject matter, on Bernhardt's Weimar output. The story, of a wealthy industrialist suffering from amnesia due to a wartime injury and now accused of having been a criminal prior to the war, not only resonated with the larger German Jewish predicament but would share its basic premise with one of Bernhardt's later Hollywood noirs, *High Wall* (1947), to be discussed in greater detail below.[13]

Bernhardt's departure from Europe, although not as dramatic as his double-barreled flight from Germany, was another harrowing affair. Panicked by the 1939 Hitler-Stalin pact into leaving France before completing *Nuit de décembre* (Night in December), the refugee director was now "wanted by the French police as a German and by the German police as a Jew."[14] With a new European war clearly imminent, the United States seemed to offer the safest haven and the greatest potential for regular film work. Like many of the émigré directors, he had to prove himself anew despite his impressive résumé. But with *Carre-four* as a calling card, and Frank Orsatti, a top agent at International Creative Management (ICM), to peddle it, he fairly quickly landed a lucrative seven-year contract with Warner Bros. He even was able to avert the B-film "training" to which several of his émigré colleagues had been subjected; his script contributions to the B-slated *My Love Came Back* (1940) impressed producer Hal Wallis enough to upgrade it to an A picture. An Olivia de Havilland vehicle, the film also—partly due to Bernhardt's apparent knack for such projects, and partly to Warner's stable of independent-minded female stars (de Havilland, Bette Davis, Joan Crawford, Barbara Stanwyck)—carved the first notch in his "woman's director" belt. And indeed, in near-perfect symmetrical contra-distinction to his European output, only two of Bernhardt's Warner produc-tions, *Juke Girl* (1941) and *Conflict* (1943), would *not* feature women as the central characters.

Along with the directorial typecasting came, for different reasons, a new name. Although Warner Bros. had recently come under fire from the govern-ment for its "prematurely antifascist" films such as *Confessions of a Nazi Spy* (1939) and *The Mortal Storm* (1940), with U.S. entry into the war the studio's concern suddenly became just the opposite: the fear of appearing "too German." Bernhardt was one of the first victims of the image makeover, as Jack Warner's personal request made painfully clear: "Kurt, we are about to go to war with Germany. 'Kurt' is a very German-sounding name. Can you do something about this?"[15] Bowing to studio pressure, but also because "every refugee, when he comes to a foreign country, is more patriotic than the locals," Bernhardt did his duty and had his given name legally changed to Curtis—"but my family name remained the same."[16]

The Psychiatrist's Director

Two of Bernhardt's three noirs for Warner Bros. feature women protagonists: *A Stolen Life* (1946) and *Possessed* (1947). His lone MGM noir, *High Wall* (1947), does not. This film, however, along with two of the Warner noirs (*Conflict* and *Possessed*), foreground psychiatrists; and *High Wall* further overcompensates by making its psychiatrist, in a unique conflation of Jewish émigré noir tropes, a woman.

Conflict, the first of Bernhardt's American film noirs (filmed in 1943, released in 1945), was based on an original story by Robert Siodmak and Alfred Neuman. Although Bernhardt, on this as with most of his films, worked on the script, was consulted on casting, and "cut with the camera," he was perhaps a little too quick to dismiss Siodmak's contribution ("He was not around while it was written or when it was made").[17] Siodmak biographer Deborah Lazaroff Alpi, for example, believes that the film "clearly bears the mark of Siodmak" in both its "exploration of noir themes he had first explored" in some of his French films and its plot elements, which are "similar to what would emerge in future films" like *The Suspect* and *The Strange Affair of Uncle Harry*. "*Conflict* might be best summed up," Alpi contends, "as the Siodmak film that got away."[18]

Whoever deserves the most credit, the film's look and theme, at a comparatively early period in the cycle, are classic noir. In a cynical portrait of middle-class marriage as searing as any in the canon, engineering-firm executive Richard Mason (Humphrey Bogart) murders his wife, Katherine (Rose Hobart), to rid himself of her shrewishness and frigidity but mainly to make way for her much younger sister Evelyn Turner (Alexis Smith), with whom he is "madly" in love—in both senses of the word, since Evelyn does not share his feelings. The film's indictment of bourgeois nuptials are given a Freudian inflection in an early scene in which close family friend Dr. Mark Hamilton (Sydney Greenstreet) psychoanalyzes the problem: "Marriage is a very tricky business. People have impulses, compulsions, *drives*, let us say, towards escape, escape from loneliness. They seek that escape in the companionship of someone else. And lo, when they think they've achieved it, they find they've put on handcuffs."

The emphasis on the word "drive" is intentional on Dr. Hamilton's and my part, for the irony here is threefold: Mason's drive is to escape *from* as much as *to* someone; his murder scheme is hatched after his own car accident and culminates with his wife's drive up a desolate mountain road; and he will be driven insane by Dr. Hamilton himself and brought to justice. The "good" doctor accomplishes this by managing to convince Mason, with the police's help, that his wife, whom he had killed before sending her car down a cliff, is still alive. The ambivalence in the treatment of both Mason and Hamilton comes partly from the casting, of course, but also from Bernhardt's own conflicted attitudes toward the two characters. In his interview with Kiersch, the director expressed both skepticism toward psychiatry and sympathy for his homicidal protagonist, whom he saw not as a psychopath but as a deeply alienated victim of greed (fig. 33).[19]

Bernhardt's alleged mistrust of psychiatrists makes it all the more noteworthy that three of his four noirs should feature such figures, each more sympathetically portrayed than the last. Before returning to the psychiatric theme, however, he would make another film that "clearly bears the mark of Siodmak," only this time the mark serves to undermine rather than support Siodmak's influence. Although *A Stolen Life*, a Betty Davis vehicle in which she plays identical twins (one good, the other evil), begs comparison to Siodmak's Olivia de Havilland–starring *The Dark Mirror*, Siodmak's film was made a year *after* Bernhardt's. And from a Jewish émigré noir standpoint, Bernhardt's film must be given the nod as well. Although *A Dark Mirror* is the lone Siodmak noir to feature a psychiatrist and *A Stolen Life* is the lone Bernhardt noir not to, the concentration on the psychological conflict in the former

Figure 33.   Not in *Casablanca* anymore: Humphrey Bogart in *Conflict* (1945).
(Photofest)

film compared to the exploration of broader social conflict in the latter
belie Schwab's ideological critique of Bernhardt's work as mired in the
mundane and apolitical.

The three main characters who provide the moral anchor in *A Stolen
Life* exist at oblique angles to mainstream society. Kate Bosworth, the good
twin, is an aspiring but alienated artist; Bill Emerson (Glenn Ford), her unrequited (until the end) true love, works in a lighthouse; and Karnock (Dane
Clark), Kate's artistic mentor, is a proto-1950s beatnik. All, to varying degrees,
are "pariahs," in Hannah Arendt's sense of the Jewish type who maintains
a position of moral righteousness through marginality (as opposed to the
"parvenu," who cedes the moral high ground through material acquisitiveness
and social climbing).[20] The fourth main character, the evil twin, Pat, in her
stealing of Emerson from Kate and her using him as a means of attaining
wealth and social status, exemplifies, in perfect narrative symmetry, the ethical
bankruptcy of the parvenu position. The transcendentally named Emerson

implies just such a distinction when, in his first intimate encounter with Kate, he confides that she's the first person to understand his lack of material ambition. Their spiritual compatibility is further suggested soon thereafter when she completes his sentence: "It's difficult for lonely people to find—" "—other lonely people."

Mincing words (or actions) is not how the ethnically named (and appearing) Karnock works—he goes right for the jugular. At an upscale gallery exhibit of Kate's paintings, the avant-garde artist not only tells her that her work stinks but also shows her why (in comparison to his own uncompromisingly sensual work). His attempt to do a life-imitating-art number on Kate indicates a sexist chink in Karnock's armor; at the film's climax, however, it is revealed that keen insight and even compassion lie behind his boorish facade. When, after evil twin Pat's death in a boating accident, Kate surreptitiously takes on Pat's identity to win back Bill, Karnock is the only person (besides Kate's avuncular guardian, Freddie [Charles Ruggles]) who sees through the subterfuge.

Karnock's odd-man-out position in the triangular relationship with Kate and Bill is preordained, of course, and not only by his supporting-actor casting and uncouth behavior. His coding as the lone Jew in a staunchly New England setting assures his perpetual pariah status. It also aligns his narrative function with that of black characters in classical Hollywood, whose collective history of suffering and oppression made them a favored moral compass for the film's protagonist, assuring that the white hero never strayed too far from true north. Of course, to retain their moral superiority, and the political status quo, blacks had to remain outsiders. And so too must the stubbornly bohemian Karnock, as only Kate and Bill are permitted both ultimate entry into the bourgeois fold and attainment—however compromised by "error and deception"—of romantic bliss.[21]

In *Possessed* and *High Wall*, the psychiatrist replaces the artist as the narrative, and ethical, fulcrum. Unlike in *Conflict*, however, the doctors in these two films serve a beneficently therapeutic role vis-à-vis their troubled protagonist patients, who themselves are more victims than perpetrators of the crimes in which they're implicated. That Louise Howell (Joan Crawford) in *Possessed* represents not just an individual mental case but an epidemiological syndrome is made explicit in Dr. Harvey Willard's (Stanley Ridges) conversation with a nurse following Louise's confinement in a Los Angeles County hospital:

DR. WILLARD: How many does this make?

NURSE: Twenty today. One manic, three seniles, six alcoholics, and ten schizos.

DR. WILLARD: And going up all the time. This civilization of ours is a worse disease than heart trouble or tuberculosis, and we can't escape it.

Moreover, as during Freud's heyday, a seemingly disproportionate female vulnerability to modern society's pathologies is apparent: "Beautiful woman. Talented, frustrated, like all the rest. Unable to cope" (fig. 34).

It takes hypnotherapy to bring out the syndrome's Jewishness. Once injected with Sodium Pentothal, noir's "prototypical drug of choice," Louise's illness is clinically diagnosed as a persecution complex.[22] Jewish enough in general, Louise's variation on the condition is lent Jewish émigré specificity in her choice of Los Angeles as a sanctuary from her alleged persecutors. The narrative illogic of her choice of the world's entertainment capital as a safe haven, except as an ironically self-reflexive allusion with decidedly Jewish émigré implications, emerges in her drug-induced explanation for why she has come all the way to L.A. from Washington, D.C.: "To get away from *them*. But they must never know. That's why I came here. I wanted to disappear."

Most of the remainder of the film takes place in flashback, adumbrating Louise's descent into paranoid delusion and the eventual murder of engineer David Sutton (Van Heflin), triggered by her frustrated love for the man whom she once had an affair with but who no longer loves her (if he ever did).

Figure 34.   Beautiful woman, unable to cope: Joan Crawford in *Possessed* (1947). (USC Special Collections)

David's European sensibility is signaled the first time we meet him, playing Schumann on the piano in a mountain cottage. His philosophical rationalization of their declining romantic relationship also exhibits a Continental bent: "We're all on the outside of people's lives looking in. . . . All I have are a lot of mathematical equations and question marks." The more specific he gets about his alienated affection, the more his explanation resonates with German-Jewish relations: "Blame it on the army, blame it on the war, blame it on anything you like, but that's the way it is. I can't love you the way you love me."

A kind of reverse femme fatale, driven to seek revenge for her jilting by an erstwhile lover, Louise begins to think that everyone, not merely David, is against her. She starts to hallucinate, believing that the ghost of the dead wife of Dean Graham (Raymond Massey)—the wealthy older man she marries in vain hope of forgetting David—is driving her to suicide. Finally, at the peak of her paranoia, she confronts David over his affair with Dean's daughter Carol (Geraldine Brooks); when he gets rough with her, she pulls a gun and shoots him. Or does she? Given Louise's previous hallucinations, which we as viewers had also initially been led to believe were actually happening, our ability to distinguish between reality and illusion has become, at this point, as suspect as that of Dr. Williard's tenth schizophrenic patient of the day. And although a post-flashback visit by Dean Graham to the hospital "assures" us that Louise did indeed kill David (and therefore we are not "all Jews now"), Dr. Williard's Holocaust-evoking prognosis for Louise's cure is decidedly not reassuring: "It's pain that made her this way, and only through greater pain and suffering beyond belief can she get well again."

Things would get worse before they got better in Bernhardt's last film noir, *High Wall*. A reworking of *Carrefour* transposed from Europe to the United States and from World War I to World War II, *High Wall* concerns a former bomber pilot, Steven Kenet (Robert Taylor), who is confined to a police mental hospital following his attempted suicide in a car accident after apparently killing his wife, Helen (Dorothy Patrick). Kenet's troubles are exacerbated by amnesia surrounding the circumstances of his wife's death, a condition that the police believe is a ploy to cop an insanity plea, but which actually is tied to a wartime head injury aggravated by the car crash. Drug-facilitated hypnotherapy, administered by another compassionate psychiatrist, Dr. Ann Lorrison (Audrey Totter), again yields positive results (fig. 35). Kenet retreats in his mind to the scene of the crime, where he recalls being driven to strangle his wife after discovering that she had been cheating on him while he was off working as a private pilot in Burma. Subsequent investigation, however, reveals that not he, but rather the man with whom his wife had the affair, Willard Whitcombe (Herbert Marshall), is the actual murderer. And sure enough, in a pharmaceutical deus ex machina, Whitcombe confesses under the involuntary influence of the "truth serum."

Figure 35.   Separation anxiety: Robert Taylor and Audrey Totter in *High Wall* (1947). (USC Special Collections)

High Wall, *A Stolen Life*, and *Possessed*, Kiersch points out, "all have charac-ters suffering guilt for crimes they didn't commit."[23] Guilt is also one of the main motifs that Fritz Göttler isolates in his auteurist analysis of Bernhardt's work—guilt, especially when combined with an obsession with the past, that "makes characters prisoners of their memories."[24] As much as false guilt, wartime trauma, and repressed memory can be related to Jewish émigré issues, however, *High Wall*'s main claim on Jewish émigré noir is supplied by the film's primary setting in the mental hospital, whose resemblance to a concentration camp is palpable.

The patients' plain white, pajama-like clothing is much closer to that of death camp inmates than the striped uniforms typically worn by prisoners in American films of the time. The chain-link rather than iron-bar barriers that secure the hospital's interior and exterior spaces also conform more to concentration camp than American prison aesthetics. The crowning touch, however, is the use of classical music. A Chopin sonata is piped into the mess hall, and one crazy inmate is obsessed with Beethoven's "Eroica"—a far cry from proto-typical U.S. prison fare, to be sure, yet a painfully precise correlative of the Kafkaesque mixture of high culture and horror that characterized the Nazi lagers, where inmate orchestras accompanied less fortunate comrades on their death march to the ovens.[25]

From Oppenheimer to Ophuls

Max Ophuls, as he came to be known in Hollywood in the late 1940s, began his life in 1902 in Saarbrücken, Germany, as Maximilian Oppenheimer. Son of a wealthy Jewish textile merchant, Max changed his last name to Ophüls (umlaut later dropped) when, already as a teenager, he became interested in stage acting. Allegedly chosen to disassociate the family name from what his parents, and bourgeois society, regarded as a disreputable profession, his new name also clearly de-Judaized its source and, more subtly but equally tellingly, feminized its substitution—Ophuls friend and mentor, director Fritz Holl, had chosen the appellation "in amorous recollection of a Danish actress by that name."[26]

Another wunderkind, Ophuls would outdo his contemporaries Ulmer, Bernhardt, and even Preminger in his precocious rise in the theater world. He directed his first professional play at the age of twenty-one, and in 1926, at age twenty-four, became the youngest director ever to head Vienna's Burgtheater. Recalling that Preminger was offered the same position some ten years later but was turned down because he refused to renounce his Jewishness, some explanation for Ophuls's privileging—which entailed not an escape from the "Jewish question" but rather a delayed reaction to it—seems in order.

Austria, like Germany, due to the more tolerant attitude of a Social Demo-cratic government in the early postwar years, experienced a comparative lull in official anti-Semitism, which allowed Jews to assume previously excluded positions of power and influence. Once the right-wing National Socialist Party replaced the Social Democrats in 1926, however, the briefly opened window of opportunity just as quickly slammed shut. Ophuls's experience at the Burgtheater exemplifies this abrupt turnaround, as he was dismissed from his prestigious impresario's post less than a year after his appointment.[27] Moving to Berlin following this personal insult and career setback, he continued to work in the theater but also branched into mass culture, writing radio plays and working for UFA. In 1930, after a stint as a dialogue coach on an early sound film directed by the Ukrainian Jewish immigrant Anatole Litvak, Ophuls directed his first picture, *Dann schon lieber Lebertran* (*I'd Rather Take Cod Liver Oil*), on which the ubiquitous Eugen Schüfftan did the camera work. Ophuls's two "most important" films from his Weimar period, *Die verkaufte Braut*

(*The Bartered Bride*, 1932) and *Liebelei* (*Flirtation*, 1933), also mark the beginning of his preoccupation with "women's subjects"—more specifically, with "victim-ized" women who became the object of exchange, and with whose plight the director appeared to identify "in hysterical fashion."[28]

As with the majority of the Jewish émigré noir directors, Ophuls left Berlin for Paris after the Nazi assumption of power in 1933. Although he also made films in Holland and Italy, including *La Signora di Tutti* (*Everybody's Woman*), which won a Venice Film Festival prize in 1934, he worked and resided mainly in France, where he became a citizen in 1938. After serving briefly in the French army and writing anti-Nazi radio broadcasts during the first years of the war, Ophuls fled first to Switzerland and then to the United States, arriving in Los Angeles, with the help of Varian Frey's Emergency Rescue Committee, in 1941.[29]

Despite Paul Kohner's help and a solid film career behind him, Ophuls would have the hardest time of any of the major émigré directors—"a second exile," Lutz Bacher calls it—finding work in Hollywood.[30] It didn't help that he had spurned an offer from MGM in 1936, that the wartime European market had dried up and with it much of the audience for the European-type art films Ophuls specialized in, and that he didn't properly socialize (although he partici-pated cursorily in the émigré salons). He was "not gregarious," Jewish émigré screenwriter Walter Reisch recalled. "He was much too elegant and artistic a man to be really able to conquer Hollywood, to become even a member of the Hollywood clan."[31] Perhaps the biggest obstacle to his landing a directing job was his refusal to make B films, something to which several of the émigrés had resorted as the admission price to the industry.[32]

Finally, after a frustrating and ultimately abortive effort with Preston Sturges and Howard Hughes's California Pictures, Ophuls, with Siodmak's assistance, completed his first Hollywood project. Made in 1947 for the newly merged Universal-International, the film was appropriately titled, at least from an extratextual standpoint, *The Exile*. The movie itself, however, dealt neither contemporaneously nor allegorically with the refugee's plight, but was rather a Restoration-era drama and star vehicle for Douglas Fairbanks Jr., ostensibly playing Charles II but essentially paying homage to his legendary father's silent swashbucklers. The most eponymously pertinent aspect of *The Exile* was Ophuls's directorial screen credit. No doubt following the same Germano-phobic logic that moved Kurt to become Curtis Bernhardt, Ophuls dropped the umlaut in his last name for the credits of this and all three of his subsequent Hollywood films. These three, *Letter from an Unknown Woman* (1948), *Caught* (1949), and *The Reckless Moment* (1949), built on and extended Ophuls's reputa-tion as a "woman's director," a reputation he would apotheosize with his last four films, all made upon his return to France: *La Ronde* (1950), *Le Plaisir* (1952),

The Earrings of Madame de . . . (1953), and *Lola Montez* (1955). Ophuls died of a chronic heart ailment in Hamburg, Germany, where he had been directing a play, in 1957.

Caught

Susan M. White's *The Cinema of Max Ophuls* is the lone analysis of any of the Jewish émigré noir directors that explicitly and to any serious degree examines Jewishness as an element in their work.[33] White's Jewish reading of Ophuls's body of films, much as mine of Jewish émigré noir in general, leans heavily on the rhetorical link between Jews and women. Although grounding this linkage in both groups' historical marginalization, White additionally emphasizes Jews' and women's shared ideological construction as carriers and victims in a capitalist system "of exchange divorced from that of production."[34] Production is meant here in both its political-economic and film-industrial senses, with the movie director regarded as a figurative and literal "middleman" in the exchange process.

Ophuls, specifically, through a "dialectic of mastery and humiliation" arising from his position as director and Jew, gets it both ways—indeed, doubly so, via his films' myriad "director surrogates . . . theatrical managers, agents, pimps, *entremetteurs*, and so on."[35] Although the director surrogates tend to be ambivalent figures, "the fallen woman" (Ophuls's favorite subject) is more fully "demythicized" as the victim rather than the agent of her fall; it is she with whom Ophuls, the Jewish refugee and "woman's director" par excellence, identifies most strongly.[36] Moreover, both woman and director surrogates, as marginalized figures who function as "scapegoats for the negative effects of interlocking systems of exchange," not only achieve a certain salvation through degradation, but also, if only unconsciously, "reveal the mechanisms that make the system work."[37]

Caught serves as a veritable primer for the dialectical relation among "'the feminine,' directorship, and inflationary exchange."[38] When its gender-based, anticapitalist content is combined with its low-key lighting and deep-focus cinematography, the film also functions (as *Ruthless* did for Ulmer), as Ophuls's *Citizen Kane*.[39] Smith Ohlrig (Robert Ryan) is the Kane analogue here, representing a composite of Howard Hughes and Preston Sturges, who, from their misbegotten film project with Ophuls, had become his prime Hollywood nemeses.[40] Leonora (Barbara Bel Geddes) plays Susan Alexander's kissing cousin in this schema, except that in Ophuls's hands the role is expanded from supporting player to protagonist. As the titular main character, Leonora is "caught" both internally and externally: internally by her desire "to be desired" and to overcome her working-class origins; and externally by her marriage to the pathological Ohlrig (oil rig?) and by her confinement in his Xanadu-like mansion, which, as in *Citizen Kane*, is more prison than palace (fig. 36).

Figure 36. Role reversal: Barbara Bel Geddes and Robert Ryan in *Caught* (1949). (USC Special Collections)

The film features two relational triangles: the first consists of Leonora, Ohlrig, and Ohlrig's pimp-like factotum, Franzi Kartos (Curt Bois); and the second of Leonora, Ohlrig, and Leonora's eventual true love and savior, Dr. Larry Quinada (James Mason). Both Franzi and Quinada, beyond their "middleman" status, possess several attributes that connote if not outright Jewishness, then the next best thing. Although White describes Franzi as "of uncertain nationality and sexual preference," one need not be so noncommittal.[41] Besides his foreign-sounding name, European accent, and penchant for playing "Tales from the Vienna Woods" on the piano, noted Jewish character actor Bois portrays Franzi with a barely disguised gayness that scarcely eluded PCA chief Joe Breen. (In his production memos, Breen continually objected to Franzi's appearing "too much like . . . a pimp? a homosexual? A Jew?"[42]) Ohlrig, whose own name and obsessive-compulsiveness suggest an "uncertainty of nationality and sexual preference," brings out all three of Breen's taboos when he calls Franzi "a dirty little parasite."[43] Quinada, if of less uncertain sexual preference, is of even more questionable nationality. Mason's undisguised British accent conveys a connection with the United Kingdom, but the Spanish-sounding Quinada points to Iberia. And when one considers that Quinada is not only a doctor but also one who works in an inner-city ghetto making house calls to families with names like Radecki, and that his office partner is Dr. Hoffmann (Frank Ferguson), the leap from Hispanic to Sephardic seems an easy one to make.

An additional biographical connection between Quinada and Ophuls reinforces the Jewish attribution. On a dinner date with Leonora, Quinada's complaint about his parents' dissatisfaction with his idealistic, rather than materialistic, choice of medical practice rhymes with Ophuls's parents' antipathy toward his theatrical ambitions: "My parents made themselves absolutely miserable by having an exaggerated idea about the importance of money. . . . They just wasted their lives pretending to be rich—finagling, never working, of course." The allusions to "finagling," "never working," and, perhaps most of all, the "of course," lend this quasi-Marxist indictment of the bourgeoisie a distinctly Jewish self-hating odor.

The self-loathing aspect is of more than passing interest for a Jewish émigré filmmaker who, despite the strong symbolic Jewish elements in his work, also exhibited a "certain avoidance of history" in regard to anti-Semitism, especially in his European-set films and specifically in his sanitized treatment of Vienna in *Letter from an Unknown Woman* (1948) and *La Ronde* (1950).[44] Such avoidance-cum-obfuscation is curious because not only was Vienna a city where "anti-Semitism was part of Ophuls' personal experience" but was also, indeed, where violent anti-Jewish uprisings preceded those of *Kristallnacht* and where "the first public programs for the elimination of Jews from the life of Europe were devised and proclaimed."[45] Virginia Wright Wexman interprets this "historical contradiction" in Ophuls's oeuvre partly "as a conflict between nationalism and internationalism—a conflict displaced onto the female body and into the private realm."[46] Ophuls himself, singing the standard frustrated filmmaker's tune, described how "the international producer anxiously avoids any political avowals."[47]

The problem with Ophuls's (and critics') *disavowal* of responsibility is threefold. First, the early postwar period was one in which American social-problem films, despite the HUAC hearings and the incipient blacklist, flourished as never before, including the first two Hollywood features on anti-Semitism in the United States, *Crossfire* and *Gentleman's Agreement* (both 1947).[48] Second, *Caught* was produced by Max Reinhardt's son Wolfgang for Enterprise Studios, a fledgling independent company formed along the lines of Frank Capra, William Wyler, and George Stevens's Liberty Films, and noted for its commitment to creative freedom.[49] Such freedom is certainly evident in *Caught*'s anticapitalist content, as well as in its aesthetic fidelity to what Lutz Bacher terms Ophuls's "deviant visual style": deep-focus long takes, sinuous camera movement, and a dearth of close-ups, all of which flew in the face of the classical Hollywood format.[50] Third, and the greatest blow to Ophuls's declaration of innocence, is his own autobiography, a cultural form far less subject to commercial constraints and Jewish defensiveness than a Hollywood movie, yet which also displays "conspicuous silence on the topic" of anti-Semitism.[51]

One can't help but wonder, along with White, whether Ophuls's son Marcel Ophuls, director of the acclaimed Holocaust-themed documentaries *The Sorrow and the Pity* (1969), *The Memory of Justice* (1976), and *Hotel Terminus* (1988), wasn't driven to make his rigorous and unflinching examinations of anti-Semitism "partly in reaction to his fathers' seeming ahistoricism."[52] Whatever Ophuls fils's motivation, his films, White adds acutely, in a manner applicable to the Jewish émigré directors as a whole, "respond not only to what is 'lacking' in his father's work but also to what they produce as historical documents that express as well as repress, place as well as displace, the problems of nationalism, sexual and religious identity, historical change, and artistic desire."[53]

The Reckless Moment

The "Jewish" woman and middleman figures are split into two characters, then recombined in complex ways, in Ophuls's second and only other film noir, *The Reckless Moment*.[54] Suburban housewife/mother Lucia Harper (Joan Bennett), though the dominant of the two main female characters, functions thematically alongside and in tandem with her aspiring-artist daughter Bea (Geraldine Brooks); gangster go-between Martin Donnelly (James Mason) is a kinder, gentler version of shady art dealer Ted Darby (Shepperd Strudwick), with whom Bea has an affair and whom Donnelly replaces in Darby's "business" and romantic roles (albeit vis-à-vis Lucia rather than Bea).

Lucia is the catalyst of both the splitting and the recombination. Her attempt to dislodge Bea from her relationship with Darby leads to his accidental death after a bitter confrontation with Bea. Believing that Bea murdered Darby, Lucia tries to cover up the crime, only to become entangled with Donnelly; on behalf of his mob boss Nagel (Roy Roberts), Donnelly blackmails Lucia with Bea's love letters to Darby, which implicate her in his death. In a twist on the femme fatale (and the homme fatal), Donnelly falls for Lucia, which redeems him morally ("I never wanted to do a decent thing till you came along") but also leads to his death. Donnelly stands up to Nagel, kills him in a fight, and, before dying in a car crash trying to escape, gives Bea's letters to Lucia and falsely confesses to Darby's killing. With all the "evildoers" conveniently in caskets, justice—in PCA terms at least—has been served. But as in all film noir, an ambivalent aftertaste remains.

Lucia's suburban, middle-class family (still missing her traveling salesman husband) may once again be intact, but any illusion of the separation of her

Figure 37.   Shining light on the situation: James Mason and Joan Bennett in *The Reckless Moment* (1949). (USC Special Collections)

Donna Reed–like existence from life's dark side has been irrevocably shattered. And the cracks in the facade were evident even before Donnelly came along, and not merely due to Bea's sordid affair or Lucia's bungled cover-up of Darby's death. That the fissures penetrated to the very foundation of bourgeois life was illustrated in an early complaint that Lucia confessed to Donnelly: "You don't know how a family can surround you at times," to which Donnelly responded—mockingly, perhaps, but not self-righteously—"Quite a prisoner, aren't you?" for just as quickly he added, "I'm not on my own. We're all involved with each other one way or another. You have your family, I have my Nagel" (fig. 37).

The name Nagel ("nail" in German), combined with Donnelly's Irish name and accent, lend a Catholic aspect to Donnelly's side of the equation: Nagel, in other words, is Donnelly's cross to bear. Family, however, despite Lucia's equally Catholic-sounding name, is arguably more of a Jewish trope. This notion is reinforced by the film's structuring absence: the missing husband/father. Mr. Harper is away on business, to Berlin of all places! He makes two long-distance calls to the house, one at the outset and one at the close, but we never see him or hear his voice. This disembodied figure has several associations. Retrospectively, it can relate to American servicemen absented, temporarily or permanently, by the war. Contemporaneously, it can allude to postwar U.S. business involvement in Germany encouraged by the Marshall Plan. But it can also, in a feminist context, refer to the missing "middleman" in White's Jewish trinity of "'the feminine,' directorship, and inflationary exchange." Assigning the "director's surrogate" role to Mr. Harper, in this schema, receives biographical support from Ophuls's remark to Curtis Bernhardt around this time: "We don't belong here. We belong in Europe."[55]

Following *A Reckless Moment* and his own advice, in 1950 Ophuls and his non-Jewish wife, Hilde, "finally did what we so long had yearned for, but which we also very much feared: we drove to Germany."[56] Illustrating their profoundly mixed feelings, when on their last stop before entering the country a boy shouted out to them, "Much happiness in your old homeland," Ophuls lowered his head to the steering wheel and burst into tears.[57] Siodmak would make the return journey soon thereafter, and Lang a few years after that, along with several other émigré artists and intellectuals, Jewish and non-Jewish alike. The reasons for changing continents were many and varied.[58] Besides a sense that Europe, in spite of everything, was indeed where the former refugees belonged, there were, especially for the filmmakers, significant practical concerns: the rise of McCarthyism, the downturn in the Hollywood film industry, and incentives provided from abroad. Upon arrival in their "old homeland," however, a new tragedy unfolded, one that Billy Wilder described upon his brief, early-postwar return to Germany ("Where was home?") and that Lang elaborated on years later in a filmed interview: "The German poet Börriss Freiher von Münchhausen wrote a poem he called 'The Emigrant.' The last two lines of the poem are: 'And when he then comes home, he is a stranger in a strange land.' That, I believe, is the tragedy of emigration."[59]

Those among the Jewish émigré noir directors who chose to make the transatlantic leap were in the minority: in the end only Siodmak and Ophuls stayed in Europe for keeps, with Lang returning to the States after a decade.[60] The others, whether from more successful acculturation to the United States or from greater ability to adapt to Hollywood's industrial paradigm shift, remained and continued to work in their adopted homeland. One of the adaptations meant at least leaving oneself open to working in the new medium of television. After all, if legendary Weimar cinematographer Karl Freund (*The Golem, The Last Laugh, Variety, Metropolis*) could go from *Caligari* to *Lucy* (he was chief cinematographer on the *I Love Lucy* show from 1951 to 1959), what was to stop an émigré noir director from giving the boob tube a try?[61]

10 Pathological Noir, Populist Noir, and an Act of Violence

JOHN BRAHM, ANATOLE LITVAK,
FRED ZINNEMANN

The Twilight Zone, The Outer Limits, Alfred Hitchcock Presents, Thriller, Suspicion, Gunsmoke, Wagon Train, Dr. Kildare, Medic, Johnny Staccato, Naked City, M Squad, and *The Defenders*, as well as the anthology series *Playhouse 90, Lux Playhouse, Screen Directors Playhouse, Schlitz Playhouse of Stars, Studio 57, Alcoa Premiere, General Electric Theater*—these are only the most prominent of the television programs for which John Brahm directed multiple episodes in the 1950s and 1960s. For some critics, such as auteurist patriarch Andrew Sarris, this wholesale migration to the small screen signaled, almost by definition, a sharp decline in Brahm's career.[1] For more television-tolerant observers, such as blogger C. Jerry Kutner, Brahm not only "hit some kind of peak" in his televisual phase but also, through his work on "some of the best-ever episodes" of *The Twilight Zone, The Outer Limits, Alfred Hitchcock Presents*, and *Thriller*, "became the greatest director of TV horror."[2] Whatever the comparative critical assessment of his film and television oeuvre, Brahm's career trajectory from Weimar-era theater to American film noir to television horror is unique among the Jewish émigré directors.

Born Hans Brahm in Hamburg, Germany, in 1893, John Brahm was the son of Jewish stage actor Ludwig Brahm and the nephew of noted theater impresario Otto Brahm. The towering figure of German theater until Max Reinhardt came on the scene, Otto Brahm founded the Deutsches Theater in Berlin in 1894 and, after Reinhardt took over its directorship in 1904, founded the Freie Bühne (Free stage) the same year. Unlike Preminger, Ulmer, or Ophuls, who faced varying degrees of familial resistance to their embarking on a stage career, John Brahm's entry into the world of European theater was all but preordained. As for his ethno-religious identification, Brahm's relation to his Jewishness can easily compete with Lang's and Ulmer's for its complexity and convolution.

"My parents considered it an advantage to be taken as a Christian," he recalled in an interview in 1971. "So [the Jewish] religion was out of my life." More than just taken *as* a Christian, however, Brahm was actually taken *in* by a Lutheran pastor and his family when he was nine years old: "I was a very

185

bad child . . . taking money and going to the zoo without permission . . . and staying away from school . . . and my parents didn't know what to do with me." The upshot of his foster upbringing was not only improved behavior ("I became a very pious boy . . . singing in the little Lutheran choir, ringing the church bells"); the whole experience so impressed him that he asked his parents to become Christians, and, according to Brahm, "they were only too happy to follow my request."[3]

The pious Christian phase was just that, however, and Brahm left both his homes at twelve years old, continued his schooling in Lübeck, eventually served in World War I, and returned to his theatrical, if not his Jewish, roots, after the war. Shuttling among Berlin, Vienna, and Paris in the 1920s, Brahm established himself as resident director in several prestigious theaters and married, in succession, two German-Jewish stage and film actresses, Johanna Hofer and Dolly Haas.[4] Despite both the conjugal connection with cinema, and contact with future Jewish émigré filmmakers Anatole Litvak, Kurt Bernhardt, and Henry Koster, Brahm remained theater-bound throughout the Weimar era and only began directing movies once he immigrated to England (following Hitler's ascension).[5] "Like many other non-religious Jews," Brahm's daughter Sumishta relates, "anti-Semitism and Nazism made him more Jewish conscious—as did his relationship to his uncle Otto Brahm."[6] He literally saw the writing on the wall when a young brownshirt painted over his name on a poster for a play that he was directing and blurted out, "You're not going to be around long!"[7]

He wouldn't be in England long either, although his departure from the Isle of Albion was more consensual than commandeered. His first film, a 1936 remake of D. W. Griffith's 1919 silent classic *Broken Blossoms*, on which Brahm took over directing chores from Griffith himself in mid-production, led to an offer from Columbia Pictures that would jump-start both his Hollywood career and the film noir cycle. Among Brahm's early A-minus and B films for the second-tier Hollywood studio were not only his first full-fledged noirs, but also two of the three films that Arthur Lyons regards as foundational to the series: "Although many critics cite RKO's *Stranger on the Third Floor* (1940) as the first true film noir, 1939 was actually the year that inaugurated the film noir with the release of three prototypical films: *Let Us Live, Rio,* and *Blind Alley.*"[8] *Blind Alley* was by first-wave Jewish immigrant Charles Vidor; *Let Us Live* and *Rio* were by Brahm. Extending the Jewish émigré connection, and perhaps Lyons's noir-cycle starting point as well, *Let Us Live*, in its title and in Henry Fonda's reprise of his working-class antihero role in a "wrong man" scenario, is an obvious nod to Lang's *You Only Live Once* (1937); and in its bitter rebuke of the U.S. justice system, the film owes as much if not more to Lang's *Fury* (1936).[9]

Like *Fury*'s Joe Wilson, *Let Us Live*'s Brick Tenant undergoes a Jekyll and Hyde transformation after coming within a whisker of being executed for a murder he did not commit. Moments after proclaiming to his fellow falsely convicted friend, "The flag isn't just a piece of cloth, it's a symbol, of freedom, justice, and all the things men fight for," he confides in his trusting fiancée, Mary (Maureen O'Sullivan), that he no longer believes in those ideals: "I've grown up, that's all. We got no chance, us little people." Although Brick's life is ultimately spared when the actual murderers are apprehended, Mary lets the DA know the irreparable damage that's been done: "Up there's a man who believed in truth and honesty and fairness. Oh, he still hears and breathes and sees, but what's inside him his dead." The DA's, and the film's, final words cynically reinforce Mary's condemnation of the system: "Well, I've convicted two innocent men. Now I've got to try to convict three guilty ones. Probably be a whole lot harder."

In allowing neither romance, patriotism, nor religion to soften its message, *Let Us Live* trumps both *Fury* and *You Only Live Once* as societal critique and therefore also, at least thematically, as film noir. Although not surpassing Lang's two films in expressionist mise-en-scène, *Let Us Live* and *Rio*—the latter especially in its extreme-high-contrast, neon-light-flashing climax—demonstrate Brahm's knack for the noir aesthetic as well. Given that this knack came despite little hands-on filmmaking experience in Weimar-era Berlin indicates, as with Preminger, that such experience was not a prerequisite for the development of an expressionist "consciousness." Exposure to the films and the aura surrounding them might suffice, which, for Brahm, occurred through "the dark and fantastic" aspect of pictures such as *Faust* and *Die Nibelungen*, which he recalled being "fascinated with" during the Weimar period.[10]

Moving on, and up, to Twentieth Century Fox in the early 1940s, Brahm gained more attention with the horror film *The Undying Monster* (1942), in which his darkly stylish mise-en-scène once again overshadowed an otherwise "fairly flaccid genre piece."[11] His breakthrough into classier A-film territory, and also his first fully realized noir, *The Lodger* (1944), came (just as his directing break in England had come) via a remake of a classic silent film of the same name by a famous director. Both Alfred Hitchcock's 1927 original and Brahm's reworking are fictionalizations of the Jack the Ripper serial murder case, set in late nineteenth-century England. The significance to Jewish émigré noir of Brahm's *The Lodger* lies not only in the film itself but also in its having sired, through its box-office success, another quasi remake: Ulmer's B-film knockoff and first film noir, *Bluebeard*.

"Psychopaths Are Like Hotcakes"

This is the glib response of *Sunset Boulevard*'s Joe Gillis to screenwriting partner/love interest Betty Schaefer (Nancy Olsen), when Betty suggests deleting the portion of Joe's script that explores "a killer's sick mind." The repartee is doubly ironic. Diegetically, it foreshadows Joe's own killing by his spurned lover, demented former silent screen star Norma Desmond (Gloria

Swanson). Intertextually, it conjures an actual spate of Hollywood films of the time featuring pathological killers. Twenty years later, noir historian Paul Schrader would famously date the trend from 1949 to 1953, identify it with "psychotic action and suicidal impulses," and label it the third and final phase of the classical noir cycle.[12] A closer look at Brahm's six 1940s noirs, however, starting with *The Lodger*, invites a reassessment of Schrader's periodization.

Four of the six films—*The Lodger*, *Guest in the House* (1944), *Hangover Square* (1945), and *The Locket* (1946)—were released during Schrader's first noir phase (1941–1946). Labeled the "private eye and lone wolf" grouping, this period is marked, for Schrader, by the Hammett/Chandler detective heroes and is regarded stylistically as favoring a "studio look" and a "film gray" muting of expressionist effects.[13] Yet all four of Brahm's first-phase noirs feature pathological protagonists more befitting Schrader's third phase, and all the films' styles are as darkly expressionistic as any in the cycle. Moreover, Brahm's sole detective noir (less darkly shot than his previous films), *The Brasher Doubloon* (1947), was made during Schrader's second, "postwar realism" phase (1945–1949), and the last of the six, *Singapore* (1947), is a romantic thriller that barely qualifies as a noir at all.[14] Schrader, of course, was a shrewd enough historian not to claim absolutism for his schema, admitting to some overlap, as his time frames suggest, and occasional exceptions, such as *Double Indemnity*, which he regards as "a bridge to the postwar phase."[15] Brahm's entire body of film noirs, however, is so exceptional as to exist in an alternative chronological universe from the one mapped by Schrader, a universe bounded not only by the parameters of the noir cycle but also, once again, by those of its Jewish émigré subset.

Brahm's four pathological noirs can be bracketed into pairs: one pair, *The Lodger* and *Hangover Square*, features psychotic males; and the other, *Guest in the House* and *The Locket*, deranged females. As Patrice Petro (among others) has shown, the feminine and the monstrous or deviant are always already iconically linked by their signification as Other.[16] The hypersensitivity of the male maniacs in their two films, and the casting of Laird Cregar in both roles, further narrows (or Judaizes) the gender gap. A hulking presence with an incongruously vulnerable sensibility, Cregar (a homosexual conflicted by his orientation) invests his serial killers with a cultured piety and an unmistakable effeminacy.[17] His Jack the Ripper character in *The Lodger*, calling himself Mr. Slade, exhibits other attributes with decidedly émigré Jewish connotations. The most notable of these is his self-characterization as a wanderer. Introducing himself to the Buntings (Cedric Hardwicke and Sara Allgood), the kindly elderly couple that takes him in as a boarder, Slade calls their house "a refuge" and asks them to regard him "as a lodger, not as a guest." Later, he admits, "I've been asked to move several times, because I was no longer welcome."

Of course, one need not reach for metaphorical links to Jewishness when dealing with the historical, though also mythic, figure of Jack the Ripper. The never apprehended perpetrator of the brutal murders and disembowelments of several prostitutes in the Whitechapel district of London in 1888 was widely believed at the time, and even controversially to the present, to be a Jew. The *Times* of London reported as late as 2006 that handwritten notes newly acquired from Scotland Yard's Black Museum confirmed what had long been suspected: that an eyewitness's identification pointed to the Polish Jew Aaron Kosminski as the diabolical killer.[18] That others contest this assertion, based on handwriting and linguistic analysis, cannot erase the historical connection of Jews and Jack the Ripper among late nineteenth-century Londoners.[19] This previously discursive connection, inscribed in the Christian popular imaginary via long-standing associations of Jews and monsters, was given demographic support by the large influx of "alien" Ostjuden to working-class districts such as Whitechapel in the mid-to-late 1800s.[20]

Slade's medical pathologist occupation also builds on historical and discursive associations with Jews. The Ripper's method of mutilation through surgically precise disembowelment led investigators to attribute to "him" professional medical training; Jews, as we know, were disproportionately represented in the medical profession by this time. The act of ritual mutilation itself has even more damning, if less historically substantiated, ties to Jews, via the notorious blood libel. And had anti-Semites dug a little deeper, they would have found perhaps the most telling Jewish correlation to the serial murderer in the organ around which "he" wrapped his only note to the police: a kidney. Kidneys (*kelayot*, in Hebrew) are mentioned more than thirty times in the *Tanach* (Old Testament), generally in the context of sacrificial offerings. In books following the Torah, Garabed Eknoyan has shown, kidneys become the figurative locus "of temperament, emotions, prudence, vigor, and wisdom," and are frequently cited "as the organs examined by God to judge an individual." They are always cited "in conjunction with the heart as mirrors of the psyche," and, particularly in the book of Job, are regarded "as the site of divine punishment for misdemeanors, committed or perceived."[21]

Any mention of excavated organs, no matter what the scriptural cachet, was of course taboo in the Production Code era; Darryl Zanuck even demanded that actresses be substituted for prostitutes as Slade's murder victims.[22] As it turns out, the latter substitution actually expanded the psychosexual dimension of the film by encouraging exploration of the conflicted relations among sexuality, popular culture, and art. Not an artist himself, as Ulmer's Gaston Morrell would be, Slade is, however, obsessed with his deceased beloved brother's self-portraits to the point of incestuousness. Indeed, his serial murders of female theater performers are rationalized as revenge for his brother's artistic ruin and eventual suicide, which Slade blames on a woman of the stage. The role played by sexual repression in his hatred of such women is revealed in his extreme dread of the female gaze (he even covers the photos of actresses that hang in

his room because their eyes follow him when he moves), and in his comment
to Kitty Langley (Merle Oberon), the music-hall star who is also the Buntings'
niece: "You're so exquisite, more wonderful than anything I've ever known. It
is such lovely women like you who drag men down" (fig. 38). But his misogyny
is also rationalized in Old Testament terms, as when he tells Mrs. Bunting:
"Solomon says a strange woman lieth in wait as for prey. She increases trans-
gressors among men."

Jewishness is figured explicitly in the bravura opening scene of *Hangover
Square*. The film opens on an organ-grinder in the bustling nighttime streets
of working-class London in 1903. Then, amid the cacophony of street sounds,
in one fluid, serpentine move, the camera swoops up and across the street to
the second-floor window of an antique dealer's shop, not only observing but
participating in, via the point of view of an unseen killer, the brutal murder of
the bearded, skull-cap-wearing merchant. The murderer, we soon discover, is
an actual artist this time, and also based on an actual historical figure, British
classical composer George Harvey (his name barely but ominously fictionalized
into George Harvey Bone). Again played by Cregar (obviously building on the
success of *The Lodger*), Bone is driven to kill not by hatred of women, or men,
but rather by raucous or discordant sounds that drive him into a homicidal rage
from which he shortly emerges with no conscious knowledge of his murderous

Figure 38.   Splitting the difference: Merle Oberon and Laird Cregar in *The Lodger*
(1944). (USC Special Collections)

actions. Sexual repression is again posited as probable cause for Bone's killer instinct: a Scotland Yard psychiatrist (George Sanders, who played the chief inspector in *The Lodger*) recommends less work and more play as a potential cure. But the greater, though not unrelated, conflict here—a veritable leitmotif in Jewish émigré noir—is between high art and mass culture.

"Play," for Bone, consists of writing music for popular ballads and romantic musicals tailored to the talents of his new love, chorus girl Nette Longdon (Linda Darnell). Nette, like any "good" femme fatale, is also playing with Bone (to benefit her own career), but he cannot resist her charms even when he realizes her opportunistic motives and, worse, her romantic betrayal. Bone's cultural frustrations, similar to Brahm's and other émigré artists,' are revealed in a conversation he has with Nette over her insistence that he write a new musical for her:

BONE: I've already put my own work aside far too long for you.
NETTE: Just one more.
BONE: It's always one more. They get stale so fast I never have time to do anything else. . . . These songs mean nothing to me! What do I get out of it?

But Nette's persistence pays off. Adding lyrics to an excerpt from the concerto he's been working on, she seduces him into converting the classical piece into her new musical.

On Guy Fawkes's Eve, Bone proposes to Nette, only to find that she's already engaged to the musical's producer, Eddie Carstairs (Glenn Langan). Driven mad by another cacophonous noise, he ends up strangling Nette, carrying her mask-faced body along the Guy Fawkes parade, and stacking it atop the refuse heap–cum–ritual bonfire. Having achieved seeming closure with Nette and pop culture, Bone returns to his concerto, which he plays at a formal concert that ends the film in even more bravura fashion than it began. Rhyming the opening serpentine camera move up to and through the Jewish merchant's window, the camera does a sinuous dance to Bone's music, swirling around the hall, up and down, back and forth, from audience, to orchestra, to Bone engrossed in his piano playing. The music is not of the more melodic sort that we heard him play earlier, however, before being distracted by Nette. It has turned eerily atonal, as if having absorbed some of mass culture's cacophony and transmuted it into high modernism—a Schoenbergian metamorphosis not dissimilar to what Brahm and his fellow Jewish expatriates were attempting with film noir.

As successful as it may be thematically for *The Lodger*, the synthesis of high and low culture, sexuality and sublimation—befitting both modernism's and film noir's ties to the Romantic tradition—turns out to be a Faustian bargain for Bone himself. His own discordant concerto triggers a deranged episode accompanied by flashbacks of his various crimes. Unable to complete his masterpiece, and accosted by the police, he tosses a kerosene lamp into the crowd, starting a fire. As the panicked crowd and orchestra rush from the scene, only Bone remains, returning to play the final stanzas of his concerto amid a swirl of smoke and flame—an image uncannily resonant of the holocaust (and Holocaust) then raging across Europe and much of the rest of the world (fig. 39).

Femme Fatale as Sociopath

The first of Brahm's female psychodramas, *Guest in the House*, a film made between *The Lodger* and *Hangover Square*, carries the latter's World War II metaphor throughout the entire narrative. The film's voice-over narrator, Aunt Martha (Aline McMahon), sets the allegorical stage to nighttime images of lashing surf, overcast skies, and a lone house perched atop a seaside promontory: "A strange story happened in the happiest house I know. There's always been laughter in that house, and love. But down under the cliff a wild sea pounds. We were safe and snug above it, but suddenly the pounding sea seemed to invade our house, a wild and evil force swept through it. We were as powerless as if we were being beaten by the wild and tearing rocks."

This demonic force of nature, we soon learn, is not a tsunami or a hurricane, though it does bear a woman's name. Evelyn Heath (Anne Baxter),

Figure 39.   Cregar playing a Holocaust (and his farewell) sonata in *Hangover Square* (1945). (USC Special Collections)

fiancée of Dr. Dan Proctor (Scott McKay), is what wreaks havoc on the once happy and loving household of Dan's painter brother, Doug (Ralph Bellamy); his wife, Ann (Ruth Warrick); daughter Lee (Connie Laird); and live-in model, Miriam (Marie McDonald). If there was a weak link in this seemingly wholesome if unconventional setup before Evelyn's arrival it was surely Miriam, who poses provocatively for Doug's fashion designs that pay the bills, and sometimes even in the nude for his personal creative work. Evelyn, who suffers from a weak heart and a fragile psyche, and whom Dan brings to the seaside house for recuperation, quickly zeroes in on Miriam and Doug's working relationship as the household's Achilles' heel, through which she hopes to make a romantic conquest of Doug, with whom she falls, again quite literally, madly in love (fig. 40).

Just as in *The Lodger* and *Hangover Square*, and as we will find again in *The Locket*, the main male figures are associated with medicine and the arts, their twinning reinforced here through attachment to two brothers with similar-sounding first names. Although these occupations, especially when the

Figure 40.   Femme fatale as fascist threat: Anne Baxter in *Guest in the House* (1945). (USC Special Collections)

fashion aspect is appended, once more conjure Jewish associations, the diegetic emphasis on the Proctor family name and Doug's desire to paint Evelyn as Saint Cecilia tends to de-Judaize them. Miriam, however, whose last name is never uttered (nor is it listed in the credits), through its ur-Jewish derivation from Moses's wife in Exodus, reclaims Jewishness in ways that well serve the wartime allegory. Miriam, after all, is also a guest in the house, and the first to be banished from it when Evelyn's scheming falsely implicates her in an unseemly affair with Doug.

Perhaps the strongest basis for a World War II reading of *Guest in the House* is the attitude of the Proctor brothers toward Evelyn, whose symbolic (Evil-in) relation to Nazi Germany, in such a scenario, should by now be apparent. Dan, the doctor, is only too aware of Evelyn's dark side; indeed, he has read portions of her diary that openly admit not only her lack of love for him but her outright contempt both for him and his mother, Martha. Dan, then, is the willing appeaser and unwitting accomplice of the Nazis, not because he agrees with their ideas but because he either believes he can temper their worst aspects or hopes they will dissipate of their own accord.

Doug's childlike naïveté is both his greatest charm and his greatest liability. His obliviousness to Evelyn's evil intentions, long after the others have grown wise to them, nearly spells disaster both for him and all he holds dear. His "it can't happen here" insouciance plays into Evelyn's hands as much if not more than Dan's "it can't last long" rationalization; although Dan may reluctantly countenance Evelyn's destructiveness, Doug ignorantly encourages it. His persistent flirtation with Miriam, even after clouds of suspicion begin to form around their innocent teasing, is what opens the way for Evelyn's rear-guard action (and eventual frontal attack). Doug is the "good German" who chose to see only the thrilling, uplifting side to Nazism, the call to glory and greatness, and the Nietzschean Übermensch, all of which is exemplified in his bitterly ironic choice of Evelyn as his model for Saint Cecilia.

That it takes someone from outside the house, Aunt Martha, to ultimately vanquish Evelyn is also telling. Despite full disclosure of Evelyn's past evil deeds and full awareness of her mental derangement, Dan remains faithful to the end and still plans to marry her. Therefore, Martha, to save her son—and God knows how many others, as she informed us in the opening voice-over—felt compelled to counterattack: "So I committed a crime. There would have been worse crimes so I chose mine." Exploiting Evelyn's own Achilles' heel, her phobia of birds, Martha tells Evelyn that the Proctor's caged bird, which actually had died, has been let loose in the house. Driven into a frenzy at the prospect—of what, facing her shadow self, or a palace revolt?—Evelyn hurtles from the house toward the promontory and plunges to the "wild and tearing rocks" below.

Brahm's *The Locket*, generally regarded as his finest cinematic achievement, is certainly the most structurally complex of his pathological noirs. *Hangover*

Square and *Guest in the House* surpass it in camera work and overall mise-en-scène; and *The Lodger*'s mirror symbolism, chiaroscuro lighting, and climactic theater chase (all of which presage similar effects in Welles's legendary *The Lady from Shanghai*, 1947) are incomparable. In narrative technique, however, *The Locket*'s multiple flashbacks, and flashbacks within flashbacks, make those in Siodmak's *The Killers*, released the same year, seem pedestrian by comparison. A filmic correlative of the unconscious motivation and repressed memory of the sociopathic femme fatale, Nancy Morris-Blair-Patton (Lorraine Day), *The Locket*'s Chinese box–like structure can rightfully be termed, with ample support from the film, Talmudic.

The Talmud, and its companion text, the Midrash, employ a convoluted hermeneutical method in which spiritual questions are not adjudicated with singular finality, but rather are rendered multivocally and left open-ended. That this process mimics, and perhaps even informs Freudian psychoanalysis, has long been acknowledged.[23] The notion that the "royal road to the unconscious" is a tortuous route, only traversable with the aid of an experienced guide adept at reading verbal signs, conforms remarkably with the principles of Talmudic exegesis. Analogously, in *The Locket* the psychoanalytic method is posited as central to unlocking the narrative's mystery.

The main story line is related in a series of interlocking flashbacks by psychiatrist Dr. Henry Blair (Brian Aherne), one of the ex-husbands of Nina, an alluring kleptomaniac who, just the opposite of *Whirlpool*'s Ann Sutton, uses her affliction to drive her various *suitors* insane. Blair himself was one of these, although he regained his sanity and now seeks to warn Nina's latest victim, John Willis (Gene Raymond), on his wedding day, of the disastrous consequences of marrying Nina. Blair explains how painter Norman Clyde (Robert Mitchum), another erstwhile paramour of Nina's, was not so lucky. Clyde had tried in vain to warn Blair about Nina before jumping to his death from Blair's office window. In the ensnarement of both the doctor and the artist by the femme fatale, *The Locket* thus parallels these figures' alignment in *Guest in the House*. The difference in *The Locket* is that art precedes science in its ability to discern the black widow's true nature.

Clyde's first painting of Nina is as Cassandra, the mythic Trojan soothsayer who, despite accurately foreseeing the future, was initially disbelieved and judged insane. Clyde's prophetic twist is to depict Nina's Cassandra as a blind woman with empty eye sockets. Besides its variation on the theme of the dreaded female gaze, as in *The Lodger*, the painting, which propels Clyde's rise from obscurity to fame and fortune, mirrors Brahm's other pathological noirs in its meditation on the Faustian interplay of morality, creation, and success—all of which come packaged in *The Locket* in the ambivalent figure of Nina.

Nina's uniqueness as a femme fatale lies in her class-inflected mixture of victimizer and victim. Other noted noir temptresses, from Phyllis Dietrichson in *Double Indemnity* to Cora Smith in *The Postman Always Rings Twice* to Norma Desmond in *Sunset Boulevard*, have had their destructiveness rendered, if not justifiable, at least partially explicable as psychosocial responses to a patriarchal, capitalist society. Only in *The Locket*, however, are the oppressive forces clearly delineated. This occurs in a third flashback (within Clyde's flashback within Blair's flashback) in which Nina relates a childhood trauma to Clyde to help explain her theft of a bracelet. After her father, a painter, died when Nina was a young girl, Nina's mother was forced to find work as a maid in a wealthy woman's household. There Nina was given a locket as a special gift by the woman's daughter, with whom she had become close friends. But the woman not only took the locket away, because of its great value, but also, when it went missing, accused Nina of stealing and beat her—even after Nina's mother found the locket among the woman's daughter's dirty clothes.

Given Nina's untrustworthiness from this point on in the film, however, the viewer is forced, retrospectively, to regard Nina's class-inflected tale as unreliable—until the very end. Just before she walks down the aisle to marry John (who was unconvinced by Blair's cautionary tale), John's mother, who turns out to be the same wealthy woman who took away Nina's childhood locket, gives it to her now (unaware of her identity) as a pre-wedding gift. At first Nina is thrilled by this ultimate retribution, until the music from a music box she knocks over (the same music box she knocked over as a child) unleashes a flood of repressed memories—including those related to her betrayal of Clyde and Blair. Her subsequent retreat into a catatonic state, which precludes her marrying John and sends her off to a mental hospital, once again placates the Production Code. But the nervous breakdown also deflects much of the responsibility for her wrongdoing onto the economic disparity and materialistic ideals that laid the groundwork for them.

Bad for Noir, Good for the Jews?

Merle Davis (Nancy Guild), the femme fatale in Brahm's last true film noir, *The Brasher Doubloon*, is rendered even more sympathetically than Nina.[24] But she is only a quasi femme fatale to begin with, à la Lauren Bacall's Vivian Rutledge in *The Big Sleep*, who will ultimately get the man (in the romantic sense) and not lure him to his doom. The kinship between Davis and Rutledge is hardly coincidental: *The Brasher Doubloon* is also based on a Raymond Chandler novel (*High Window*) and features the same private detective, Philip Marlowe. But the similarity ends there. Although his pathological noirs more than justify critical assessment of Brahm "as a unique stylist," the Chandler adaptation also supports, however anomalously, those who would dismiss him as a "rank imitator of better directors."[25] Although *The Brasher Doubloon*'s inferior quality may detract from Brahm's overall body of work, the weakness, in this particular case, actually further benefits the Jewish émigré noir thesis.

As the lone Jewish émigré noir with a private-eye protagonist, and only the second one based on a hard-boiled novel (*Double Indemnity* is the other), *The Brasher Doubloon* is the exception that proves the rule: namely, that Jewish refugee directors were far less drawn to tough-guy material than to stories featuring female or sensitive male leads. The sense that Brahm lacked either the knack or the heart for the project starts with George Montgomery's portrayal of the Marlowe character, which Andrew Dickos deems "perhaps the least effective of the period." At best predicting Ralph Meeker's Mike Hammer in *Kiss Me Deadly* (1955), sans the satirical edge, Montgomery's Marlowe "was translated as a cross between a smug womanizer and a matinee idol."[26] Not helped by a half-baked plot that mashes up the precious-object conceit of *The Maltese Falcon*, the upper-class milieu of *The Big Sleep*, and the gather-all-the-suspects payoff of *The Thin Man*, even *The Brasher Doubloon*'s mise-en-scène is "comparatively understated." Except for the palpable presence of the Santa Ana winds, there "is little out of the ordinary or flamboyant in Brahm's hard-boiled world."[27]

The film, however, is not without its redeeming features. Chandler's telling turns of phrase surface sporadically, such as in Marlowe's voice-over about Los Angeles's Bunker Hill district: "It used to be a choice place to live. Now people live there because they have no choice." And a couple of grotesque, foreign-coded characters make their appearance, such as the German-accented gangster Eddie Prue (Alfred Linder) and the newsreel cameraman/numismatist Rudolph Vannier (Fritz Kortner). Kortner's casting and Vannier's character are easily the strongest Jewish émigré noir elements in the film. Kortner, of course, who starred in Willy Wilder's *The Victim*, was "a veteran actor molded in the expressionist cinema of Germany in the 1920s."[28] Vannier, meanwhile, literalizes the Weimar connection, with a touch of émigré-inflected pathos, when he tells Marlowe that, prior to his becoming a cameraman in Hollywood, he had been a filmmaker in Germany . . . ten years ago.

Anatole Litvak

As a Jewish refugee who left Weimar Germany on the eve of the Nazi takeover, and as a director of some of the earliest U.S. film noirs and a handful overall, Anatole Litvak would seem to deserve higher billing than his penultimate treatment here. The reason for the "second-class citizenship" is largely geopolitical: Litvak was neither born nor raised in a German-speaking country, but rather in Kiev in the Ukraine. The Slavic rather than Teutonic sociocultural backdrop, although it certainly did not preclude Litvak's exposure to anti-Semitism, did minimize a key component of the Jewish émigré noir dynamic: intense ambivalence toward Germany, and less virulent but still mixed feelings toward an American nation at war with the erstwhile homeland.

Litvak did not lack all contact with German culture or society. Following a stage-to-film trajectory similar to that of many of the Jewish émigré noirists, he attended the State Theatre School in Leningrad; worked as a stage actor, designer, and director; and then spent two years with the Soviet branch of the Danish film company Nordisk before moving to Berlin in 1925.[29] After a stint as assistant editor on G. W. Pabst's *Joyless Street* (1925) and four years as assistant to émigré Russian director Alexander Wolkoff in Paris, Litvak returned to Germany, where he directed his first two films, the musical *Dolly macht Karriere* (*Dolly Gets Ahead*, 1930) and the comedy *Nie wieder Liebe* (*No More Love*, 1931). Another inter-émigré link occurred with *Dolly*, on which Max Ophuls, apparently due to Litvak's lack of command of German, served as dialogue director. Before returning to Berlin for his last German film, *Das Lied einer Nacht* (*The Song of Night*, 1932), another musical, Litvak directed two films in France, the comedy *Calais-Douvres* (1931) and the policier *Coeur de Lilas* (*Lilac*, 1932). The second of these, starring Jean Gabin, is of note both in relation to its crime-drama theme and its fledgling association with poetic realism.

An émigré from Germany in an ethno-religious rather than a national sense, Litvak would trade time between England and France from 1933 to 1936, gradually moving from musicals and comedies to more dramatic fare; after scoring a major international success with the French production of *Mayerling* (1936), he landed a directing contract with Warner Bros. Fluctuating in his early Hollywood years once more between comedy (*Tovarich*, 1937; *The Amazing Dr. Clitterhouse*, 1937) and drama (*The Woman I Love*, 1937, a remake of his *L'Equipage* [*Flight into Darkness*], 1935; *The Sisters*, 1938), a turning point in his U.S. career came with *Confessions of a Nazi Spy* (1939), one of only three overtly anti-Nazi films made in Hollywood before U.S. entry into World War II.[30] The film itself wasn't a hit either critically or financially, but Litvak's personal relationship to the material seems to have laid the groundwork for a string of serious films to follow, many with a distinctly political thrust. Broken only by the war film *This Above All* (1942) and the war itself, during which he joined Frank Capra's contingent on the Office of War Information–produced *Why We Fight* documentary series, the string would include all of Litvak's quasi, hybrid, and full-fledged noirs.

These qualifying adjectives point to my own fluid take, as well as a marked discrepancy among the encyclopedias, on the films' noir credentials. The most inclusive of the taxonomists, Michael Keaney, lists six Litvak films within the noir cycle: *City for Conquest* (1940), *Blues in the Night* (1941), *Out of the Fog* (1942), *The Long Night* (1947), *Sorry, Wrong Number* (1948), and *Snake Pit* (1948). Paul Duncan rejects *Snake Pit*, rightfully in my opinion, because this is clearly a social-problem film with no crime element. Spencer Selby additionally drops *City for Conquest*, which is a problematic noir for other reasons (to be discussed below). Alain Silver and Elizabeth Ward curiously retain *City for Conquest* but otherwise include only *The Long Night* and *Sorry, Wrong Number*.

My own approach both broadens and narrows the above selections. Although I regard only two films—*The Long Night* and *Sorry, Wrong Number*—as unequivocally noir, I believe that all the others except *Snake Pit* warrant consideration, to varying degrees, and I additionally include two earlier, "peripheral" noirs, for their considerable interest from a Jewish émigré perspective.

Peripheral Noir

The gangster/prison film *Castle on the Hudson* (1940) stars Jewish actor John Garfield (born Julius Garfinkel) in the first of his two small-time mobster roles for Litvak. Unlike the later film *Out of the Fog*, where Garfield's Harold Goff plays the heavy, his Tommy Gordon in *Castle* is an antihero in the *You Only Live Once* vein: a penny-ante crook who goes straight while in prison only to be executed for a crime he didn't commit. An added Jewish émigré noir twist in *Castle* is that Tommy (who hails from the East Side and has Garfield's dark, curly-haired looks) has a Saturday complex. Although the biblical "seventh day's" relation to the Jewish Sabbath remains unspecified, Tommy refuses to participate in an attempted prison break on Saturday and only reluctantly accepts the warden's pass from prison because his conditional release also happens to fall on his "bad-luck day."

All This and Heaven Too (1940), although also only peripherally noir, could serve, at least thematically, as a period prototype for the romantic-triangle subset of the noir cycle, and one with even more Jewish émigré trimmings. A kind of *Mayerling* in French coitteur, the film stars Bette Davis as a governess in a Parisian ducal palace in 1848 whose tragically chaste romance with the duke, played by Charles Boyer (the male lead in *Mayerling*), not only leads to scandal and murder (of the insanely jealous duchess by the duke) but also, somewhat fancifully, triggers the revolution of 1848. The personal tragedy is compounded when the duke commits suicide to spare the life of the governess, who had been unjustifiably suspected of abetting the duchess's killing.

A Jewish émigré sensibility appears from the start, when the ostracized governess, hired as a French teacher at an American girls' school, finds that the scandal that drove her from her homeland has followed her to the United States. Her sad story is then recounted in flashback to her students by the governess, but in the third person. The first flashback scene, on a boat carrying the governess from England back to France, where she is to take up her duties in the ducal palace, reinforces the exilic theme through the governess's Ophuls-like voice-over: " . . . and she looked forward to the distant invisible shores of her native country with mingled feelings of hope and apprehension." Her post-flashback summation to the students clinches the refugee connection: "What future was there in a country where she was hated, where their love, faulted in life, had been twisted into an ugly horror? . . . But people can be as cruel in one country as another. Gossip can spread here too, until there is no peace for her, even in America. It is for you to end this story. Can she continue her work, here where so many before her have found refuge?"

Quasi Noir

Litvak's first film noir in Keaney's and Duncan's estimation, *City for Conquest*, in my view plays more like a city symphony than an urban crime drama. The only murder in the film occurs away from the main line of action and affects only secondary characters. The protagonist, Danny Kenny (James Cagney), though he does suffer partial blindness from foul play in a boxing match, clearly is on the road to regaining his sight by film's end due to the abiding love of his girlfriend, Peggy (Ann Sheridan). The kinship with the city symphony, meanwhile, is literalized in Danny's brother Eddie's (Arthur Kennedy) Magic Isle Symphony, an orchestral ode to New York that Eddie conducts at Carnegie Hall at the film's climax. Despite Eddie's claim, in his cramped apartment at the start of the film, that his symphony would present the modern metropolis "with all its proud passionate beauty and all its sordid ugliness," beauty is all that remains in the elegant concert-hall finale.

Out of the Fog, although it comes closer to full-fledged noir, also hedges its bets. Violence and murder ground the action; an homme fatal (Garfield's Goff, the inverse of "fog") is the prime antagonist; and the wharf section of Brooklyn, where most of the entire film (based on Irwin Shaw's play) is set, exclusively at night, is painted in thickly fogged, claustrophobic strokes. Yet an incongruously bright tinge seeps through the expressionist veneer. This comes partly from the comedic interplay between the buffoonish cook, Olaf Johnson (John Qualen), and his similarly foreign-accented tailor pal, Jonah Goodwin (Thomas Mitchell), both of whom dream of cashing in their dreary domesticated existences for a deep-sea fishing adventure off some tropical isle. Even less noirish is the film's payoff, which finds Olaf and Jonah unable to pull off the murder of their nemesis Goff, whose escalating shakedown tactics threaten their plans, but whose accidental drowning (and their subsequent retrieval of the shakedown money) makes the plans even more realizable. Yet what churlish fate gives with one hand it takes with the other, as the dream enabled by Goff's death, for Olaf and Jonah, quashes that of Jonah's daughter Stella (Ida Lupino), who was all set to sail for Cuba with Goff, courtesy (unbeknownst to her) of Jonah's shakedown money.

Before this improbable ending applies a glossy Hollywood finish to an intermittently noir undercoat, the film had occasionally peeled away its comedic and melodramatic layers to reveal wide ideological fissures. Besides the by-now clichéd analogy between organized crime and big business, as in Goff's likening himself to a "good corporation," Jonah's inchoate sense that "the system" is responsible for "pushing us" little people around is articulated with Marxist sophistication by the recently bankrupted Russian Jewish dry goods salesman Igor Kropotkin (George Tobias), as he sits with Jonah in a sauna: "I sweat and the profit system comes right out my pores. They push you, they push you. They take everything from you. They strip you naked, naked as a mule. Misery grows like a boil."

His own misery level pushed to the boiling point, Jonah spews his own voluble mix of Marxism, social Darwinism, and Jewish émigré noir: "A situation like this could make me an anarchist. If you live in a jungle and a tiger stole your children, what would you do? We wanted peace, but can you convince air planes and bombs, and men with guns in their pockets?" But Jonah's antifascist rhetoric is as thin as a silver dollar. When destiny, rather than his own activism, rids him of the child-robbing tiger and plops a windfall profit in his and Olaf's lap, the jungle suddenly becomes a tropical isle. And when, Goff's ill-gotten gains in hand, Jonah comforts Stella with the nostrum that she's an ordinary girl "but there's nothing wrong with being ordinary," any noir tartness *Out of the Fog* may have harbored dissipates in the studio set's pea soup.

Hybrid Noir

The populist voice that gets muffled in *Out of the Fog* rings loud and clear in *Blues of the Night* (1942). Yet this film noir—at least according to Keaney, Selby, and Duncan—still only ranks desultorily as one in my estimation due to a generic hybridization all but postmodern in its "radical eclecticism." Both the eclecticism and the populist strain can be traced to the film's jazz music theme and to the band of anarchist musicians who carry its banner. The ragtag combo's improvisational riffs not only motivate the spatial trajectory from freight-car jams to roadhouse gigs to fancy club engagements and back again, but they also propel the generic shifts from musical to comedy to gangster noir to populist fable. Noir only enters the picture midway, literally through the freight-car door, when escaped convict Del Davis (Lloyd Nolan) hops aboard, befriends the group, and sets them up in his roadhouse hideaway.

Davis's joint—aptly named, from both jazz and noir angles, the Jungle—is where the closest thing to a protagonist, piano virtuoso and bandleader Jigger Pine (Richard Whorf), falls hard for femme fatale Kay (Betty Field). Jigger also articulates the film's populist theme. During the semi-comical opening, with the band holed up in jail after a farcical barroom brawl, Jigger passionately expounds his vision of the ideal musical group: "It's gotta be *our* kinda music, *our* kinda band, the songs we've listened to, knockin' about the country! Blues, *real* blues, the kind that come outta people, *real* people! Their hopes and their dreams, what they've got and what they want! The whole USA in one chorus! Five guys, no more, who feel, play, live, even think the same way! That ain't a band, it's a *unit*! It's one guy multiplied by five! It's got a style that's theirs and nobody else's!"

Well, not quite nobody else's, as Jigger's music is clearly inspired, as was *City for Conquest*'s Eddie Kenny's Gershwin-esque symphony, by black blues, ragtime, and dixie. Nor will Jigger remain a populist purist. Stung by Kay's rejection, he sets off on his own and briefly headlines for a big-time swing band. This sellout only disillusions him further, and after bumming around he nearly dies—until his old buddies find and revive him. Finally, after a last unrequited fling with Kay—who dies in a car accident after killing her unrequited love, Del—Jigger and the boys end up where they started, tearing it up on a freight train headed for who knows where but who cares: "We're in a groove!"

Jazz and noir unmistakably intersect with Jewishness in the person, and name, of Jigger Pine. Jigger's dark, curly locks are not surprising given that he was played by Jewish actor Richard Whorf. And of course Jews were inextricably linked with the jazz scene, in some ways even more distinctively than with the movies, due to their disproportionate representation, compared to other whites, in a predominantly black cultural form. Besides their profusion among songwriters, record producers, musicians, bookers, and club owners, famed Jewish bandleaders include Benny Goodman, "Bix" Beiderbecke, Stan Kenton, and Artie Shaw. As for Jigger's nickname, if "wigger" is the slang term of choice for a "white Negro," then what better moniker than "Jigger" to specify a Jewish black wannabe? The band's clarinetist, Nickie Haroyen, extends the Jewish-jazz trope. Played by the Greek-born but arguably Jewish-looking Elia Kazan, Nickie is the film's comic foil, always making with the jokes, including the movie's running gag: incessant calls to his mother.

Full-Fledged Noir

Litvak's most uncompromising noirs were made after the war, which is not surprising given the war's cumulative effects, knowledge of the Holocaust, and the cycle's greater maturation. Yet despite the distinctly darker turn of *The Long Night* (1947) and *Sorry, Wrong Number* (1948), a populist strand still shines through—at least in *The Long Night*, a remake of Marcel Carné's poetic-realist classic *Le Jour se lève* (*Daybreak*, 1939). The casting of Henry Fonda in the Jean Gabin role is interesting in this regard. Although generally regarded as an actor not particularly suited to noir roles—unlike, say, Humphrey Bogart, Robert Mitchum, Dick Powell, and Gabin himself—Fonda, as we've seen, carved out somewhat of a Jewish émigré noir niche with his "wrong man" roles in *You Only Live Once* and *Let Us Live*.[31] The working-class pedigree required for those roles, and the one in *The Long Night*, was further reinforced by his iconic performance as Tom Joad in John Ford's adaptation of John Steinbeck's *The Grapes of Wrath* (1940). Intertextuality, then, if not the law, was on Fonda's side in his portrayal of Joe Adams, a working-class stiff who barricades himself, following the shooting of his romantic rival, in the upstairs room of an apartment house subsequently surrounded by police.

Another American twist to the remake, besides the casting and small-town steel-country setting, is that (GI) Joe is also a World War II vet. The film's ambivalence toward this nationalistic aspect is evident from the start. Following a voice-over introduction whose documentary-like effect ("Our story could happen anywhere to anyone. . . . They were just average human beings in an average town") is undercut by a mock-patriotic tone, we watch blind war vet Frank Dunlap (Elisha Cook Jr.) stumble past a war memorial statue and into Joe's apartment building just as the shots from Joe's crime of passion ring out. Later, in one of Joe's flashbacks that make up the bulk of the narrative, a similar disconnect exists between the "Peace and Prosperity" billboard behind Joe and his true love, Jo Ann (Barbara Bel Geddes), and the grim fate that we sense awaits them. Finally, as the entire town gathers in the square beneath the apartment house where Joe remains trapped like a wild animal, the memorial statue looms tauntingly above the crowd.

In the end, however, sentimental populism triumphs over mock patriotism. Instead of the truer-to-noir ending of *Le Jour se lève*, in which daybreak finds Gabin's François dead in his bed from a self-inflicted gunshot, Fonda's Joe gets a reprieve. Jo Ann manages to slip past the police cordon up to his room and convinces him to surrender. Countering his earlier, class-based critique—"People take you for where you came from, what your name is"—she insists (and the crowd's shouts support her): "The people believe in you! Because we're people just like them, not strangers. No matter what name, what family, it doesn't matter!"

Although Jo Ann's homily counts as one of the most cherished American myths, earlier conversations lent the populist sentiment a distinctly post-Holocaust air. When Joe and Jo Ann first met at the steel mill and discovered that they had both been raised in orphanages, Joe observed, "We got the same name almost, and we got the same family—I mean on account of we haven't got no family at all." Then, glancing from the flowers Jo Ann was holding to the grimy surroundings, he added poetically, "Sand and flowers, flowers and smoke." The most explicit wartime allusion occurred when Joe's smarmy rival, Maximilian (Vincent Price), lied that he was Jo Ann's father and told Joe to back off, and Joe likened the effete, European-ish magician to "the people who claim now they weren't real Nazis!"

Litvak's most indisputable film noir, *Sorry, Wrong Number* (1948), is also, unsurprisingly, rife with Jewish émigré noir features. These begin with another of that grouping's, by now almost obligatory, female protagonists: Leona Stevenson (Barbara Stanwyck). A cough-drop magnate's daughter and psychosomatic invalid, Leona overhears a telephone conversation about an impending murder that turns out to be her own—planned by her husband, Henry (Burt Lancaster), who hoped to use her inheritance to pay off the mob wanting in on his drug-dealing scheme.

The most Jewish aspect of the film, however, is its multi-flashback, flashback-within-flashback structure. This arguably Talmudic element, also found in Siodmak's *The Killers* and extended in Brahm's *The Locket*, is expanded exponentially in *Sorry, Wrong Number*, almost to the point where, in Rabbi Simcha Weinstein's words, "questions never reach a suitable conclusion and end with the word *taiku*, meaning 'the question stands.'"[32] The "question" here pertains to the meaning of the ominous phone call Leona receives, which, due to her hypochondriacal confinement, she can only investigate via telephone interrogations of others and the probing of her own memories. Then there are the flashbacks themselves: ten in all, two of them flashbacks within flashbacks. But unlike those in *The Killers*, which tell a chronologically progressive story in the past that is paralleled by the forward motion of the insurance investigator in the present, and those in *The Locket*, which also follow a temporally coherent pattern, those in *Sorry, Wrong Number* jump, *Citizen Kane*–style, back and forth in time. Yet even in Welles's bio-epic, arguably the model for complex multi-flashback storytelling, the disjointedness of the flashback chronology is anchored by the temporal and spatial coherence of the reporter's "Rosebud" quest.

In *Sorry, Wrong Number*, paradoxically, an extra measure of uncanniness (in the Freudian sense of *Unheimlichkeit*, or "un-homeliness") comes from the extreme temporal and spatial contraction. The filmic present here is one short evening, with the threatening call overheard in the early evening and the murder deadline set for 11:15 P.M. This foreshortened time frame is mirrored spatially by Leona's confinement in the upstairs bedroom of a cavernous mansion whose multiple floors conversely (or concavely?) mirror the multi-flashback structure. As if all this weren't *Unheimlich* enough, the intercession of the disembodied telephone, through which all the flashbacks are transmitted, adds another level of spatiotemporal discombobulation that, narrative closure notwithstanding, cries out for *taiku*.

I have said little so far about Litvak's cinematic style, which, as Richard Schickel aptly remarks, is "noirish in manner but usually not in spirit," and generally "self-effacing."[33] The final scene in *Sorry, Wrong Number* is a notable exception. As the near-midnight deadline approaches, Leona is on the phone with Henry, who has come to rue his homicidal decision and urges her, with police visible behind him, to go to the window and cry out for help. As loud street noise and Leona's extreme frailty render such an attempt moot, we start in close on Leona's terrified expression, then, in a bravura *plan sequence* (complex long take) reminiscent of Brahm's *Hangover Square*, the camera retreats through the capacious bedroom to the open window, continues receding to the exterior of the building, swoops down sloping walls and past drooping foliage to the side steps, where we glimpse a shadow flitting past. Back inside, we view the indoor spiral staircase from Leona's point of view as the shadowy presence slowly ascends the circular wall and Leona finally, desperately, calls for help on the phone (fig. 41). With the phantom now visible to her but not to us, Leona cringes backward in the bed and screams. A shadow slowly crosses her face, a black glove reaches out and clutches her neck, and, as the camera pans to the telephone on the nightstand beside her, death voids her final scream.

Act of Violence

One of the phalanx of Austro-German Jewish filmmakers who got his start on *Menschen am Sonntag*, Fred Zinnemann, at that time the least experienced of the group, went on to a Hollywood directing career whose critical and box-office success, among the Jewish émigré noirists, is matched only by Billy Wilder. In addition to winning Best Short Subject and Documentary Short Oscars for *That Mothers Might Live* (1938) and *Benjy* (1951), two of Zinnemann's feature films, *From Here to Eternity* (1953) and *A Man for All Seasons* (1966), won Academy Awards for Best Picture and Best Director. He also directed four other Oscar-nominated films—*The Search* (1948), *High Noon* (1951), *The Nun's Story* (1959), and *Julia* (1977)—as well as the Broadway musical *Oklahoma!* (1955) and the hit thriller *The Day of the Jackal* (1973). For all this, however, Zinnemann's identification with Jewish émigré noir remains tenuous, for two reasons: first, because he made only one consensus film noir, *Act of Violence* (1949); and second, because

Figure 41. Destiny calling: Barbara Stanwyck in *Sorry, Wrong Number* (1948). (USC Special Collections)

his émigré credentials are (except for Willy Wilder's) the most compromised of the group.[34]

Born in Vienna in 1907 to a prominent Jewish family, Zinnemann received a law degree from the University of Vienna before going to Paris in 1927 to study film and to Berlin in 1929 to start directing. Although he belongs to the "Second Viennese School" of directors—those who came to the United States in the early-to-mid-1930s rather than the early-to-mid-1920s—he was the least driven from Europe by the specter or reality of Nazism.[35] Rather, his prime motivation in coming to the United States, by his own admission, was pragmatic. Following the smash success of *Menschen am Sonntag*, "We all thought that we would find it easy to get work as a result. But just about that time sound pictures were introduced in America with *The Jazz Singer* and *The Singing Fool* and so on. The coming of the sound era took Berlin by storm, and the German industry wasn't prepared for it. Jobs were non-existent, so I went to America to see what sound was also about at first hand."[36] As with Billy and Willy Wilder, however, psychological (if less Oedipally based) factors also informed Zinnemann's decision to come to the States: "Like a lot of young people living in the congestion of a big city, I loved to go to Westerns, not so much for the violence, but for the huge vistas and the big sky that they pictured. Hence I was attracted subconsciously to America all along."[37]

Attraction and ambition counted for something, but immigrant-Jewish connections helped most. These included a letter of recommendation to Universal's Carl Laemmle that got Zinnemann his first film job, and apprentice work with Austrian director Berthold Viertel that gained him access to Berthold's wife Salka's salons. There Zinnemann met the pioneering documentary filmmaker Robert Flaherty, who would become his strongest cinematic (and overall) influence, and with whom he would return to Berlin to prepare a film sponsored by the Soviet Union. When this project fell through, Zinnemann returned to the United States to stay, working briefly on an Eddie Cantor musical, *The Kid from Spain* (1932), then directing his first film, *The Wave* (1934).[38] A proto-neorealist social-problem film made in Mexico at the behest and with the assistance of avant-garde photographer/filmmaker Paul Strand, *The Wave* established what would be a lifelong leaning of Zinnemann's toward social themes and a documentary style.

Following an extended apprenticeship with the MGM shorts unit from 1938 to 1942, Zinnemann skirted the edges of noir with a couple of low-budget feature thrillers, *Kid Glove Killer* (1942) and *Eyes in the Night* (1943), the second of which also nudged closer to Jewishness with its antifascist plot.[39] His first A film for MGM, *The Seventh Cross* (1944), more emphatically incorporated Jewish and noir elements, in style and in theme. Although it maintained Hollywood's aversion to emphasizing the anti-Jewish specifics of Nazism, *The Seventh Cross* was the first major American film to deal with, much less depict, a Nazi concentration camp.[40] Starring Spencer Tracy as a political prisoner, George Heisler, who escapes from a camp in 1936 with six others, including a token Jew, the only hint of official anti-Semitism comes when a doctor, who treats Heisler knowing that he's a fugitive, tells him it's his duty to inform him that he's a Jew. The film's secondary casting, including refugee actors Felix Bressart, Alexander Granach, Kurt Katch, Kaaren Verne, and Brecht's wife, Helene Veigel, furthers the émigré subtext. As for style and theme, the opening fog-drenched escape scene, shot by legendary Weimar cinematographer Karl Freund, is imported straight from UFA, while the story of a man pursued through the streets of his hometown, and the casting of Tracy in the innocent fugitive's role, clearly evoke Lang's *M* and *Fury*.[41] Yet, curiously for someone whose parents perished in the Holocaust, but echoing the ambivalent sentiments of many in the émigré Jewish community, Zinnemann envisioned *The Seventh Cross* not solely as an indictment of Nazism but also as a corrective to the wartime U.S. demonizing of the German people as a whole. "I felt it was very important to get across the fact," he said in a 1976 interview, "that just because you were a German it didn't mean automatically that you were a monster."[42]

Rehabilitation of the "good German" notwithstanding, Zinnemann's next important film (following a studio suspension for rejecting inferior material) would mark another first in the anti-Nazi genre: this time dealing not just with concentration camps but with the Holocaust itself. *The Search* (1948) concerns the postwar humanitarian crisis posed by the orphaned children of World War II in general and the Final Solution in particular. It stars Montgomery Clift (in his first screen performance) as a U.S. soldier confronted with the plight of one of the "orphan" boys—whose mother, however, is alive and searching desperately for her son among the displaced persons camps.[43] Betraying his Flaherty–esque bent, as well as the neorealist and semidocumentary influences that were reshaping postwar Hollywood film (most notably, film noir), Zinnemann visited some of the camps in researching the film; shot the film on location in Munich, Nuremberg, and Frankfurt; and cast an actual concentration camp survivor, Jandl, as the main orphan boy.

Zinnemann's next film, and the first in which he felt totally "in command," was also his first and only full-fledged film noir: *Act of Violence*.[44] And though the word "Jew" does not make even a token appearance here, the film is noteworthy from a Jewish émigré noir perspective in its focus on a post-Holocaust topic left largely unexplored by the other émigré directors: survivor guilt. The narrative centers around two World War II veterans and onetime close friends, Frank Enley (Van Heflin) and Joe Parkson (Robert Ryan), who ended up in a Nazi prison camp after their bomber plane was shot down. Captain Enley, as the senior officer, was responsible for his fellow American prisoners. When they planned an escape, however, Enley not only did not participate, but, hoping to avert a disaster similar to that which had befallen the camp's British prisoners, informed the Nazi commandant, who promised to go easy on the escapees. When the commandant reneged, all the men were killed—with the exception of Parkson, who managed to escape but was left with a gimp leg.

The film starts with Parkson, hell-bent on revenge for his former buddy's betrayal, hopping a bus from New York to Los Angeles, where Enley now lives a comfortable family life in the fictional suburb of Santa Lisa.[45] Recalling the opening big-city/small-town setup of Hitchcock's *Shadow of a Doubt* (1942), Parkson's introduction as a lone crippled figure shuffling through dark, deserted city streets with a gun stashed in his overcoat pocket contrasts sharply with our first view of Enley on a bright sunny day—infant son on his shoulders, beautiful wife at his side, and a small crowd applauding his role as chief contractor on a new housing development. Dark and light elements ironically clash but also dialectically intersect when Parkson arrives in Santa Lisa in the middle of a Memorial Day parade. As he "walks across the road between that point which separates soldiers and civilians, momentarily disrupting its smooth continuity," his passage not only "represents the limbo between wartime and civilian life in which Parkson now moves," as Neil Sinyard aptly observes, but also the limbo between the wartime and post-Holocaust worlds that émigrés such as Zinnemann were forced to negotiate.[46]

Befitting Zinnemann's Weimar-cinema exposure, his documentary background, and the postwar realist turn, *Act of Violence*'s aesthetics, like much of Zinnemman's work, also combine expressionist and documentary modes.[47] Some scenes emphasize one style over the other: Parkson's departure from New York, for example, favors expressionism; his pursuit of Enley up to a California mountain lake leans toward the newsreel. The most powerful scenes interweave the two styles, such as those at Enley's suburban house, or in his climactic late-night trek through the streets of downtown Los Angeles. The film's most original functionally expressionist touch is the manner in which Enley's prison-camp experience is conveyed to his wife, Edith (Janet Leigh), and to the viewer. Eschewing noir's standard flashback device, Enley tells his sordid story in the backroom of a downtown Los Angeles convention hall. As building-industry conventioneers revel in a high-key-lit scene redolent of a carnival-cum–meat market, Ensley unburdens himself to Edith among shadowy stairways, cinder-block walls, and chain-link fence reminiscent, symbolically and literally, of the prison-camp environment in which his tragic tale unfolds.

Unlike at the house earlier, however, when in first broaching the incident he had defended his actions as well-meaning, he now humbly confesses, "I was an informer. It doesn't make any difference why I did it. I betrayed my men. They were dead. The Nazis even paid me a price and I ate it." When Edith tries to reassure him—"You had your reasons. . . . You tried. You made a mistake. You can't suffer all your life for one mistake"—he will have none of it: "You can always find reasons. Even the Nazis had reasons. . . . I hadn't done it just to save their lives. I talked myself into believing it, that [the commandant] would keep his word. But in my guts from the start I think I knew he wouldn't. And maybe I didn't even care. They were dead and I was eating and maybe that's all I did it for, to save one man—me."

What makes the film's disquisition on survivor guilt most interesting is that Parkson's pathological drive for revenge is yet another (far more complex) manifestation of it. Although Parkson's ostensible goal, to avenge his fellow prisoners' deaths, is (like Enley's aim to spare them) seemingly laudable, it masks a similarly self-interested motive: namely, to compensate for his own physically deformed (and symbolically emasculated) condition, and, of course, to bring about his own conviction and death for killing Enley. The sexual motive is disclosed in a scene with Parkson's girlfriend, Ann (Phyllis Thaxter), who has followed after him in hopes of convincing him to give up his vengeful (and self-destructive) plan. In a last-ditch effort to change his mind, she blurts, "You're as crippled in your mind as in—!" Although the punch line is left unspoken, its psychological effect is all the more potent for Parkson's need to fill the gap. That he has connected the dots is evident in the sudden change in his previously steely expression, which subtly but poignantly exhibits the first signs of self-recognition.

Enley's "crime" has already been committed, however, and thus, per the PCA, cannot go unredeemed. After a soul-searching nighttime odyssey through Bunker Hill's half-documentary/half-expressionist alleyways, staircases, flophouses, tunnels, and bars (playing like a recap montage of most-favored film-noir sites), Enley hires a hit man to kill Parkson. Enley closes the deal in a drunken stupor and under duress, thus mimicking his prison-camp complicity and setting the stage for his atonement—which comes only after barely fore-going suicide by having a train (that iconic symbol of the Holocaust) run him down (fig. 42). Instead, Enley jumps in front of the hit man's bullet meant for Parkson. Critically wounded, Enley clings to the getaway car and struggles with the hit man at the wheel, causing the car to crash into a lamppost (that iconic symbol of film noir), killing them both. Parkson, meanwhile, is not only spared going to prison for a second time (and likely for good); as he limps away from the crash scene arm-in-arm with Ann, he also appears to be leaving at least a portion of his psychological deformity behind.

Beyond the indirect association with the Holocaust, Enley's prison-camp informer, as Wheeler Winston Dixon points out, also recalls the HUAC hearings just concluded, and soon to resume, in Washington—hearings that, as we know, had an undisguised anti-Semitic aspect.[48] Enley's survivor guilt, as Dixon further suggests, goes beyond the Nazi death camps or the McCarthyist witch hunts to the nuclear family and rampant consumerism that was radically transforming postwar American society. The "new life" that

Figure 42.   Facing survivor guilt head-on: Van Heflin in *Act of Violence* (1949). (USC Special Collections)

Enley has built for himself in Southern California, like the shabbily built houses he has constructed, "is a lie, and has no foundation," and thus "must and will collapse."[49] The ultimate message of *Act of Violence*, like much of Jewish émigré noir, thus combines the refugee's hyperawareness of the horrors of Nazism, the dangers of McCarthyism, and the vapidity of American materialism; or, as Dixon summarizes, "that the one-family home of the 1940s is no refuge from the world, but rather a self-imposed prison; that World War II and the social hatred it engendered have scarred us all; . . . that the surfaces of any community . . . hide a wealth of corruption, violence, and false fronts; . . . that precisely those who are most boosterish are those who are most suspect."[50]

Conclusion

In its compendium of noir elements and its confrontation with survivor guilt, *Act of Violence* seems a fitting conclusion to this study of Jewish émigré noir. The Jewish refugee condition was grounded to a large degree in discomfiture over their narrow escape from the deadly fate of European Jews less fortunate than themselves. This discomfiture grew in direct relation to the number, familial connection, and tragic fate of the loved ones left behind, and was further complicated in comparative relation to their ties to German culture.

Film noir, although certainly no cure-all for the Jewish émigré complex, offered a unique creative outlet for addressing some of the conflicts and alleviating some of the pain.

Film noir was made to order for Jewish émigré directors on several levels, which operated conceptually both forward and backward in time, and extended to both European and American culture. Noir enabled, indeed encouraged, an expressionist cinematic style that not only derived from Weimar Germany and bore the traces of German high culture, but that also had two additional benefits: it had been crucially affected by Jews and had, because of its modernist imprimatur, allowed for—indeed demanded—a critique of German society. Similarly, because émigré Jewish directors' ambivalence extended, in uneven portions, to the political economy of the United States and to the commercial constraints of Hollywood, film noir's thematic critique of American society, and its aesthetic mode at the margins of the classical Hollywood style, offered as powerful a weapon for confronting the culture industry as was available within mass media. Such an "entrist" approach (in the Gramscian sense of working for change from within the system) may have been anathema to Adorno and Horkheimer (although it didn't hamper social relations between Adorno and Lang), but for filmmakers less antithetically inclined toward popular culture than the Frankfurt School theorists, and with no avant-garde alternative in the United States to speak of, film noir at least supplied a vehicle for challenging "the absence of culture, the mindless materialism, and the new barbarism" that the twentieth-century United States had come to represent.[51] The unavoidable irony, of course, is that by obliquely critiquing Germany and more directly indicting the United States, Jewish émigré noirists also paid homage to the German cultural patrimony and bolstered the Hollywood film industry.

Besides its psychological and ideological function for Jewish émigré directors in general, film noir also allowed for specific, if largely disguised and possibly unconscious, Jewish references, which varied from film to film and from filmmaker to filmmaker. To summarize from the foregoing case studies, these references include: a preponderance of both un-"tough guy" antiheroes and female protagonists; allusions to blood libel and ritual sacrifice; high-low cultural conflict; the trauma of exile; the persistence of anti-Semitism and the continuing threat of fascism, here and abroad; and survivor guilt and the Holocaust.

Of course some of these aspects may be partially attributable, in certain instances, to collaboration from producers, authors of story sources, screenwriters, and so forth. Nor does the privileging of a particular noir predisposition among Jewish émigré directors preclude a similar orientation among first-wave Jewish immigrants, non-Jewish émigrés, American-born Jews, or non-Jews. As I have frequently indicated, several of the tropes identified with Jewish émigré noir can also be found, if to a less consistent and concentrated degree, in the work of non-Jewish émigré noir directors. The purpose of this book is not to claim proprietary exclusivity for Jewish émigré noir, much less to produce the definitive account of the Jewish émigré noir phenomenon, but simply to make the case for both its prevalence and its inclusion in the broader film noir discourse. If in the process I have enriched the understanding of film noir, enlivened the debate around this highly complex cultural form, and provided a rewriting of noir history that itself becomes subject to rewriting, then *Driven to Darkness* has achieved its goal.

Appendix

AMERICAN FILM NOIRS
BY JEWISH ÉMIGRÉ DIRECTORS

1. FRITZ LANG (15)

Fury (1936)

You Only Live Once (1937)

Hangmen Also Die! (1943)

Ministry of Fear (1944)

The Woman in the Window (1945)

Scarlet Street (1945)

Cloak and Dagger (1946)

Secret Beyond the Door (1948)

House by the River (1950)

Clash by Night (1952)

The Big Heat (1953)

The Blue Gardenia (1953)

Human Desire (1954)

While the City Sleeps (1956)

Beyond a Reasonable Doubt (1956)

2. ROBERT SIODMAK (10)

Phantom Lady (1944)

Christmas Holiday (1944)

The Suspect (1944)

The Strange Affair of Uncle Harry (1945)

The Spiral Staircase (1945)

The Dark Mirror (1946)

The Killers (1946)

Cry of the City (1948)

Criss Cross (1949)

The File on Thelma Jordan (1949)

3. JOHN BRAHM (8)

Rio (1939)

Let Us Live (1939)

The Lodger (1944)

Guest in the House (1944)

Hangover Square (1945)

The Locket (1946)

The Brasher Doubloon (1947)

Singapore (1947)

4. W. LEE WILDER,
AKA WILLY WILDER (8)

The Glass Alibi (1946)

The Pretender (1947)

Once a Thief (1950)

Three Steps North (1951)

The Big Bluff (1955)

Fright (1956)

Manfish (1956)

Bluebeard's Ten Honeymoons (1960)

5. OTTO PREMINGER (6)

Laura (1944)

Fallen Angel (1945)

Whirlpool (1949)

Where the Sidewalk Ends (1950)

The Thirteenth Letter (1951)

Angel Face (1953)

6. EDGAR G. ULMER (6)

Bluebeard (1944)
Detour (1945)
Strange Illusion (1945)
The Strange Woman (1946)
Ruthless (1948)
Murder Is My Beat (1955)

7. CURTIS BERNHARDT (5)

Conflict (1945)
A Stolen Life (1946)
Possessed (1947)
High Wall (1947)
Sirocco (1951)

8. ANATOLE LITVAK (5)

Out of the Fog (1940)
City for Conquest (1940)
Blues in the Night (1941)
The Long Night (1947)
Sorry, Wrong Number (1948)

9. BILLY WILDER (3)

Double Indemnity (1944)
Sunset Boulevard (1950)
Ace in the Hole, aka *The Big Carnival*
   (1951)

10. MAX OPHULS (2)

Caught (1949)
The Reckless Moment (1949)

11. FRED ZINNEMANN (1)

Act of Violence (1949)

Notes

CHAPTER I — INTRODUCTION

1. George Santayana, *The Life of Reason* (1905, 1906; repr., New York: C. Scribner, 1953), 397.

2. Tom Gunning, *The Films of Fritz Lang: Allegories of Vision and Modernity* (London: British Film Institute, 2006), 206; James A. Paris, "'Murder Can Sometimes Smell Like Honeysuckle': Billy Wilder's *Double Indemnity*," in *Film Noir Reader* 4, ed. Alain Silver and James Ursini (New York: Proscenium, 2004), 21; and Foster Hirsch, *Film Noir: The Dark Side of the Screen* (New York: Da Capo Press, 1981), 115.

3. Susan M. White, *The Cinema of Max Ophuls: Magisterial Vision and the Figure of Women* (New York: Columbia University Press, 1995); and Neil Sinyard, *Fred Zinnemann: Films of Character and Conscience* (Jefferson, N.C.: McFarland, 2003).

4. Given the still unresolved dispute over film noir's status as a genre, to be addressed later in this chapter, I will refer to it variously as a film cycle, form, or type.

5. Vidor (né Vidor Károly) was born in Budapest and worked at UFA before coming to the United States in 1924. Other prominent German/Austrian Jewish film personnel who came to Hollywood in the 1920s included writer Carl Mayer, cinematographer Karl Freund, set designer Hans Dreier, and composer Max Steiner. Of course, several major non-Jewish émigré filmmakers, and not merely Germans or Austro-Hungarians, came to Hollywood after World War I. The Austrian-born Josef von Sternberg came to the United States in the early 1900s. For a detailed study of the "foreign filmmaker" phenomenon, see Graham Petrie, *Hollywood Destinies: European Directors in America, 1922–1931* (Detroit: Wayne State University Press, 2002).

6. Quoted in Gene D. Phillips, *Exiles in Hollywood: Major European Film Directors in America* (Bethlehem: Lehigh University Press, 1998), 13. In an interview, Wilder further stated, "Even without the Nazis, I think I would have wound up in Hollywood. But not so quickly." Burt Prelutsky, "An Interview with Billy Wilder" [1996], in *Billy Wilder: Interviews*, ed. Robert Horton (Jackson: University Press of Mississippi, 2001), 183.

7. The ongoing controversy surrounding the expressionist influence on film noir will be touched on later in this chapter and examined in detail in subsequent chapters.

8. Peter Gay, *Weimar Culture: The Outsider as Insider* (New York: Norton, 2001). The ascendant "outsiders" of Gay's title include "democrats" and "avant-garde artists" as well as Jews, but Jews were well represented and highly influential in these areas also. The Weimar Constitution itself was drafted by a Jew, Hugo Preuss.

9. The percentage of Jews in Germany in 1933 was 0.8 percent, 525,000 out of 65 million. Herbert A. Strauss, "The Movement of People in a Time of Crises," in *The Muses of Hitler: Cultural Transfer and Adaptation, 1930–1945*, ed. Jarrell C. Jackman and Carla M. Borden (Washington, D.C.: Smithsonian Institution Press, 1983), 47.

10. Walter Laqueur, *Weimar: A Cultural History* (New York: Capricorn, 1976), 73.

11. Quoted in Paul Hoffmann, *The Viennese: Splendor, Twilight, and Exile* (New York: Anchor, 1998), 39. Although their numbers were small in Austria as a whole (185,000), the Jewish population of Vienna by the 1900s was about 9 percent. Strauss, "The Movement of People," 47.

12. Quoted in ibid., 40.

13. Expressionism with an uppercase *E* will be used to refer to the Expressionist art movement and its cinematic offshoot. Expressionism with a lowercase *e* will refer to Expressionist-influenced applications. This distinction will be explained further in chapter 3, as will Jewish involvement with the Expressionist movement. For more on the Jewish "invention" of Hollywood, see Neal Gabler, *An Empire of Their Own: How the Jews Invented Hollywood* (New York: Anchor Books, 1989).

14. The Jewish identity of these filmmakers are according to Klaus Kreimeier, *The Ufa Story: A History of Germany's Greatest Film Company, 1918–1945*, trans. Robert and Rita Kimber (New York: Hill and Wang, 1996), 134–135; and S. S. Prawer, *Between Two Worlds: The Jewish Presence in German and Austrian Film, 1910–1933* (New York: Berghahn, 2007). Prawer's appendix offers a quite comprehensive listing of Jewish filmmakers, going well beyond my "short list."

15. Cited in Patrick McGilligan, *Fritz Lang: The Nature of the Beast* (New York: Faber and Faber, 1997), 169.

16. Raymond Borde and Etienne Chaumeton, *A Panorama of American Film Noir, 1941–1953*, trans. Paul Hammond (1955; repr., San Francisco: City Lights Books, 2002), 23.

17. Ginette Vincendeau, "Noir Is Also a French Word: The French Antecedents of Film Noir," in *The Book of Film Noir*, ed. Ian Cameron (New York: Continuum, 1993), 49–58. Anatole Litvak worked in France and in England between 1933 and 1936.

18. Marcel Carné remained in France, Julien Duvivier made no film noirs, and Renoir made only one film noir, *Woman on the Beach* (1947). Maté also served as cinematographer on *Gilda* (1946) and (uncredited) on *The Lady from Shanghai* (1947).

19. Gay, *Weimar Culture*, vi.

20. Lawrence Weschler, "Paradise: The Southern California Idyll of Hitler's Cultural Exiles," in *Exiles and Émigrés: The Flight of European Artists from Hitler*, exhibition catalogue, ed. Stephanie Barron and Sabine Eckmann (Los Angeles: Los Angeles County Museum of Art, 1997), 350.

21. Janet Burstein, "Recalling 'Home' from Beneath the Shadow of the Holocaust,"

in *You Should See Yourself: Jewish Identity in Postmodern American Culture*, ed. Vincent Brook (New Brunswick: Rutgers University Press, 2006), 37–54, quote 41.

22. Max Horkheimer and Theodor Adorno, *Dialectic of Enlightenment: Philosophical Fragments*, trans. Edmond Jephcott (1944; repr., Stanford: Stanford University Press, 2002), xvi. The quote is gleaned from Ehrhard Bahr, *Weimar on the Pacific: German Exile Culture in Los Angeles and the Crisis of Modernism* (Berkeley and Los Angeles: University of California Press, 2007), 36.

23. Bahr, *Weimar on the Pacific*, 36.

24. Michael Meyer, "Refugees from Hitler's Germany: The Creative Elite and Its Middles-Class Audience in Los Angeles in the 1930s and 1940s—Film Noir and Orders of Sunny-Side Up," in *Festschrift zum Geburtstag von Julius H. Schoeps*, ed. Willi Jasper (Hildesheim, Germany: Georg Olms Verlag, 2002), 361.

25. Ibid.

26. Bahr, *Weimar on the Pacific*, 1, 10.

27. Joseph Horowitz, *Artists in Exile: How Refugees from Twentieth Century War and Revolution Transformed the American Performing Arts* (New York: HarperCollins, 2007), 19.

28. Lutz Bacher, *Max Ophuls in the Hollywood Studios* (New Brunswick: Rutgers University Press, 1996), 3.

29. Weschler, "Paradise," 345.

30. Meyer, "Refugees from Hitler's Germany," 370. The statistics are from David S. Wyman, *The Abandonment of the Jews: America and the Holocaust, 1942–1945* (New York: Pantheon, 1984), 8. See also Stephanie Barron, "European Artists in Exile: A Reading Between the Lines," in Barron and Eckmann, *Exiles and Émigrés*, 19.

31. Barron, "European Artists in Exile," 19.

32. Ibid.

33. Weschler, "Paradise," 346.

34. Jon Lewis, "'We Do Not Ask You to Condone This': How the Blacklist Saved Hollywood," *Cinema Journal* 39, no. 2 (2000): 3–30.

35. The quote is from http://en.wikipedia.org/wiki/Hanns_Eisler (accessed February 7, 2009). Bertolt Brecht, who followed the Ten to the stand, would depart the day after his testimony. Brecht was one of the so-called Unfriendly Nineteen, which included the Hollywood Ten. Twelve of the Nineteen, and six of the Ten, were American-born Jews.

36. There are several versions of this incident. See, for example, Vincent Deveau, "Honoring the Artistry of Fred Zinnemann" [1994], in *Fred Zinnemann: Interviews*, ed. Peter Brunette (Jackson: University of Mississippi Press, 2005), 141. Lang's alleged blacklisting will be examined in subsequent chapters.

37. Judith, Billy's first wife, became politically radicalized during their marriage, held political meetings in their home, and later married a leading Communist figure in San Francisco. Phone interview with Myles Wilder, May 17, 2008. Ulmer's information is from an e-mail from Arianné Ulmer Cipes.

38. Richard and Clara Winston, ed., *Letters of Thomas Mann, 1989–1955* (New York: Vintage Books, 1975).

39. Quoted in Philip K. Scheuer, "Wilder Seeks Films 'with Bite' to Satisfy 'Nation of Hecklers'" [1950], in Horton, *Billy Wilder*, 15–20, quote 17.

40. Michael Chopra-Gant, *Hollywood Genres and Postwar America: Masculinity, Family, and Nation in Popular Movies and Film Noir* (London: I. B. Tauris, 2006), 3. Chopra-Gant regards "Zeitgeist theory" (whose identification he credits to Richard Maltby) as oversimplified in its application to film noir, at least in the cycle's postwar formation. He argues that the mood of the postwar United States wasn't "either entirely gloomy or totally optimistic: in reality it was a complicated and often contradictory mixture of both" (4).

41. French critics Nino Frank and Jean-Pierre Chartrier are credited with coining the term "film noir" upon viewing, for the first time in 1946, the darker type of American film that had emerged during the war. Nino Frank, "Un Nouveau Genre 'policier': L'Adventure criminelle," *L'Ecran Français* 61 (August 28, 1946): 8–9, 14–16; and Jean-Pierre Chartrier, "Les Americains aussi font des films noirs," *Revue du cinéma* 2 (November 1, 3, 1946): 66–70. Two Frenchmen also wrote the first book about film noir: Raymond Borde and Etienne Chaumeton, *Panorama du film noir Americain, 1941–1953* (Paris: Editions du Minuit, 1955). For various positions on the "genre question" in regard to film noir, see Cameron, *The Book of Film Noir*; Alain Silver and Elizabeth Ward, ed., *Film Noir: An Encyclopedic Reference to the American Style*, 3d ed. (Woodstock, N.Y.: Overlook Press, 1992); James Naremore, *More Than Night: Film Noir in Its Contexts* (Berkeley and Los Angeles: University of California Press, 1998); David Bordwell, Janet Staiger, and Kristin Thompson, *The Classical Hollywood Cinema: Film Style and Mode of Production to 1960* (New York: Columbia University Press, 1985), 74–77; and Marc Vernet, "Film Noir: On the Edge of Doom," in *Shades of Noir: A Reader*, ed. Joan Copjec (New York: Verso, 1993), 1–31.

42. Raymond Durgnat, "Paint It Black: The Family Tree of Film Noir," in *Film Noir Reader*, ed. Alain Silver and James Ursini (New York: Limelight, 1993), 37–51.

43. Michael F. Keaney, *Film Noir Guide* (Jefferson, N.C.: McFarland, 2003); Spencer Selby, *Dark City: Film Noir* (Jefferson, N.C.: McFarland, 1997); Paul Duncan, *Film Noir: Films of Trust and Betryal* (North Pomfret, Vt.: Pocket Essentials, 2000); and Silver and Ward, *Film Noir*.

44. Vidor was also from Hungary, and Milestone from Russia. I credit Curtiz with five noirs, Vidor and Wyler with two, and Milestone with one, but among these are the canonical *Mildred Pierce* (Curtiz), *Gilda* (Vidor), and *The Strange Love of Martha Ivers* (Milestone).

45. Horowitz, *Artists in Exile*, 9. Weimar-era Expressionism's relation to American film noir has not gone unquestioned, in particular by Vernet, "Film Noir"; Barry Salt, "From Caligari to Who?" *Sight and Sound* 48 (Spring 1979): 119–123; Barry Salt, "From German Stage to German Screen," in *Before Caligari: German Cinema, 1895–1920*, ed. P. Cherchi Usai and L. Codelli (Pordenone, Italy: Edizoni Biblioteca dell'Immagine, 1990); and Thomas Elsaesser, *Weimar Cinema and After: Germany's Historical Imaginary* (New York: Routledge, 2000). The debate surrounding the Weimar-noir relation will be addressed in subsequent chapters.

46. Several film scholars consulted in the research for this book, including one who was writing specifically on émigré filmmakers, were not even aware of Willy Wilder's existence; a common response, when I mentioned the name, was to correct me and suggest that I meant William *Wyler* instead.

47. Alain Silver, "Introduction," in Silver and Ursini, *Film Noir Reader* 4, 3. American-born noir Jewish directors, besides Lewis and Mann, include Jack Arnold, Jack Bernhard, William Castle, George Cukor, Jules Dassin, Felix Feist, Richard Fleischer, Sam Fuller, Michael Gordon, Phil Karlson, Stanley Kubrick, Mervyn LeRoy, Arthur Lubin, Joseph Mankiewicz, Sam Newfield (aka Sherman Scott and Peter Stewart), Irving Pichel, Abraham Polonsky, Mark Robson, Robert Rossen, Vincent Sherman, Don Siegel, Alfred Werker, Richard Whorf, Robert Wise, Franz Wysbar, and Alfred Zeisler. Non-Jewish European noir directors, besides Hitchcock, Maté, and Tourneur, include John H. Auer, William Dieterle, Jean Negulesco, Steve Sekely, Douglas Sirk, and Andre de Toth.

48. Karl Popper, *The Open Society and Its Enemies* (1945; repr., New York: Routledge, 2002), 547.

49. For a brief but thorough summary of these "determinants," see Paul Kerr, "Out of What Past? Notes on the B Film Noir," in Silver and Ursini, *Film Noir Reader*, 106–127.

50. *Scarlet Street* was a remake of the French film *La Chienne* (*The Bitch*, 1931), directed by Jean Renoir.

51. Quoted in Frank Krutnik, *In a Lonely Street: Film Noir, Genre, Masculinity* (London: Routledge, 1991), 42–43.

52. Sander Gilman, *The Jew's Body* (New York: Routledge, 1991), 52, 76.

53. Karoly Benkert coined the term "homosexuality" in 1869; Wilhelm Marr coined "anti-Semitism" in 1879. Gilman, *The Jew's Body*, 126.

54. Ibid., 53.

55. According to historian Peter Levine, between 1910 and 1939 Jews continuously held at least one boxing championship (except in 1913), and in seven of those years, "Jews held three titles simultaneously. . . . So prominent were Jewish boxers in certain weight divisions that nine times between 1920 and 1934, Jews fought each other in championship bouts." Quoted in Stephen Whitfield, "A Stereotype with Muscle," in *Jews, Sport, and the Rites of Citizenship*, ed. Jack Kugelmass (Urbana: University of

Illinois Press, 2006), 26. For more on American Jewish gangsters, see Rich Cohen, *Tough Jews: Fathers, Sons, and Gangster Dreams in Jewish America* (New York: Simon and Schuster, 1998).

56. Quoted in Whitfield, "A Stereotype," 147.

57. Ibid. Harvard's anti-Jewish quotas, along with those of other U.S. universities, were testament, of course, that Jews were by no means inferior in *mental* stature and development. For more on the anti-Jewish quotas, see Leonard Dinnerstein, *Antisemitism in America* (New York: Oxford University Press, 1994).

58. Quoted in Whitfield, "A Stereotype," 147.

59. Irving Howe, with Kenneth Libo, *World of Our Fathers* (New York: Harcourt Brace Jovanovich, 1976), 182.

60. Daniel Boyarin, *Unheroic Conduct: The Rise of Heterosexuality and the Invention of the Jewish Man* (Berkeley and Los Angeles: University of California Press, 1997). For more on Jewish masculinity see Daniel Boyarin, Daniel Itzkovitz, and Ann Pellegrini, eds., *Queer Theory and the Jewish Question* (New York: Columbia University Press, 2003).

61. Philip Roth, *American Pastoral* (New York: Grove Press, 1997), 25.

62. For more on the luftmensch, see Ruth Wisse, *The Schlemiel as Modern Hero* (Chicago: University of Chicago Press, 1971).

63. Sheri Chinen Biesen, *Blackout: World War II and the Origins of Film Noir* (Baltimore: Johns Hopkins University Press, 2005), 3, 5–6.

64. Ibid., 3–8. By our strict terms, of course, Curtiz was not an émigré.

65. Ibid., 13; and Borde and Chaumeton, *A Panorama of American Film Noir*, 1. Borde and Chaumeton also identify three *post*war U.S. films that reinforced French critics' noir designation: *The Killers* (Siodmak, 1946), *The Big Sleep* (Hawks, 1946), and *Lady in the Lake* (Montgomery, 1947).

66. Biesen, *Blackout*, 13.

67. Silver and Ward, *Film Noir*, 334.

68. Leonard J. Leff and Jerold L. Simmons, *The Dame in the Kimono: Hollywood Censorship, and the Production Code from the 1920s to the 1960s* (New York: Anchor, 1990), 127.

69. Biesen, *Blackout*, 2, 3.

70. Ibid., 12.

71. Thomas Schatz, *The Genius of the System: Hollywood Filmmaking in the Hollywood Era* (New York: Metropolitan Books, 1988); Richard Maltby, *Hollywood Cinema*, 2d ed. (New York: Blackwell, 2003); and Steve Neale and Murray Smith, ed., *Contemporary Hollywood Cinema* (London: Routledge, 1998). See also Tino Balio, ed., *Grand Design: Hollywood as a Modern Business Enterprise, 1930–1939* (Berkeley and Los Angeles: University

of California Press, 1993); and Thomas Schatz, ed., *Boom and Bust: American Cinema in the 1940s* (Berkeley and Los Angeles: University of California Press, 1997).

72. Robert Siodmak, *Zwischen Berlin und Hollywood: Erinnerungen eines grossen Filmregisseurs*, ed. Hans C. Blumenberg (Munich: Goldmann Verlag, 1980), 102.

73. For more on Zanuck, see Denise Mann, *Hollywood Independents: When Talent Became Management* (Minneapolis: University of Minnesota Press, 2007). Mann gleans much of her information from J. A. Aberdeen, *Hollywood Renegades: The Society of Independent Motion Picture Producers* (Van Nuys, Calif.: Cobblestone Entertainment Press, 2000).

74. Curtis Bernhardt and Mary Kiersch, *Curtis Bernhardt: A Directors Guild of America Oral History* (Metuchen, N.J.: Directors Guild of America and Scarecrow Press, 1986); and Joel Greenberg, *Oral History with John Brahm*, 1971 (Beverly Hills, Calif.: American Film Institute Center for Advanced Studies, 1975).

75. Bacher, *Max Ophuls*.

76. Todd McCarthy and Charles Flynn, eds., *Kings of the Bs: Working Within the Hollywood System* (New York: Dutton, 1975).

77. Interview with Myles Wilder, November 24, 2007.

78. Arthur Lyons, *Death on the Cheap: The Lost B Movies of Film Noir* (New York: Da Capo Press, 2000), 38.

79. Bacher, *Max Ophuls*, 29.

80. Ibid.

81. Mann, *Hollywood Independents*.

82. Ibid.

83. Biesen, *Blackout*, 2.

84. Quoted in Thomas Schatz, *Hollywood Genres: Formulas, Filmmaking, and the Studio System* (New York: Random House, 1981), 111.

85. Kreimeier, *The Ufa Story*, 40–41.

86. Paul Schrader, "Notes on Film Noir," in *Film Noir Reader*, ed. Alain Silver and James Ursini (New York: Limelight, 1996), 53–63.

87. Janey Place, "Women in Film Noir," in *Women in Film Noir*, ed. E. Ann Kaplan (London: British Film Institute, 2000), 47–68, quote 50. The conjunction of Schrader and Place was drawn from Jane Root, "Film Noir," in *The Cinema Book*, ed. Pam Cook (London: British Film Institute, 1994), 93–97.

88. Place, "Women in Film Noir."

89. Schrader, "Notes," 59.

90. This last phrase is of course lifted from Siegfried Kracauer's classic history of Weimar cinema, *From Caligari to Hitler: A Psychological Study of the German Film* (1947; repr., New York: Noonday Press, 1959).

91. Wilder's actual words, to Cornelius Schnauber (no doubt among others), were: "It was through Hitler that I became aware that I was a Jew." E-mail from Cornelius Schnauber, September 9, 2008. In *Cinema's Exiles* (a 2008 documentary by Karen Thomas), Lutzi Korngold, wife of Jewish émigré composer Erich Wolfgang Korngold, is quoted as saying, "We thought of ourselves as Viennese; Hitler made us Jewish."

92. Bernhardt and Kiersch, *Curtis Bernhardt*, 72.

93. Bacher, *Max Ophuls*, 22, 27.

94. R. Barton Palmer, "'Lounge Time' Reconsidered: Spatial Discontinuity and Temporal Contingency in *Out of the Past* (1947)," in Silver and Ursini, *Film Noir Reader* 4, 54.

95. For more on issues surrounding auteurist criticism, see Virginia Wright Wexman, ed., *Film and Authorship* (New Brunswick: Rutgers University Press, 2003); and David A. Gerstner and Janet Staiger, eds., *Authorship and Film* (New York: Routledge, 2003).

CHAPTER 2 — JEWS IN GERMANY: TORN BETWEEN TWO WORLDS

1. Johann Wolfgang von Goethe, *Goethe's Faust*, trans. Walter Kaufmann (1790; repr., New York: Random House, 1961), 145.

2. Henry Bean, *The Believer: Confronting Jewish Self-Hatred* (Emeryville, Calif.: Thunder's Mouth Press, 2002), 19.

3. The Marquis D'Argens's *Lettres juives*, published between 1735 and 1738, though not as influential as Lessing's work, were the first pro-Jewish writings by a non-Jew. A sympathetic Jewish character also appears in German novelist Christian Geller's *Leben der Schwedischen Gräfinn von G*** (Life of the Swedish Countess of G**), published in 1746.

4. Paul Hoffmann, *The Viennese: Splendor, Twilight, and Exile* (New York: Anchor, 1989), 38; and Emily D. Bilski, "Introduction," in *Berlin Metropolis: Jews and the New Culture, 1890–1918*, ed. Emily D. Bilski (Berkeley and Los Angeles: University of California Press, 1999), 5.

5. Bilski, "Introduction," 5.

6. Ibid., 5.

7. Ibid., 7.

8. Ibid., 5; and Paul Mendes-Flohr, "The Berlin Jew as Cosmopolitan," in Bilski, *Berlin Metropolis*, 17.

9. Mendes-Flohr, "The Berlin Jew," 17.

10. Ferdinand Avenarius, "*Aussprachen mit Juden*" [Dialogue with Jews], *Der Kunstwart* 25, no. 22 (August 2, 1912): 225–236. The references to Avenarius were gleaned from Paul Mendes-Flohr, *German Jews: A Dual Identity* (New Haven: Yale University Press, 1999), 46–47.

11. Steven A. Aschheim, *Brothers and Strangers: The East European Jew in German Consciousness, 1800–1923* (Madison: University of Wisconsin Press, 1982), 65.

12. Ibid.

13. Ibid., 66.

14. Mendes-Flohr, "The Berlin Jew," 18.

15. Peter Paget, "Modernism and the 'Alien Element' in German Art," in Bilski, *Berlin Metropolis*, 33.

16. Moritz Goldstein, "German-Jewish Parnassus," *Der Kunstwart* 25, no. 11 (March 1, 1912), 283, 286. Goldstein's article actually preceded Stauff's anti-Semitic diatribe, which was published in 1913.

17. Mendes-Flohr, "The Berlin Jew," 22.

18. Ibid., 402.

19. Thorstein Veblen, "The Intellectual Pre-eminence of Jews in Modern Europe," *Political Science Quarterly* 34 (March 1919), reprinted in *The Writings of Thorstein Veblen: Essays in Our Changing Order*, ed. Leon Ardrooni (New York: N. Kelly, 1964), 219–231.

20. Mendes-Flohr, "The Berlin Jew," 21.

21. As paraphrased in ibid.

22. Bilski, "Introduction," 10.

23. Quoted in Naomi Seidman, "Fag Hags and Bu-Jews," in *Insider/Outsider: American Jews and Multiculturalism*, ed. David Biale, Michael Galchinsky, and Susannah Herschel (Berkeley and Los Angeles: University of California Press, 1998), 258. Philosopher Hannah Arendt, echoing Jean-Paul Sartre's sentiments in *Anti-Semite and Jew* (1948; repr., New York: Grove Press, 1960), similarly championed Jewish "outsiderness" in her descriptive and prescriptive binary of pariah and parvenu, in which the former's qualities were favored for their Jewish translation into ethical concern, humor, and "disinterested intelligence." *The Jew as Pariah: Jewish Identity and Politics in the Modern Age* (New York: Grove Press, 1978), 15.

24. Mendes-Flohr, *German Jews: A Dual Identity*, 25–44.

25. Ibid., 27.

26. Ibid., 31. The term "meta rabbis" is from George Steiner, "Some 'Meta-Rabbis,'" in *Next Year in Jerusalem: Jews in the Twentieth Century*, ed. Douglas Villiers (New York: Viking Press, 1976), 26.

27. Aschheim, *Brothers and Stranger*, 6.

28. Michael A. Meyer, *The Origins of the Modern Jew: Jewish Identity and European Culture, 1749–1824* (Detroit: Wayne State University Press: 1967, 1984), 13, 15.

29. Quoted in Aschheim, *Brothers and Strangers*, 7.

30. Quoted in ibid., 6.

31. Ibid., 11.

32. Ibid., 33, 34.

33. Wilhelm Marr is "credited" with coining the term. See Sander L. Gilman, *Jewish Self-Hatred: Anti-Semitism and the Hidden Language of the Jews* (Baltimore: Johns Hopkins University Press, 1986), 211.

34. Inka Bertz, "Jewish Renaissance—Jewish Modernism," in Bilski, *Berlin Metropolis*, 165; and Aschheim, *Brother and Strangers*, 35.

35. Meyer, *Origins of the Modern Jew*, 49.

36. Because Karl Marx's mother remained a Jew, Karl himself, avowed atheist and anti-Semite that he was, can still be considered a Jew according to traditional Jewish law. This is certainly what contemporaneous and subsequent anti-Semites and Jews claim him to be.

37. Aschheim, *Brothers and Strangers*, 65; and Omer Bartov, "Faraway So Close," review of *Five Germanys I Have Known*, by Fritz Stern, *The Nation*, January 8/15, 2007, 28–32.

38. Nathan Ausubel, *Pictorial History of the Jewish People* (New York: Crown, 1958), 161. Another, initially less successful attempt to cut Jewish cloth to fit the modern age was the Society for the Promotion of Jewish Culture and Science. Also founded in Berlin in 1819, this group foundered a few years later due to the opportunistic conversion of many of its officers. As short-lived as it was, the group initiated the scientific method in the study of Jewish religion and is regarded as the forerunner of Jewish studies.

39. Bertz, "Jewish Renaissance," 165.

40. Ibid., 166.

41. Ibid., 165.

42. Ibid., 175–176.

43. Aschheim, *Brothers and Strangers*, 108.

44. Ibid., xxviii, 55–56.

45. Ibid., 56.

46. Quoted and paraphrased in Bertz, "Jewish Renaissance," 183.

47. Martin Buber, *Drei Reden über das Judentum* (Frankfurt: Literarische Anstalt Rütten, and Loening, 1911), 24 (the English translation is from Bertz, "Jewish Renaissance," 183).

48. Bertz, "Jewish Renaissance," 184.

49. For more on the cult of the Ostjuden, see Aschheim, *Brothers and Strangers*, 185–214.

50. Bilski, "Introduction," 12.

51. Aschheim, *Brothers and Strangers*, 215.

52. Mendes-Flohr, *German Jews*, 75–76.

53. Ibid., 82.

54. Ibid.

55. Aschheim, *Brothers and Strangers*, 215.

56. Cited in ibid., 215

57. Peter Gay, *Freud, Jews, and Other Germans* (New York: Oxford University Press, 1978), 201; and Aschheim, *Brothers and Strangers*, 224.

58. Jakob Wassermann, *My Life as German and Jew*, trans. S. N. Brainin (1921; repr., New York: Allen and Unwin, 1933), 196–197. The quotes used here are cited in Aschheim, *Brothers and Strangers*, 225.

59. Quoted in Aschheim, *Brothers and Strangers*, 197–198, 234, 220–221.

60. Aschheim, *Brothers and Strangers*, 242.

61. The cartoon's German captions read as follows. For the first image: "Moische Pisch handelte in Carnopel mit abgelente Kleidern" (Moische Pisch in Carnopel dealt in secondhand clothing); for the second: "als Moritz Wasserstrahl siedelte er nach Posen über und handelte Pariser Modewaren" (as Moritz Wasserstrahl he moved on to Posen and dealt in Paris fashion ware); for the third: "jetzt lebt er als Maurice Lafontaine in Berlin, wo er eine neue Kunstrichtung gegründet hat und mit abgelegter Pariser Kunstmode handelt" (now he lives as Maurice Lafontaine in Berlin, where he has started a new business and deals in secondhand Parisian artwork).

62. Eduard Meyer, *Gegen L. Börner, den Warheit-, Recht- und Ehvergessnen Briefsteller aus Paris* (Altona, 1831), 14, quoted in Jacob Katz, *From Prejudice to Destruction* (Cambridge: Harvard University Press, 1980), 178.

63. Aschheim, *Brothers and Strangers*, 69.

64. In the original German, the caption reads: "Wie die Giftpilze oft schwer von den guten zu entscheieden sind, so ist es oft sehr schwer, die Juden als Gauner und Verbrecher zu erkennen." The cover illustration of *Der Giftpilz* is visually even more offensive: a bearded man with a hook nose, a broad mushroom cap for a hat, and a Jewish star pinned to his chest. For more on the Jewish double bind, see Gilman, *Jewish Self-Hatred*.

65. Quoted in Omer Bartov, "Faraway, So Close," 30. Stern's father's experience, although particularly repugnant, should not be taken as an isolated incident. Frankfurt School member Franz Neumann stated that after the war anti-Semitism was "openly preached by university professors." Quoted in Peter Gay, *Weimar Culture: The Outsider As Insider* (New York: Norton, 2001), 44.

66. Siegfried Kracauer, *From Caligari to Hitler: A Psychological Study of the German Film* (1947; repr., New York: Noonday Press, 1959), 66. Lang's involvement with *Caligari* is also mentioned in Patrick McGilligan, *Fritz Lang: The Nature of the Beast* (New York: St. Martin's, 1997), 61; and Tom Gunning, *The Films of Fritz Lang: Allegories of Vision and Modernity* (London: British Film Institute, 2000), 147.

67. Quoted in McGilligan, *Fritz Lang*, 61. All the parties mentioned were Jewish.

68. Kracauer, *From Caligari to Hitler*, 70.

69. Ibid.

70. Ibid.

71. Mayer would get the "last laugh," in more ways than one, in another Weimar-era film that he wrote, titled *The Last Laugh* (1924) in English, and *Der Letzte Mann* (The last man) in German. This film's "happy ending," added this time by producer Pommer to boost its prospects in the foreign (read: U.S.) market, is not only an absurd deus ex machina tacked on to an otherwise tragic tale, but the stranger who miraculously bequeaths his inheritance to the lowly protagonist is an American millionaire named "Money."

72. Cited by Sigrid Bauschinger, "The Berlin Moderns: Else Lasker-Schüler and Café Culture," in Bilski, *Berlin Metropolis*, 67. See also Norbert Wolf, *Expressionism* (Cologne, Germany: Taschen, 2004), 8; and Dietmar Elger, *Expressionism: A Revolution in German Art* (Cologne, Germany: Taschen, 1988), 14.

73. Elger, *Expressionism*, 5–6.

74. Ibid., 17.

75. Ibid.

76. Quoted in Gay, *Freud, Jews and Other Germans*, 171.

77. Quoted in George L. Mosse, *The Crisis of German Ideology* (1964; repr., New York: H. Fetig, 1998), 23. Gay, himself a Jew, is quick to caution, as must I, that Jews were not the only outsiders among the artists, intellectuals, and politicians to become influential insiders during the Weimar period. A significant number of non-Jews had filled the ranks of the avant-garde and the political opposition before the war and would continue to do so up until the Nazi ascension. Weimar certainly cannot be regarded as a "Jewish" republic, as both anti- and philo-Semites have suggested; it did, however, "give Jews unprecedented prominence across a wide scope" (Gay, *Freud, Jews, and Other Germans*, vi).

78. Gay, *Freud, Jews, and Other Germans*, 120.

79. Ibid., 8.

CHAPTER 3 — JEWS AND EXPRESSIONISM:
"PERFORMING HIGH AND LOW"

1. Norbert Wolf, *Expressionism* (Cologne, Germany: Taschen, 2004), 8; Dietmar Elger, *Expressionism: A Revolution in German Art* (Cologne, Germany: Taschen, 1988), 7; Timothy O. Benson, "Introduction," in *Expressionist Utopias: Paradise, Metropolis, Architectural Fantasy*, ed. Timothy O. Benson (Los Angeles: Los Angeles County Museum of Art, 1993), 8; and Lotte Eisner, *The Haunted Screen: Expressionism in the German Cinema and the Influence of Max Reinhardt* (1952; repr., Berkeley and Los Angeles: University of California Press, 1977), 12.

2. Walter Laqueur, *Weimar: A Cultural History* (New York: Capricorn, 1976), 111.

3. Wolf-Dieter Dube, *Expressionism*, trans. Mary Whittall (New York: Praeger, 1979), 19.

4. Wolf, *Expressionism*, 6.

5. Marit Werenskiold, *The Concept of Expressionism: Origin and Metamorphoses* (New York: Columbia University Press, 1984), cited in Robin Reisenfeld, "Collecting and Collective Memory: German Expressionist Art and Modern Jewish Identity," in *Jewish Identity in Modern Art History*, ed. Catherine M. Soussloff (Berkeley and Los Angeles: University of California Press, 1999), 125.

6. Hanni Mittelman, "Expressionismus und Judentum," in *Condito Judaica: Judentum, Antisemitismus und deutschsprachige Literatur vom Ersten Weltkrieg bis 1933/38*, ed. Horst Denkler (Tübingen, Germany: Niemeyer, 1993), 251–259, quoted in Sigrid Bauschinger, "The Berlin Moderns: Else Lasker-Schüler and Café Culture," in *Berlin Metropolis: Jews and the New Culture, 1890–1918*, ed. Emily D. Bilski (Berkeley and Los Angeles: University of California Press, 1999), 63.

7. Laqueur, *Weimar*, 142.

8. Schoenberg later reverted to Judaism.

9. Religious aniconism is based on the Second Commandment, which, in Deuteronomy 5:7–8, states, "Thou shalt not make for yourself a graven image, or any likeness of anything that is in heaven above, or that is on the earth beneath, or that is in the water under the earth." *The Holy Bible*, Revised Standard Edition (New York: Thomas Nelson and Sons, 1953). On Jews and aniconism, see Kalman B. Bland, "Antisemitism and Aniconism: The Germanophone Requiem for Jewish Visual Art," in Soussloff, *Jewish Identity*, 41–66. See also Peter Gay, *Freud, Jews, and Other Germans* (New York: Oxford University Press, 1978), 103; and Reisenfeld, "Collecting and Collective Memory," 115.

10. For more on the Berlin café scene, see Bauschinger, "The Berlin Moderns."

11. Deborah Lazaroff Alpi, *Robert Siodmak* (Jefferson, N.C.: McFarland, 1998), 11. For more on Berlin salons, see Barbara Hahn, "Encounters at the Margins: Jewish Salons Around 1900," in Bilski, *Berlin Metropolis*, 188–207; and Emily D. Bilski and Emily Braun, *Jewish Women and Their Salons: The Power of Conversation* (New Haven: Yale University Press, 2005).

12. Wolf, *Expressionism*, 72.

13. Benson, "Introduction," 8.

14. Wolf, *Expressionism*, 20, 72.

15. Quoted in David Frisby, "Social Theory, the Metropolis, and Expressionism," in Benson, *Expressionist Utopias*, 105.

16. Peter Gay, *Weimar Culture: The Outsider as Insider* (New York: Norton, 2001), 113.

17. Wolf, *Expressionism*, 6. Gay, in *Weimar Culture*, lists the play as premiering in 1914.

18. Gay, *Weimar Culture*, 34.

19. Laqueur, *Weimar*, 213.

20. See Otto Friedrich, *City of Nets: A Portrait of Hollywood in the 1940s* (New York: Harper and Row, 1986); and Thomas B. Kirsch, *Jungians: A Comparative Historical Perspective* (London: Routledge, 2000).

21. Paul Mendes-Flohr, "Introduction," in Martin Buber, *Ecstatic Confessions: The Heart of Mysticism*, trans. Esther Cameron (1909; repr., Syracuse: Syracuse University Press, 1996), xix.

22. Inka Bertz, "Jewish Renaissance—Jewish Modernism," in Bilski, *Berlin Metropolis*, 171.

23. Wolf, *Expressionism*, 8.

24. Ibid.

25. Ibid.

26. Quoted in Timothy O. Benson, "Fantasy and Functionality: The Fate of Utopia," in Benson, *Expressionist Utopias*, 16.

27. Benn's quote is in Wolf, *Expressionism*, 8. Huebner's assertion is cited in Frisby, "Social Theory," 97.

28. Quoted in Frisby, "Social Theory," 99.

29. Ibid., 97. Some of the quotes here are from Simmel, others from Frisby's gloss. I'm indebted to Frisby for his extensive analysis of Simmel's piece.

30. Georg Simmel, "The Metropolis and Modern Life," in *The Sociology of Georg Simmel*, ed. and trans. Kurt H. Wolff (Glencoe, Ill.: Free Press, 1950), 409.

31. Quoted in Frisby, "Social Theory," 100 (emphasis added).

32. Frisby, "Social Theory, 100.

33. Meidner's quotes are in Benson, "Fantasy and Functionality," 25, 14; Endell's are on pp. 24, 25.

34. Benson, "Fantasy and Functionality," 27.

35. Ibid., 28.

36. Quoted in ibid., 28.

37. Elger, *Expressionism*, 13.

38. Quoted in ibid.

39. Curtis Bernhardt and Mary Kiersch, *Curtis Bernhardt: A Directors Guild of America Oral History* (Metuchen, N.J.: Directors Guild of America and Scarecrow Press, 1986), 19.

40. Wolf, *Expressionism*, 23.

41. Benson, "Fantasy and Functionality," 27–28.

42. Eisner, *The Haunted Screen*, 47.

43. Siegfried Kracauer, *From Caligari to Hitler: A Psychological Study of the German Film* (1947; repr., New York: Noonday Press, 1959),, 75.

44. Eisner, *The Haunted Screen*, 47.

45. Ibid., 44; and Klaus Kreimeier, *The Ufa Story: A History of Germany's Greatest Film Company, 1918–1945*, trans. Robert and Rita Kimber (New York: Hill and Wang, 1996), 134.

46. Kreimeier, *The Ufa Story*, 1.

47. Of these, Bergner, Fein, Granach, Grüne, Kortner, Lubitsch, Poelzig, and Richter were Jewish.

48. Eisner, *The Haunted Screen*, 47–48.

49. Ibid., 48. Similar financial concerns confronting producer Erich Pommer during the making of *Caligari* apparently dictated the film's "groundbreaking" (but also cheaper) use of painted backdrops. Herbert G. Luft, "Erich Pommer," *Films in Review* 10, no. 8 (1959): 461. Further discussion on this topic can be found in Wolfgang Davidson, ed., *Erich Pommer* (Berlin: Argon, 1989), 38–42; Kristen Thompson, "Expressionistic Mise-en-Scène," in *Ivan the Terrible* (Princeton: Princeton University Press, 1981), 127–139; and Ursula Hardt, *From Caligari to California: Eric Pommer's Life in the International Film Wars* (Providence, R.I.: Berghahn Books, 1996), 45–51.

50. Eisner, *The Haunted Screen*, 51.

51. Ibid., 113.

52. Ibid., 51, 55.

53. Ibid., 56.

54. Gottfried Reinhardt, *The Genius: A Memoir of Max Reinhardt, by His Son Gottfried Reinhardt* (New York: Knopf, 1979), 4.

55. Ibid., 24.

56. Ibid., 17.

57. Ibid., 4–5.

58. Quoted in Peter Jelavich, "Performing High and Low: Jews in Modern Theater, Cabaret, Revue, and Film," in Bilski, *Berlin Metropolis*, 213.

59. Quoted in Sarah Blacher Cohen, ed., *Jewish Wry: Essays on Jewish Humor* (Detroit: Wayne State University Press, 1987), 2 (emphasis added).

60. Ibid.

61. Jelavich, "Performing High and Low."

62. Eli Barnavi, ed., *A Historical Atlas of the Jewish People* (New York: Schocken, 2002), vi.

63. Ibid., vi. For more on Jews and postmodern consciousness, see Vincent Brook, ed., *You Should See Yourself: Jewish Identity and Postmodern American Culture* (New Brunswick: Rutgers University Press, 2006).

64. Herman Kienzl, "Theater und Kinematograph," *Der Strom* 1 (1911–1912), quoted in Anton Kaes, "Introduction," in *Kino-Debatte: Texte zum Verhältnis von Literatur und Film,* 1909–1929, ed. Anton Kaes (Tübingen, Germany: Max Niemeyer Verlag, 1978), 6, cited in Patrice Petro, *Joyless Streets: Women and Melodramatic Representation in Weimar Germany* (Princeton: Princeton University Press, 1989), 6–7.

65. Petro, *Joyless Streets,* 8.

66. Ibid., 8.

67. Sander Gilman, *The Jew's Body* (New York: Routledge, 1991).

68. Petro, *Joyless Streets,* 40, 34.

69. Ann Pellegrini, "Whiteface Performances," in *Jews and Other Differences: The New Jewish Cultural Studies,* ed. Jonathan and Daniel Boyarin (Minneapolis: University of Minnesota Press, 1997), 110.

70. Jelavich, "Performing High and Low," 223. To gain permission from the authorities to present the play, Reinhardt was forced to eliminate scenes dealing with masturbation and homosexuality (223).

71. Reinhardt, *Genius,* 16.

72. Jelavich, "Performing High and Low," 220.

73. According to Jelavich, in *Ghosts,* when actors moved past a bright light, they cast "enormous shadows on the back wall that gave the impression they were being pursued by demons" ("Performing High and Low," 220).

74. Barry Salt, "From Caligari to Who?" *Sight and Sound* (Spring 1990): 119–123.

75. Emily D. Bilski, "Images of Identity and Urban Life: Jewish Artists in Turn-of-the-Century Berlin," in Bilski, *Berlin Metropolis,* 104, 105.

76. Ibid., 108.

77. Salt, in a later essay, although granting Reinhardt's influence on German cinema, also draws attention to the significant impact of other theater artists, such as Piscator and Jessner. "From German Stage to German Screen," in *Before Caligari: German Cinema,* 1895–1920, ed. Paolo Cherchi Usai and Lorenzo Codelli (Pordenone, Italy: Edizioni Biblioteca dell'Immagine, 1990), 402–422. On German filmmakers' collaborative propensities, see Eisner, *The Haunted Screen*; Thomas Elsaesser, *Weimar Cinema and After: Germany's Historical Imaginary* (New York: Routledge, 2000); and Sabine Hake, *German National Cinema* (New York: Routledge, 2002), among others.

78. Kracauer, *From Caligari to Hitler,* 17.

79. From most accounts (e.g., Kracauer, Jelavich), the two films—*Die Insel der Seligen* (The isle of the blessed, 1913) and *Eine Venezianische Nacht* (A Venetian night, 1914)— were undistinguished.

80. Kracauer, *From Caligari to Hitler,* 17–18.

81. Quoted in Kreimeier, *The Ufa Story*, 17.

82. Hake, *German National Cinema*, 13; and Elsaesser, *Weimar Cinema and After*, 26–27.

83. Kracauer, *From Caligari to Hitler*, 29.

84. Geoffrey Dennis, *The Jewish Encyclopedia of Jewish Myth, Magic, and Mysticism* (Woodbury, Maine: Llewellyn, 2007). According to Eisner, the 1914 version of *The Golem*, which is lost, "mixed contemporary events (the Golem being discovered in Prague) with the legend." The extent 1920 remake sticks to the legend (Eisner, *The Haunted Screen*, 41).

85. Quoted in Eisner, *The Haunted Screen*, 40.

86. Kracauer, *From Caligari to Hitler*, 29.

87. Eisner, *The Haunted Screen*, 40 (emphasis added).

88. Quoted in ibid., 40.

89. Salt, "German Stage to German Screen," 198.

90. Hake, *German National Cinema*, 26.

91. Kracauer, *From Caligari to Hitler*, 156.

92. Quoted, respectively, in Elger, *Expressionism*, 181; Wolf, *Expressionism*, 7; Elger, *Expressionism*, 133; and Benson, "Fantasy and Functionality," 22.

93. Kracauer, *From Caligari to Hitler*, 69

94. John D. Barlow, *German Expressionist Film* (Boston: Twayne, 1982), 186.

95. Jelavich, "Performing High and Low," 225.

96. Quoted in Eisner, *The Haunted Screen*, 177, cited in Petro, *Joyless Streets*, 175.

97. Ibid.

98. Marc Vernet, "Film Noir on the Edge of Doom," in *Shades of Noir: A Reader*, ed. Joan Copjec (New York: Verso, 1993), 1–31, quote on 7–8.

99. Ibid., 7.

100. Among the pre-Weimar films to which Vernet, directly or indirectly, is referring, those of the Dane Bernard Christensen perhaps come closest to the sophisticated expressionist mode of the Kammerspiel/street films.

101. A useful analogy here is Griffith's contribution to the development of montage; although undeniable and considerable, it in no way minimizes the significance of Soviet filmmakers of the 1920s (Vertov, Kuleshov, Eisenstein, Pudovkin) in advancing these developments and codifying them into a coherent set of principles.

102. Interview in *Hollywood (aka Hollywood: A Celebration of the American Silent Film)*, "The Directors" episode (multipart documentary series, directed by Kevin Brownlow and David Gill, 1980).

103. Vernet, "Film Noir," 8. *Two Seconds* also owes much, at least in content, to von Sternberg's *The Blue Angel* (1930) and Renoir's *La Chienne* (1931).

CHAPTER 4 — THE FATHER OF FILM NOIR: FRITZ LANG

1. Georges Sturm, *Fritz Lang: film/texts/references* (Nancy, France: Presses Universitaires de Nancy, 1990), quoted in Patrick McGilligan, *Fritz Lang: The Nature of the Beast* (New York: Faber and Faber, 1997), 485.

2. McGilligan, *Fritz Lang*, 74.

3. David Wallace, *Exiles in Hollywood* (New York: Limelight, 2006), 34. Alain Silver and Elizabeth Ward, ed., *Film Noir: An Encyclopedic Reference to the American Style*, 3d ed. (Woodstock, N.Y.: Overlook Press, 1992).

4. Eddie Muller, *Dark City: The Lost World of Film Noir* (New York: St. Martin's Griffin, 1998), 45. Bob Porfirio, in a review of Joseph Losey's *M*, calls this classic American noir of 1951 "an almost exact remake of the Fritz Lang film." Silver and Ward's *Film Noir*, which focuses on American film noir, lists Joseph von Sternberg's *Underworld* (1927) as the first film noir, but this was not a sound film (178).

5. McGilligan, *Fritz Lang*, 228.

6. For a more complete account of the discrepancies in Lang's story, see McGilligan, *Fritz Lang*, 174–184. Lang's situation with Goebbels is similar to that of Leni Riefenstahl, who claimed that Goebbels disliked her intensely, that the feeling was mutual, and that she avoided him like the plague; yet his diaries describe their relationship as quite cordial and list numerous pleasant social contacts between them. Also similar to Lang in general, Riefenstahl was notorious for twisting the truth to spare her reputation.

7. Ibid., 178–182, 207–209. As for Lang's Nazi ties, both Gottfried Reinhardt, Max's son, and Seymour Nebenzahl, one of Lang's Weimar producers, insist that Lang cozied up to the Nazis; on the other hand, Conrad von Molo, a crew member and confidant of Lang's, claims that Lang was horrified by a Nazi gathering that he attended out of curiosity in 1932 and refused to give the Nazi salute (ibid., 157, 163).

8. Ibid., 227.

9. Ibid., 365–377. It is true that Lang had been targeted by the HUAC for his leftist affiliations as early as 1940, and his signing on to the Committee for the First Amendment, not to mention his collaborations with Bertolt Brecht, Hanns Eisler, Albert Malz, and Ring Lardner, certainly didn't help his standing with the witch-hunters.

10. Ibid., 57. Rosenthal's background, indeed her very existence, is a mystery (see note 17, below).

11. Ibid., 76–80.

12. Ibid., 79.

13. Thomas Elsaesser, *Weimar Cinema and After: Germany's Historical Imaginary* (New York: Routledge, 2000), 74; and McGilligan, *Fritz Lang*, 79.

14. There are two additional suicides in *Spies*: that of the Japanese diplomat, Matsumoto, and of the eastern European spy, Jellusic.

15. McGilligan, *Fritz Lang*, 80.

16. Quoted in ibid., 80. Film critic Kevin Thomas, another of Lang's close friends in the United States, in a phone interview confirmed Schnauber's appraisal of Lang's moods: "He could be incredibly loving, with a tremendous capacity for devotion, concern, encouragement, and support. But he could be a devil!"

17. McGilligan, *Fritz Lang*, 80. McGilligan adds this caveat in his "Notes and Sources" section on the Rosenthal case: "As the text makes clear, there is no proof positive of her death, marriage to Fritz Lang, or even existence of the director's first wife. The reputable French scholar Bernard Eisenschitz told me he was half-inclined to believe it was all a clever fiction Lang had managed to concoct to dramatize his otherwise humdrum life" (516).

18. Ibid., 56.

19. For more on Viennese and Austrian anti-Semitism, see Paul Hoffmann, *The Viennese: Splendor, Twilight, and Exile* (New York: Anchor Books, 1989).

20. Ibid., 1.

21. Quoted in Erwin Ringel, *Die Österreichische Seele* (Vienna: Europaverlag, 1986), 25 (the translation is from Hoffmann, *The Viennese*, 1).

22. Hoffmann, *The Viennese*, 4.

23. Ibid., 10–12.

24. Kevin Thomas, in our May 21, 2007, interview, related two contrasting personal views concerning Lang's legendary authoritarianism as a director: the French cineaste and close friend of Lang's, Pierre Rissient, believes that actors and other film professionals were perfectly capable of discerning, and responding to, the film artist behind the tantrums; Roddy McDowell, on the other hand, who worked with Lang as a child actor on *Man Hunt* and became a close friend, admitted after Lang's death that the director "really could be a monster."

25. McGilligan, *Fritz Lang*, 47.

26. Siegmund Hurwitz, *Lilith, the First Eve: Historical and Psychological Aspects of the Dark Feminine*, trans. Robert Hinshaw (1980; repr., Zürich: Daimon, 1992).

27. McGilligan, *Fritz Lang*, 47.

28. Anthony Heilbut, *Exiled in Paradise: German Refugee Artists and Intellectuals in America from the 1930s to the Present* (1983; repr., Berkeley and Los Angeles: University of California Press, 1997), 242. Oddly, McGilligan fails to mention the *Golem* project in his

more recent, and otherwise meticulously researched, biography. For his part, Heilbut, without access to McGilligan's later-published work, swallows Lang's Goebbels and blacklisting tales whole.

29. Schnauber published this story, with his commentary, in a collection of other Lang stories and movie treatments, listed under Fritz Lang, *Der Berg des Aberglaubens und andere Geschichten* (Wien-Zurich: Europaverlag, 1988), along with a similar collection, with commentary, listed under Fritz Lang, *Der Tod eines Karrieregirls und andere Geschichten* (Wien-Zürich: Europaverlag, 1987).

30. David Daube, "Ahasver," *The Jewish Quarterly Review*, n.s., 45, no. 3 (January 1955): 243–244. Other common names for the Wandering Jew include *Melmoth*, Matathias, Buttadeus, Cartophilus, Isaac Laquedem (in France and the Low Countries), Juan Espera a Dios (*Spanish* for "John who waits for God"), and Jerusalemin suutari ("Shoemaker of Jerusalem," in *Finnish*).

31. Interview with Cornelius Schnauber, May 31, June 1, 2007.

32. Lang told Schnauber that his ties to Catholicism were not religiously based, but rather stemmed from his strict Catholic upbringing by his mother, the converted Catholic Jew (ibid.).

33. McGilligan, *Fritz Lang*, 170, 174, 171, 176, 184.

34. Ibid., 258, 326, 288, 296

35. Ibid., 288.

36. Ibid., 337, 344, 350, 385, 331. As for von Harbou's relation to Nazism, according to McGilligan, "she had always been a conservative nationalist, while at the same time she demonstrated progressive tendencies" (particularly on women's issues). During the Hitler period, despite her secret marriage to a much younger, Indian man, she fared quite well, and Goebbels mentions her favorably in his diaries (ibid., 157).

37. Ibid., 425.

38. Quoted in ibid., 461.

39. Ibid., 475.

40. Quoted in ibid., 475. The late wedding was performed mainly for estate-settlement purposes. Schnauber, meanwhile, in our interview, claimed that he could find no specific reference to a Jewish wedding in Lang's papers, only that the wedding to Latté took place in Las Vegas.

41. Heilbut, *Exiled in Paradise*, 230–231.

42. Tom Gunning, *The Films of Fritz Lang: Allegories of Visions and Modernity* (London: British Film Institute, 2001), 88.

43. Ibid., 89.

44. Ibid., 94.

45. Quoted in ibid., 94.

46. This assertion is mentioned in several secondary sources, and repeated by Lang in later interviews.

47. McGilligan, *Fritz Lang*, 87.

48. Siegfried Kracauer, *From Caligari to Hitler: A Psychological Study of the German Film* (1947; repr., New York: Noonday Press, 1959), 82.

49. Quoted in ibid., 83–84.

50. Gunning, *The Films of Fritz Lang*, 97.

51. Interview with Fritz Lang in the "Special Features" on the King Video DVD of *Dr. Mabuse: The Gambler* (2004); and Kracauer, *From Caligari to Hitler*, 83.

52. Kracauer, *From Caligari to Hitler*, 83; and Gunning, *The Films of Fritz Lang*, 87–116.

53. Lang interview in the *Dr. Mabuse: The Gambler* DVD.

54. Quoted in McGilligan, *Fritz Lang*, 103.

55. Alleged by Lotte Eisner in Lotte H. Eisner, *Fritz Lang* (New York: Da Capo Press, 1976), 79.

56. Although one can argue that Caligari and Nosferatu, to whom Mabuse bears no small resemblance, are also exoticized, this does not at all compromise his—or their—Jewish aspect. Caligari's appearance could easily pass for Jewish, and his psychiatrist's occupation definitely does. Nosferatu's "Jewish" credentials, given his anti-Christian agenda and large hook nose, are even more pronounced.

57. The Austrian author Vicki Baum and the American author L. Frank Baum would have provided contemporary audiences with ready support for the surname's Jewishness.

58. Walter Laqueur, *Weimar: A Cultural History* (New York: Capricorn, 1976), 6.

59. Gunning, *The Films of Fritz Lang*, 119.

60. Lang interview in the *Dr. Mabuse: The Gambler* DVD.

61. Hannah Arendt, "We Refugees" [1943], in *The Jew as Pariah: Jewish Identity and Politics in the Modern Age*, ed. Ron H. Feldman (New York: Grove Press, 1978), 55–66.

62. Peter Jalevich, "Performing High and Low: Jews in Modern Theater, Cabaret, and Review," in *Berlin Metropolis: Jews and the New Culture, 1890–1918*, ed. Emily D. Bilski (Berkeley and Los Angeles: University of California Press, 1999), 225, 216.

63. Ibid., 232.

64. Ibid., 233.

65. Ibid., 217.

66. The film's full title is *Borat: Cultural Learnings of America for Make Benefit Glorious Nation of Kazakhstan*.

67. Eisner, *Fritz Lang*, 79.

68. For more on Jewish self-hatred, see Sander L. Gilman, *Jewish Self-Hatred: Anti-Semitism and the Hidden Language of the Jews* (Baltimore: Johns Hopkins University Press, 1986); and Albert Memmi, *The Liberation of the Jew*, trans. Judy Hyun (New York: Orion, 1966).

69. McGilligan, *Fritz Lang*, 81.

70. Gunning, *The Films of Fritz Lang*, 173.

71. See Kracauer, *From Caligari to Hitler*, 54; Lotte Eisner, *The Haunted Screen: Expressionism in the German Cinema and the Influence of Max Reinhardt* (1952; repr., Berkeley and Los Angeles: University of California Press, 1977), 163; and Gottfried Reinhardt, *The Genius: A Memoir of Max Reinhardt, by His Son Gottfried Reinhardt* (New York: Knopf, 1979).

72. Kracauer, *From Caligari to Hitler*, 150.

73. Ibid., 250. Mabuse's Nazi-esque lines: "The ultimate purpose of crime is to establish an empire of complete uncertainty and anarchy, founded upon shattered ideals of a world doomed to annihilation. When the people are ruled by terror and go mad from horror and dread, when chaos is elevated to a supreme law, then the time of the empire of crime will have come."

74. Kracauer, *From Caligari to Hitler*, 250.

75. *Citizen Kane* was itself consciously influenced by Weimar cinema and would subsequently "return the favor" by influencing film noir.

76. Kracauer, *From Caligari to Hitler*, 221–222.

77. Ibid., 222.

78. Ibid., 30.

79. Ibid., 99.

80. Gunning, *The Films of Fritz Lang*, 164.

81. Underplaying acts of violence and murder was a consistent feature of Lang's films. In this case the indirection was partly due to the special heinousness of the crimes, but also, as he explained in his filmed interview with William Friedkin, to allow the audience to become his "collaborators" (*Dr. Mabuse: The Gambler* DVD).

82. Gunning, *The Films of Fritz Lang*, 164.

83. Ibid.

84. Ibid., 191

85. Quoted in McGilligan, *Fritz Lang*, 157.

86. Gunning, *The Films of Fritz Lang*, 198.

87. Ibid., 197.

88. Gilman, *Jewish Self-Hatred*, 7.

89. Quoted in ibid., 7.

90. Quoted in ibid., 8.

91. As late as 1946 a pogrom relating to blood libel resulted in the killing of thirty-seven Jews and the wounding of eighty-two in Kielce, Poland. Arab countries, sometimes with state sponsorship and media complicity, have remained the most ardent promulgators of the myth, particularly since the 1967 Six-Day War and subsequent Israeli occupation of Palestine. A popular book upholding the blood libel, *The Matzoh of Zion*, was written by the Syrian defense minister in 1986, and a 2003 Syrian miniseries, shown throughout the Muslim world, not only presents the myth as fact but also adds *The Protocols of the Elders of Zion* to its calumnies. One can be sure that the Middle Eastern madrassas also continue to promote the falsehood.

92. McGilligan, *Fritz Lang*; and Kracauer; *From Caligari to Hitler*, 219.

CHAPTER 5 — FRITZ LANG IN HOLLYWOOD

1. John Russell Taylor, *Strangers in Paradise: The Hollywood Émigrés, 1933–1950* (New York: Holt, Rinehart and Winston, 1983), 57.

2. For more on the émigrés' living conditions, see, besides individual biographies: Taylor, *Strangers in Paradise;* Anthony Heilbut, *Exiled in Paradise: German Refugee Artists and Intellectuals in America from the 1930s to the Present* (1983; repr., Berkeley and Los Angeles: University of California Press, 1997); David Wallace, *Exiles in Hollywood* (New York: Limelight, 2006); Ehrhard Bahr, *Weimar on the Pacific: German Exile Culture in Los Angeles and the Crisis of Modernism* (Berkeley and Los Angeles: University of California Press, 2007); Joseph Horowitz, *Artists in Exile: How Refugees from Twentieth Century War and Revolution Transformed the American Performing Arts* (New York: HarperCollins, 2007); Otto Friedrich, *City of Nets: Hollywood in the 1940s* (New York: Harper and Row, 1986); John Baxter, *Hollywood Exiles* (New York: Taplinger, 1976); and Salka Viertel, *The Kindness of Strangers* (New York: Holt, Rinehart and Winston, 1969).

3. For more on *Die Gruppe*, see Ruth E. Wolman, *Crossing Over: An Oral History of Refugees from Hitler's Reich* (New York: Twayne, 1996). My father (a lawyer in Berlin) worked as a gardener for several notable émigrés, including some with film noir connections, such as Lang, Peter Lorre, Karl Freund, and Douglas Sirk; other famous foreigners, such as Bruno Walter and Hildegard Knef; and non-Jewish American actors, such as Judy Garland, Robert Ryan, and Cornell Wilde.

4. Emily D. Bilski and Emily Braun, *Jewish Women and Their Salons: The Power of Conversation* (New Haven: Yale University Press, 2005), 31.

5. Quoted in Barbara Hahn, "Encounters at the Margins: Jewish Salons Around 1900," in *Berlin Metropolis: Jews and the New Culture, 1890–1918*, ed. Emily D. Bilski (Berkeley and Los Angeles: University of California Press, 1999), 203 (emphasis added).

6. Bilski and Braun, *Jewish Women and Their Salons*, 3, 4.

7. Gottfried Reinhardt, *Genius: A Memoir of Max Reinhardt, by His Son Gottfried Reinhardt* (New York: Knopf, 1979), 284. Viertel had numerous lesbian affairs as well, most famously with Greta Garbo.

8. Quoted in ibid., 145.

9. Quoted in Heilbut, *Exiled in Paradise*, 34.

10. Quoted in Gottfried Reinhardt, *The Genius: A Memoir of Max Reinhardt, by His Son Gottfried Reinhardt* (New York: Knopf, 1979), 304. This legendary anecdote has many variations: see Heilbut, *Exiled in Paradise*, 236; Lawrence Weschler, "Paradise: The Southern California Idyll of Hitler's Cultural Exiles," in *Exiles and Émigrés: The Flight of European Artists from Hitler*, exhibition catalogue, ed. Stephanie Barron and Sabine Eckmann (Los Angeles: Los Angeles County Museum of Art, 1997), 346; and Horowitz, *Artists in Exile*, 298.

11. Bilski and Braun, *Jewish Women and Their Salons*, 145.

12. Shira Bisman, "Biographies," in Bilski and Braun, *Jewish Women and Their Salons*, 211. The manifesto was never issued due to a lack of consensus among the committee members (Bahr, *Weimar on the Pacific*).

13. Viertel, *The Kindness of Strangers*, 250.

14. Bisman, "Biographies," 211.

15. Quoted in Reinhardt, *The Genius*, 160.

16. Cornelius Schnauber, in our interview, claims that émigré filmmakers like Lang, Wilder, and Zinnemann were not regular visitors to the salons because people tended to speak German, whereas the filmmakers—Preminger's anecdote notwithstanding—wanted to improve their English.

17. Reinhardt, *The Genius*, 299.

18. Bilski and Braun, *Jewish Women and Their Salons*, 21.

19. Bahr, *Weimar on the Pacific*, 226.

20. Ibid., 227. Mann would elaborate on the concept of a dialectically fractured Germany in a lecture he delivered at the Library of Congress in Washington, D.C., in May 1945, where he stated, "There are *not* two Germanys, a good and a bad one, but only one, whose best turned into evil through devilish cunning. Wicked Germany is merely good Germany gone astray, good Germany in misfortune, in guilt, and ruin" (quoted in Bahr, *Weimar on the Pacific*, 243). For the full speech, see Thomas Mann, *Germany and the Germans* (Washington, D.C.: Library of Congress, 1945).

21. Bertolt Brecht to Karl Korsch, [August 1941], in Bertolt Brecht, *Letters*, ed. John Willer, trans. Ralph Mannheim (London: Methuen, 1990), 339. Found in Bahr, *Weimar on the Pacific*, 44.

22. Patrick McGilligan, *Fritz Lang: The Nature of the Beast* (New York: Faber and Faber, 1997), 157.

23. Ibid., 217.

24. Interview with Schnauber, May 31, 2007.

25. Bertolt Brecht, "On Thinking about Hell," trans. Nicholas Jacobs, in *Poems, 1913–1956* (New York: Methuen, 1976), 367.

26. Quoted in Bahr, *Weimar on the Pacific*, frontispiece epigraph (cited as Bertolt Brecht, *Refugee Conversations* [GBA 18: 264]).

27. Bahr, *Weimar on the Pacific*.

28. See Lotte Eisner, *The Haunted Screen: Expressionism in the German Cinema and the Influence of Max Reinhardt* (1952; repr., Berkeley and Los Angeles: University of California Press, 1977); Kristin Thompson, "Early Alternatives to the Hollywood Mode of Production: Implications for Europe's Avant-Garde," *Film History* 5, no. 4 (December 1993): 386–404; and David Bordwell, Janet Staiger, and Kristin Thompson, *The Classical Hollywood Cinema: Film Style and Mode of Production to 1960* (New York: Columbia University Press, 1985).

29. Tom Gunning, *The Films of Fritz Lang: Allegories of Vision and Modernity* (London: British Film Institute, 2006), 205.

30. A prominent exception is Thomas Elsaesser's article "Fritz Lang und Lily Latté. Die Geschichte zweier Umwege," *Filmblatt* 15 (2001): 40–54.

31. McGilligan, *Fritz Lang*, 159–164. Additional support for Latté's leftist leanings during this period comes from my interview with Schnauber, May 31, 2007.

32. McGilligan, *Fritz Lang*, 163–164.

33. Rolf Aurich, Wolfgang Jacobsen, and Cornelius Schnauber, ed., *F.L.: Fritz Lang— His Life and Work* (Berlin: Filmmuseum Berlin, Deutsche Kinemathek, Jovis Verlag GmbH, 2001), 231, 236.

34. For more on relations between Theodor/Gretel Adorno and Fritz Lang/Lily Latté (which were apparently predominantly between the two women), see Elsaesser, "Fritz Lang und Lily Latté: Die Geschichte zweier Umwege," 40–54.

35. Schnauber interview, May 31, 2007, also quoted in McGilligan, *Fritz Lang*, 178.

36. Gunning, *The Films of Fritz Lang*, 212–213.

37. The most prominent of these include *The Big House* (1930), *Little Caesar* (1931), *Public Enemy* (1931), *I Am a Fugitive from a Chain Gang* (1931), *Hell's Highway* (1932), *Hallelujah, I'm a Bum* (1933), *Heroes for Sale* (1933), *Our Daily Bread* (1934), *Imitation of Life* (1934), *Black Fury* (1935), *Riffraff* (1936), *Mr. Deeds Goes to Town* (1936), and *Modern Times* (1936). For a more complete survey, see Peter Roffman and Jim Purdy, *The Hollywood Social Problem Film: Madness, Despair, and Politics from the Depression to the Fifties* (Bloomington: Indiana University Press, 1981).

38. Gunning, *The Films of Fritz Lang*, 213.

39. Ibid., 32.

40. Horowitz, *Artists in Exile*, 285.

41. Ibid.

42. Gunning, *The Films of Fritz Lang*, 215.

43. Alain Silver, "Fury," in *Film Noir: An Encyclopedic Reference to the American Style*, ed. Alain Silver and Elizabeth Ward, 3d ed. (Woodstock, N.Y.: Overlook Press, 1992), 110.

44. From his performance in *Fury*, it's no surprise that Tracy was cast in 1941's *Dr. Jekyll and Mr. Hyde*.

45. McGilligan, *Fritz Lang*, 227. Two scenes with marginal black characters did make it into the film: one a somewhat clichéd *Porgy and Bess* moment of blacks outside Katherine's window singing while they work; and a second, more politically potent, shot of a black man outside the bar where the mob is gathered, scurrying for cover as they exit onto the street.

46. Several films inspired by the Leo Frank lynching were made before *Fury*—*The Gunsaulus Mystery* (1921), *Murder in Harlem* (1935), and *Lem Hawkins' Confession* (1935)—and *They Won't Forget* (1937) afterward. The 1988 TV movie *The Murder of Mary Phagan* was the first filmic treatment to deal explicitly with the tragic incident.

47. D. K. Holm, *Film Soleil* (North Pomfret, Vt.: Trafalgar Square Publishing, 2005). Unfortunately, Holm neither rigorously defines nor illuminatingly applies the "film soleil" concept.

48. Alain Silver, "*You Only Live Once*," in Silver and Ward, *Film Noir*, 320–321.

49. Ibid., 321.

50. Gunning, *The Films of Fritz Lang*, 245.

51. Ibid., 256.

52. Ibid.

53. Quoted in McGilligan, *Fritz Lang*, 228–229.

54. Gunning, *The Films of Fritz Lang*, 260.

55. Ibid.

56. Ibid., 260.

57. Ibid., 262.

58. This trailer, titled "A Tabloid Story of America's Men and Women on Parole," precedes the film on the Universal video release.

59. *The Goldbergs* (created by and starring Gertrude Berg) aired on radio from 1929 to 1951 and on television from 1949 to 1956. It was the second-highest-rated series, after *Amos 'n' Andy*, in much of its U.S. radio run, and was the first successful sitcom on television. Vincent Brook, *Something Ain't Kosher Here: The Rise of the "Jewish" Sitcom* (New Brunswick: Rutgers University Press, 2003), 21–42.

60. Gunning, *The Films of Fritz Lang*, 295.

61. Ibid., 297.

62. Ibid., 296 (emphasis added).

63. Quoted in ibid., 296. The line is from Andrew Sarris, ed., *Interviews with Film Directors* (Indianapolis: Bobbs-Merrill, 1967), 257.

64. Quoted in Victor S. Navasky, *Naming Names* (New York: Penguin, 1981), 369. Adding absurdity to insult, Rankin also misidentified June Havoc (née June Hovick) as Jewish.

65. The extramarital discrepancy was partly due to PCA strictures on the Hollywood film, of course, although Lang managed to wangle an ending—in which the murderer is punished internally but not by the law—that severely tested the agency's moral guidelines.

66. Foster Hirsch, *Detours and Lost Highways: A Map of Neo-noir* (New York: Limelight, 1999), 73.

67. Siegfried Kracauer, *From Caligari to Hitler: A Psychological Study of the German Film* (1947; repr., New York: Noonday Press, 1959), 219–220.

68. Gunning, *The Films of Fritz Lang*, 291; the last quote is from Kracauer, *From Caligari to Hitler*, 220.

69. McGilligan, *Fritz Lang*, 312.

70. Gunning, *The Films of Fritz Lang*, 289.

71. Ruth D. Johnston, "Jewish Disappearing Acts and the Construction of Gender," *Journal of Homosexuality* 52, nos. 1–2 (2006): 216.

72. Sander Gilman, *Freud, Race, and Gender* (New York: Routledge, 1993), 38–39.

73. Johnston, "Jewish Disappearing Acts," 234.

74. Gilman, *Freud, Race, and Gender*, 47.

75. Johnston, "Disappearing Acts," 217; Daniel Boyarin, "What Does a Jew Want?; or, The Political Meaning of the Phallus," in *The Psychoanalysis of Race*, ed. C. Lane (New York: Columbia University Press, 1998), 229.

76. On production conditions for *The Woman in the Window*, see McGilligan, *Fritz Lang*, 307–308. The formation of Diana Productions, under the auspices of Universal Pictures, was brokered by Walter Wanger, husband of Joan Bennett; McGilligan strongly suggests, however, that Lang was having an affair with the actress (ibid., 315–316).

77. Female leads in film noir were not the exclusive province of Jewish émigré directors, of course, as Hitchcock's *Rebecca* (1940), *Suspicion* (1941), and *Shadow of Doubt* (1943); Curtiz's *Mildred Pierce* (1945); and Joseph Lewis's *My Name Is Julia Ross* (1945) attest. But the fact that Curtiz was a first-wave Jewish immigrant and Lewis an American-born Jew only reinforces the Jewish-European connection.

CHAPTER 6 — THE FRENCH CONNECTION: ROBERT SIODMAK

1. Michael Walker, "Robert Siodmak," in *The Book of Film Noir*, ed. Ian Cameron (New York: Continuum, 1993), 110; and Mark Bould, *Film Noir: From Berlin to Sin City* (New York: Wallflower, 2005), 24. Joseph Greco also ranks Siodmak ahead of Lang, with twelve film noirs. *The File on Robert Siodmak in Hollywood: 1941–1951* (Park-

land, Fla.: Dissertation.com [Brown Walker Press], 1999), 4. The numerical dispute hinges on whether some of Lang's espionage thrillers or his 1930s films *Fury* and *You Only Live Once* are considered full-fledged noirs, and on whether Siodmak's *Fly-By-Night* (1942), *The Great Sinner* (1949), and *Portrait of a Sinner* (1959) are considered as such.

2. Legend has it that Siodmak was born in Memphis, Tennessee, to a German father who came to the United States as a teenager and returned to Germany when Robert was one year old. Although this story was concocted by Siodmak to get a visa to the United States in Paris, he relates it as truth in his memoirs, *Zwischen Berlin und Hollywood: Erinnerungen eines grossen Filmregisseurs* (Between Berlin and Hollywood: Memoirs of a famous director), ed. Hans C. Blumenberg (Munich: Herbig, 1980), 9.

3. The credits for this film are notoriously unreliable, with substantial differences in various texts and Web sites (http://www.imdb.com/title/tt0020163/fullcredits#directors, for example, lists Zinnemann as one of the directors and Ulmer as producer). The actual individual contributions are even more contested, with each participant tending to maximize his own input at the others' expense. Siodmak, for example, claims in his memoirs that Ulmer left early on in the shooting after Siodmak insulted Ulmer's wife, and that Wilder contributed "nur einen einzigen Gag" (only one single gag) (Siodmak, *Zwischen Berlin und Hollywood*, 42–43). See also Ed Sikov, *On Sunset Boulevard: The Life and Times of Billy Wilder* (New York: Hyperion, 1998), 59.

4. Thomas Elsaesser, *Weimar Cinema and After: Germany's Historical Imaginary* (New York: Routledge, 2000), 428.

5. Sikov, *On Sunset Boulevard*, 68. Ludwig Hirschfeld is also given co-screenwriting credit on *Der Mann, der seinen Mörder sucht*.

6. Elsaesser, *Weimar Cinema*, 433.

7. Ginette Vincendeau, "Noir Is Also a French Word: The French Antecedents of Film Noir," in Cameron, *The Book of Film Noir*, 51–52.

8. Ibid., 52.

9. Elsaesser, *Weimar Cinema*, 422, 26.

10. Vincendeau, "Noir Is Also a French Word," 52. Schüfftan, Curant, and Heller were also Jewish.

11. Ibid., 49, 53.

12. Ibid., 52; Foster Hirsch, "The French Connection," in *Detours and Lost Highways: A Map of Neo-noir* (New York: Limelight, 1999), 72–74.

13. Thomas Elsaesser, "Pathos and Leave-Taking," *Sight and Sound* 53, no. 4 (Autumn 1984): 278–283.

14. Vincendeau, "Noir Is Also a French Word," 50.

15. Ibid., 51.

16. Luchino Visconti's Italian adaptation of *Postman*, titled *Ossessione* (*Obsession*, 1943), also preceded the first U.S. version.

17. Michael F. Keaney, *Film Noir Guide* (Jefferson, N.C.: McFarland, 2003), 145. Tourneur also made the atmospheric horror films *Cat People* (1942), *I Walked with a Zombie* (1943), *The Leopard Man* (1943), and *Night of the Demon* (1957), the first three of which Keaney (but neither Selby nor Duncan, in their encyclopedias) lists as noirs. Born in France in 1904, Tourneur came to the United States with his French director father, Maurice Tourneur, in the 1910s and became a naturalized U.S. citizen in 1919. He worked with his father in France in the 1930s. Maté worked briefly as a cinematographer in France in the early to mid-1930s, including on Lang's romantic fantasy *Liliom* (1934), and as mentioned in chapter 1, note 18, was cinematographer on *Gilda* (1946) and (uncredited) on *The Lady from Shanghai* (1947).

18. Vincendeau, "Noir Is Also a French Word," 52.

19. Siodmak, *Zwischen Berlin und Hollywood*, 8, 96.

20. Universal was then one of the "Little Three" studios with Columbia and United Artists; the "Big Five" were Paramount, MGM, Twentieth Century Fox, Warner Bros., and RKO.

21. Thomas Schatz, *The Genius of the System: Hollywood Filmmaking in the Studio Era* (New York: Henry Holt, 1988), 250.

22. Greco, *The File on Robert Siodmak*, 12; and John Izod, *Hollywood and the Box Office: 1895–1986* (New York: Columbia University Press, 1988), 126.

23. Greco, *The File on Robert Siodmak*, 12, 13.

24. Ibid., 13.

25. Ibid.

26. Ibid.; and Siodmak, *Zwischen Berlin und Hollywood*, 101.

27. Greco, *The File on Robert Siodmak*, 26.

28. Ibid., 76, 50, 18.

29. Ibid., 27.

30. Andrew Sarris, *American Cinema: Directors and Directions, 1929–1968* (Chicago: University of Chicago Press, 1968), 138.

31. Proportionately, the comparison with the "woman's directors" is more equivocal. Five of Siodmak's ten noirs feature female protagonists, two of Bernhardt's five noirs do, and both of Ophuls's noirs are woman-centered.

32. The name Marlow was changed from Lombard in the novel.

33. Walker, "Robert Siodmak," 116. The first quote is from Deborah Thomas, "Psychoanalysis and Film Noir," in Cameron, *The Book of Film Noir*, 71–87, quote 82.

34. Besides its only nominally expressionist mise-en-scène, *The Suspect* falls short of paradigmatic noir in other respects as well (e.g., it's a period piece, set in early nineteenth-century London).

35. Although most film noir references list *Woman in the Window* as a 1944 film, Alain Silver and Elizabeth Ward, in *Film Noir: An Encyclopedic Reference to the American Style*, 3d

ed. (Woodstock, N.Y.: Overlook Press, 1992), specify the official release date as January 25, 1945; Deborah Lazaroff Alpi, in *Robert Siodmak* (Jefferson, N.C.: McFarland, 1998), shows *The Suspect* premiering on January 26, 1945, and *Uncle Harry* on August 17, 1945. *Scarlet Street*, again according to Silver and Ward, opened on December 28, 1945.

36. Another interesting resemblance among these four films is that the same actress plays the love interest in each of the director's two films: Joan Bennett in *Woman in the Window* and *Scarlet Street*, and Ella Raines in *The Suspect* and *Uncle Harry*.

37. Although Milton Krasner was the film's cinematographer, Siodmak, in *Zwischen Berlin und Hollywood*, credits Eugen Schüfftan, a close friend and colleague from his Weimar days, with some of the more striking special effects.

38. Walker, "Robert Siodmak," 128.

39. Greco, *The File on Robert Siodmak*, 89, 93.

40. Walker, "Robert Siodmak," 113.

41. The gay subtext is noticeably stronger in Maugham's novel.

42. Walker, "Robert Siodmak," 138–139.

43. Richard Dyer, "Postscript: Queers and Women in Film Noir," in *Women in Film Noir*, ed. E. Ann Kaplan, 2d ed. (London: British Film Institute, 2000), 115; and Jonathan Buchsbaum, "Tame Wolves and Phony Claims: Paranoia and Film Noir," *Persistence of Vision*, nos. 3–4 (Summer 1986): 41.

44. Buchsbaum, "Tame Wolves and Phony Claims," 41, 38; and Robert J. Corber, *Homosexuality in Cold War America: Resistance and the Crisis of Masculinity* (Durham: Duke University Press, 1997), 10. Also see Vincent Brook and Allan Campbell, "Pansies Don't Float: Gay Representability, Film Noir, and *The Man Who Wasn't There*," *Jump Cut* 46 (2003), http://ejumpcut.org/archive/jc46.2003/brook.pansies/index.html.

45. Daniel Boyarin, *Unheroic Conduct: The Rise of Heterosexuality and the Invention of the Jewish Man* (Berkeley and Los Angeles: University of California Press, 1997).

46. David Biale, *Eros and the Jews: From Biblical Israel to Contemporary America* (New York: Basic Books, 1992), 161.

47. Ibid., quoted in Boyarin, *Unheroic Conduct*, 330.

48. Boyarin, *Unheroic Conduct*, 70.

49. Ibid., 69.

50. Ibid., 183, 55.

51. Jewish women's influence was nowhere more seminal than in second-wave feminism, which is virtually unthinkable without the contributions of Betty Friedan, Gloria Steinem, Bella Abzug, Phyllis Chesler, and Letty Cottin Pogrebin, to name only the most famous of the movement's leaders.

52. In regard to the feminist attributes of the femme fatale, see E. Ann Kaplan, ed., *Women in Film Noir* (London: British Film Institute, 1989); Mary Ann Doane, *Femme*

Fatales: Feminism, Film Theory, Psychoanalysis (New York: Routledge, 1991); and Jans B. Wager, *Dames in the Driver's Seat: Rereading Film Noir* (Austin: University of Texas Press, 2005).

53. Lawrence Kasdan, writer-director of the seminal neo-noir *Body Heat* (1981), revealed, in a documentary interview, a consciously feminist position in regard to his film's femme fatale: "The villainess—*if she can be called that*—just wants to have it all" (*American Cinema: Film Noir*, PBS video, 1995).

54. Lang's anti-Nazi films have already been mentioned. Others by Jewish émigré noir directors include Billy Wilder's *Five Graves to Cairo* (1943); Preminger's *Margin for Error* (1943); Brahm's *Tonight We Raid Calais* and *Bomber's Moon* (both 1943); Litvak's *Confessions of a Nazi Spy* (1939), and several of the *Why We Fight* documentary series (1943–1945); and Zinnemann's *Forbidden Passage* (1941), *Eyes in the Night* (1942), and *The Seventh Cross* (1944). Ulmer contributed substantially to the preproduction and direction of *Hitler's Madman* (1943), although Douglas Sirk received sole directorial credit.

55. Lutz Kopenick, *The Dark Mirror: German Cinema Between Hitler and Hollywood* (Berkeley and Los Angeles: University of California Press, 2002), 173.

56. Ibid., 177. The quote within the quote is from Ernest Krieck, *Volk im Werden* (Oldenburg: Stalling, 1932), 53.

57. Kopenick, *The Dark Mirror*, 187.

58. Siodmak, *Zwischen Berlin und Hollywood*, 83 (translation mine).

59. Lang returned to the United States in the mid-1960s and remained there until his death in 1976; Siodmak continued to work in Europe, mainly Germany, until 1968, and died in Ascona, Switzerland, in 1973.

60. Patrick McGilligan, *Fritz Lang: The Nature of the Beast* (New York: Faber and Faber, 1997), 149; and Bernard Hemingway, "The Devil Strikes at Night," *Senses of Cinema* 29 (November–December 2003), available online at http://www.sensesofcinema.com/contents/cteq/03/29/devil_strikes_at_night.html.

61. Hemingway, "The Devil Strikes at Night."

62. Ibid.

63. Ibid.

64. Ibid.

65. Ibid.

66. His 1955 film *Die Ratten* (*The Rats*), based on Gerhart Hauptmann's darkly naturalist play, comes the next closest.

67. Greco, *The File on Robert Siodmak*.

68. Theodor W. Adorno, *Minima Moralia: Reflections from a Damaged Life*, trans. E.F.N. Jephcott (London: New Left Books, 1951), 33, paraphrased in Kopenick, *The Dark Mirror*, 14.

CHAPTER 7 — VIENNESE TWINS: BILLY AND WILLY WILDER

1. Quoted in Ed Sikov, *On Sunset Boulevard: The Life and Times of Billy Wilder* (New York: Hyperion, 1998), 15.

2. Ibid.

3. Maurice Zolotow, *Billy Wilder in Hollywood* (New York: Limelight, 1987), 21; Kevin Lally, *Wilder Times* (New York: Henry Holt, 1996), 1; and Sikov, *On Sunset Boulevard*, 5. At least this is the story that Billy recounted to his various biographers. Willy's son Myles, however, claimed in an interview with me (held November 24, 2007) that his father never mentioned this story as the source of Billy's nickname. This does not negate Billy's story; indeed, it potentially further complicates the sibling rivalry aspect, whether through Billy's need to concoct such a fabulous story or through Willy's need to deny its validity.

4. Sikov, *On Sunset Boulevard*, 5.

5. Joseph's attempted killing by his jealous older brothers, Solomon's usurpation of the throne, and his own sons' subsequent battle for control of the Holy Land are other prominent biblical variations on the sibling rivalry theme.

6. Sikov, *On Sunset Boulevard*, 5, 7.

7. Frank Sullaway, "Birth Order and Evolutionary Psychology: A Meta-analytic Overview," *Psychological Inquiry* 6 (1995): 75–80, paraphrased in Steven Pinker, *How the Mind Works* (New York: Norton, 1997), 453. More recent research reaffirms the overweening importance of birth order in personality formation. See Jeffrey Kluger, "The Power of Birth Order," *Time*, October 29, 2007, 42–48.

8. "In one study, fully two-thirds of British and American mothers confessed to loving one of their children more" (Pinker, *How the Mind Works*, 452).

9. Ibid., 455.

10. Melanie Klein, *New Directions in Psychoanalysis* (New York: Basic Books, 1957).

11. Ibid., 6.

12. For more on Wilder's life, see Zolotow, *Billy Wilder in Hollywood*; Lally, *Wilder Times*; Sikov, *On Sunset Boulevard*; Cameron Crowe, *Conversations with Wilder* (New York: Knopf, 1999); and Charlotte Chandler, *Nobody's Perfect: Billy Wilder: A Personal Biography* (New York: Simon and Schuster, 2002).

13. Zolotow, *Wilder Times*, 24–25.

14. Sikov, *On Sunset Boulevard*, 14. Sikov's additional claim that Billy stood an imposing five feet, ten inches tall at fifteen years of age is disputed both by photographs of him in later years, and by Myles Wilder, who met Billy in the 1940s, had contact with him for several decades thereafter, and remembers his uncle as, "at most," five feet eight (interview with Myles Wilder, May 17, 2008).

15. Not only did Joe May not direct any Jewish émigré noirs, but he had difficulty

making anything but low-budget Bs during his seventeen-year career in Hollywood, after which he tried his hand, also unsuccessfully, at the restaurant business.

16. Zolotow (on whom Sikov bases his information) doesn't specify that Willy didn't graduate high school, but if Billy met Willy, "whom he had not seen for twelve years," in New York in 1934, Willy would have had to have left Vienna in 1922 (when he could have been no older than eighteen) (*Billy Wilder in Hollywood*, 53; and Sikov, *Sunset Boulevard*, 98). Willy told Myles, however, that he had not only graduated high school but attended the University of Vienna before coming to the United States—"perhaps as an incentive for *me* to go to college," Myles speculated in our May 17, 2008, interview. Interestingly, Billy also claimed to have gone to the University of Vienna, although there are no records of his having attended (Sikov, *Sunset Boulevard*, 16).

17. November 24, 2007, interview with Myles Wilder.

18. Willy was also sitting on the biggest windfall of his business career, having landed the extremely lucrative government contract for WAC handbags during World War II (May 2008 interview with Myles Wilder).

19. November 24, 2007, interview with Myles Wilder.

20. Sikov, *On Sunset Boulevard*, 161.

21. Quoted in ibid., 101.

22. Ibid., 230.

23. Crowe, *Conversations*, 324.

24. Ibid.

25. November 24, 2007, interview with Myles Wilder. Bobbe was present at the interview and contributed to it.

26. Ibid. Myles stated in the November 24, 2007, interview that Billy "was the least family-oriented man I have ever met in my life." He also corrected a misrepresentation in Zolotow's biography, however, about Billy's treatment of him personally. Although Billy was indeed "a rotten uncle," his introduction of Myles to his neighbor Edward G. Robinson's rambunctious son Manny was not, as Zolotow conveys, an example of this. On the contrary, Manny and Myles became fast friends in junior high school, and although Manny was indeed a "bad influence," mainly on himself (he died in his thirties from the complications of alcoholism), he never became so for Myles.

27. Kluger, "The Power of Birth Order." My own case, as an "entitled"-feeling younger brother, adds anecdotal evidence.

28. Quoted in Crowe, *Conversations*, 324; Lally, *Wilder Times*, 141; and Chandler, *Nobody's Perfect*, 28–29.

29. Myles related in our November 24, 2007, interview that Billy forced Willy to change his name because the similarity was "screwing up the mail."

30. Quoted in Sikov. *On Sunset Boulevard*, 253.

31. Todd McCarthy, "Through a Lens Darkly: The Life and Films of John Alton,"

in John Alton, *Painting with Light* (Berkeley and Los Angeles: University of California Press, 1995), x.

32. Ibid., xviii; and Spencer Selby, *Dark City: The Film Noir* (Jefferson, N.C.: McFarland, 1984), 171.

33. Mann was uncredited as director on *He Walked by Night*, whose sole credit went to Alfred Werker.

34. F. Gwynplaine MacIntyre, "Strictly from Hungary," available online at http://www.imdb.com/title/tt0040941/#comment (accessed September 5, 2007).

35. November 24, 2007, interview with Myles Wilder. Of his father's films, Myles wrote or cowrote the story or screenplay for *Phantom from Space*, *Killers from Space*, *The Snow Creature*, *Manfish*, *Fright*, *Spy in the Sky!* and *Bluebeard's Ten Honeymoons*. His television writing credits include work on, among others, *The Dukes of Hazard*; *Diff'rent Strokes*; *Welcome Back, Kotter*; *The Flying Nun*; *Get Smart*; *McHale's Navy*; *Bonanza*; *My Three Sons*; *The Addams Family*; *The Ghost and Mrs. Muir*; and *The Doris Day Show*.

36. The Clytemnestra allusion is from Raymond Durgnat, "Paint It Black: The Family Tree of the *Film Noir*" [1970], in *Film Noir Reader*, ed. Alain Silver and James Ursini (New York: Limelight, 1996), 37.

37. The interview is in the documentary film *The Exiles*, directed by Robert Kaplan (Connoisseur Video Collection, 1999).

38. Zolotow, *Billy Wilder in Hollywood*.

39. Quoted in ibid., 339, 340. Chuck Tatum in *Ace in the Hole* and Sefton in *Stalag 17*, to be discussed later in the chapter, must be added to the list of Billy's crassly opportunistic male characters.

40. Zolotow, *Billy Wilder in Hollywood*, 343, 342.

41. Ibid., 342.

42. Jans B. Wager, *Dames in the Driver's Seat: Reading Film Noir* (Austin: University of Texas Press, 2005), 4.

43. November 24, 2007, interview with Myles Wilder.

44. Willy was, like Billy and most of the other émigré Jewish directors, a died-in-the-wool Democrat (November 24, 2007, interview with Myles Wilder).

45. Myles says that the main reason his father remade *The Glass Alibi* was that "he liked the story and thought it could be remade" (May 17, 2008, interview).

46. The most famous Landru-based film is Chaplin's *Monsieur Verdoux* (1947). The first version was the German silent *Landru, der Blaubart von Paris* (Hans Otto, 1922), and Claude Chabrol made a French version, *Landru*, in 1963.

47. Group auteurist considerations come into play here as well. In their exposure and indictment of the "ugly American," Willy and Billy joined Lang and Siodmak, and other Jewish émigré directors yet to be discussed, in taking a stance toward their

adopted homeland that went beyond the already uncommonly "self-critical" thrust of classical noir as a whole.

48. Rossellini embarked on a hybridized variant of neorealism in his early 1950s work with Ingrid Bergman (*Stromboli*, 1950; *Europa '51*, 1952; *We, the Women*, 1953; *Journey to Italy*, 1954), in which star turns and melodramatic treatment mesh, and sometimes clash, with unvarnished, documentary-like moments.

49. The more comprehensive noir surveys—such as Michael F. Keaney's *Film Noir Guide* (Jefferson, N.C.: McFarland, 2003); Selby's *Dark City;* and Duncan's *Film Noir: Films of Trust and Betrayal* (North Pomfret, Vt.: Pocket Essentials, 2000)—are more generous in their W. Lee Wilder listings, neglecting only *Bluebeard's Ten Honeymoons*, *Fright*, and *Manfish*. Keaney even goes so far (*too* far, in my opinion) as to include *Vicious Circle.*

50. Billy observed that *Mauvais Graine* "looked ahead" to Jean-Luc Godard's *Breathless* (Sikov, *On Sunset Boulevard*, 92).

51. Sikov, *On Sunset Boulevard*, 112.

52. Ibid., 243; and Crowe, *Conversations*, 121.

53. Myles stated that Willy never spoke of his mother's or grandmother's perishing in the Holocaust, which is certainly no indication of their tragic deaths' psychic effect on him. Reticence about the Holocaust was, understandably, quite common in the generation that suffered its consequences, as I can attest from my own parents' reluctance to bring up the loss of their closest relatives in the death camps (November 24, 2007, interview).

54. On-camera interview in *The Exiles*.

55. Quoted in Sikov, *On Sunset Boulevard*, 236.

56. Ibid., 18.

57. Ibid., 21–26.

58. Keaney, in *Film Noir Guide*, calls *Vicious Circle* a "ridiculous, low-budget film" (455). F. Gwynplaine MacIntyre, in an online commentary, deems it a "bad movie" and "rubbish" ("Strictly from Hungary"). Myles, on the other hand, recalled the film, in our November 24, 2007, interview, as his father's best work.

CHAPTER 8 — THE ABZS OF FILM NOIR: OTTO PREMINGER
AND EDGAR G. ULMER

1. Richard Maltby, *Hollywood Cinema*, 2d ed. (Malden, Mass.: Blackwell, 2003), 132. The eight major studios were divided into a Big Five—Paramount, MGM, Warner Bros., Twentieth Century Fox, and RKO—and a Little Three—Universal, Columbia, and United Artists. Monogram and Republic were regarded as mini-majors.

2. Myron Meisel, "Edgar G. Ulmer: The Primacy of the Visual" [1972], in *Kings of the Bs: Working Within the Hollywood System*, ed. Todd McCarthy and Charles Flynn (New York: Dutton, 1975), 148.

3. Preminger's autobiography fudges both his Viennese origins and the time frame of his father's career success, eliding his own eastern European roots and his father's hard-won rise from poverty. For more on the discrepancies, compare pertinent passages in Otto Preminger, *Preminger: An Autobiography* (Garden City, N.Y.: Doubleday, 1977); Foster Hirsch, *Otto Preminger: The Man Who Would Be King* (New York: Knopf, 2007); and Chris Fujiwara, *The World and Its Double: The Life and Work of Otto Preminger* (New York: Faber and Faber, 2008).

4. Ulmer claims that Fox chief Darryl Zanuck offered him the chance to direct Shirley Temple films in the late 1930s, but he refused; as for MGM chief Louis B. Mayer, "I prided myself that he could never hire me! I did not want to be ground up in the Hollywood hash machine." Peter Bogdanovich, "Edgar G. Ulmer," in *Who the Devil Made It: Conversations with Legendary Film Directors* (New York: Ballantine Books, 1997), 592.

5. The biographical information is gleaned from Hirsch, *Otto Preminger*; and Preminger, *Preminger*.

6. His mother relocated from Vienna to a farm in Olomouc for his birth, and the Ulmer family spent summer vacations there (e-mail from Arianné Ulmer Cipes, November 3, 2007; Ulmer Cipes's information is based on her father's unpublished short biography).

7. Bogdanovich, "Edgar G. Ulmer," 577.

8. The notion that the Jewish star's function was purely pragmatic was gleaned from a phone interview with Arianné Ulmer Cipes on October 10, 2007, and is again based on Ulmer's unpublished short biography. The same information can be found in Stefan Grissemann, *Mann im Schatten: Der Filmmacher Edgar G. Ulmer* (Vienna: Paul Szolnay Verlag, 2003).

9. The postwar "Red Vienna" period, in which Jews played a prominent part, came to an abrupt end in 1927 when right-wing militias quelled a mob uprising and the Social Democrats lost their hold on power. Paul Hofmann, *The Viennese: Splendor, Twilight, and Exile* (New York: Doubleday, 1988), 185.

10. He had apparently done some film acting and set designing as early as 1918 (Bogdanovich, "Edgar G. Ulmer," 562–563).

11. Ibid., 561–563. In the Bogdanovich interview and the unpublished biography, "Ulmer recalled working in one capacity or another on films by Murnau, Lang, Lubitsch, Stiller, Pabst, Leni, Wegener, Curtiz, Griffith, Vidor, von Stroheim, Walsh, DeMille, Mamoulian, Maurice Tourneur, Clarence Brown, Chaplin, Borzage, [Feyder,] and Eisenstein (on *Que Viva Mexico*)." Bill Krohn, "King of the B's," *Film Comment* 19, no. 4 (July–August 1983): 60–64. This list must be taken with a large grain of salt, if not a saltshaker, for Ulmer, as much as if not more than Lang, Wilder, and others, notoriously embellished his past. Among his wildest claims were to have almost single-handedly invented German Expressionist cinema, served as the subject for one of Freud's psychoanalytic studies, and been related to Arthur Schnitzler (Grissemann, *Mann im*

Schatten, 12). If you read what he alleged about himself, Bertrand Tavernier observed, Ulmer would had to have been "everywhere at the same time" (quoted in Grissemann, *Mann im Schatten*, 12).

12. According to Ulmer, during the Weimar period the production designer served as a second director: "There were two directors on each picture: a director for the dramatic action and for the actors, and then the director for the *picture* itself, who established the camera angles, camera movements, et cetera; there had to be teamwork" (Bogdanovich, "Edgar G. Ulmer," 563).

13. E-mail from Arianné Ulmer Cipes, November 3, 2007.

14. E-mail from Arianné Ulmer Cipes, December 26, 2007. *The Loves of Three Queens* (1954) is the film of Ulmer's that Viertel would cowrite, with Marc Allegret, Vittorio Nino Novarese, and Vladim Penianikoy.

15. Bill Krohn, "King of the B's," 61.

16. J. Hoberman, *Bridge of Light: Yiddish Film Between Two Worlds* (Philadelphia: Temple University Press, 1991); and Vincent Brook, "Forging the 'New Jew': The Yiddish Films of Edgar G. Ulmer," in *Edgar G. Ulmer: From Detour to Poverty Row*, ed. Bernd Herzogenrath (New York: Scarecrow Press, 2009).

17. Thomas Elsaesser, *Weimar Cinema and After: Germany's Historical Imaginary* (New York: Routledge, 2000), 433.

18. Hirsch, *Otto Preminger*, 34.

19. This was one of several Nazi film-character roles for Preminger, the most famous of which was as the German prison-camp commandant in Billy Wilder's *Stalag 17*.

20. Hirsch, *Otto Preminger*, 89.

21. *Angel Face* (1950) was produced for RKO during his semi-independent period.

22. For several instances of the latter, see Hirsch, *Otto Preminger*.

23. Preminger gave LaShelle his first cinematographer's job, on *Laura*, and used him in another of his darker-tinted noirs, *Where the Sidewalk Ends*.

24. June's claim of gleaning the quote from one of her books is a self-reflexive conceit, for the words actually stem from Marty Holland's novel *Fallen Angel*, from which the film was adapted.

25. Grissemann, *Mann im Schatten*, 195.

26. Quoted in ibid., 168 (translation mine).

27. Ibid., 179.

28. Ibid., 168. For the majors, the average B-film budget ranged between fifty thousand and one hundred thousand dollars (Maltby, *Hollywood Cinema*, 132).

29. Grissemann, *Mann im Schatten*, 168 (translation mine).

30. Bret Wood, "Edgar G. Ulmer: Visions from the Second Kingdom," *Video Watchdog* 41 (1997): 22–31.

31. Grissemann, *Mann im Schatten*, 169.

32. Ibid., 197.

33. Ulmer's claim of having studied music with Richard Strauss in Vienna is no doubt another of his biographical embellishments.

34. Steve Jenkins, "Edgar G. Ulmer and PRC: A Detour down Poverty Row," *Monthly Film Bulletin*, July 1982, cited in Grissemann, *Mann im Schatten*, 203.

35. Bogdanovich, "Edgar G. Ulmer," 603.

36. Grissemann, *Mann im Schatten*, 200 (translation mine).

37. Ibid., 192–193. Schüfftan would eventually be admitted to the ASC and, somewhat compensating for his earlier slighting by the industry, would receive the Academy Award for Best Cinematography for *The Hustler* (1961).

38. The Schüfftan effect played perhaps its most famous role in the Mount Rushmore sequence in Hitchcock's *North by Northwest* (1957).

39. Grissemann, *Mann im Schatten*, 231; Ulmer quoted in ibid., 207 (translation mine).

40. Pedophiles appear in several other Ulmer films, including *Moon over Harlem* (1938), *Tomorrow We Live* (1942), and *The Strange Woman* (1945).

41. The opening also strikingly resembles the dream scenes in Laurence Olivier's 1948 film version of *Hamlet*.

42. Alexander Horwath, *"Das Shining,"* in *Schatten, Exil, Europäische Emigranten in Film Noir*, ed. Christian Cargnelli and Michael Omasta (Vienna: PVS Verlegen, 1997), 335, quoted in Grissemann, *Mann im Schatten*, 211.

43. "Boyish heroes" abound in Ulmer's non-noirs as well: Michael Goldstein in *Green Fields* (1937), David Patashu in *The Light Ahead* (1939), Eugene Eglesias in *The Naked Dawn* (1955), and Jean-Louis Trintignant in *L'Atlantide* (1961) (Grissemann, *Mann im Schatten*, 211).

44. Young Jenny was originally to be played by Ulmer's daughter Arianné, and footage of the opening scene with her in the role was shot. But, according to Arianné: "What very few know is that producer Hunt Stromberg and Hedy Lamarr decided I was not mean enough and therefore I landed on the cutting room floor. My mother was furious and refused to let Edgar do the reshoot with another little girl. Robert Siodmak, Dad's friend, stepped in and did the two-day shoot of the required shots. The painful thing about it was that since they needed the replay of the exact shots of the sequence, both my mother, who was the script supervisor, and I were on the set to work with the little girl you now see in the film" (e-mail to the author, January 13, 2008).

45. Grissemann, *Mann im Schatten*, 244 (translation mine).

46. Ulmer himself was neither blacklisted nor called before the HUAC. Certainly left-leaning, he was never actively involved in politics and belonged to no political party. Due to his friendships and associations with communists and other stigmatized leftists,

however, he was understandably concerned about the possible negative consequences to him as well. "He lived on the edge," daughter Arianné recalls (quoted in Grissemann, *Mann im Schatten*, 253).

47. Meisel, "Edgar G. Ulmer," 150.

48. Grissemann, *Mann im Schatten*, 248–249 (translation mine).

49. Quoted in ibid., 249.

50. Ibid., 249 (translation mine).

51. *Detour* was shot in six days rather than the legendary three, and the budget was not under $30,000 (as were most of Ulmer's films) but actually $89,000, with a final cost of $117,000—still cheap by Hollywood standards but lavish by PRC's. Glenn Erickson, "Fate Seeks the Loser: Edgar G. Ulmer's *Detour* (1945)," in *Film Noir Reader 4: The Crucial Films and Themes*, ed. Alain Silver and James Ursini (New York: Limelight, 2004), 26.

52. Grissemann, *Mann im Schatten*, 226 (translation mine).

53. The "program notes" are courtesy of ibid., 221.

54. James Naremore, in *More Than Night: Film Noir in Its Contexts* (Berkeley and Los Angeles: University of California Press, 1998), has insightfully analyzed the surrealist element in film noir, which is also strongly apparent in *Detour's* hotel room scene: after Roberts accidentally strangles Vera with the telephone cord, the camera pans around the room to various objects, moving in and racking in and out of focus on each one.

55. Paul Mendes-Flohr, *German Jews: A Dual Identity* (New Haven: Yale University Press, 1999).

56. Joseph Jacobs and Maurice Fishberg, "Consumption (Tuberculosis)," available online at http://www.jewishencyclopedia.com/view.jsp?artid=751&letter=C (accessed January 16, 2009).

57. Ibid.

58. Ibid.

59. Ulmer's last noir, *Murder Is My Beat* (1955), is not included for discussion here because, despite several interesting aspects, both aesthetically and thematically, it was made toward the end of the noir cycle. The quite distinguished *The Naked Dawn* (1955) was excluded because, despite noir elements, it's a western.

CHAPTER 9 — WOMAN'S DIRECTORS:
CURTIS BERNHARDT AND MAX OPHULS

1. Curtis Bernhardt and Mary Kiersch, *Curtis Bernhardt: A Directors Guild of America Oral History* (Metuchen, N.J.: Directors Guild of America and Scarecrow Press, 1986), 102. Other Hollywood filmmakers typed as "woman's directors" include another émigré (albeit a non-Jew), Douglas Sirk; another Jew (albeit a non-émigré), Joseph von Sternberg; and (neither a Jew nor an émigré) John Stahl.

2. Ibid., 10, 12.

3. Ibid., 19.

4. Ibid., 157. Bernhardt himself, appropriately, refused to name the informant.

5. Ibid., 43; and Lothar Schwab, "Im Labyrinth der Männerängste: Kurt Bernhardts deutsche Filme," in *Aufruhr der Gefühle: Die Kinowelt des Curtis Bernhardt*, ed. Frank Arnold, Helga Belach, Gero Gandert, and Hans Helmut Prinzler (Munich: Verlag C. J. Bucher, 1982), 27. All translations from German mine.

6. Fritz Göttler, "Gestolenes Leben, fictive Existenze: Kurt Bernhardts französiche Filme," in *Aufruhr der Gefühle*, 50

7. Bernhardt and Kiersch, *Curtis Bernhardt*, 78.

8. Göttler, "Gestolenes Leben," 50.

9. Schwab, "Im Labyrinth," 26, 32, 34; and Heinz-Gerd Rasner and Reinhardt Wulf, "Sehnsucht, Schuld und Einsamkeit," in *Aufruhr der Gefühle*, 62.

10. Bernhardt and Kiersch, *Curtis Bernhardt*, 55.

11. Ibid., 59.

12. Ibid.

13. *Carrefour* was remade in Great Britain, by Thomas Bentley, as *Dead Man's Shoes* (1940), and in the United States, by Jack Conway, as *Crossroads* (1942).

14. Bernhardt and Kiersch, *Curtis Bernhardt*, 70.

15. Ibid., 91.

16. Ibid., 84; Warner Bros. bore the brunt of a 1941 Senate committee's charges of making anti-Nazi films at a time when, despite President Roosevelt's anti-Axis animus and secret U.S. aid to Great Britain, the country had not yet entered the war and was still officially neutral.

17. Ibid., 95. Apropos of his slighting of Siodmak, Bernhardt told Kiersch that he didn't know many refugees in Hollywood "because every refugee was jealous of the next one" (ibid., 72).

18. Deborah Lazaroff Alpi, *Robert Siodmak* (Jefferson, N.C.: McFarland, 1998), 113.

19. Bernhardt and Kiersch, *Curtis Bernhardt*, 96–98.

20. Hannah Arendt, *The Jew as Pariah: Jewish Identity and Politics in the Modern Age* (New York: Grove Press, 1978).

21. Claudia Lenssen, "Durehlöcherte Finsternis," in *Aufruhr der Gefühle*, 18.

22. Wulf, "Sensucht," 63.

23. Bernhardt and Kiersch, *Curtis Bernhardt*, 113.

24. Wulf, "Sensucht," 67

25. Bernhardt's *Sirocco* (1951), which is listed as a film noir in the encyclopedias, barely qualifies as one in my estimation. Starring Humphrey Bogart as a sleazy night-

club owner in French-occupied Syria in 1925, the film is a failed attempt to repeat the magic of *Casablanca*, which itself, despite its expressionist look and ambivalent (until the end) protagonist, is more wartime romance than noir.

26. Susan M. White, *The Cinema of Max Ophuls: Magisterial Vision and the Figure of Women* (New York: Columbia University Press, 1995), 8. In his autobiography, Ophuls claims that Holl insisted on maintaining the initials "MO" (so that Max could use the same stage clothes) and scribbled the name "Max Ophuls" on a piece of paper. Max Ophuls, *Spiel im Dasein* (Stuttgart: Henry Goverts Verlag, 1959), 36–37.

27. White, *The Cinema of Max Ophuls*, 50.

28. Ibid., 23.

29. Lutz Bacher, *Max Ophuls in the Hollywood Studios* (New Brunswick: Rutgers University Press, 1996), 20–21. Fry's organization was formed in 1940 to rescue not all those seeking to escape Nazi extermination, but rather primarily political and intellectual refugees.

30. Ibid., 4.

31. Quoted in ibid., 31.

32. Bacher, *Max Ophuls*, 33.

33. As cited in the introductory chapter, Neil Sinyard, in *Fred Zinnemann: Films of Character and Conscience* (Jefferson, N.C.: McFarland, 2003), also mentions, though largely in passing, the "Jewish question" in regard to Zinnemann's work as a whole.

34. White, *The Cinema of Max Ophuls*, 38.

35. Ibid., 13.

36. Ibid., 5, 16.

37. Ibid., 39.

38. Ibid., 37.

39. Ibid. 241.

40. Ibid., 359.

41. Ibid.

42. Ibid. White also sees Franzi as "almost a parody of the 'Viennese' Ophuls" himself (251).

43. Ohlrig's favorite pastimes are playing pinball in his mansion and, most perversely, endlessly hand rolling a pool ball against the sides of the pool table.

44. White, *The Cinema of Max Ophuls*, 190.

45. Ibid.; and George Steiner, "Dream City," *New Yorker*, January 28, 1985, 92, cited in Virginia Wright Wexman, "The Transfiguration of History: Ophuls, History, and *Letter from an Unknown Woman*," in *Letter from an Unknown Woman: Max Ophuls, Director*, ed.

Virginia Wright Wexman and Karen Hollinger (New Brunswick: Rutgers University Press, 1986), 11.

46. Wexman, "The Transfiguration of History," 12.

47. Max Ophuls, "Der Kampf," in *New Theater and Film, 1934–1937: An Anthology*, ed. Herbert Kline (New York: Harcourt Brace Jovanovich, 1985), 342, cited in Wexman, "The Transfiguration of History," 12.

48. Ironically, both films were produced and directed by non-Jews (*Crossfire* was even written by a gentile), and in the case of *Gentleman's Agreement*, several Jewish moguls actually urged Twentieth Century Fox head Darryl Zanuck not to make the film. Zanuck's experiences were parodied in the film, when board members of the magazine planning to run the investigative series on anti-Semitism (some of whom appear to be Jewish) urge the publisher to drop the project (*Gentleman's Agreement*, DVD, Special Features documentary, 20th Century Fox Movie Classics).

49. Bacher, *Max Ophuls*, 204.

50. Ibid., 2.

51. White, *The Cinema of Max Ophuls*, 317.

52. Ibid., 190.

53. Ibid., 193.

54. *The Reckless Moment* was made at Columbia for Walter Wanger, who worked well with directors and, according to Bacher, "was the first producer to speak in favor of meeting the expectations of European audiences." On this particular film, however, despite Wanger's best efforts, Ophuls experienced far more studio intrusion than he had on *Caught* (*Max Ophuls*, 265, 264–320).

55. Bernhardt and Kiersch, *Curtis Bernhardt*, 129.

56. Hilde Ophüls, "Nachwort," in Ophüls, *Spiel im Dasein*, 237 (translation mine).

57. Ibid.

58. On reasons for the return of the non-filmmakers, see Ehrhard Bahr, *Weimar on the Pacific: German Exile Culture in Los Angeles and the Crisis of Modernism* (Berkeley and Los Angeles: University of California Press, 2007).

59. *Shadows in Paradise* (2008), documentary film produced and directed by Peter Rosen, and coproduced and written by Sara Lukinson.

60. Zinnemann would relocate to England, but only in the 1970s.

61. Freund also directed *The Mummy* (1932), and photographed, among countless other American films, *Dracula* (1931), two major film noirs—*Undercurrent* (1946) and *Key Largo* (1948)—and the anti-Nazi film *The Seventh Cross* (1944), directed by Fred Zinnemann (to be discussed in the next chapter).

CHAPTER 10 — PATHOLOGICAL NOIR, POPULIST NOIR, AND
AN ACT OF VIOLENCE: JOHN BRAHM, ANATOLE LITVAK, FRED ZINNEMANN

1. Andrew Sarris, *The American Cinema: Directors and Directions, 1929–1968* (New York: Da Capo Press, 1968), 253.

2. C. Jerry Kutner, "Overlooked Noir—John Brahm and *Let Us Live* (1939)," *Bright Lights After Dark*, February 10, 2008, available online at http://brightlightsfilm. blogspot.com/2008/02/overlooked-noir-john-brahm-and-let-us.html (accessed January 19, 2008). The "best-ever episodes" quote is from Hal Erickson, "John Brahm: Full Biography," *All Movie Guide*, available online at http://allmovie.com/artist/82771.

3. Joel Greenberg, *Oral History with John Brahm, 1971* (Beverly Hills, Calif.: American Film Institute, Center for Advanced Studies, 1975), 1.

4. Dolly Haas left with Brahm for France and came with him to the United States. He married his third wife, non-Jewish Italian actress Anna Benson, in the United States when she was twenty-eight and he was in his sixties.

5. Imdb.com lists Brahm as assistant director on a few films during the Weimar period (http://www.imdb.com/find?s=all&q=john+brahm&x=16&y=11), but in Joel Greenberg's *Oral History*, Brahm insists that he had had no professional involvement with filmmaking in Germany "whatsoever" (10). Koster is one of the few Jewish émigré directors who did not make any American film noirs, but instead specialized in comedies, musicals, and costume dramas.

6. Interview with Sumishta Brahm, January 12, 2008.

7. Ibid. Sumishta also recalls her father having his own regular quasi-salons at their house in Malibu, attended by "mainly film people he had worked with, including several Europeans and/or Jews."

8. Arthur Lyons, *Life on the Cheap: The Lost B Movies of Film Noir* (New York: Da Capo Press, 2000), 35.

9. Alain Silver and Elizabeth Ward's list of proto-noirs—that is, American noirs that predate the cycle—goes back to *Underworld* (1927) and, for sound films, to *City Streets* (1931), *Beast of the City* (1932), *I Am a Fugitive from a Chain Gang* (1932), and *The Scoundrel* (1935). *Film Noir: An Encyclopedic Reference to the American Style*, 3d ed. (Woodstock, N.Y.: Overlook Press, 1992), 333. Other critics, such as Marc Delazel and even Arthur Lyons himself, unofficially regard *Two Seconds* (1932) as a proto-noir, with *Skyscraper Souls* (1932) and *Crime Without Passion* (1932) receiving honorable mention (e-mail from Marc Delazel, August 23, 2008).

10. "John Brahm: The Last Interview by David Del Valle," available online at http://www.sumishta.com/pages/johnbrahminterview.html (accessed February 7, 2009), 2. As for creative control, Brahm, like many of the Jewish émigré directors, claims to have assured this in Hollywood by "pre-shooting" and "cutting in the camera" (Greenberg, *Oral History*, xv, 17–18, 44, 52, 53).

11. Paul Duder, "Fox Horror Classics: Directed by John Brahm," available online at http://exclaim.ca/motionreviews/generalreview.aspx?csid1=118&csid2=774&fid1=29071 (accessed February 2009).

12. Paul Schrader, "Notes on Film Noir" [1972], in *Film Noir Reader*, ed. Alain Silver and James Ursini (New York: Limelight, 1996), 59.

13. Ibid. 58.

14. Brahm blames *The Brasher Doubloon*'s uncharacteristically un-noirish look on budget and time constraints (Greenberg, *Oral History*, 77).

15. Schrader, "Notes on Film Noir," 59.

16. Patrice Petro, *Joyless Streets: Women and Melodramatic Representation in Weimar Germany* (Princeton: Princeton University Press, 1989).

17. Uncomfortable with his size as well as his homosexuality, which he felt limited his ability to play romantic leads on the one hand, and to lead a "normal life" on the other, Cregar underwent a primitive stomach-stapling procedure during the filming of *Hangover Square*, "apparently hastening a fatal heart attack just weeks before the film's release" ("John Brahm: The Last Interview"; Duder, "Fox Horror Classics"; and David Del Valle, "The Auteur on the Hill," in "Camp David August 2006," available online at http://www.filmsinreview.com/2006/08/01/camp-david-august-2006-john-carradine/, accessed February 2009).

18. Stewart Tendler, "Official: Jack the Ripper Identified," *Times (London)*, July 14, 2006, available online at http://www.timesonline.co.uk/tol/news/uk/crime/article687489.ece (accessed February 2009). The eyewitness identification could not be used as evidence at the time because, according to the chief inspector's notes, the witness, also a Jew, refused to swear to it.

19. Beth Schwartzapfel, "Handwriting Analyst: Jack the Ripper Not Jewish," *Jewish Daily Forward*, December 15, 2006, available online at http://www.forward.com/articles/9664/Jac+the+r (accessed January 19, 2009).

20. Jeremy Dauber, "Demons, Golems, and Dybbuks," available online at http://www.nextbook.org/ala/demonsgolems-color-letter.pdf (accessed March 2009).

21. Garabed Eknoyan, "The Kidneys in the Bible: What Happened?" *American Society of Nephrology* 16 (2005): 3464.

22. "John Brahm: The Last Interview," 2.

23. Sander Gilman, *The Jew's Body* (New York: Routledge, 1991); Peter Gay, *Freud: A Life for Our Time* (New York: Norton, 1988); and Jerry V. Diller, *Freud's Jewish Identity: A Case Study in the Impact of Ethnicity* (Madison: Fairleigh Dickenson University Press, 1991), among others.

24. Brahm's *Singapore* (1947) is listed as a noir in all the encyclopedias except Silver and Ward's. I side with the latter's estimation that this lightweight, postwar romance barely qualifies, and thus I refrain from including it in my discussion.

25. Erickson, "John Brahm."

26. Andrew Dickos, *Street with No Name: A History of the Classical Film Noir* (Lexington: University of Kentucky Press, 2002), 108.

27. Carl Macek, *"The Brasher Doubloon,"* in Silver and Ward, *Film Noir*, 42.

28. Ibid.

29. Michael Walker, "Anatole Litvak, *Film Dope* 31 (February–March 1992): 34–36. This information was gleaned largely from Litvak himself, Walker states, and, as with most of the Jewish émigré noir directors I have discussed, "his various statements concerning his early career are as a whole somewhat confusing and contradictory" (35).

30. The two others were PRC's *Beast of Berlin* (1939) and Warner Bros.'s *The Mortal Storm* (1940). The latter, however, failed to even mention anti-Semitism; indeed, director Sidney Lumet, in a documentary interview, recalls Charlie Chaplin's *The Great Dictator* (1940) as the first Hollywood film that deigned to utter the word "Jew" (in *Imaginary Witness: Hollywood and the Holocaust*, 2008). For more on U.S. anti-Nazi films, see Jan-Christopher Horak, "Anti-Nazi-Film der deutschsprachigen Emigration von Hollywood 1939–1945" (PhD diss., Westfälischen Wilhelms-Universität zu Münster, 1984).

31. This pattern would culminate with Fonda's titular lead in Hitchcock's *The Wrong Man* (1957), and be complimented the same year by his wrong-man-saving role in *Twelve Angry Men*.

32. Simcha Weinstein, *Shtick Shift: Jewish Humor in the 21st Century* (Lanham, Md.: National Book Network), 88–89.

33. Richard Schickel, "Anatole Litvak: Oceanside Retreat of *The Snake Pit*'s Director," *Architectural Digest: Academy Awards Collector's Edition!* April 1992, 1. I must part company with Schickel, however, on another point. Although it is true that most of Litvak's so-called noirs are not long on "cynical bite," *Out of the Fog*, *Blues in the Night*, and *The Long Night* hardly can be said to lack "the fondness for low American life, language and places that other refugees from Hitler's Europe—Billy Wilder is a good example—so enthusiastically developed and exploited" (1).

34. Anomalous listings of "noirs" by Zinnemann include *A Hatful of Rain* (1957), in Michael F. Keaney's *Film Noir Guide* (Jefferson, N.C.: McFarland, 2003), and *Kid Glove Killer* (1942), in Arthur Lyons's *Death on the Cheap: The Lost B Movies of Film Noir* (New York: Da Capo Press, 2000).

35. Neil Sinyard, *Fred Zinnemann: Films of Character and Conscience* (Jefferson, N.C.: McFarland, 2003), 3.

36. Gene Phillips, "Fred Zinnemann Talking to Gene Phillips (1973)," in *Fred Zinnemann Interviews*, ed. Peter Brunette (Jackson: University of Mississippi Press, 2005), 38.

37. Ibid.

38. The Flaherty project fell through, unsurprisingly, because "he wanted the film to be a monument to a lost culture, whereas the Russians wanted to make a propaganda picture showing how miserable these people had been until the Revolution" (Phillips, "Fred Zinnemann," 39).

39. Zinnemann had made two other antifascist shorts before this: *While America Sleeps* (1939) and *Forbidden Passage* (1941).

40. For an overview of Hollywood's filmic treatment of the Holocaust and Jewish themes in general, see the documentary film *Imaginary Witness: Hollywood and the Holocaust* (2008), directed by Daniel Anker.

41. The *M* and *Fury* allusion is derived from Sinyard, *Fred Zinnemann*, 24.

42. Gordon Gow, "Individualism Against Machinery (1976)," in Brunette, *Fred Zinnemann Interviews*, 58.

43. Clift finished shooting *Red River* before *The Search*, but the latter film was released earlier (Sinyard, *Fred Zinnemann*, 33).

44. Arthur Nolletti Jr., "Conversations with Fred Zinnemann (1993)," in Brunette, *Fred Zinnemann Interviews*, 116.

45. The actual location was Santa Monica (Drew Casper commentary on the "Special Features" section of the *Act of Violence* DVD, Warner Home Video, 2007).

46. Sinyard, *Fred Zinnemann*, 39.

47. Brian Neve, "A Past Master of His Craft: An Interview with Fred Zinnemann (1996)," in Brunette, *Fred Zinnemann Interviews*, 148. The expressionist side of Zinnemann's approach found a ready and willing ally in cinematographer Bob Surtees, who had studied and even met Zinnemann in Berlin.

48. For more on the connection between the HUAC, McCarythism in general, and anti-Semitism, see, among the vast literature on the subject: Victor Navasky, *Naming Names* (New York: Penguin, 1981); and Jon Lewis, "'We Do Not Ask You to Condone This': How the Blacklist Saved Hollywood," *Cinema Journal* 39, no. 21 (Winter 2000): 3–30.

49. Wheeler Winston Dixon, "*Act of Violence* (1949) and the Early Films of Fred Zinnemann," in *The Films of Fred Zinnemann: Critical Perspectives*, ed. Arthur Nolletti Jr. (Albany: State University of New York Press, 1999), 52.

50. Ibid.

51. Walter Laqueur, *Weimar: A Cultural History* (New York: Capricorn, 1976), 32.

Bibliography

Adorno, Theodor W. *Minima Moralia: Reflections from a Damaged Life*. Trans. E.F.N. Jephcott. London: New Left Books, 1951.

Adorno, Theodor, and Max Horkheimer, *Dialectic of Enlightenment* (1944). Trans. Edmond Jephcott. Stanford: Stanford University Press, 2002.

Alpi, Deborah Lazaroff. *Robert Siodmak*. Jefferson, N.C.: McFarland, 1998.

Alton, John. *Painting with Light*. Berkeley and Los Angeles: University of California Press, 1995.

Arendt, Hannah. *The Jew as Pariah: Jewish Identity and Politics in the Modern Age*. New York: Grove Press, 1978.

Arnold, Frank, Helga Belach, Gero Gandert, and Hans Helmut Pinzler, eds. *Aufruhr der Gefühle: Die Kinowelt des Curtis Bernhardt*. Munich: Verlag C. J. Bucher, 1982.

Aschheim, Steven E. *Brothers and Strangers: The East European Jew in German Consciousness, 1800–1923*. Madison: University of Wisconsin Press, 1982.

Aurich, Rolf, Wolfgang Jacobsen, and Cornelius Schnauber, eds. *F.L.: Fritz Lang—His Life and Work*. Berlin: Filmmuseum Berlin, Deutsche Kinemathek, Jovis Verlag GmbH, 2001.

Ausubel, Nathan. *Pictorial History of the Jewish People*. New York: Crown, 1958.

Bacher, Lutz. *Max Ophuls in the Hollywood Studios*. New Brunswick: Rutgers University Press, 1996.

Bahr, Ehrhard. *Weimar on the Pacific: German Exile Culture in Los Angeles and the Crisis of Modernism*. Berkeley and Los Angeles: University of California Press, 2007.

Barlow, John D. *German Expressionist Film*. Boston: Twayne, 1982.

Barnavi, Eli, ed. *A Historical Atlas of the Jewish People*. New York: Schocken, 2002.

Barron, Stephanie, and Sabine Eckmann, eds. *Exiles and Émigrés: The Flight of European Artists from Hitler* . Exhibition catalogue. Los Angeles: Los Angeles County Museum of Art, 1997.

Baxter, John. *Hollywood Exiles*. New York, Taplinger, 1976.

Benson, Timothy O., ed. *Expressionist Utopias: Paradise, Metropolis, Architectural Fantasy*. Los Angeles: Los Angeles County Museum of Art, 1993.

Bernhardt, Curtis, and Mary Kiersch. *Curtis Bernhardt: A Directors Guild of America Oral History*. Metuchen, N.J.: Directors Guild of America and Scarecrow Press, 1986.

Biale, David. *Eros and the Jews: From Biblical Israel to Contemporary America*. New York: Basic Books, 1992.

Biesen, Sheri Chinen. *Blackout: World War II and the Origins of Film Noir*. Baltimore: Johns Hopkins University Press, 2005.

Bilski, Emily D., ed. *Berlin Metropolis: Jews and the New Culture, 1890–1918*. Berkeley and Los Angeles: University of California Press, 1999.

Bilski, Emily D., and Emily Braun. *Jewish Women and Their Salons: The Power of Conversation*. New Haven: Yale University Press, 2005.

Bogdanovich, Peter. *Who the Devil Made It: Conversations with Legendary Film Directors*. New York: Ballantine, 1997.

Borde, Raymond, and Etienne Chaumeton. *A Panorama of the American Film Noir, 1941–1953* (1955). Trans. Paul Hammond. San Francisco: City Lights Books, 2002.

Bordwell, David, Janet Staiger, and Kristin Thompson. *The Classical Hollywood Cinema: Film Style and Mode of Production to 1960*. New York: Columbia University Press, 1985.

Bould, Mark. *Film Noir: From Berlin to Sin City*. New York: Wallflower, 2005.

Boyarin, Daniel. *Unheroic Conduct: The Rise of Heterosexuality and the Invention of the Jewish Man*. Berkeley and Los Angeles: University of California Press, 1997.

Boyarin, Daniel, Daniel Itzkovitz, and Ann Pellegrini, eds. *Queer Theory and the Jewish Question*. New York: Columbia University Press, 2003.

Boyarin, Jonathan, and Daniel Boyarin. *Jews and Other Differences: The New Jewish Cultural Studies*. Minneapolis: University of Minnesota Press, 1997.

Brunette, Peter, ed. *Fred Zinnemann: Interviews*. Jackson: University of Mississippi Press, 2005.

Buber, Martin. *Ecstatic Confessions: The Heart of Mysticism* (1909). Trans. Esther Cameron. Syracuse: Syracuse University Press, 1996.

Cameron, Ian, ed. *The Book of Film Noir*. New York: Continuum, 1993.

Cargnelli, Christian, and Michael Omasta, eds. *Schatten, Exil, Europäische Emigranten in Film Noir*. Vienna: PVS Verlegen, 1997.

Chandler, Charlotte. *Nobody's Perfect: Billy Wilder, a Personal Biography*. New York: Simon and Schuster, 2002.

Chopra-Gant, Michael. *Hollywood Genres and Postwar America: Masculinity, Family, and Nation in Popular Movies and Film Noir*. London: I. B. Tauris, 2006.

Cohen, Rich. *Tough Jews: Fathers, Sons, and Gangster Dreams in Jewish America*. New York: Simon and Schuster, 1998.

Cohen, Sarah Blacher, ed. *Jewish Wry: Essays on Jewish Humor*. Detroit: Wayne State University Press, 1987.

Copjec, Joan, ed. *Shades of Noir: A Reader*. New York: Verso, 1993.

Corber, Robert J. *Homosexuality in Cold War America: Resistance and the Crisis of Masculinity.* Durham: Duke University Press, 1997.

Crowe, Cameron. *Conversations with Wilder.* New York: Knopf, 1999.

Davidson, Wolfgang, ed. *Erich Pommer.* Berlin: Argon, 1989

Dennis, Geoffrey. *The Jewish Encyclopedia of Jewish Myth, Magic, and Mysticism.* Woodbury, Maine: Llewellyn, 2007.

Dickos, Andrew. *Street with No Name: A History of the Classical Film Noir.* Lexington: University of Kentucky Press, 2002.

Diller, Jerry V. *Freud's Jewish Identity: A Case Study in the Impact of Ethnicity.* Madison: Fairleigh Dickenson University Press, 1991.

Dinnerstein, Leonard. *Antisemitism in America.* New York: Oxford University Press, 1994.

Doane, Mary Ann. *Femme Fatales: Feminism, Film Theory, Psychoanalysis.* New York: Routledge, 1991.

Dube, Wolf-Dieter. *Expressionism.* Trans. Mary Whittall. New York: Praeger, 1979.

Duncan, Paul. *Film Noir: Films of Trust and Betrayal.* North Pomfret, Vt.: Pocket Essentials, 2000.

Eisner, Lotte. *Fritz Lang.* New York: Da Capo Press, 1976.

———. *The Haunted Screen: Expressionism in the German Cinema and the Influence of Max Reinhardt* (1952). Berkeley and Los Angeles: University of California Press, 1977.

Elsaesser, Thomas. *Weimar Cinema and After: Germany's Historical Imaginary.* New York: Routledge, 2000.

Friedrich, Otto. *City of Nets: A Portrait of Hollywood in the 1940s.* New York: Harper and Row, 1986.

Fujiwara, Chris. *The World and Its Double: The Life and Work of Otto Preminger.* New York: Faber and Faber, 2008.

Gabler, Neal. *An Empire of Their Own: How the Jews Invented Hollywood.* New York: Anchor, 1989.

Gay, Peter. *Freud: A Life for Our Time.* New York: Norton, 1988.

———. *Freud, Jews, and Other Germans.* New York: Oxford University Press, 1978.

———. *Weimar Culture: The Outsider as Insider.* New York: Norton, 2001.

Gerstner, David A., and Janet Staiger, eds. *Authorship and Film.* New York: Routledge, 2003.

Gilman, Sander. *Freud, Race, and Gender.* New York: Routledge, 1993.

———. *The Jew's Body.* New York: Routledge, 1991.

———. *Jewish Self-Hatred: Anti-Semitism and the Hidden Language of the Jews.* Baltimore: Johns Hopkins University Press, 1986.

Greco, Joseph. *The File on Robert Siodmak in Hollywood: 1941–1951.* Parkland, Fla.: Dissertation.com [Brown Walker Press], 1999.

Greenberg, Joel. *Oral History with John Brahm, 1971.* Beverly Hills: American Film Institute Center for Advanced Studies, 1975.

Grissemann, Stefan. *Mann im Schatten: Der Filmmacher Edgar G. Ulmer.* Vienna: Paul Szolnay Verlag, 2003.

Gunning, Tom. *The Films of Fritz Lang: Allegories of Vision and Modernity.* London: British Film Institute, 2006.

Hake, Sabine. *German National Cinema.* New York: Routledge, 2002.

Hardt, U. *From Caligari to California: Eric Pommer's Life in the International Film Wars.* Providence, R.I.: Berghahn, 1996.

Heilbut, Anthony. *Exiled in Paradise: German Refugee Artists and Intellectuals in America from the 1930s to the Present* (1983). Berkeley and Los Angeles: University of California Press, 1997.

Herzogenrath, Bernd, ed. *The Films of Edgar G. Ulmer.* New York: Scarecrow Press, 2009.

Hess, Jonathan. *Germans, Jews and the Claims of Modernity.* New Haven: Yale University Press, 2002.

Hirsch, Foster. *Detours and Lost Highways: A Map of Neo-noir.* New York: Limelight, 1999.

———. *Film Noir: The Dark Side of the Screen.* New York: Da Capo Press, 1981.

———. *Otto Preminger: The Man Who Would Be King.* New York: Knopf, 2007.

Hoberman, J. *Bridge of Light: Yiddish Film Between Two Worlds.* Philadelphia: Temple University Press, 1991.

Hoffmann, Paul. *The Viennese: Splendor, Twilight, and Exile.* New York: Anchor, 1998.

Holm, D. K. *Film Soleil.* North Pomfret, Vt.: Trafalgar Square Publishing, 2005.

Horak, Jan-Christopher. "Anti-Nazi-Film der deutschsprachigen Emigration von Hollywood 1939–1945." PhD diss., Westfälischen Wilhelms-Universität zu Münster, 1984.

Horowitz, Joseph. *Artists in Exile: How Refugees from Twentieth Century War and Revolution Transformed the American Performing Arts.* New York: HarperCollins, 2007.

Horton, Robert, ed. *Billy Wilder: Interviews.* Jackson: University of Mississippi Press, 2001.

Howe, Irving, with Kenneth Libo. *World of Our Fathers.* New York: Harcourt Brace Jovanovich, 1976.

Hurwitz, Siegmund. *Lilith, the First Eve: Historical and Psychological Aspects of the Dark Feminine* (1980). Trans. Robert Hinshaw. Zurich: Daimon, 1992.

Izod, John. *Hollywood and the Box Office: 1895–1986.* New York: Columbia University Press, 1988.

Jackman, Jarrell C., and Carla M. Borden, ed. *The Muses of Hitler: Cultural Transfer and Adaptation, 1930–1945*. Washington, D.C.: Smithsonian Institution Press, 1983.

Kaplan, E. Ann, ed. *Women in Film Noir*. London: British Film Institute, 2000.

Keaney, Michael F. *Film Noir Guide*. Jefferson, N.C.: McFarland, 2003

Klein, Melanie. *New Directions in Psychoanalysis*. New York: Basic Books, 1957.

Kopenick, Lutz. *The Dark Mirror: German Cinema Between Hitler and Hollywood*. Berkeley and Los Angeles: University of California Press, 2002.

Kracauer, Siegfried. *From Caligari to Hitler: A Psychological Study of the German Film* (1947). New York: Noonday Press, 1959.

Kreimeier, Klaus. *The Ufa Story: A History of Germany's Greatest Film Company, 1918–1945*. Trans. Robert and Rita Kimber. New York: Hill and Wang, 1996.

Krutnik, Frank. *In a Lonely Street: Film Noir, Genre, Masculinity*. London: Routledge, 1991.

Lally, Kevin. *Wilder Times*. New York: Henry Holt, 1996.

Langman, Larry. *Destination Hollywood: The Influence of Europeans on American Filmmaking*. Jefferson, N.C.: McFarland, 2000.

Laqueur, Walter. *Weimar: A Cultural History*. New York: Capricorn, 1976.

Lyons, Arthur. *Death on the Cheap: The Lost B Movies of Film Noir*. New York: Da Capo Press, 2000.

Maltby, Richard. *Hollywood Cinema*. 2d ed. New York: Blackwell, 2003.

McCarthy, Todd, and Charles Flynn, eds. *Kings of the Bs: Working Within the Hollywood System*. New York: Dutton, 1975.

McGilligan, Patrick. *Fritz Lang: The Nature of the Beast*. New York: Faber and Faber, 1997.

Memmi, Albert. *The Liberation of the Jew*. Trans. Judy Hyun. New York: Orion, 1966.

Mendes-Flohr, Paul. *German Jews: A Dual Identity*. New Haven: Yale University Press, 1999.

Meyer, Michael A. *The Origins of the Modern Jew: Jewish Identity and European Culture, 1749–1824*. Detroit: Wayne State University Press, 1967.

Mosse, George L. *The Crisis of German Ideology* (1964). New York: H. Fetig, 1998.

Muller, Eddie. *Dark City: The Lost World of Film Noir*. New York: St. Martin's Griffin, 1998.

Naremore, James. *More Than Night: Film Noir in Its Contexts*. Berkeley and Los Angeles: University of California Press, 1998.

Navasky, Victor S. *Naming Names*. New York: Penguin, 1981.

Nolletti, Arthur, Jr., ed. *The Films of Fred Zinnemann: Critical Perspectives*. Albany: State University of New York Press, 1999.

Ophuls, Max. *Spiel im Dasein*. Stuttgart: Henry Goverts Verlag, 1959.

Petrie, Graham. *Hollywood Destinies: European Directors in America, 1922–1931*. Detroit: Wayne State University Press, 2002.

Petro, Patrice. *Joyless Streets: Women and Melodramatic Representation in Weimar Germany*. Princeton: Princeton University Press, 1989.

Phillips, Gene D. *Exiles in Hollywood: Major European Film Directors in America*. Bethlehem: Lehigh University Press, 1998.

Pinker, Steven. *How the Mind Works*. New York: Norton, 1997.

Prawer, S. S. *Between Two Worlds: The Jewish Presence in German and Austrian Film, 1910–1933*. New York: Berghahn, 2007.

Preminger, Otto. *Preminger: An Autobiography*. Garden City, N.Y.: Doubleday, 1977.

Reinhardt, Gottfried. *The Genius: A Memoir of Max Reinhardt, by His Son Gottfried Reinhardt*. New York: Knopf, 1979.

Roffman, Peter, and Jim Purdy. *The Hollywood Social Problem Film: Madness, Despair, and Politics from the Depression to the Fifties*. Bloomington: Indiana University Press, 1981.

Sarris, Andrew. *The American Cinema: Directors and Directions, 1929–1968*. New York: Da Capo Press, 1968.

———, ed. *Interviews with Film Directors*. Indianapolis: Bobbs-Merrill, 1967.

Schatz, Thomas. *The Genius of the System: Hollywood Filmmaking in the Hollywood Era*. New York: Metropolitan Books, 1988.

Schnauber, Cornelius. *Fritz Lang in Hollywood*. Vienna: Europaverlag, 1986.

Selby, Spencer. *Dark City: The Film Noir*. Jefferson, N.C.: McFarland, 1997.

Sikov, Ed. *On Sunset Boulevard: The Life and Times of Billy Wilder*. New York: Hyperion, 1998.

Silver, Alain, and James Ursini, eds. *Film Noir Reader*. New York: Limelight, 1996.

———. *Film Noir Reader 4: The Crucial Films and Themes*. New York: Limelight, 2004.

Silver, Alain, and Elizabeth Ward, eds. *Film Noir: An Encyclopedic Reference to the American Style*. 3d ed. Woodstock, N.Y.: Overlook Press, 1992.

Sinyard, Neil. *Fred Zinnemann: Films of Character and Conscience*. Jefferson, N.C.: McFarland, 2003.

Siodmak, Robert. *Zwischen Berlin und Hollywood: Erinnerungen eines grossen Filmregisseurs*. Ed. Hans C. Blumenberg. Munich: Goldmann Verlag, 1980.

Soussloff, Catherine M., ed. *Jewish Identity in Modern Art History*. Berkeley and Los Angeles: University of California Press, 1999.

Taylor, John Russell. *Strangers in Paradise: The Hollywood Émigrés, 1933–1950*. New York: Holt, Rinehart and Winston, 1983.

Usai, Paolo Cherchi, and Lorenzo Codelli, eds. *Before Caligari: German Cinema 1895–1920*. Pordenone, Italy: Edizoni Biblioteca dell'Immagine, 1990.

Viertel, Salka. *The Kindness of Strangers*. New York: Holt, Rinehart and Winston, 1969.

Villiers, Douglas, ed. *Next Year in Jerusalem: Jews in the Twentieth Century*. New York: Viking Press, 1976.

Wager, Jans B. *Dames in the Driver's Seat: Rereading Film Noir*. Austin: University of Texas Press, 2005.

Wallace, David. *Exiles in Hollywood*. New York: Limelight, 2006.

Wexman, Virginia Wright, ed. *Film and Authorship*. New Brunswick: Rutgers University Press, 2003.

Wexman, Virginia Wright, and Karen Hollinger, eds. *Letter from an Unknown Woman: Max Ophuls, Director*. New Brunswick: Rutgers University Press, 1986.

White, Susan M. *The Cinema of Max Ophuls: Magisterial Vision and the Figure of Women*. New York: Columbia University Press, 1995.

Wisse, Ruth. *The Schlemiel as Modern Hero*. Chicago: University of Chicago Press, 1971.

Wolf, Norbert. *Expressionism*. Cologne, Germany: Taschen, 2004.

Wolff, Kurt H., ed. *The Sociology of Georg Simmel*. Trans. Hans Gerth. Glencoe, Ill.: Free Press, 1950.

Wolman, Ruth E. *Crossing Over: An Oral History of Refugees from Hitler's Reich*. New York: Twayne, 1996.

Zolotow, Maurice. *Billy Wilder in Hollywood*. New York: Limelight, 1987.

Index

About the Author

Vincent Brook has a PhD in film and television from the University of California, Los Angeles (UCLA). He teaches media and cultural studies at UCLA and the University of Southern California. He has written numerous essays on film and television for anthologies, encyclopedias, and leading journals in the field; authored *Something Ain't Kosher Here: The Rise of the "Jewish" Sitcom* (2003); and edited the anthology *You Should See Yourself: Jewish Identity in Postmodern American Culture* (2006).